Wikipedia @ 20

Wikipedia @ 20

Stories of an Incomplete Revolution

Edited by Joseph Reagle and Jackie Koerner

The MIT Press
Cambridge, Massachusetts
London, England

The open access edition of this book was made possible by generous funding from Knowledge Unlatched, Northeastern University Communication Studies Department, and Wikimedia Foundation.

 Knowledge Unlatched

This book was set in Stone Serif and Stone Sans by Westchester Publishing Services. Printed and bound in the United States of America.

Library of Congress Cataloging-in-Publication Data

Names: Reagle, Joseph, editor. | Koerner, Jackie, editor.
Title: Wikipedia @ 20 : stories of an incomplete revolution / edited by
   Joseph M. Reagle and Jackie Koerner.
Other titles: Wikipedia at 20
Description: Cambridge, Massachusetts : The MIT Press, [2020] |
   Includes bibliographical references and index.
Identifiers: LCCN 2020000804 | ISBN 9780262538176 (paperback)
Subjects: LCSH: Wikipedia--History.
Classification: LCC AE100 .W54 2020 | DDC 030--dc23
LC record available at https://lccn.loc.gov/2020000804

10   9   8   7   6   5   4   3   2   1

Contents

III   Vision

Preface

This book was not an easy undertaking and is unusual in a number of ways.

Even though this is a collection of essays from an academic press, our contributors are not exclusively academics. Many of the essayists make use of Wikipedia as part of their work: scholars, teachers, librarians, journalists, and activists. Many are more than one of these things. Many of the essayists are also multilingual, and not all are writing in their native language. This variety is a strength, speaking to the connections among languages, professions, and enthusiasms across the movement.

Also, we hope to reach a general audience. Our intention is to speak to the nonspecialist reader interested in Wikipedia. Perhaps our readers are fond of using Wikipedia, or perhaps they follow stories about it with interest. Perhaps they even contribute to Wikipedia, a little or a lot. Or, perhaps, Wikipedia is part of their work. This isn't an introduction to Wikipedia; rather, it is a set of reflections from those who have given a lot of thought to the online encyclopedia as its twentieth year approaches.

The process for this book was also unusual. With the approach of Wikipedia's anniversary, we aspired to move quickly and create an accessible and coherent work. Gita Devi Manaktala, MIT Press's editorial director, suggested we make use of PubPub, a new online collaborative publishing platform. Each essay began as a proposed abstract; those selected were given editorial feedback. Later, full drafts were posted on PubPub and open to peer, public, and editorial review. Finally, revised essays underwent external review before selections were made for the printed book.

Completing such a work requires the generosity and patience of many—especially when there's a change of editorship midstream.

Skill and patience could not be better exemplified than by Gita Devi Manaktala, Maria Isela Garcia, and Jessica Lipton at MIT Press. Their editorial and logistical savvy was paramount to this project's completion. Other consummate professionals who contributed to the polish, production, and presentation of this work include Elizabeth Granda, Marcy Ross, Kate Elwell, Gregory Hyman, Matthew White, Ori Kometani, and Susan Clark.

This book is the result of a collective effort. Unfortunately, we could not include all of the pieces here, and the website remains a broader and useful hypertextual collection from all those who participated. John Broughton, Stephane Coillet-Matillon, Jake Orlowitz, and Denny Vrandečić were especially generous with their feedback on PubPub. The editors benefited from the guidance and expertise of Phoebe Ayers, Siko Bouterse, Anasuya Sengupta, and Adele Vrana. Samantha Lien and Nadee Gunasena from the Wikimedia Foundation helped to facilitate the capstone piece. And the external reviewers for MIT Press went above and beyond by providing helpful feedback on a large manuscript in a short period of time. Thank you to all.

Like any technology, a publishing platform can prompt moments of confusion. PubPub's Catherine Ahearn, Gabe Stein, and Travis Rich were quick to respond to the many questions we sent their way.

The open access edition of this book was made possible with generous funding from Knowledge Unlatched, the Northeastern University Communication Studies Department, and a Wikimedia Foundation rapid grant.

We hope you will enjoy this unusual collection. It was produced in the wiki-spirit of open collaboration, contains varied voices, and speaks to insights from hindsight and visions for the future. What might you learn in reading these pages? Though Wikipedia was revolutionary twenty years ago, it has yet to become the revolution we need. The important work of sharing knowledge, connecting people, and bridging cultures continues.

Introduction: Connections

Joseph Reagle and Jackie Koerner

Twenty years ago, Wikipedia set out on its path to provide humanity with free access to the sum of all knowledge. Even if this is a mission that can't be finished, Wikipedia has made remarkable progress toward the impossible. How so? Wikipedia is an encyclopedia built on a wiki. And never has an application (gathering the sum of human knowledge) been so suited to its medium (easily interconnected web pages).

Encyclopedias have long been reliant on interconnections. In 1755, the *Encyclopédie's* Denis Diderot wrote that the use of cross-references (or *renvois*) was "the most important part of our encyclopedia scheme."[1] This feature allowed the *Encyclopédie's* editors to depict the connective tissue of Enlightenment knowledge and to dodge state and church authorities by way of facetious and satirical references. For example, they linked to articles on the Christian rite of communion, wherein "the body and blood of Christ" is consumed, from the article on "Cannibals."

At the onset of each new informational medium—from paper, to microfilm, to silicon—connectivity was the impetus. Among the documentalists of the early twentieth century, there was Wilhelm Ostwald's *Brücke*, a bridge, and Suzanne Briet's *indice*, an indicator. Such documentalists advanced indexing and classification schemes to improve interconnections between information. Then, on the cusp of the digital age, Vannevar Bush famously wrote of the power of an electromechanical memex laced with "associative trails."[2] This inspired the hyperlinks of the 1960s and the URLs of the 1990s.

Creating HTML web pages interspersed with links, however, is not so easy; the first wiki was launched in 1995 to fix this. To create and link to a new page, you simply wrote the page's title in CamelCase, so-called because capitalizing "camel" and "case," when conjoined, has two humps. Your lumpy title is now a link that, when clicked, takes you to a fresh page awaiting new content.

Wikipedia, then, appeared in 2001, almost by way of accident.[3] Efforts at collaboratively creating an online encyclopedia had faltered for years. When a wiki was added to one such project, as an experimental scratchpad, it took off beyond anyone's expectation: Wikipedia was born.

Just as the history of two centuries, from print to digital, reveals the importance of connection—call it a reference, bridge, indicator, trail, or link—Wikipedia's two decades are also a story of connection. The following essays speak of and exemplify those connections across disciplines and borders, across languages and data, and across the professional and personal.

What Has Changed

This is a collection of essays about Wikipedia as the English-language edition and larger movement approach their twentieth year. Many of the contributors are astonished by this milestone because we've been so close to Wikipedia and remember when it was young. So we pause to look back on those two decades, to see what has changed, and to connect the past with the present, looking toward the future.

In Wikipedia's early days, those of us concerned with history argued Wikipedia was the fulfillment of a long-pursued vision of a universal encyclopedia: the rousing end of a long story. But, of course, the story didn't end; a good story never ends.

Other contributors have sought to explain how Wikipedia worked in practice given that it was not easily explained by theory. New theories, including commons-based peer production, prompted hope that Wikipedia's success would be followed by similar examples. Yet there have been disappointments on the road to an imagined utopia and back.

Those of us following the public discourse about Wikipedia remember it as the new kid on the block, upsetting traditional knowledge authorities. We can recall a former president of the American Library Association calling Wikipedia the dietary equivalent of a Big Mac.[4] Now, Wikipedia is reported on in the press as the grown-up of the web and as a bastion of (mostly) reasoned interaction.

Many of the educators among us first encountered Wikipedia when we were students. Even if our teachers were suspicious of the new site, we were thrilled to collaborate with others on something people would actually read. Now, as Alexandria Lockett notes in her essay, our students have never lived in a world without Wikipedia. Helping students contribute to Wikipedia is one of the most rewarding assignments we offer. And rather than dismissing Wikipedia as junk food, some librarians see rigorous engagement with Wikipedia as a staple of their profession.

Finally, those of us who recognized the limitations of Wikipedia in its first decade hoped that the obstacles of complicated syntax, entrenched biases, and complex policies were tractable. A lot of effort has been spent on these concerns, and progress has been made. Though it took time to develop and deploy, the VisualEditor is now the predominant default on most Wikipedia editions. And there are now vigorous projects working to increase representation and participation. Even so, these problems are far from solved.

Insight from Hindsight, in Three Parts

The intention behind this collection was to pause and ask: what have we learned?

Often, technology is seen as a stepping stone to the future. Near its start, Wikipedia was labeled as an extraordinary revolution and a degenerate hive mind. Yet people are so caught up in tech's present novelty and future implications they rarely look back to consider what actually happened. Wikipedia's twentieth anniversary is a moment to do so. It's not often we have such a hyped and controversial tech phenomenon still doing what it was doing from its start—most become advertising platforms, like Facebook and Google.

Consequently, in late 2018, this book project was launched with a request for essay proposals related to "Wikipedia @ 20." Prospective contributors were asked what insights they had gained from these two decades of history. The saying that "hindsight is twenty-twenty" is sometimes used dismissively; we wanted to use it constructively. Contributors were asked to tell us about lessons learned, insights gained, and myths busted during their engagement with Wikipedia.

The resulting chapters are grouped into three sections: hindsight, connection, and vision. This is an arbitrary division as each essay has elements of each—but some organization never hurt.

The first set of chapters are retrospective; they are mini-histories on how Wikipedia has been produced and discussed relative to internal and external tensions—such as the encyclopedia's conflict of interest policy. And the insight from these hindsights is that events flow in ways contrary and unexpected. Wikipedia has far exceeded its creators' expectations and outlived the many predictions of its death. Similarly, as the authors of "From Anarchy to Wikiality, Glaring Bias to Good Cop" write, Wikipedia's press coverage "has evolved from bewilderment at the project, to concern and hostility at its model, to acceptance of its merits and disappointment at its shortcomings, and finally to calls to hold it socially accountable and reform it like any other institution." The peer-based production that the encyclopedia heralded had much utopian potential, but time has revealed unforeseen limitations. And among the many things Wikipedia is not, it is not a newspaper, but its content and readership is driven by the news.

The second set of chapters demonstrate the richness of connections. Not only is the link essential in the story of encyclopedias and the web, it is a motif in many of the essays. Wikipedia spans national, cultural, and linguistic divides as well as those between people, data, and machines. Wikipedia has even become "the most important laboratory for social scientific and computing research in history," as one pair of contributors show. And the connections between Wikipedia and the many platforms that use its data are not as close as they should be, severing the context and verifiability of knowledge.

In "Three Links," the authors write that "working with the encyclopedia and its community has been a valuable forging ground, shaping each of us into links in a wide-reaching mesh of personal and professional connections." Wikipedia connects volunteers, teachers, librarians, scholars, and activists. Many of our contributors bridge these communities by serving in multiple roles—not always easy. There's also evidence of Wikipedia's place in our personal lives, of long-lasting collaborations and friendships.

The final set of chapters speak to Wikipedia's founding vision, best expressed in the famous provocation to "imagine a world in which every single person on the planet is given free access to the sum of all human knowledge."[5] This Enlightenment-inspired promise has yet to be fulfilled.

Obviously, not everyone who'd like to read Wikipedia can do so, and we include the story of some of those making it available to people without internet and those within censorious regimes. However, "free access" is more than *read only*; it also includes contribution. As coeditor Jackie Koerner writes, Wikipedia's relationship with knowledge equity is complex: the summation of human knowledge is biased by those documenting it. We include essays from those working to remedy this shortfall, from the Art+Feminism and Black Lunch Table projects, from an educator at a historically Black Women's college, and from those at Wiki Education. A path forward, "Toward a Wikipedia For and From Us All," is illuminated by the contributors from *Whose Knowledge?*

We conclude with a capstone from Katherine Maher, executive director of the Wikimedia Foundation. As we finished work on this volume, the Wikimedia movement had finished a process for envisioning the Wikipedia of 2030. Wikipedia will continue its development from a wiki website toward an accessible platform for knowledge. And the community will redouble its efforts to include people and bodies of knowledge previously overlooked. Maher eloquently articulates what is required to continue the journey toward a world that no longer need only be imagined.

Notes

1. Denis Diderot, "The Encyclopedia," in *University of Chicago Readings in Western Civilization, Vol. 7: The Old Regime and the French Revolution*, John W. Boyer, Keith M. Baker, Julius Kirshner (Chicago: University of Chicago Press, 1987), 82.

2. Michael Zimmer, "Renvois of the Past, Present and Future: Hyperlinks and the Structuring of Knowledge from the Encyclopédie to Web 2.0," *New Media & Society* 11, no. 95 (2009), http://nms.sagepub.com/cgi/content/abstract/11/1-2/95.

3. Joseph Reagle, "Wikipedia: The Happy Accident," *Interactions* 16, no. 3 (2009): 42–45, http://doi.acm.org/10.1145/1516016.1516026.

4. Michael Gorman, "Jabberwiki: The Educational Response, Part II," *Encyclopædia Britannica Blog*, June 26, 2007, http://blogs.britannica.com/2007/06/jabberwiki-the-educational-response-part-ii/.

5. Jimmy Wales, "Wikipedia Founder Jimmy Wales Responds," *Slashdot*, July 28, 2004, https://slashdot.org/story/04/07/28/1351230/wikipedia-founder-jimmy-wales-responds.

1 Hindsight

1 The Many (Reported) Deaths of Wikipedia

Joseph Reagle

Wikipedia's death has been predicted many times in its twenty years through four periods of dour prognostication. Though this history shows making predictions is foolhardy, Wikipedia, no doubt, has many years of life ahead of it.

Many Wikipedians can recall a favorite article that has since been deleted. My forsaken favorite is "Failed Predictions," one of the two thousand articles deleted on a November day over a decade ago. I appreciated how the article evidenced shortsighted thinking about technology given the many dismissals of the radio, telephone, and computer. Some quotes were apocryphal, such as Bill Gates's purported claim that "640K [of memory] ought to be enough for anybody," but I believed the article could have been improved with time. Despite similar lists having survived, "Failed Predictions" was expunged in 2007 from the English-language version of Wikipedia—the focus of this essay.

Although we lost Wikipedia's article on failed predictions, we gained Wikipedia itself as a topic of prognostication. Some have claimed that the young Wikipedia was a joke, that it wasn't an encyclopedia, that it would fail; mid-life, some claimed that the English Wikipedia was dying or dead; more recently, we have seen claims of its demise and extinction. Claims about Wikipedia's death are not included in its "List of Premature Obituaries," but the topic does have a stub.

I began following Wikipedia in 2004 as a graduate student interested in wikis and blogs. When it came time to choose between the two, I chose Wikipedia. Blogs tended to be insular and snarky. Wikipedia had its conflicts, but people were at least attempting to work together on something worthwhile. Plus, its historical antecedents and popular reception were fascinating. In 2010 I published a book about Wikipedia's history, culture, and controversies: *Good Faith Collaboration*.[1] And at that point, I thought the dismal predictions about Wikipedia were over. Yet they continued.

As Wikipedia's twentieth-anniversary approaches, I look back on those who spoke about the project's future to understand why they doubted the "encyclopedia anyone can edit" could make it this long. (See chapter 2 for a broader take on Wikipedia press coverage.) I discern four periods of prognostication within which people expressed skepticism or concern about Wikipedia's early growth, nascent identity, production model, and contributor attrition. Given how often such bleak sentiments are expressed as premature obituaries, we'll see that I am not alone in thinking of Mark Twain's quip about exaggerated reports of his death.

Early Growth (2001–2002)

Not all predictions about Wikipedia falling short have been from its critics. The earliest predictions, from its founders no less, were not ambitious enough.

As I've written before, Wikipedia can be thought of as a happy accident—a provocation to those who confuse Wikipedia's eventual success with its uncertain origins.[2] The encyclopedia that anyone can edit was initially part of a project of an elect few. Jimmy Wales, the entrepreneur behind Bomis, a men's oriented web portal, had hired Larry Sanger, a new philosophy PhD, to launch Nupedia, an encyclopedia for the new millennium. Although Nupedia was online and inspired by open source, Nupedia's experts worked within a rigorous multitiered process. And it was slow going: by the end of 2000, only two articles had been completed. Wales likened Nupedia's process to being back in graduate school: an intimidating grind.

To shake things up, Wales and Sanger set up a wiki in January 2001. They hoped it would lead to some drafts for Nupedia, but their expectations were modest. Wales feared that the wiki would be overrun with "complete rubbish" and that Nupedians "might find the idea objectionable."[3] My reconstruction of the first ten thousand edits to Wikipedia does show a lot of dreck, but it was fertile stuff, being produced and improved at a remarkable rate.[4] Wikipedians hoped to one day have 100,000 articles—a scale a bit larger than most print encyclopedias. In July, Sanger predicted that if Wikipedia continued to produce a thousand articles a month, it would be close to that in about seven years. Amazingly, in less than seven years, in

September 2007 the English Wikipedia reached two million articles, some twenty times Sanger's estimate.

Wales's initial pessimism and Sanger's modest estimate are humbling in hindsight. Yet such mistakes can now be taken as a source of pride. This is not true of the modest expectations of Wikipedia's first critic.

Peter Jacso, a computer science professor, regularly published "Peter's Picks & Pans" in a journal for information professionals. In the spring 2002 issue, he panned Wikipedia, likening it to a prank, a joke, or an "outlet for those who pine to be a member in some community." Jacso dismissed Wikipedia's goal of producing one hundred thousand articles; he wrote, "That's ambition," as this "tall order" was twice the number of articles in the sixth edition of the *Columbia Encyclopedia*.

When I asked Jacso about this pan from seventeen years ago, he had not given it much thought. To be fair, he published over eighty "Picks & Pans" between 1995 and 2009. And he now concedes that Wikipedia has "worked exceptionally well" thanks to the thousands of contributors working under "constantly updated guidelines." Jacso's early skepticism arose because so many other projects had failed: "I did not anticipate that the free Wikipedia service could realize what even the richest companies such as Microsoft failed to do, as demonstrated by the trials and tribulation of the subscription-based *Encarta*."[5]

Jacso and Wikipedia's founders exemplify three ways of thinking about the future. Like Jacso, people look to similar projects to get a sense of what is feasible: even established and well-funded projects had failed to create sustainable online encyclopedias. Or, like Sanger, people extrapolate linearly; in this case, taking the first six months of Wikipedia as the norm for the next seven years. The only model people didn't make use of was exponential growth, which characterized Wikipedia article creation until about 2007. In "Why Technology Predictions Go Awry," Herb Brody identified this cause as *underestimating a revolution*.[6] Now, hopeful entrepreneurs default to this model in their predictions, but this is only because of early examples such as Wikipedia.

Nascent Identity (2001–2005)

Just as Wikipedia's emergence and initial growth confounded early expectations, the identity that we now take for granted, the nonprofit "encyclopedia anyone can edit," was not a given at the start.

First, Wikipedia was conceived by Wales as a possible commercial undertaking. Wikipedia was originally hosted at wikipedia.com, and by 2002 Sanger and Wales were hinting that Bomis might start selling ads on Wikipedia, in part to pay Sanger's salary. Wikipedians objected—Spanish Wikipedians even left to create their own. Given these objections and the deflation of the dot-com bubble, Sanger was laid off. Wales changed the site over to a .org domain and began work to establish the nonprofit Wikimedia Foundation, which happened in 2003.

Second, there was the question of whether Wikipedia was a wiki, an encyclopedia, both, or neither. In Wikipedia's first year, Wales visited the wiki of Ward Cunningham to put this question to the inventor of the wiki.[7]

> My question, to this esteemed Wiki community, is this: Do you think that a Wiki could successfully generate a useful encyclopedia? —JimboWales

> Yes, but in the end it wouldn't be an encyclopedia. It would be a wiki. —WardCunningham

This interaction is a storied part of Wikipedia's history, and in subsequent years Cunningham was often asked about Wikipedia and his prediction. When he was asked if Wikipedia was still a wiki in 2004, he responded, "Absolutely. A certain amount of credit drifts my way from Wikipedia. I'm always quick to remind people that my wiki is not Wikipedia, and that there's a lot of innovation there. I'm proud of what the Wikipedia community has done, I think it's totally awesome." He thought Wikipedia's talk pages, where contributors discuss their work on an article, were especially useful. Cunningham also conceded that Wikipedia was an encyclopedia: "If someone were to ask me to point to a modern encyclopedia, I would choose Wikipedia. Wikipedia defines encyclopedia now."[8] However, Cunningham's concession did not settle the matter. Elsewhere, the debate over Wikipedia's identity continued.

Shortly after being laid off, Sanger resigned from all participation in Nupedia and Wikipedia. He was unemployed, looking for work, and didn't see his contribution as a part-time hobby. However, he remained in Wikipedia's orbit, defending his status as a cofounder and, eventually, becoming one of Wikipedia's most prominent critics and competitors. This began in December 2004 with an essay on "Why Wikipedia Must Jettison Its Anti-Elitism." Sanger objected to Wikipedia's culture of "disrespect toward expertise": while Wikipedia was open to contributions from all,

Wikipedians still ought to defer to experts.[9] This deference to expertise was something he would attempt to restore at Citizendium, his 2006 fork of Wikipedia.

Sanger's essay led to another discussion about Wikipedia's identity, with two media scholars, danah boyd and Clay Shirky, taking opposing positions. (Boyd lowercases her name and pronouns.) Boyd recognized that though Wikipedia was useful, its content was uneven and often embarrassingly poor, leading her to conclude: "It will never be an encyclopedia, but it will contain extensive knowledge that is quite valuable for different purposes." She prefaced this with the sentiment that "this does not mean that i dislike Wikipedia, just that i do not consider it to be equivalent to an encyclopedia. I believe that it lacks the necessary research and precision." Anticipating Citizendium, she suggested this lack of quality could be remedied by "a vetted version of Wikipedia, one that would provide a knowledge resource that is more accountable and authoritative."[10]

Alternatively, Clay Shirky recognized that although Wikipedia's content was sometimes inferior to traditional encyclopedias, it was sometimes superior, especially on contemporary topics on which *Britannica* was silent. He also believed that it was myopic not to recognize Wikipedia as an encyclopedia.

> The idea that the Wikipedia will never be an encyclopedia is in part an ahistorical assertion that the definition and nature of encyclopediahood is fixed for all time, and that works like *Britannica* are avatars of the pattern. Contra boyd, I think Wikipedia will be an encyclopedia when the definition of the word expands to include peer production of shared knowledge, not just *Britannica's* institutional production.[11]

I was partial to Shirky's argument then and remain so. Yet boyd maintains her position though her concern has shifted. Boyd believes *Britannica* had its shortcomings and biases, and Wikipedia has improved; yet the latter is special given "how Wikipedia ends up serving as a form of data infrastructure." Wikipedia is relied on as "an information backbone that shapes the core network structure of search engines." This means it has an outsized effect on the world and is then "made vulnerable by those who seek to control algorithmic systems."[12] For boyd, to label and understand Wikipedia merely as an encyclopedia ignores its importance.

Clearly, questions of identity are not as easy to resolve as those about growth. As David Nye wrote about the "Promethean problem" of technology prediction, a technology's symbolic meaning is as important as any technical utility in shaping its often unforeseen uses.[13]

Production Model (2005–2010)

Wikipedia's supplanting of Nupedia demonstrated the benefits of open and easy peer production. In 2005, law professor Eric Goldman predicted that this same model meant that "Wikipedia will fail within 5 years."[14]

Communities, especially online ones, struggle with scale. As a community grows, personal interactions are no longer sufficient for making decisions. This is the endogenous challenge of scale. The exogenous challenge is that a larger community is also a larger target. For example, at the beginning of 2005, white nationalists were marshaling off-site to save their pet article "Jewish Ethnocentrism" from deletion. Wikipedians weren't sure how to quickly and effectively respond to this threat.

In response, Jimmy Wales said he could, reluctantly, play the part of benign dictator. Wales responded, "If 300 NeoNazis show up and start doing serious damage to a bunch of articles, we don't need to have 300 separate ArbCom cases and a nightmare that drags on for weeks. I'll just do something to lock those articles down somehow, ban a bunch of people, and protect our reputation and integrity." And as the crisis is dealt with, "we can also work in parallel to think about the best way to really take care of such problems in the long run."[15]

Throughout 2005, Wikipedians struggled with such problems, prominently reported as "growing pains." This was the year that John Seigenthaler Sr. condemned the project for falsely implicating him in John F. Kennedy's assassination. This was also the year that Goldman not only predicted Wikipedia's death but made a bet of it with fellow law blogger, Mike Godwin, over dinner.

> I remarked to Mike that Wikipedia inevitably will be overtaken by the gamers and the marketers to the point where it will lose all credibility. There are so many examples of community-driven communication tools that ultimately were taken over—USENET and the Open Directory Project are two that come top-of mind—that I didn't imagine that my statement would be controversial or debatable. Instead, I was surprised when Mike disagreed with my assertion. Mike's view is that Wikipedia has shown remarkable resilience to attacks to date, and this is evidence that the system is more stable than I think it is.[16]

Mike Godwin is best known for his eponymous "law" that "as an online discussion grows longer, the probability of a comparison involving Nazis or Hitler approaches 1." If this maxim reflected some cynicism, his bet against Goldman—and his joining Wikimedia as general counsel in 2007—reflected some optimism. Godwin believed Wikipedia could manage its growing pains. For example, in 2005, Wikipedia experimented with semi-protection, which limited edits to regularly vandalized pages to accounts older than four days. This was one of the "long run" solutions Wales alluded to at the start of the year. As Godwin wrote, "I think part of the design of Wikipedia was to allow for the evolution of contributor standards, even though as a 'foundational' principle anonymous contributors will always be allowed to edit it. Such evolution ought to be enough to keep Wikipedia alive and vital in the face of a changing digital environment."[17]

In 2006, Goldman affirmed his belief in Wikipedia's predicted demise. Its success made it a target, and defending the project would lead to Wikipedian burnout. Those who remained would be overloaded, and "thus, Wikipedia will enter a death spiral where the rate of junkiness will increase rapidly until the site becomes a wasteland."[18] Media critic Nicholas Carr had less patience, announcing the death of Wikipedia that very year. Unlike Goldman, Carr did not have a plausible theory; he simply wanted to bury the myth of openness as Wikipedia ceded to the "corrosive process of compromise." Others rightly called Carr on his histrionics, with Shirky responding that "news of Wikipedia's death is greatly exaggerated."[19]

By 2009, Goldman had agreed with Shirky and conceded his bet with Godwin. Though Wikipedia had introduced some barriers to vandalism and bad-faith edits, "in total Wikipedia's current technological restrictions are fairly modest."[20] In 2010, Goldman wrote, "My 2005 prediction of Wikipedia's failure by 2010 was wrong." Competitor projects might arise, but they too would have to follow Wikipedia's model of balancing openness with limited protections. (And competitors tend to presage Wikipedia's death in the headlines: "Google Knol—Yup, it's a Wikipedia Killer," "Wolfram Alpha: Wikipedia Killer?," and "Is Owl AOL's Wikipedia-Killer?"[21]) Goldman remained an active user and was pleased to wish the site a happy tenth anniversary. Wikipedia's model of peer production remained its lifeblood, rather than a source of sickness or external threat.

As Wikipedia approaches its twentieth anniversary, Goldman has confirmed his assessment of Wikipedia's success, though he remains concerned about the quality of lesser-visited articles and the lack of new contributor growth (discussed in the next section). Additionally, he noted that two things he did not anticipate were the effectiveness of nofollow web links—such links are ignored by search engines, making them less attractive to spammers—and the growth of Wikimedia's staff: "I don't know what Wikipedia would look like without the active support of 100+ full-time staff."[22]

In any case, Goldman's prediction shows what *not* to do as a successful tech prognosticator. Like those of a neighborhood fortune teller, predictions ought to be nonspecific in content and time. Goldman predicted Wikipedia's death (rather than subtle changes in openness) in a five-year horizon (rather than "soon") and specified the process of its demise (a death spiral). Although this weakens the likelihood of a prediction, it clarifies rather than obfuscates the concerns discussed. Kudos.

Contributor Attrition (2009–2017)

I underestimated Wikipedia in its first few years, as did everyone. However, in subsequent years, I was confident Wikipedia would continue as a wiki and as an encyclopedia, despite the dismal prognostications by some.

However, in 2009, it became clear that the English Wikipedia was facing possible senescence. That year, researchers found evidence that Wikipedia's new article growth had slowed or plateaued. Additionally, new contributions were being increasingly deleted and reverted, and the balance of activity was favoring experienced editors over newcomers. Over the next five years, researchers, Wikipedians, and the Wikimedia Foundation documented similar changes and attempted remedies. Headlines reported on an "aging" Wikipedia that was on the "decline" and "slowly dying."[23]

Though one prominent Wikipedian invoked Twain's "exaggerated death" quip again in Wikipedia's defense, the trend was undeniable and the concern was widespread. Attempts to retain contributors, to make the site easier to use, and to recruit newcomers were belied by a 2014 story. *The Economist* reported that the past seven years had seen the number of active editors with five or more edits in a given month fall by a third.[24] Wikipedia's statistics page shows that the active editors fell from a peak of fifty-three thousand in 2007 to around thirty thousand in 2014. Without the efforts to shore up Wikipedia, these numbers could have been even worse, but things weren't getting better.

Through 2017, the prognostications remained dismal as people spoke of Wikipedia's "extinction event" and wrote that "Wikipedia Editors Are a Dying Breed." A 2015 *New York Times* opinion piece asked, "Can Wikipedia Survive?"[25] The fear in many of these pieces was that Wikipedia's problems were being compounded by peoples' move to smartphones, where editing Wikipedia is not easy.

Nonetheless, it appears that the number of active editors has been stable since 2014, never dropping below twenty-nine thousand, and that this pattern of fast growth and plateau is not unusual for wikis.[26] Therefore, the English Wikipedia's growth to maturity might be likened to that of the quaking aspen (*populus tremuloides*). The tree grows aggressively toward maturity, sending out roots from which new trees grow. Even if the English Wikipedia has slowed, the larger Wikimedia grove continues to grow.

Conclusion (2020–)

At this point, it's foolish for anyone to predict Wikipedia's death. While such a prognostication makes for catchy headlines—which will probably continue—Wikipedia persists. It has survived modest expectations, an identity crisis, spammers, and contributor attrition. Wikipedia is undoubtedly an encyclopedia; it's the go-to reference of the twenty-first century. Although getting a handle on Wikipedia's hundreds of templates and policies is daunting, some continue to make the effort.

It isn't wrong, of course, to be concerned about Wikipedia. It's an important website that has become even more so in its last decade. Wikipedia is among only a handful of significant noncommercial websites. It's doing a decent job at resisting large-scale misinformation and manipulation. And its data is increasingly relied on by other web services.

It isn't wrong to think about the future, but there's a difference between the future and hype. I appreciate Goldman's five-year prediction. Unlike clickbait, his prediction was based on a plausible theory with specific implications. This kind of prediction can sharpen our discussions rather than muddle them.

The only prediction that I'd hazard for the next ten years is that Wikipedia will still exist. The platform and community have momentum which no alternative will supplant. And by then, the Wikimedia Endowment, started in 2016, should have raised its goal of a $100 million toward maintaining its projects "in perpetuity." The English Wikipedia community will no doubt face challenges and crises as it always has, but I don't foresee anything so profound that only a husk of unchanging articles remains.

I predict Wikipedia will live.

Acknowledgments: I was able to improve this essay with the help of LiAnna L. Davis, Jackie Koerner, Jake Orlowitz, Ian Ramjohn, and Denny Vrandečić. Thank you.

Notes

1. Joseph Reagle, *Good Faith Collaboration: The Culture of Wikipedia* (Cambridge, MA: MIT Press, 2010), https://reagle.org/joseph/2010/gfc/.

2. Joseph Reagle, "Wikipedia: The Happy Accident," *Interactions* 16, no. 3 (2009): 42–45, http://doi.acm.org/10.1145/1516016.1516026.

3. Stacy Schiff, "Know It All: Can Wikipedia Conquer Expertise?" *The New Yorker*, July 31, 2006, 3, http://www.newyorker.com/archive/2006/07/31/060731fa_fact; Larry Sanger, "Let's Make a Wiki," nupedia-l, January 10, 2001, http://web.archive .org/web/20030822044803/http://www.nupedia.com/pipermail/nupedia-l/2001 -January/000676.html.

4. Joseph Reagle, "Wikipedia 10K Redux," *Open Codex* (blog), December 16, 2010, https://reagle.org/joseph/blog/social/wikipedia/10k-redux.html.

5. Peter Jasco, email message to author, February 22, 2019.

6. Herb Brody, "Great Expectations: Why Technology Predictions Go Awry," in *Technology and the Future*, ed. Albert H. Teich, 7th ed. (New York: St. Martin's Press, 1997), 113.

7. Ward Cunningham, Jimmy Wales, and Larry Sanger, "Wiki Pedia," C2, January 2001, http://wiki.c2.com/?WikiPedia.

8. Ward Cunningham, "Interview/Ward Cunningham," *Wikimedia Quarto* 1 (2004), http://wikimediafoundation.org/wiki/Interview/Ward_Cunningham.

9. Larry Sanger, "Why Wikipedia Must Jettison Its Anti-Elitism," Kuro5hin, December 31, 2004, http://www.kuro5hin.org/story/2004/12/30/142458/25.

10. Danah boyd, "Academia and Wikipedia," *Many-to-Many* (blog), January 4, 2005, https://web.archive.org/web/20060316184224/http://many.corante.com/archives /2005/01/04/academia_and_wikipedia.php.

11. Clay Shirky, "Wikipedia: Me on Boyd on Sanger on Wales," *Many-to-Many* (blog), January 5, 2005, https://web.archive.org/web/20050107003720/www.corante.com /many/archives/2005/01/05/wikipedia_me_on_boyd_on_sanger_on_wales.php.

12. Danah boyd, email message to author, February 21, 2019.

13. David Nye, "Technological Prediction: A Promethean Problem," in *Technological Visions: The Hopes and Fears That Shape New Technologies*, ed. Marita Sturken, Douglas Thomas, and Sandra Ball (Philadelphia: Temple University Press, 2004), 171.

14. Eric Goldman, "Wikipedia Will Fail Within 5 Years," *Technology & Marketing Law Blog* (blog), December 5, 2005, http://blog.ericgoldman.org/archives/2005/12/wikipedia_will.htm.

15. Jimmy Wales, "Re: Neo-Nazis to Attack Wikipedia," wikien-l, February 7, 2005, http://marc.info/?i=20050207162911.GO29080@wikia.com.

16. Goldman, "Wikipedia Will Fail Within 5 Years."

17. Mike Godwin, "Will Wikipedia Fail in Five Years?" *Godwin's Law Blog* (blog), December 6, 2005, https://web.archive.org/web/20060206175448/www.godwinslaw.org/weblog/archive/2005/12/06/will-wikipedia-fail-in-five-years.

18. Eric Goldman, "Wikipedia Will Fail in Four Years," *Technology & Marketing Law Blog* (blog), December 5, 2006, http://blog.ericgoldman.org/archives/2006/12/wikipedia_will_1.htm.

19. Ross Mayfield, "Nick Carr Is the New Dave Winer," *Ross Mayfield's Weblog* (blog), May 25, 2006, http://ross.typepad.com/blog/2006/05/nick_carr_is_th.html; Clay Shirky, "News of Wikipedia's Death Greatly Exaggerated," *Many-to-Many* (blog), May 25, 2006, http://many.corante.com/archives/2006/05/25/news_of_wikipedias_death_greatly_exaggerated.php.

20. Eric Goldman, "Wikipedia's Labor Squeeze and Its Consequences," *Journal of Telecommunications and High Technology* 8, 2009, 6, http://papers.ssrn.com/sol3/papers.cfm?abstract_id=1458162.

21. Christopher Dawson, "Google Knol—Yup, It's a Wikipedia Killer," ZDNet, July 28, 2008, https://www.zdnet.com/article/google-knol-yup-its-a-wikipedia-killer/; Christopher Dawson, "Wolfram Alpha: Wikipedia Killer?" ZDNet, May 17, 2009, https://www.zdnet.com/article/wolfram-alpha-wikipedia-killer/; TechCrunch, "Is Owl AOL's Wikipedia-Killer?" *Mediapost*, January 18, 2010, https://www.mediapost.com/publications/article/120803/is-owl-aols-wikipedia-killer.html.

22. Eric Goldman, email message to author, April 29, 2019.

23. Julia Angwin and Geoffrey A. Fowler, "Volunteers Log Off as Wikipedia Ages," *The Wall Street Journal*, November 27, 2009, https://www.wsj.com/articles/SB125893981183759969; Adrian Chen, "Wikipedia Is Slowly Dying," *Gawker* (blog), August 4, 2011, https://gawker.com/5827835/wikipedia-is-slowly-dying; Tom Simonite, "The Decline of Wikipedia," *MIT Technology Review*, October 22, 2013, https://www.technologyreview.com/s/520446/the-decline-of-wikipedia/.

24. Kaldari, "Reports of Wikipedia's Demise Greatly Exaggerated," *WikiVoices* (blog), August 19, 2009, http://web.archive.org/web/20120127062644/wikivoices.blogspot

.com/2009/08/reports-of-wikipedias-demise-are.html; "The Future of Wikipedia: Wiki-Peaks?" *The Economist*, March 4, 2014, https://www.economist.com/international/2014/03/04/wikipeaks.

25. Andrew Lih, "Can Wikipedia Survive?" *The New York Times*, June 20, 2015, https://www.nytimes.com/2015/06/21/opinion/can-wikipedia-survive.html.

26. "Wikipedia Statistics English," Wikimedia, January 31, 2019, https://stats.wiki media.org/EN/TablesWikipediaEN.htm; Nathan TeBlunthuis, Aaron Shaw, and Benjamin Mako Hill, "Revisiting 'the Rise and Decline' in a Population of Peer Production Projects," in *CHI '18: Proceedings of the 2018 CHI Conference on Human Factors in Computing Systems*, ed. R. Mandryk and M. Hancock (New York: Association for Computing Machinery, 2018), http://dx.doi.org/10.1145/3173574.3173929.

2 From Anarchy to Wikiality, Glaring Bias to Good Cop: Press Coverage of Wikipedia's First Two Decades

Omer Benjakob and Stephen Harrison

Media coverage of Wikipedia has radically shifted over the past two decades: once cast as an intellectual frivolity, it is now lauded as the "last bastion of shared reality" online. To increase diversity and digital literacy, journalists and the Wikipedia community should work together to advance a new "wiki journalism."

"Jimmy Wales has been shot dead, according to Wikipedia, the online, up-to-the-minute encyclopedia." That was the opening line of a blatantly false 2005 news report by the online magazine the *Register*.[1] Rather than being an early example of what we may today call "fake news," the report by the tech site was a consciously snarky yet prescient criticism of Wikipedia and its reliability as a source for media. Wales was still alive, of course, despite what it had briefly stated on his Wikipedia entry, but by attributing his death to English Wikipedia, the *Register* sought to call out a perceived flaw in Wikipedia: on Wikipedia, truth was fluid, and facts were exposed to anonymous vandals who could take advantage of its anyone-can-edit model to spread disinformation.

Over the past twenty years, English Wikipedia has frequently been the subject of media coverage, from in-depth exposés to colorful features and critical op-eds. But if you randomly sample the words used to describe Wikipedia from the headlines in this period, you might conclude that the press has no idea what it thinks about the free internet encyclopedia. Should we refer to it as "the hive" as the *Atlantic* did in 2006 or rather as the "good cop of the internet" as the *Washington Post* did in 2018? Is Wikipedia "impolite" as the *New York Times* claimed in 2008 or rather a "ray of light" as the *Guardian* suggested in 2018?[2] Is there a logical progression to how the press has described Wikipedia over the past two decades, or does seemingly every reporter possess a dramatically different opinion?

Both of us are journalists who have regularly covered Wikipedia in recent years, and before that we were frequent consumers of knowledge on the site (like many of our journalist colleagues). Press coverage of Wikipedia during the past twenty years has undergone a dramatic shift, and we believe it's important to highlight how the media's understanding of Wikipedia has shifted along with the public's understanding. Initially cast as the symbol of intellectual frivolity in the digital age, Wikipedia is now being lauded as the "last bastion of shared reality" in Trump's America.[3] Coverage, we claim, has evolved from bewilderment at the project to concern and hostility at its model, to acceptance of its merits and disappointment at its short-comings, and finally to calls to hold it socially accountable and reform it like any other institution.

We argue that press coverage of Wikipedia can be roughly divided into four periods. We have named each period after a major theme: "Authorial Anarchy" (2001–2004/2005); "Wikiality" (2005–2008); "Bias" (2011–2017); and "Good Cop" (2018–present). We note upfront that these categories are not rigid and that themes and trends from one period can and often do carry over into others. But the overall progression reveals how the dynamic relationship between Wikipedia and the press has changed since its inception and might provide further insight into how the press and Wikipedia will continue to interact with each other in the internet's knowledge ecosystem.

In short, we argue for what we term "wiki journalism" and the need for media to play a larger role in improving the general public's "Wikipedia literacy." With the help of the Wikimedia Foundation and the Wikipedia community, we claim that the press can play a more substantial role in explaining Wikipedia to the public and in serving as a civilian watchdog for the online encyclopedia. Encouraging critical readership of Wikipedia and helping to increase diversity among its editorship will ensure greater public oversight over the digital age's preeminent source of knowledge.

Authorial Anarchy (2001–2004/2005)

When Wikipedia was launched in 2001, mainstream media as well as more technology minded outlets treated it as something between a fluke and quirky outlier. With quotes from cofounders Jimmy Wales and Larry Sanger, early coverage tended to focus on what seemed like Wikipedia's most novel aspects: how it is written by anyone, is edited collaboratively, is free to access, and in the case of tech media, extends the culture of open software development to the realm of encyclopedias.

"Anyone who visits the site is encouraged to participate," the *New York Times* wrote in its first piece on Wikipedia, titled "Fact-Driven? Collegial? This Site Wants You." Reports like these laid out the basic tenets of English Wikipedia, focusing on how collaborative technology and the volunteer community regulated what was termed "authorial anarchy."[4] Many of these reports included a colorful lede ("What does Nicole Kidman have in common with Kurt Godel?" Hint: Both have Wikipedia articles) showcasing the quirky diversity of content on the new site, where "you don't even have to give your real name" to contribute.[5]

Despite Wales's lofty claims that Wikipedia was creating a world in which everyone could have "free access to the sum of all human knowledge," throughout the early 2000s mainstream media remained skeptical toward Wikipedia.[6] Reports from 2002–2003 mostly documented with some surprise its rapid growth in scale and scope as well as its expansion into other languages. *MIT Technology Review* ran a report called "Free the Encyclopedias!," which described Wikipedia as "intellectual anarchy extruded into encyclopedia form" and "a free-wheeling Internet-based encyclopedia whose founders hope will revolutionize the stodgy world of encyclopedias"[7]—then still dominated by the Enlightenment-era *Britannica* and its more digital savvy competitor *Encarta*.

Repeated comparison with *Encarta* and *Britannica* is perhaps the most prominent characteristic of early media coverage, one that will disappear in later stages as Wikipedia cements its status as a legitimate encyclopedia. *MIT Technology Review*, for example, unironically claimed that Wikipedia "will probably never dethrone *Britannica*, whose 232-year reputation is based upon hiring world-renowned experts and exhaustively reviewing their articles with a staff of more than a hundred editors."[8] The demise of the status of experts would later become a hallmark of coverage of Wikipedia (discussed in the next section), but its seeds can be found from the onset: for example, in its first *exposé* on Wikipedia in 2004, the *Washington Post* reported that *Britannica*'s vaunted staff was now down to a mere twenty editors. Only a year prior, Wikipedia editors noted that the prestigious paper "brushed off" Wikipedia almost entirely and instead focused on CD-ROM encyclopedias[9]—all the rage since *Encarta* launched a decade earlier and mounted what seemed at the time to be the bigger threat toward *Britannica*. Within a year, however, the newspaper's take on Wikipedia changed dramatically, and it was now concerned by the long-term effect of Wikipedia's success, suggesting "the Internet's free dissemination of knowledge will eventually decrease the economic value of information."[10]

At the end of 2005, this tension between the English encyclopedia of the Enlightenment and that of the digital age would reach its zenith in a now infamous *Nature* news study that compared Wikipedia and *Britannica* (also discussed in chapter 13). Published in December 2005, *Nature's* "Internet Encyclopaedias Go Head to Head" found Wikipedia to be as accurate as its Enlightenment-era competitor based on experts' comparisons of randomly selected science articles.[11] News that Wikipedia successfully passed scientific scrutiny—that its ever-changing content was deemed to be as reliable as the static entries of a vaunted print-era encyclopedia like *Britannica*—made headlines around the world.[12] The *Nature* study was the final stage in a process that peaked in 2005 and cemented Wikipedia's shift from a web novelty whose value was to be treated skeptically at best to a cultural force to be reckoned with.

In March 2005, Wikipedia had crossed the half million article mark, and some intellectuals began to discuss the "the *wikification* of knowledge."[13] Wales, increasingly an internet celebrity, took his pitch about "a ragtag band of volunteers" revolutionizing encyclopedias to *TED*.[14] In the widely popular talk, titled "The Birth of Wikipedia," Wales failed to reference Sanger, who had left the project in 2002. In the early days Sanger was a leading voice that spoke to the internet community from which Wikipedia's first volunteers were enlisted, penning guest blog posts as part of early outreach efforts. However, as the 2005 *TED* speech symbolized, Wikipedia was now mainstream and no longer aiming at early internet adopters but rather the general public—and Wales had taken on the role of public face of the project.

Tellingly, 2005 was also the year that the Wikipedia community first began recording its coverage in the media in an organized fashion. Initially focused on instances of "Wiki love" from the press, in 2005 the community created categories like "America's Top Newspapers Use Wikipedia" for its early press clippings.[15] The *Signpost*, the online newspaper for English Wikipedia, was also founded in 2005 to report on events related to Wikipedia.[16] Over time the community grew increasingly conscious of its public role, and by 2006 an organized index of all media references to Wikipedia was set up—first with a list for every year and then, as coverage swelled, one for every month as well.[17] Categories were also created for times when Wikipedia was cited as a source of information by mainstream media[18]—a rare reversal of roles that highlighted the mutually affirming relationship between Wikipedia and the media that would develop over later periods.

Indeed, 2005 was to be a key year for Wikipedia: it saw its biggest vindication—the *Nature* report—alongside its biggest vilification—the so-called Seigenthaler affair. John Seigenthaler, a journalist and friend of US President John F. Kennedy, had his Wikipedia article falsely accuse him of playing a role in the president's and the president's brother's assassinations. The error—introduced by an anonymous editor—was eventually erased by Wales himself, but it was online for a number of months and garnered numerous negative headlines for the open encyclopedia and its collaborative model.[19] The author of the *Nature* study made a point of addressing the "Wikipedia Seigenthaler biography incident," writing in the report that in his view "such high-profile examples are the exception rather than the rule."[20] The fallout even caused Wikipedia to reform its policy on articles dealing with the biographies of living people,[21] arguably the first example of successful media-driven public pressure on the community-run encyclopedia.

By 2005, Wikipedia was no longer quirky. Now it was to be viewed within a new framework which contrasted its popularity with its accuracy and debated the risks it posed.[22] The *New York Times*, for example, claimed that the Seigenthaler "case triggered extensive debate on the Internet over the value and reliability of Wikipedia, and more broadly, over the nature of online information."[23] In the next phase, Wikipedia's effect on the popular understanding of truth would be the overriding theme.

Wikiality (2005–2008)

Stephen Colbert launched his satirical news program the *Colbert Report* with a segment dedicated to what would be dubbed 2005's word of the year: *truthiness*.[24] "We're not talking about truth, we're talking about something that seems like truth—the truth we want to exist," Colbert explained.[25] He even urged viewers to take the truth into their own hands and "save" the declining populations of elephants in Africa by changing their numbers on Wikipedia, causing its server to crash. The wider point resonated.[26] "It's on Wikipedia, so it must be true," the *Washington Post* wrote that year.[27] Wikipedia was no longer taken to be just another website; it was now a powerhouse undermining intellectual institutions and capable of changing our very perception of reality.

Colbert followed up his infamous segment with another potent neologism: *wikiality*. "Wikiality," he charged, was the reality created by Wikipedia's model, in which "truth" was based on the will of the majority and not on facts. This was a theme that had a deep political resonance in post-9/11 America, buoyed by the presidency of George W. Bush and the rise to prominence of Fox News—and Wikipedia was increasingly cast as providing its underlying intellectual conditions. This framing peaked in 2005 and 2006 but was omnipresent when Wikipedia launched in 2001, when for example "populist editing" was selected as one of the year's "big ideas."[28] The culture of *truthiness* and the *wikiality* it created were taken to be the real-world manifestations of the Wikipedia philosophy—and the fallout was taking on an increasingly political undertone. "Who is *Britannica* to tell me that George Washington had slaves? If I want to say he didn't, that's my right," Colbert charged. "Thanks to Wikipedia, it's also a fact. [We're] bringing democracy to knowledge."[29]

During 2006–2009, the dominance of Wikipedia's encyclopedic model was solidified. In 2008, the *New York Times* published a "eulogy" for print encyclopedias and flagged the need to understand the "epistemology of Wikipedia" and the "wikitruth" it bred.[30] Wikipedia's underlying philosophy—its model's effects on the very nature of facticity—was now deserving of more serious and critical examination. *MIT Technology Review* ran a piece on "Wikipedia and the Meaning of Truth," asking "why the online encyclopedia's epistemology should worry those who care about traditional notions of accuracy."[31] The manner Wikipedia constructed knowledge and offered an alternative justification to that of expert-based print encyclopedias was taking central stage.

Concerns that Wikipedia's epistemological model was replacing expertise loomed large. In 2006, the *New York Times* debated the merits of "the nitpicking of the masses vs. the authority of the experts," and the *Independent* asked: "Do we need a more reliable online encyclopedia than Wikipedia?"[32] In a report that profiled Wikipedians, the *New Yorker* wondered: "Can Wikipedia conquer expertise?"; and Larry Sanger, who had left the project by then, lamented "the fate of expertise after Wikipedia."[33] Though largely negative, these in-depth reports also permitted a more detailed treatment of Wikipedia's theory of knowledge. Articles like Marshal Poe's "The Hive," published in the *Atlantic's* September 2006 edition, laid out for intellectual readers Wikipedia's history and philosophy like never before.

Epistemic and social fears of Wikipedia were also fueled by Wikipedia's biggest public media storm to date—the so-called Essjay scandal of 2007, in which a prolific Wikipedia editor profiled by the *New Yorker* was revealed to be a fraud. The user Essjay claimed to be a professor of theology but turned out to be a twenty-four-year-old college dropout, Ryan Jordan. Jordan's outing prompted a rare correction from the magazine and made headlines.[34] It even spurred calls to reform Wikipedia.[35] The fact that Jordan held an official status within Wikipedia's community seemed to echo an increasingly accepted political truism: facts were being manipulated by those with power.

During 2004 and 2005, Wikipedia dealt with a number of media storms regarding errors in its political content: notably, the articles of George W. Bush and John Kerry during the 2004 presidential election.[36] The ambiguity of the election's contested results reverberated on Wikipedia in the form of "edit wars," and political vandalism continued to plague Wikipedia throughout Bush's second term, turning his article into one of the "most controversial" ever.[37] Knowledge was increasingly being politicized, and much of Capitol Hill was banned from editing Wikipedia anonymously during 2006 after politicians' articles were whitewashed in what the *Washington Post* called "wikipolitics."[38] During this period Wikipedia also first faced allegations of having a liberal bias—for example, by "evangelical Christians" who opened a conservative *wiki* of their own.[39] Reports like these helped grant social currency to the claim that knowledge was political like never before.

The politicization of knowledge, alongside a proliferation of alternative wikis—exacerbated in part by Wales's for-profit website Wikia, launched in 2006—all served to highlight the *wikiality* of America's political and media landscape.[40] It was at this time that the first cases of "citogenesis"—circular and false reporting originating from Wikipedia—appeared. These incidents showed how dependent classic media was on Wikipedia—and therefore how politically vulnerable and unreliable it was by proxy. They included reports that cited the unfounded claim regarding Hillary Clinton's being the valedictorian of her class at Wellesley College, an error born from false information introduced to her Wikipedia article.[41] The edit wars on Bush's Wikipedia page highlighted the online encyclopedia's role in what the *New York Times* termed the "separate realities" existing within America.[42]

By 2007, Wikipedia was among the top ten most popular websites in the world. Though it was a nonprofit, it enjoyed the top spots on Google's search engine results, sparking concerns of a "googlepedia" by internet thinkers.[43]

Wikipedia was now a primary source of knowledge for the information age, and its internal workings mattered to the general public.[44] Coverage shifted in accordance. Reports began to focus on the internal intellectual battles raging within the community of editors. For example, the *Guardian* wrote about the two different encyclopedic schools of thought active on Wikipedia—the "deletionists," who want to delete low quality articles, as opposed to the "inclusionists," who are more forgiving.[45] For the first time, coverage of Wikipedia was no longer monolithic, and the community was permitted diverging opinions by the press. Wikipedia was less a unified publisher and more a vital discursive arena. Policy changes were debated in the media, and concerns over Wikipedia's "declining user base" were also covered—mostly by Noam Cohen, who covered the encyclopedia for the *New York Times*.[46] Wikipedia was now a beat, its worldview fully embedded within our social and political reality. The question was what was it telling us, who was writing it, and who was being excluded.

Bias (2011–2017)

In February 2011, the *New York Times* ran a series of articles on the question "Where Are the Women of Wikipedia?" in its opinion pages. These 2011 articles have very different headlines than the paper's coverage of Wikipedia in the prior decade. Between roughly the years 2006 to 2009, reporting focused on the reliability of Wikipedia's model, with headlines like "Growing Wikipedia Refines Its 'Anyone Can Edit' Possibility" (2006) and "Without a Source, Wikipedia Can't Handle the Truth" (2008).[47]

By 2011, however, the press coverage had zeroed in on the site's gender imbalance. Headlines were much more openly critical of the community itself than in the past, with a series published in the *New York Times* calling out "trolls and other nuisances" and Wikipedia's "antisocial factor."[48] Press coverage had shifted from the epistemological merits of Wikipedia to legitimate concerns about bias in its contributor base.

The 2011 series about gender on Wikipedia followed a 2010 survey conducted by the United Nations University and UNU-MERIT that indicated only 12.64 percent of Wikipedia contributors were female among the survey's respondents.[49] Although the results of that study were later challenged,[50] the fact that the study received an entire series of articles indicates how the results struck a cultural nerve. What did it say about Wikipedia—and internet knowledge generally—that a disproportionate number of the contributors were men?

One could argue that this shift—from grappling with the underpinnings of Wikipedia's model of knowledge production to a critique of the actual forces and output of the *wiki* way of doing things—symbolized an implicit acceptance of Wikipedia's status as the preeminent source of knowledge in the digital age. Media coverage during this period no longer treated Wikipedia as an outlier, a fluke, or as an epistemological disaster to be entirely rejected. Rather, the press focused on negotiating with Wikipedia as an existing phenomenon, addressing concerns shared by some in the community—especially women, predating the Gamergate debate of 2014.

Press coverage of Wikipedia throughout the period of 2011 to roughly 2017 largely focused on the online encyclopedia's structural bias. This coverage also differed markedly from previous years in its detailed treatment of Wikipedia's internal editorial and community dynamics. The press coverage highlighted not only the gender gap in percentage of female *contributors* but also the gender gap in the *content* of biographical articles and the efforts by some activists to change the status quo. Publications ranging from the *Austin Chronicle* to the *New Yorker* covered feminist edit-a-thons, events to increase and improve Wikipedia's content for female, queer, and women's subjects, linking contemporary identity politics with the online project's goal of organizing access to the sum of human knowledge.[51] In addition to gender, the press covered other types of bias such geographical blind spots and the site's exclusion of oral history and other types of knowledge that did not meet the Western notions of verifiable sources.[52]

During this period, prestigious publications also began profiling individual Wikipedia contributors, giving faces and names to the forces behind our knowledge. "Wikipedians" were increasingly cast as activists and recognized outside the community. The *Washington Post*, for example, covered Dr. Adrianne Wadewitz's death in 2014, noting that Wadewitz was a "Wikipedian" who had "empower[ed] everyday Internet users to be critical of how information is produced on the Internet and move beyond being critical to making it better."[53] The transition from covering Wikipedia's accuracy to covering Wikipedians themselves perhaps reflects an increased concern with awareness about the human motivations of the people contributing knowledge online. Many times this took on a humorous tone, like the case of the "ultimate WikiGnome" Bryan Henderson whose main contribution to Wikipedia was deleting the term "comprised of" from over 40,000 articles.[54] Journalists (including the authors of this chapter) have continued this trend of profiling Wikipedians themselves.

A 2014 YouGov study found that around two-thirds of British people trust the authors of Wikipedia pages to tell the truth, a significantly higher percentage than those who trusted journalists.[55] At the same time, journalists were increasingly open to recognizing how crucial Wikipedia had become to their profession: with the most dramatic decline in newsroom staffs since the Great Recession, Wikipedia was now used by journalists for conducting initial research[56]—another example of the mutually affirming relationship between the two.

As more journalists used and wrote about Wikipedia, the tone of their writing changed. In one of his reports for the *New York Times*, Noam Cohen quoted a French reporter as saying, "Making fun of Wikipedia is so 2007."[57] When Cohen first began covering Wikipedia, most people saw Wikipedia as a hobby for nerds—but that characterization had now become passé. The more pressing concern, according to Cohen, was "seeing Wikipedia as *The Man*."[58] Overall, press coverage of Wikipedia during this period oscillates between fear about the site's long-term existential prospects[59] and concern that the site is continuing the masculinist and Eurocentric biases of historical encyclopedias. The latter is significant as it shows how Wikipedia's pretenses of upending the classic print-model of encyclopedias have been accepted by the wider public, which, in turn, is now concerned or even disappointed that despite its promise of liberating the world's knowledge from the shackles of centralization and expertise, it has in fact recreated most of the biases of yesteryear.

Good Cop (2018–Present)

In April 2018, Cohen wrote an article for the *Washington Post* titled "Conspiracy Videos? Fake News? Enter Wikipedia, the 'Good Cop' of the Internet."[60] For more than a decade, Cohen had written about Wikipedia in the popular press, but his "Good Cop" piece was perhaps his most complimentary and it signaled a wider change in perception regarding Wikipedia. He declared that "fundamentally ... the project gets the big questions right."

Interestingly, Cohen's "Good Cop" article is not unique for its positive press treatment of Wikipedia during this period and marks the latest shift in coverage of Wikipedia, one that embarks from the issue of *truthiness* and reexamines its merits in the wake of "post-truth" politics and "fake news"—2016 and 2017's respective words of the year.

The *Wall Street Journal* credited English Wikipedia's top arbitration body, Arbcom, with "keep[ing] the peace at [the] internet encyclopedia."[61] Other favorable headlines from 2018 and 2019 included "There's a Lot Wikipedia Can Teach Us About Fighting Disinformation" and "In a Hysterical World, Wikipedia Is a Ray of Light—and That's the Truth."[62] Wikipedia was described by the *Atlantic* as "the last bastion of shared reality" online, and for its eighteenth birthday, it was lauded by the *Washington Post* as "the Internet's good grown up."[63]

What caused press coverage of Wikipedia to pivot from criticizing the encyclopedia as "the man" to recognizing Wikipedia's importance as the *good cop*? Several factors converged to cast Wikipedia in a more favorable light. Since the election of President Trump in the United States, the mainstream press has expressed concerns about whether traditional notions of truth and reality-based argument can survive under an administration that is infamous for lying and for its so-called alternative facts. The "truthiness" culture of intellectual promiscuity represented by the presidency of George W. Bush had deteriorated into the post-truth culture of the Trump White House. Wikipedia's procedural answers for the question "What is a fact?," initially hailed as flawed, could now be taken in a different light.[64]

Wikipedia's emphasis on a neutral point of view and the community's goal to maintain an objective description of reality represent an increasingly striking contrast to politicians around the world whose rhetoric is not reality-based.[65] Moreover, the Wikipedia community's commitment to sourcing claims (exemplified by Wikipedia's community ban on the *Daily Mail* in 2017 and of Breitbart News Network in 2018) highlighted how Wikipedia's model was seemingly more successful than the traditional media in fighting "fake news."[66]

In 2018, Wikipedia locked horns with some of those who were considered supportive of Trump and the "post-truth" discourse, including Breitbart and even Russian media. The so-called "Philip Cross affair"[67] saw a British editor face an accusation that he was in fact a front for the UK's Ministry of Defense or even the American CIA, claims that were parroted out by both Sputnik News and Breitbart, with the latter all but declaring war on the online encyclopedia (running no less than ten negative reports about it in as many months, including headlines like "Wikipedia Editors Paid to Protect Political, Tech, and Media Figures" and "Wikipedia Editors Post Fake News on Summary of Mueller Probe").[68] The year 2018 also saw the clearest example of Russian intervention in Wikipedia, with Russian agent Maria Butina being outed by the community for trying to scrub her own Wikipedia page.[69]

The shift toward more positive press treatment of Wikipedia also overlaps with a general trend toward negative coverage of for-profit technology sites. In recent years, Facebook, Google, Twitter, and YouTube have been chastised in the press for privacy violations and election hacking and for being a platform for hateful content. But Wikipedia has largely dodged these criticisms. Complimentary journalists have noted the site's rare position as a nonprofit in the most visited websites in the world—the only site in the global top ten that is not monetized with advertising or by collecting and selling personal information of users. Journalists have also praised Wikipedia's operating model. As Brian Feldman pointed out in a *New York Magazine* piece titled "Why Wikipedia Works," the site's norms of review, monitoring by a community of editors, and deletion of false information and inflammatory material seems vastly superior to the way social media platforms like Twitter fail to moderate similarly problematic content.[70]

It's important to note that even during this period of relatively favorable press coverage of Wikipedia, newspapers have still been publishing highly critical articles. But the focus has been on reforming Wikipedia's governance policies rather than rejecting its underlying model of crowdsourced knowledge.[71] For example, Wikipedia received significant media attention in 2018 when Donna Strickland won a Nobel Prize in physics and, at the time of her award, did not have a Wikipedia page; an earlier entry had been deleted by an editor who found that Strickland lacked sufficient notability, despite the fact her two male co-laureates had pages for the same academic research that earned the three the prestigious award. But note how the press coverage of Strickland did not dispute Wikipedia's underlying premise of community-led knowledge production. Rather, press coverage was continuing the structural critique from the previous phase. Further, by this era the Wikimedia Foundation had increasingly begun speaking publicly about matters of concern to the Wikipedia community. When it came to the Strickland incident, the Wikimedia Foundation was not overly apologetic in its public statements, with Executive Director Katherine Maher writing an op-ed for the *Los Angeles Times* titled "Wikipedia Mirrors the World's Gender Biases, It Doesn't Cause Them."[72] Maher challenged journalists to write more stories about notable women so that volunteer Wikipedians have sufficient material to source in their attempt to fix the bias. Maher's comments, in other words, advocate further awareness of the *symbiotic* relationship between the media and Wikipedia.

The Strickland incident is in some ways an outlier during a time of relatively favorable press coverage of Wikipedia. How long will this honeymoon period last? One indication that the pendulum will swing back in a more critical direction is the coverage of large technology companies that rely on Wikipedia. The press widely covered YouTube's 2018 announcement that it was counting on Wikipedia to counteract videos promoting conspiracy theories when there had been no prior notice to the Wikimedia Foundation regarding YouTube's plans. Journalists also wrote—at times critically—about Facebook's plan to give background information from Wikipedia about publications to combat "fake news," about Google's use of Wikipedia content for its knowledge panels, and how smart assistants like Siri and Alexa pull information from the site.

Prominent tech critics have questioned whether it is truly appropriate to leverage Wikipedia as the "good cop" since the site is maintained by unpaid volunteers and tech companies are using it for commercial purposes. But from a news perspective, it might not matter so much whether it's fair or prudent for technology companies to leverage Wikipedia in this way—the appearance of partnership is enough to spur a news story. The more it seems as if Wikipedia has become aligned with "*Big Tech*," the more likely the encyclopedia will receive similarly adverse coverage.

Conclusion

Over the span of nearly two decades, Wikipedia went from being heralded as the original *fake news*, a symbol of all that was wrong with the internet, to being the "grown up" of the web and the best medicine against the scourge of disinformation. This process was predicated on Wikipedia's epistemological model gaining social acceptance as well as the erosion of status of mainstream media and traditional knowledge sources. Comparisons with older encyclopedias have all but disappeared. More common are appeals like Maher's request following the Strickland affair that journalists aid Wikipedia in the attempt to reform by publishing more articles about women. This dynamic highlights how Wikipedia is now a fixture within our media landscape, increasingly both the source of coverage and the story itself.

Understanding the mutually affirming dynamic between media and Wikipedia opens up a rare opportunity to engage the public directly with some of the issues underscoring "fake news"—from critical reading of different sources to basic epistemological debates, issues that were once considered too academic for mainstream media are now finding their place in the public discourse through coverage of Wikipedia. For example, reports about Strickland's lack of a Wikipedia article helped make accessible the feminist theory regarding knowledge being "gendered." The idea that history is *his-story* was highlighted in debates about Wikipedia's gender bias, with the dire lack of articles about women scientists being easily explained by the lack of historical sources regarding women. Meanwhile, reports about Wikipedia being blocked in countries such as China and Turkey have allowed for a discussion of the politics of knowledge online as well as a debate regarding the differences among Wikipedias in different languages and their local biases. Detailed and critical reports like these are part of a new subgenre of journalism that has emerged in the past years, what we term "wiki journalism": coverage of Wikipedia as a social and political arena in its own right.[73]

Nonetheless, much more can be done—by journalists, the Wikimedia Foundation, and even the Wikipedia community of volunteers. Though Wikipedia's technology purportedly offers fully transparency, public understanding of Wikipedia's processes, bureaucracy, and internal jargon is still a massive obstacle for would-be editors and journalists alike. Despite its open format, the majority of Wikipedia is edited by a fraction of its overall editors, indicating the rise of an encyclopedic elite not too dissimilar in characteristics than that of media and academia. To increase diversity in Wikipedia and serve the public interest requires journalists to go beyond "gotcha" headlines. Much of the popular coverage of Wikipedia is still lacking and is either reductive or superficial, treating Wikipedia as a unified voice and amplifying minor errors and vandalism. Many times, reports like these needlessly politicize Wikipedia. For example, after a vandal wrote that the Republican Party of California believed in "Nazism" and the error was aggregated by Alexa and Google, reports attributed blame to Wikipedia.[74]

Instead of focusing on these, media should work to increase Wikipedia literacy, dedicating more coverage to the project's inner workings and policies. Although the Wikimedia Foundation has taken steps to make press contacts available in recent years, there is still much work to be done to enhance communication between Wikipedia and the media. For example, the Wikimedia Foundation refuses to comment on content disputes (claiming they are an internal community issue), and journalists looking to cover Wikipedia have no official spokesperson to talk to for background or practical instruction. Jimmy Wales serves as a de facto figurehead for the online encyclopedia, but only a privileged few enjoy informal exchanges with Wikipedia's "benevolent dictator."[75] A more formal media relations policy should be developed specifically for Wikipedia by the Foundation. Creating a special status for *wiki journalists*, for example, granting them read-only status for deleted articles and censored edits—a right currently reserved for official administrators—could help reporters better understand the full context of edit wars.

The community must too be more open to working with media and take a much less aggressive approach to external coverage of their debates. Many times, editors are reluctant to speak to reporters and are antagonistic toward unversed users who have come to mend an error or bias they have read about in the media. Wikipedia editors must accept their social role and not just allow the media to highlight problems within their community but proactively flag issues, help reporters sift through countless debates, and find the truly important stories instead of limiting themselves to internal forums and demanding journalists and the public fix Wikipedia themselves.

Together, journalists, the Wikimedia Foundation, and the community can help increase critical digital literacy through deeply reported coverage of Wikipedia. High-quality *wiki journalism* would not treat Wikipedia as a monolithic agent that speaks in one voice but rather would seek to understand the roots of its biases and shortcomings. This will serve to high-light the politics of knowledge production instead of politicizing knowl-edge itself.

Notes

1. Andrew Orlowski, "Wikipedia Founder 'Shot by Friend of Siegenthaler,'" *Register*, December 17, 2005, https://www.theregister.co.uk/2005/12/17/jimmy_wales_shot _dead_says_wikipedia/.

2. Marshall Poe, "The Hive," *Atlantic* 298, no. 2 (2006): 86, https://www.theatlantic .com/magazine/archive/2006/09/the-hive/305118/; Noam Cohen, "Conspiracy Videos? Fake News? Enter Wikipedia, the 'Good Cop' of the Internet," *Washington Post*, April 6, 2018, https://www.washingtonpost.com/outlook/conspiracy-videos-fake -news-enter-wikipedia-the-good-cop-of-the-internet/2018/04/06/ad1f018a-3835-11e8 -8fd2-49fe3c675a89_story.html; Noam Cohen, "Defending Wikipedia's Impolite Side," *New York Times*, August 20, 2007, https://www.nytimes.com/2007/08/20/technology /20link.html; John Naughton, "In a Hysterical World, Wikipedia Is a Ray of Light— and That's the Truth," *Guardian*, September 2, 2018, https://www.theguardian.com /commentisfree/2018/sep/02/in-hysterical-world-wikipedia-ray-of-light-truth.

3. Alexis C. Madrigal, "Wikipedia, the Last Bastion of Shared Reality," *Atlantic*, August 7, 2018, https://www.theatlantic.com/technology/archive/2018/08/jeongpedia /566897/.

4. Peter Meyers, "Fact-Driven? Collegial? This Site Wants You," *New York Times*, September 20, 2001, https://www.nytimes.com/2001/09/20/technology/fact-driven -collegial-this-site-wants-you.html.

5. Judy Heim, "Free the Encyclopedias!" *MIT Technology Review*, September 4, 2001, https://www.technologyreview.com/s/401190/free-the-encyclopedias/.

6. Rob Miller, "Wikipedia Founder Jimmy Wales Responds," *Slashdot*, July 28, 2004, https://slashdot.org/story/04/07/28/1351230/wikipedia-founder-jimmy-wales -responds. Citing Wikipedia, the *New York Times Magazine* chose "Populist edit-ing" as one of 2001's big ideas: Steven Johnson, "The Year in Ideas: A to Z; Populist Editing," *New York Times Magazine*, September 12, 2001, https://www.nytimes.com /2001/12/09/magazine/the-year-in-ideas-a-to-z-populist-editing.html.

7. Heim, "Free the Encyclopedias!"

8. Heim, "Free the Encyclopedias!"

9. Leslie Walker, "Spreading Knowledge: The Wiki Way," *Washington Post*, September 9, 2004, http://www.washingtonpost.com/wp-dyn/articles/A5430-2004Sep8.html; Wikipedia contributors, "Wikipedia: Press coverage 2003," Wikipedia, accessed August

29, 2019, https://en.wikipedia.org/w/index.php?title=Wikipedia:Press_coverage_2003 &oldid=760053436.

10. Walker, "Spreading Knowledge: The Wiki Way."

11. Jim Giles, "Internet Encyclopaedias Go Head to Head," *Nature*, December 14, 2005, https://www.nature.com/articles/438900a.

12. Dan Goodin, "Science Journal: Wikipedia Pretty Accurate," *Associated Press*, December 14, 2005. The *AP* report was reprinted in over 112 media outlets, including *Al Jazeera* and the *China Post*. The *BBC* also reported about *Nature*'s findings, writing: "Wikipedia Survives Research Test" (*BBC News Online*, December 15, 2005), as did Australia's *The Age* (Stephen Cauchi, December 15, 2005), to name a few.

13. John C. Dvorak, "The Wikification of Knowledge," *PC Magazine*, November 7, 2005, https://www.pcmag.com/article2/0,2817,1835857,00.asp; see also Jaron Lanier, "Digital Maoism: The Hazards of the New Online Collectivism," *Edge*, May 29, 2006, https://www.edge.org/conversation/jaron_lanier-digital-maoism-the-hazards-of-the -new-online-collectivism.

14. TED, "Jimmy Wales: How a Ragtag Band Created Wikipedia," YouTube, video, 20:48, January 16, 2007, https://www.youtube.com/watch?v=WQR0gx0QBZ4.

15. Wikipedia, s.v. "Wikipedia: Wikilove from the Press," last modified January 14, 2017, https://en.wikipedia.org/w/index.php?title=Wikipedia:Wikilove_from_the_ press&diff=760052982&oldid=14045772; Wikipedia, s.v. "Wikipedia: America's Top Newspapers Use Wikipedia," accessed August 29, 2019, https://en.wikipedia.org/w /index.php?title=Wikipedia:America%27s_Top_Newspapers_Use_Wikipedia&diff =760053107&oldid=21067987.

16. Wikipedia, s.v. "The Signpost," Wikipedia, accessed August 29, 2019, https://en .wikipedia.org/w/index.php?title=The_Signpost&oldid=913126984.

17. Wikipedia, s.v. "Wikipedia: Press coverage," accessed August 29, 2019, https://en .wikipedia.org/w/index.php?title=Wikipedia:Press_coverage&diff=877404926 &oldid=33446632.

18. Wikipedia, s.v. "Wikipedia: Wikipedia as a Press Source," accessed August 29, 2019, https://en.wikipedia.org/w/index.php?title=Wikipedia:Wikipedia_as_a_press _source&oldid=601134577.

19. Katherine Q. Seelye, "Snared in the Web of a Wikipedia Liar," *New York Times*, December 4, 2005, https://www.nytimes.com/2005/12/04/weekinreview/snared-in -the-web-of-a-wikipedia-liar.html; Jason Fry, "Wikipedia's Woes," *Wall Street Journal*, December 19, 2005, https://www.wsj.com/articles/SB113450010488821460-LrYQrY _jrOtOK3IiwMcglEq6aiE_20061223. It was also on the front page of *Asharq Al-Awsat*'s December 9, 2005 print edition and was even reported in Russian: S. R., "Неслана шала са Википедије," *Politika*, December 16, 2005.

20. Giles, "Internet Encyclopaedias Go Head to Head."

21. Chris Nuttall, "Wikipedia Plans Site Shake-up to Counter 'Abuse,'" *Financial Times*, December 19, 2005.

22. Laura Sydell, "Wikipedia's Growth Comes with Concerns," *NPR's Weekend Edition*, February 20, 2005, https://www.npr.org/templates/story/story.php?storyId =4506421?storyId=4506421.

23. Seelye, "Snared in the Web of a Wikipedia Liar."

24. Allan Metcalf, "Truthiness Voted 2005 Word of the Year by American Dialect Society," *American Dialect Society*, January 6, 2005, 1–7.

25. Matthew F. Pierlott, "Truth, Truthiness, and Bullshit for the American Voter," in *Stephen Colbert and Philosophy: I Am Philosophy (and So Can You!), ed.* A. A. Schiller (Peru, IL: Open Court Publishing, 2009), 78.

26. The stunt earned Colbert (or at least a user associated with him) a lifetime ban from editing Wikipedia, but others followed suit: the *Washington Post's* satirical columnist Gene Weingarten, for example, introduced errors into his own page to see how long they would stand online—a genre in its own right—see, for example, Gene Weingarten, "Wiki Watchee," *Washington Post*, March 11, 2007, http://www .washingtonpost.com/wp-dyn/content/article/2007/03/06/AR2007030601573.html.

27. Frank Ahrens, "It's on Wikipedia, So It Must Be True," *Washington Post*, August 6, 2006, https://www.washingtonpost.com/archive/business/2006/08/06/its-on-wiki pedia-so-it-must-be-true/c3668ff7-0b66-4968-b669-56c982c2c3fd/.

28. Johnson, "The Year in Ideas: A to Z; Populist Editing."

29. David Detmer, "Philosophy in the Age of Truthiness," in *Stephen Colbert and Philosophy: I Am Philosophy (and So Can You!),* ed. Aaron Allen Schiller, (Peru, IL: Open Court Publishing, 2009); *The Colbert Report*, July 31, 2016.

30. Noam Cohen, "Start Writing the Eulogies for Print Encyclopedias," *New York Times*, March 16, 2008, https://www.nytimes.com/2008/03/16/weekinreview/16n cohen.html.

31. Simson L. Garfinkel, "Wikipedia and the Meaning of Truth," *Technology Review*, 111, no. 6 (2008): 84–86.

32. George Johnson, "The Nitpicking of the Masses vs. the Authority of the Experts," *New York Times*, January 3, 2006, https://www.nytimes.com/2006/01/03/science/the -nitpicking-of-the-masses-vs-the-authority-of-the-experts.html; Paul Vallely, "The Big Question: Do We Need a More Reliable Online Encyclopedia than Wikipedia?" *Independent*, October 18, 2006.

33. Lawrence M. Sanger, "The Fate of Expertise After Wikipedia," *Episteme* 6, no. 1 (2009): 52–73.

34. Catherine Elsworth, "Wikipedia Professor Is 24-Year-Old College Dropout," *Telegraph*, March 7, 2007.

35. Brian Bergstein, "After Flap Over Phony Professor, Wikipedia Wants Writers to Share Real Names," *Associated Press*, March 7, 2007; Noam Cohen, "After False Claim, Wikipedia to Check Whether a User Has Advanced Degrees," *New York Times*, March 12, 2007; Noam Cohen, "Wikipedia Tries Approval System to Reduce Vandalism on Pages," *New York Times*, July 17, 2008.

36. Sarah Boxer, "Mudslinging Weasels into Online History," *New York Times*, November 10, 2004.

37. Andrew Griffin, "Wikipedia's Most Edited Articles: WWE and George W Bush Take Spot as Encyclopedia's Most Controversial Topics," *Independent*, June 25, 2015.

38. Yuki Noguchi, "On Capitol Hill, Playing WikiPolitics," *Washington Post*, February 4, 2006, www.washingtonpost.com/wp-dyn/content/article/2006/02/03/AR2006020302610.htm; Nate Anderson, "Congressional Staffers Edit Boss's Bio on Wikipedia," *Ars Technical*, January 30, 2006 https://arstechnica.com/uncategorized/2006/01/6079-2/

39. Bobbie Johnson, "Conservapedia—The US Religious Right's Answer to Wikipedia," *Guardian*, March 2, 2007.

40. Jacqueline Hicks Grazette, "Wikiality in My Classroom," *Washington Post*, March 23, 2007, http://www.washingtonpost.com/wp-dyn/content/article/2007/03/23/AR2007032301614.html.

41. Wikipedia, s.v. "Reliability of Wikipedia," accessed August 29, 2019, https://en.wikipedia.org/w/index.php?title=Reliability_of_Wikipedia&oldid=907354472.

42. John Schwarz, "When No Fact Goes Unchecked," *New York Times*, October 31, 2004.

43. Steve Fuller, *Post-Truth: Knowledge as a Power Game* (London, UK: Anthem Press, 2018), 125; John C. Dvorak, "Googlepedia: The End is Near," *PC Magazine*, February 17, 2005.

44. Katie Hafner, "Growing Wikipedia Refines Its 'Anyone Can Edit' Policy," *New York Times*, June 17, 2006, https://www.nytimes.com/2006/06/17/technology/17wiki.html.

45. Bobbie Johnson, "Deletionists vs. Inclusionists. Teaching People about the Wikipedia World," *Guardian*, August 12, 2009.

46. Noam Cohen, "Wikipedia May Restrict Public's Ability to Change Entries," *New York Times*, January 23, 2009.

47. Katie Hafner, "Growing Wikipedia Refines Its 'Anyone Can Edit' Policy"; Idea of the Day Series, "The Epistemology of Wikipedia," *New York Times*, October 23, 2008.

48. Terri Oda, "Trolls and Other Nuisances," *New York Times*, February 4, 2011; Anna North, "The Antisocial Factor," *New York Times*, February 2, 2011; Henry Etzkowitz and Maria Ranga, "Wikipedia: Nerd Avoidance," *New York Times*, February 4, 2011.

49. Ruediger Glott, Phillip Schmidt, and Rishab Ghoseh, "Wikipedia Survey— Overview of Results," United Nations University, March 15, 2010.

50. Benjamin Mako Hill and Aaron Shaw, "The Wikipedia Gender Gap Revisited: Characterizing Survey Response Bias with Propensity Score Estimation," *Plos One*, June 26, 2013, https://journals.plos.org/plosone/article?id=10.1371/journal.pone .006578.

51. Sarah Marloff, "Feminist Edit-a-Thon Makes Wikipedia More Diverse," *Austin Chronicle*, March 10, 2017, https://www.austinchronicle.com/daily/news/2017-03 -10/feminist-edit-a-thon-makes-wikipedia-more-diverse/.

52. Seth Stephens-Davidowitz, "The Geography of Fame," *New York Times*, March 22, 2014, https://www.nytimes.com/2014/03/23/opinion/sunday/the-geography-of -fame.html.

53. Elaine Woo, "Adrianne Wadewitz, Wikipedia Contributor, Dies at 37," *Washington Post*, April 25, 2014.

54. Andrew McMillen, "Meet the Ultimate Wikignome," *Wired*, February 3, 2015, https://www.wired.com/2015/02/meet-the-ultimate-wikignome/.

55. William Jordan, "British People Trust Wikipedia More Than the News," *YouGov*, August 9, 2014, https://yougov.co.uk/topics/politics/articles-reports/2014/08/09/more -british-people-trust-wikipedia-trust-news.

56. Holly Epstein Ojalvo, "How Do You Use Wikipedia? Media People Talking About How They Use It," *New York Times*, November 9, 2010, https://learning.blogs .nytimes.com/2010/11/09/how-do-you-use-wikipedia/.

57. Noam Cohen, "When Knowledge Isn't Written, Does It Still Count?" *New York Times*, August 7, 2011.

58. Cohen, "When Knowledge Isn't Written, Does It Still Count?"

59. Andrew Lih, "Wikipedia Just Turned 15 Years Old. Will it Survive 15 More?" *Washington Post*, January 15, 2016, https://www.washingtonpost.com/news/the -intersect/wp/2016/01/15/wikipedia-just-turned-15-years-old-will-it-survive-15 -more.

60. Noam Cohen, "Conspiracy Videos? Fake News? Enter Wikipedia, the 'Good Cop' of the Internet," *Washington Post*, April 6, 2018, https://www.washingtonpost .com/outlook/conspiracy-videos-fake-news-enter-wikipedia-the-good-cop-of-the -internet/2018/04/06/ad1f018a-3835-11e8-8fd2-49fe3c675a89_story.html.

61. Corine Ramey, "The 15 People Who Keep Wikipedia's Editors from Killing Each Other," *Wall Street Journal*, May 7, 2018, https://www.wsj.com/articles/when -wikipedias-bickering-editors-go-to-war-its-supreme-court-steps-in-1525708429.

62. Omer Benjakob, "Verified: Wikipedia Is Our Unlikely Champion in the War of Fake News," *Wired UK*, July 2019, 22–23.

63. Madrigal, "Wikipedia, the Last Bastion of Shared Reality"; Stephen Harrison, "Happy 18th Birthday, Wikipedia. Let's Celebrate the Internet's Good Grown-up," *Washington Post*, January 14, 2019, https://www.washingtonpost.com/opinions /happy-18th-birthday-wikipedia-lets-celebrate-the-internets-good-grown-up/2019 /01/14/e4d854cc-1837-11e9-9ebf-c5fed1b7a081_story.html.

64. Omer Benjakob, "Is the Sky Blue? How Wikipedia Is Fighting for Facts by Redefining the Truth," *Haaretz*, December 15, 2017, https://www.haaretz.com /science-and-health/.premium.MAGAZINE-how-wikipedia-is-fighting-for-facts-by -redefining-the-truth-1.5628749.

65. Madrigal, "Wikipedia, the Last Bastion of Shared Reality."

66. Stephen Amstrong, "Inside Wikipedia's Volunteer-run Battle Against Fake News," *Wired*, August 21, 2018, https://www.wired.co.uk/article/fake-news-wikipedia -arbitration-committee.

67. Omer Benjakob, "The Witch Hunt Against a 'Pro-Israel' Wikipedia Editor," *Haaretz*, May 17, 2018, https://www.haaretz.com/world-news/russian-and-leftists-witch-hunt -against-pro-israel-wikipedia-editor-1.6115917.

68. Omer Benjakob, "Breitbart Declares War on Wikipedia as Encyclopedia Gets Drafted into Facebook's 'Fake News' Battle," *Haaretz*, April 24, 2018, https://www .haaretz.com/us-news/.premium-breitbart-declares-war-on-wikipedia-in-facebook-s -fight-against-fake-news-1.5991915.

69. Lachlan Markay and Dean Sterling Jones, "Who Whitewashed the Wiki of Alleged Russian Spy Maria Butina?" *Daily Beast*, July 24, 2018, https://www.thedailybeast .com/who-whitewashed-the-wiki-of-alleged-russian-spy-maria-butina/.

70. Brian Feldman, "Why Wikipedia Works," *New York Magazine*, March 16, 2018, http://nymag.com/intelligencer/2018/03/why-wikipedia-works.html.

71. Martin Dittus and Mark Graham, "To Reduce Inequality, Wikipedia Should Consider Paying Editors," *Wired UK*, September 11, 2018, https://www.wired.co.uk /article/wikipedia-inequality-pay-editors.

72. Katherine, Maher, "Wikipedia Mirrors the World's Gender Biases, It Doesn't Cause Them," *Los Angeles Times*, October 18, 2018, https://www.latimes.com /opinion/op-ed/la-oe-maher-wikipedia-gender-bias-20181018-story.html.

73. Brian Feldman, "Why Wikipedia Works," *New York Magazine*, March 16, 2018, http://nymag.com/intelligencer/2018/03/why-wikipedia-works.html.

74. "Google Blames Wikipedia for Linking California GOP to Nazism," *Associated Press*, June 1, 2018.

75. Martin Dittus and Mark Graham, "To Reduce Inequality, Wikipedia Should Consider Paying Editors," *Wired UK*, September 11, 2018, https://www.wired.co.uk /article/wikipedia-inequality-pay-editors.

3   From Utopia to Practice and Back

Yochai Benkler

Wikipedia has been a useful utopia for conceiving how people could cooperate productively without market relations and hierarchies. Despite the limitations of that vision and disappointments with recent history, Wikipedia remains a critical anchor for working alternatives to neoliberalism.

Warts and all, Wikipedia and commons-based peer production more generally continue to offer an existence proof that there can be another way. People can work together, build a shared identity in a community of practice, and make things they need without resorting to enforced market exchange. The great challenge of the next twenty years is working out how we can recombine what has worked in commons-based peer production to contribute to a genuine alternative to neoliberalism: we need to understand how to generalize commons-based peer production to society at large, cognizant of its imperfections and limitations; how to enable people to satisfy their basic material needs as they work together, without being forced into working in a competitive labor market that defines their choices and trade-offs; how to integrate commons-based practices into a system that still includes and relies on both state and market processes; how to use its lessons to improve each of these other systems; and how to protect the commons from the relentless encroachment by market and state actors as we have seen in the past decade.

I first published about Wikipedia in 2002.[1] Together with Free/Libre and Open Source Software (FLOSS) and other peer-produced publications like Slashdot, I argued that Wikipedia was a core instance of what was emerging as a new mode of production—commons-based peer production. The success of these practices was radical when considered on the background of prevailing wisdom. Had you asked a room full of well-socialized policy wonks in 1996 whether a loose networks of software developers, without property rights or formal organizational structure, could outcompete the biggest software companies in the world or whether thousands of individuals could collaborate to produce an encyclopedia that would become more important than *Britannica*, similarly without anyone asserting exclusive property rights or formal organizational authority, you would have been laughed out of the room. And yet, FLOSS and Wikipedia do exist and have thrived despite the overwhelming weight of contrary theory dominant at the time. They represented the potential, I wrote at the time, that

> productivity and growth can be sustained in a pattern that differs fundamentally from the industrial information economy of the twentieth century in two crucial characteristics. First, nonmarket production ... can play a much more important role than it could in the physical economy. Second, radically decentralized production and distribution, whether market-based or not, can similarly play a much more important role.[2]

Two decades later, we've learned not only the wonders of Wikipedia but its limits as a model as well.

If the foundation of capitalism is the combination of private property, commodified exchange, and wage labor, Wikipedia (and FLOSS, Slashdot, etc.) were none of the above. The "commons-based" aspect of the practice inverted all three core attributes. First, FLOSS and Wikipedia eschewed property-based exclusion. The inputs and outputs of production were licensed so that anyone could take them and make what they wanted or needed out of them. An open access commons that anyone can use as they need it for either consumption of production was the basic form. Second, production was not for commodity exchange. People were producing for their own and each other's use and pleasure first and for sale, if at all, only secondarily. Third, most of the production occurred in social contributions and through social exchange rather than as wage labor in markets. At the time, this was true even for FLOSS, and it continues to be the case for Wikipedia. This is the first dimension of freedom that "commons-based" practices promised: freedom from markets. They suggested the ability to live our lives under the constraints of social relations other than those dictated by the need to buy and sell labor to obtain the basic necessities of life.

The "peer-production" part of the practice had to do with the displacement of hierarchy in favor of decentralized coordination or, as in the case of Wikipedia, self-governance around a set of shared social norms. It was this aspect that at the time I found most distinctive about the then-eighteen-months-old encyclopedia relative to other commons-based practices online: it was fully based on social norms rather than on technical constraints that prevented "defection" by noncooperators. It was

> a rich example of a medium sized collection of individuals, who collaborate to produce an information product of mid- to highbrow quality, and is reasonably successful. In particular, it suggests that even in a group of this size, social norms coupled with a simple facility to allow any participant to edit out blatant opinion written in by another in contravention of the social norms keep the group on track.[3]

Neither state administration nor corporate managerial hierarchy was necessary for groups to scale to large numbers and effectively produce critical information, knowledge, and cultural goods. Or so at least it seemed at the time. We can think of this as freedom from hierarchy or domination, distinct from freedom from markets.

Along both these dimensions (freedom from markets and freedom from hierarchy), Wikipedia, FLOSS, and commons-based peer production (CBPP) were both an idea and a utility (see table 3.1).

As an idea, CBPP could serve as a shining light for others, showing a very real possibility of organizing productive life differently. They were instances of a utopian project, like the Israeli Kibbutz movement and the Mondragon federation of worker cooperatives, serving as inspiring examples of the possibility of arranging production outside of market relations. Wikipedia in

Table 3.1
Wikipedia's great success: A nonmarket basic knowledge utility.

	Freedom from markets	Freedom from hierarchy
Idea	Emerging at the height of neoliberalism, CBPP offered an existence proof that nonmarket, socially embedded mechanisms could be productive and central to innovation	Allied with the Elinor Ostrom school of the commons, CBPP offered an existence proof that people could overcome "the logic of collective action"; organization did not necessarily resolve into hierarchy or markets
Utility	Affordances developed by nonmarket actors—foundations and networked individuals—create work-arounds to circumvent systems designed to extract rents	Affordances produced by anarchic, flat, cooperative networks would provide alternatives to systems that enforced submission to control relationships

particular offered an example of how tens of thousands of people could cooperate through debate, persuasion, and shared social norms rather than through benevolent dictatorship, as many FLOSS projects did; through mechanism-design-informed technical affordances, like Slashdot; through voting rules that ultimately subjected the minority to the majority; or through pricing.

As a utility, CBPP could serve as a core set of basic utilities that would give their users practical freedom to work around constraints and sources of exploitation that were built by market-centric, proprietary actors. If Microsoft's Windows enforced certain constraints on how you could use software or view video, then GNU/Linux would allow you to run the software or use the video as you chose. If Internet Explorer (now Edge) featured weak privacy protection or enforced digital rights management (DRM) that constrained fair use of cultural materials, Firefox would provide these affordances. If mobile phone carriers restricted how you could use mobile internet, spectrum-commons-based community networks would let you connect without being so constrained. If repressive governments tried to spy on you, FLOSS could provide incorruptible encryption products that couldn't be bought or coerced by governments. In each case, beyond the idea of nonmarket, cooperative production, CBPP would produce a set of technical affordances that enabled anyone to circumvent the technologically embedded control system imposed by market actors or by government authorities.

The most obvious and enduring success of the past twenty years has been the sheer quality, coverage, and usage of Wikipedia. In the first few years, debates over Wikipedia were centered on the impossibility of amateur knowledge providing anything but the most confusing and irrelevant stuff. Instead, Wikipedia has become the basic knowledge utility of contemporary society. It is not the final word on any topic. But, like other encyclopedias before it, Wikipedia has become the first cut on most subjects of significance to any meaningful number of people. Repeatedly over the first few years, reports were published expressing amazement that rigorous tests of quality found that Wikipedia was, broadly speaking, as good as other encyclopedias or similarly public-oriented sources of information, without being as good as peer-reviewed literature available only to specialists in a field. In other words, Wikipedia was at least as good and imperfect as any encyclopedia. Today we see fewer of these studies because the baseline assumptions have changed, and the reasonably high, without being perfect, quality of Wikipedia articles is accepted as a background fact.

This serves a critical role in the category of utility from nonmarket production. When we consider, on the one hand, the extensive surveillance that many commercial companies employ to fund their own offerings as knowledge utilities and, on the other hand, the reams of nonsense that commercial clickbait produces, we see quite clearly the importance of a nonmarket knowledge utility. In political debates, at least in the United States, Wikipedia has come to fulfill a rare role as a source trusted, or at least used and shared, across the partisan divide. In health, a study of the anti-vaccine movement makes quite clear that Wikipedia plays a central role in providing high quality information about the safety of vaccines while a range of commercial sites purvey clickbait to the contrary.[4] Given the high stakes of many of these debates, the incentives and efforts to shape Wikipedia's articles to represent one viewpoint or another on politics or on conspiracy theories, Wikipedia's resilience has been nothing short of remarkable.

So too is the continued resistance of the community and the Foundation to incorporating advertising, allowing Wikipedia to be the only privacy-respecting site among the top online sites. Particularly as awareness of surveillance capitalism is becoming clearer[5] and the risk that a handful of companies will use massive amounts of data they collect on each of us to shape both commercial demand and political outcomes, Wikipedia has more than justified the idea that having a significant source of knowledge that is free of markets and marches to the beat of a different drum having nothing to do with dollars is of critical importance.

At the level of nonmarket utility, then, Wikipedia's success has been largely vindicated. It has succeeded in becoming a critical piece of our knowledge infrastructure. Its resistance to market incentives has played a critical role in its adherence to a reasonable conception of truth as resulting from honest engagement by a community of practice, implemented as a facility that does not seek to manipulate and control its readers.

In retrospect, the miracle of Wikipedia did not consist in its nonhierarchical governance. We have seen a gradual formalization of governance,[6] and it has been almost a decade since the first major works developed the critique of the claim that Wikipedia represented genuinely nonhierarchical production.[7] But Wikipedia, unlike FLOSS, did retain the fundamental attribute of nonmarket production, consistently refusing to transition to advertising or other commodification of the knowledge the community produces and insisting instead on retaining the pure nonmarket form.

The Limits of Wikipedia, FLOSS, and CBPP More Generally

And yet, there are limits.

The Open Directory Project, which when Wikipedia was born was a coeval effort to produce a search utility that would be open source, nonmarket, and nonhierarchical, has largely dissipated. Open Street Map exists but has not become to navigation utility what Wikipedia or the major FLOSS projects like Apache or Linux have been in their own domain. Even if one insists that Chrome is FLOSS (in the sense that it has the Chromium development community alongside it), Google's search utility is decidedly commercial and designed to spy on its users and deliver them up to advertisers, and using Chrome to Google offers no additional protection. No peer-produced commons-based search engine has emerged to any significant degree. The handful of privacy protecting search engines (DuckDuckGo; StartPage) are built by companies, however well-intentioned their founders were. Mastodon may have had greater success than Diaspora, but there is no genuinely successful social network whose infrastructure is FLOSS and, more importantly, whose governance is in the hands of users. However one might celebrate the ubiquitous adoption of Linux in server farms and embedded devices, it is hard to see how smart devices that run on Linux will, in the normal course of their application in homes, be more open and legible to users or more resistant to their producers in embedding data collection and reporting capabilities that will render the homes in which the devices are deployed susceptible to commercial surveillance.

In the meantime, the success of the open source branch of the FLOSS movement, with its focus on innovation rather than freedom, is reflected in the widespread embrace of open source by commercial companies. As a result, most of the major FLOSS projects are produced by contributors who contribute as employees of firms that are using FLOSS as a strategy to engage in precompetitive collaboration among firms to produce critical inputs to the products they will develop on top of these collaborative innovations. Even FLOSS projects that remain governed by a foundation and dependent on volunteer contributions are forced into compromises if they want to retain users. Most prominent here was Firefox's implementation of DRM in order not to lose browser share due to users who wanted to use Netflix and Amazon Prime video on the Firefox platform. Firms have, as a practical matter, found ways to leverage the products of FLOSS as dynamic, innovative inputs into their processes, enjoying the functional benefits of decentralized innovation but circumventing the constraints on exploitation that the social model on which that innovation was grounded originally demanded.

The second way in which the promise of Wikipedia and CBPP fell short of the ideal was in the dimension of freedom from hierarchy. Beginning toward the end of the first decade of Wikipedia's life, an increasing number of studies began to focus on the limits of its egalitarianism. Gender imbalance and the power of admins came under increasing scrutiny. The iron law of oligarchy seemed to reassert itself.[8] This didn't mean that Wikipedia failed as a governance structure. In fact, the community is stable; it has developed quite elaborate procedures for settling disputes and making rules; and as I started out emphasizing, Wikipedia is an unalloyed success as the leading encyclopedia of the day. It has also succeeded in avoiding formal command hierarchies of either the state or corporate form. But it has not developed as a paragon of participatory democratic self-governance.

Nonetheless, I would argue that, like so many of the commons governance models that underlie the literature that followed Nobel laureate Elinor Ostrom's groundbreaking work, successful actual self-governance, however imperfect, still offers critically important lessons in how we might structure large scale cooperation efforts without falling back on formal hierarchy.[9] We have a lot more experience with the failure modes associated with do-ocracy—governance by those who show up and do the work. But we also understand that the authenticity of governance by people who volunteer to do work has important public value, in particular by comparison with governance by people who are out to make a profit.

Where to?

By the end of the second decade of the twenty-first century, democratic market societies find themselves facing a fundamental crisis of legitimacy. Economic insecurity for both present and future generations has become widespread in the broad middle class that makes up the demographic core across these societies.[10] Long-term trends of declining trust in government, media, and religion reflect broad and deep loss of faith in authority in a broad range of institutions throughout much of the most economically developed countries.[11] The shock of the Great Recession exacerbated these longer term trends, and one can only describe the present state in much of the world's democratic societies as an epistemic and political crisis. Swaths of the population behave as though they have lost the ability (or will) to distinguish truth from fiction that supports their biases, whether by adopting political conspiracy theories or pursuing flat earth and anti-vaccine conspiracies. Many have turned to new figures of authority peddling atavistic nationalist and racist narratives as an alternative to the hemming and hawing of neoliberalism, with its individualistic dominant frame of the past forty years, rejecting both pluralist cosmopolitan (left-spin) and globalizing market-fundamentalist (right-spin) aspects of *Homo Davosis*.

What's Wikipedia got to do with it? Remember Wikipedia the idea, and consider Wikipedia the utility.

Alongside the new ethnonationalism we see emerging as an alternative to neoliberalism, we also see two other major responses. The closest to "stay the course" we might call techno-liberalism or techno-libertarianism (both versions coexist in roughly the same class and are distinguished by how comfortable they are with redistribution; their adherents seem to have settled on universal basic income as the solution that leaves the least disagreement between them). Here, the basic understanding of neoliberalism is maintained, with a particularly strong emphasis on the failures of regulation and government and an effort to focus on private sector solutions to social problems. The main difference is the persistent belief that adding more technology will eliminate scarcity and deliver prosperity for all. A second alternative we might call "nudge progressivism." Here, the major deviation from the neoliberal settlement is a newfound confidence in the ability or government agencies to collect enough data and develop sufficiently sophisticated models to overcome the information limitations of regulation and to then translate this new confidence into "soft nudges" for people to behave in ways beneficial to their own and the public good while leaving individuals the freedom to opt out of these behaviors. Both techno-liberalism and nudge progressivism combine strong reliance on markets and a reassertion of hierarchy that depends on data to govern benevolently. The main difference is that the techno-liberals imagine the hierarchical power to be located in the hands of private companies—Facebook, Google, and so on—while the nudge progressives emphasize data-informed rational regulation by public officials.

Wikipedia's twin ideal characteristics—as nonmarket and nonhierarchical, a good-faith collaboration among people engaged with each other socially—mark it as the ideal anchor for an alternative way out after neoliberalism has run its course. In the most immediate sense, Wikipedia's core characteristics can serve as a pointer toward how we climb out of the epistemic crisis we are experiencing. Most importantly, it will not be by emphasizing market actors or reasserting a cultural authority whose luster has long dimmed.

For journalism, for example, the nonmarket attribute means that we will need a much greater investment in models that depart from advertising as a major source of income and that are not for profit. Whether through a properly insulated model of public funding, as in the model of the BBC; an endowed philanthropy trust, as in the case of the Guardian or the Poynter Institute's acquisition of Politifact; or a nonprofit organization funded by user donations, like public radio in the United States and the Wikimedia Foundation, we need the heart of professional journalism to resolve the perennial tension between the editorial side and the business side by shifting emphasis away from market-based independence for media toward society-based independence from government. Moreover, the transparent and "show me" participatory model of governance that characterizes Wikipedia (for all its faults) suggests a transition from "trust us, we're professionals" to "show your work and engage with reasons" as the central practice of responsible journalism. Internal peer review is important, as is transparency to the outside world to the very limit of what can be done without compromising confidential sources. We need parallel recommitment to public funding for science and a reversal of long-standing trends to reduce the fiscal burden on public research by shifting investment to business research and development.

Note that I focus in these areas of journalism and science not on "citizen journalism" or "citizen science," which are the direct correlates of Wikipedia, but on nonmarket journalism and science. Each of these plays an important role in the contemporary media and innovation ecosystems. But the past twenty years have also taught us their limitations. As long as we continue to live in a society in which the basic necessities of life—food, shelter, health, education—need to be purchased in markets, then we will need some method of providing at least some people a way of engaging in these pursuits as a vocation, not merely an avocation. While Wikipedia itself has provided an inspiring example of a knowledge good produced purely from volunteer work, when we look at other efforts to replicate it— particularly in areas that are time sensitive like news—we have seen that some mix of professional and amateur, rather than pure amateur efforts, have worked best. Citizen science, like Zooniverse or FoldIt, offers one such quite-tightly orchestrated mix. The looser interaction among professional commercial media, nonprofits, activists, and academics has produced a good deal of effective reporting and commentary as well as collaborative discovery of emerging stories over the past twenty years. Nonetheless, the past few years have also seen how this system has become vulnerable to manipulation and disinformation as well. When we compare the suscep- tibility of American audiences to propaganda to the relative resilience of French or German audiences, it turns out that a trusted professional core to the media ecosystem can be an important counterbalance to some of the failures of purely decentralized, volunteer networks when it comes to news, just as these latter can keep the mainstream media from falling back on their worst habits. So the lesson is to expand the idea of Wikipedia from standing purely for citizen journalism or science, and to understand that a critical part of what Wikipedia stands for is the importance of nonmarket production as a counterweight to those producers driven and directed by commercial incentives.

More generally, as we design policy interventions or think about how to arrange our affairs as a society, we need to learn from the failures of CBPP to capture a broader range of core utilities than seemed possible when Wikipe- dia was five or even ten years old. We need to develop ways of integrating the nonmarket and participatory, or nonhierarchical, aspects of Wikipedia into systems that also seek to harness the more traditional models of orga- nization—in particular the state. The literature on "democratic experimen- talism" in governance has for twenty years sought to develop regulatory mechanisms that engage participants in the regulated practices—including most importantly participants who are not market actors, academic experts, or engaged members of civil society—to develop a more responsive and adaptive regulatory system. How to do so is far from a settled problem. But the critical turning point is to recognize that solutions to the present crisis of confidence in government and governance will not come from doubling down on the strategy of privatizing provisioning of public goods or from relying on market mechanisms to solve the failures of public institutions. If we want to avoid the failures of public governance of the past forty years, we should explore the solution space that Wikipedia and CBPP has laid out—participatory, social, and not dependent on or subservient to the discipline of markets.

Notes

1. Yochai Benkler, "Coase's Penguin, or, Linux and 'The Nature of the Firm,'" *The Yale Law Journal* 112, no. 3 (December 2002): 369, https://doi.org/10.2307/1562247.

2. Yochai Benkler, "Freedom in the Commons: Towards a Political Economy of Information," *Duke Law Journal* 52 (2003): 32.

3. Benkler, "Coase's Penguin, or, Linux and 'The Nature of the Firm.'"

4. Rebekah Getman et al., "Vaccine Hesitancy and Online Information: The Influence of Digital Networks," *Health Education & Behavior*, December 21, 2017, https://doi.org/10.1177/1090198117739673.

5. Julie E. Cohen, "The Biopolitical Public Domain: The Legal Construction of the Surveillance Economy," *Philosophy & Technology*, March 28, 2017, https://doi.org/10.1007/s13347-017-0258-2; Shoshana Zuboff, *The Age of Surveillance Capitalism: The Fight for a Human Future at the New Frontier of Power* (New York: PublicAffairs, 2019).

6. Joseph Michael Reagle, *Good Faith Collaboration: The Culture of Wikipedia* (Cambridge, MA: MIT Press, 2010).

7. Daniel Kreiss, Megan Finn, and Fred Turner, "The Limits of Peer Production: Some Reminders from Max Weber for the Network Society," *New Media & Society* 13, no. 2 (March 2011): 243–259, https://doi.org/10.1177/1461444810370951.

8. Aaron Shaw and Benjamin M. Hill, "Laboratories of Oligarchy? How the Iron Law Extends to Peer Production: Laboratories of Oligarchy," *Journal of Communication* 64, no. 2 (April 2014): 215–238, https://doi.org/10.1111/jcom.12082.

9. Brett M. Frischmann, Michael J. Madison, and Katherine Jo Strandburg, eds., *Governing Knowledge Commons* (New York: Oxford University Press, 2014).

10. Organisation for Economic Co-operation and Development (OECD), *Under Pressure: The Squeezed Middle Class* (OECD, 2019), https://doi.org/10.1787/689afed1-en.

11. "Public Trust in Government: 1958–2017," Pew Research Center, April 11, 2019, https://www.people-press.org/2017/12/14/public-trust-in-government-1958-2017/; Knight Foundation and Gallup, *American Views: Trust, Media and Democracy* (Washington, DC: Gallup, January 16, 2018), https://kf-site-production.s3.amazonaws .com/publications/pdfs/000/000/242/original/KnightFoundation_AmericansViews _Client_Report_010917_Final_Updated.pdf; OECD, "Trust in Government, Policy Effectiveness and the Governance Agenda," in *Government at a Glance 2013* (Paris: OECD Publishing, 2013), https://doi.org/10.1787/gov_glance-2013-6-en.

4 An Encyclopedia with Breaking News

Brian Keegan

Wikipedia's response to the September 11 attacks profoundly shaped its rules and identity and illuminated a new strategy for growing the project by coupling the supply and demand for information about news. Wikipedia's breaking news collaborations offer lessons for hardening other online platforms against polarization, disinformation, and other sociotechnical sludge.

The web was a very different place for news in the United States between 2001 and 2006. The hanging chads from the 2000 presidential election, the spectacular calamity of 9/11, the unrepentant lies around Operation Iraqi Freedom, and the campy reality television featuring Donald Trump were all from this time. The burst of the dot-com bubble and corporate malfeasance of companies like Enron dampened entrepreneurial spirits, news publishers were optimistically sharing their stories online without paywalls, and blogging was heralded as the future of technology-mediated accountability and participatory democracy. "You" was Time Magazine's Person of the Year in 2006 because "Web 2.0" platforms like YouTube, MySpace, and Second Life had become tools for "bringing together the small contributions of millions of people and making them matter."[1]

Wikipedia was a part of this primordial soup, predating news-feed-mediated engagement, recommender-driven polarization, politicized content moderation, and geopolitical disinformation campaigns. From very early in its history, Wikipedia leveraged the supply and demand for information about breaking news and current events into strategies that continue to sustain this radical experiment in online peer production. This chapter will explore Wikipedia's earliest efforts to cover breaking news events, common features of these unique collaborations, and how these features may serve as a model for other social platforms grappling with problems like disinformation.

I first encountered Wikipedia as an undergraduate student around 2004. My introduction to Wikipedia was likely a product of the sociotechnical coupling between Google and Wikipedia during this era. Google helped Wikipedia because Google's ranking algorithms privileged Wikipedia's highly interlinked articles, which brought an influx of users, some (tiny) fraction of whom became contributing editors like myself. Wikipedia also helped Google because Wikipedia could reliably generate both general interest and up-to-date content that satisfied its users' information-seeking needs, which brought users back to Google rather than its competitors. The aftermath of natural disaster, the death of a celebrity, or a new pop culture sensation are all occasions for people to seek out background information to help them make sense of these events. Traditional journalistic offerings provide incremental updates about the immediate subject but often lack context or background: Why are there earthquakes in Indonesia? Who is Saddam Hussein? What is Eurovision? The availability and timeliness of Wikipedia content around topics of general interest would prove to be critical for its own sustainability in addition to complementing other platforms' need to serve relevant and up-to-date content.

Wikipedia also entered the popular awareness of undergraduates like myself through the pitiless warnings from instructors and librarians about its lack of reliability as a citation. While these anxieties were largely reversed through empirical research and changes in professional culture, they also missed the forest for the trees: the value and authority of Wikipedia was not in any single article's quality but in its network of hyperlinked articles. More than synthesizing knowledge as a tertiary source like traditional encyclopedias, Wikipedia's hyperlink network invited users to follow their interests, dive deeper into topics, introduce missing connections, and create new articles where none existed. Where the decentralized web created a fragmented user experience requiring directories (*e.g.*, Yahoo!) and search engines (*e.g.*, Google) for navigation, Wikipedia's hyperlinked articles foreshadowed an era of centralized web platforms that sustain user engagement with a consistent experience and "bottomless" content to consume and engage.

There are many ways to promote Wikipedia articles to its front page. Immediately to the right of "From today's featured article" is the "In the news" (ITN) box featuring "articles that have been substantially updated to reflect recent or current events of wide interest."[2] The presence of news-like content in an encyclopedia is uncanny. On the one hand, encyclopedias are supposed to be stable references of historical knowledge rather than dynamic accounts of current events. On the other hand, there is a long history of encyclopedia editors grappling with how to incorporate new knowledge and encyclopedia publishers competing to be the most up-to-date.[3] Wikipedia's choice to privilege content related to current events via the ITN is also shrewd: it simultaneously is a shortcut to content users may already be searching for, it showcases the dynamism and quality of Wikipedia articles, and it invites users to consume and contribute to content outside of their primary interests.

September 11 and Wikipedia

To understand how Wikipedia's "ITN" template and its broader culture of breaking news collaborations came about, we have to return to the immediate aftermath of the September 11, 2001, attacks. Wikipedia was ten months old at the time of the attacks, and while it already surpassed its elder sibling Nupedia in the number of articles, it was far from certain that the project would ever reach a sustainable level of activity. Although a comprehensive accounting of the editing activity in the immediate aftermath of the events has been lost to a server migration, snapshots from the Internet Archive's Wayback Machine along with listserv discussions document the extent to which the Wikipedia community at the time went into overdrive in response to the attacks.[4] Far from being an idiosyncratic case of online collaboration, the decisions made by editors at the time to use Wikipedia's unique collaborative capacities to deeply cover the September 11 attacks would fundamentally change the direction, scope, and culture of Wikipedia as a project to the present day.

A Wayback Machine snapshot of the "September 11, 2001 terrorist attack" article from October 9, 2011, captures the remarkable breadth and depth of topics that were authored and organized together about the attacks.[5] There were timelines; documentation of closings and cancellations; lists of casualties; links to donating blood and money; articles on political and economic effects; and newly created articles about the buildings, cities, flights, and perpetrators as well as topics like "terrorism," "box-cutter knife," and "collective trauma." Approximately one hundred September 11–related articles were created in total (at a time when Wikipedia as a whole had only thirteen thousand articles) but Wikipedia's content attracted links from other prominent web gateways like Yahoo! that brought in an influx of desperately-needed new users to the project.

The list of casualties enumerating each of the nearly three thousand victims (sorted by name and location and categorized by civilian or first responder) became a source of tension in the weeks following the attacks. Some editors argued this level of detailed coverage was unbecoming of the traditional encyclopedia Wikipedia was trying to emulate stylistically. Supporters referenced the rule that "Wikipedia is not paper" to justify a goal of writing biographies for thousands of victims, survivors, and leaders. As the trauma-induced altruism continued to fade, Wikipedia editors continued to raise concerns about the quality, notability, and importance of these memorialization efforts given the other demands of writing an encyclopedia. By September 2002 the community reached a consensus decision to move the September 11–related recollections and nonnotable pages to a "memorial wiki." The launch of the memorial wiki led to heated discussions about which September 11–related articles would get to stay on Wikipedia and which would be relegated to the memorial wiki. The memorial wiki ultimately failed to thrive: its stagnant content and lack of editing activity led to accumulating vandalism, and it was effectively shuttered by September 2006. The creation, rejection, and disappearance of the September 11 memorial wiki's content remains an underappreciated cautionary tale about the presumed durability of peer-produced knowledge: this content only persists when it remains integrated to the larger common project rather than being relegated to a smaller and more specialized project. Wikipedia's peer production model is not immune from "rich get richer" mechanisms.

The Wikipedia community's overreaction to the September 11 attacks and the discussions about the memorial content led to reflexive rule making about news that persists today. The "What Wikipedia is not" (WP:NOT) policy predates the attacks and enumerates that Wikipedia is not a dictionary, manual, directory, or a variety of other reference genres. In the midst of the debates in 2002 about what to do with the September 11 memorial content, the WP:NOT policy was expanded to assert that Wikipedia is not "a news report." The revised policy attempted to thread the needle between the channeling of collaborative energy following current events against diluting the mission of writing an encyclopedia. The policy emphasized that "Wikipedia should not offer news reports on breaking stories" but conceded "creating encyclopedia articles on topics currently in the news is an excellent idea"[6] as long as current events articles are written in an encyclopedic style. This "NOT NEWS" policy has persisted to the present, and the policy now emphasizes that "Wikipedia should not offer first-hand news reports on breaking stories" and "newsworthy events do not [automatically] qualify for inclusion ... breaking news should not be emphasized or treated differently from other information."[7] Another change in identity that emerged as a result of the September 11 memorial content was the addition of "Memorials" to the WP:NOT policy. The policy, revised in 2004, now emphasizes that "Wikipedia is not the place to memorialize deceased friends, relatives, acquaintances, or others who do not meet such requirements."[8] These normative guardrails remain in place today to channel the outpouring of pro-social collaborative energy and sensemaking in the aftermath of traumatic events.

Features of Breaking News Collaborations

Even as an extremely active Wikipedia editor who made hundreds of revisions per month, I was always disappointed that I was never the first to create or update an article about a major current event. Wikipedia's editors had remarkable alacrity in revising content in response to current events: articles about deceased celebrities, political scandals, and natural disasters were all updated or created seemingly within minutes of the news breaking. My disappointment at being unable to author the first revisions shifted into curiosity, and I began to explore the revision histories of these breaking news articles.[9] These explorations raised more questions about the emergent social behaviors, and I switched my dissertation research project to exploring these breaking news collaborations. I was not alone in this inquiry. The Wikipedia model of a single, central account is much more legible to search engines like Google that boosted these articles' authority and that drove the virtuous feedback loops of more traffic, more contributors, more updates, and better content. In 2009, then Google Vice President Marissa Mayer imagined a new web-oriented form of journalism where news stories did not compete against each other for authority or search engine results:

How [might] the authoritativeness of news articles grow if an evolving story were published under a permanent, single URL as a living, changing, updating entity?[10]

It is hard to imagine that Ms. Mayer's vision of the future of journalism was not influenced by the enormous volumes of traffic her search engine was referring to Wikipedia in the aftermath of current events. More than a decade later, Wikipedia's collaborations around breaking news continues to be a generative research context for myself and other researchers.[11] Several general patterns have consistently emerged from my research over the past decade into Wikipedia's breaking news collaborations.

First, the contributors to breaking news articles are drawn from editors across the Wikipedia community, not introduced by a small set of "ambulance-chasing" editors who had specialized roles and routines of breaking news editing. This suggests the motivation and ability for editors to engage in breaking news collaborations is widely shared. This distributed collaborative capacity proved to be important throughout Wikipedia's history for mobilizing when multiple major events happened simultaneously. In March 2011 while the events of the Arab Spring demanded complex revisions across articles related to Tunisia, Egypt, Libya, and Syria, a 9.0-magnitude earthquake off the coast of Japan's Tōhoku province triggered a massive tsunami that ultimately killed more than twenty thousand people and led to the most serious nuclear disaster since Chernobyl. Because of Wikipedians' distributed collaborative capacity, editors were able to process these major historical events in parallel when each event itself required a massive undertaking of synthesizing, coordinating, and deliberating across dozens of articles, talk pages, administrative processes, and language editions. Moreover, the contributors to breaking news article collaborations have diverse repertoires and roles on the project: an editor specializing in editing articles about Japanese boy bands shifted their focus to updating infrastructure damaged by the 2011 tsunami while another editor migrated their dispute resolution experience from Harry Potter articles to the Fukushima nuclear disaster article.[12] Other topical areas that are proximate to breaking news have developed specialized routines for managing common coordination problems. When a new storm happens, members of the WikiProject Tropical Cyclones shift to editing these articles and bring a wealth of experience for structure, style, references, and multimedia about storms to structure these collaborations. Pro-social responses in the aftermath of disaster and catastrophe are ubiquitous,[13] but Wikipedia uniquely channels this energy into producing enduring and highly net-worked knowledge artifacts.

Second, breaking news events are sites of large, rapid, and temporary col-laborations that were otherwise rare on Wikipedia. The average Wikipedia article has accumulated fewer than ten unique editors and revisions over a span of years while breaking news articles can have hundreds of editors and revisions over a span of days. Examining the archival "zeitgeist" sta-tistics for the English Wikipedia articles,[14] the most actively revised articles in any given month tend to be related to breaking news events or people in the news. In 2004, the articles with the most unique editors in a month included the "2004 Madrid train bombings" (112 editors in March), "Ron-ald Reagan" (114 editors in June), "2004 Summer Olympics" (92 editors in August), "Timeline of the 2004 United States Presidential election" (154 editors in November), and "2004 Indian Ocean earthquake and tsunami" (345 editors in December). The number and frequency of revisions to these articles was also extremely high: on major events, multiple revisions can be made in the same minute, complicating efforts for longer-form writing or copyediting.

The MediaWiki software on which Wikipedia runs did not anticipate this kind of synchronous editing behavior, so editors revert to strategies for working around the limitations of the software such as making smaller and more frequent edits, merging in changes from a sandbox, or request-ing an administrative lock on the article to incorporate requested changes. These collaborations are often temporary, involving editors with disparate expertise and interests to come together to collaborate, with most of them never having worked together before and with no expectations of collabo-rating again in the future. In the absence of social relationships to shape these emergent collaborations, editors are guided by common interests and shared values around writing an encyclopedia. Even if most participants in breaking news collaborations return to editing their usual topics afterward, these breaking news collaborations play a crucial role as "watering holes" where different groups' norms are reaffirmed and best practices are synthe-sized and then diffused back out through the rest of the project. Breaking news collaborations arguably play an important role in the viability of the broader Wikipedia project by engaging editors in challenging experiences,

validating the investments of volunteer editors, and circulating innovations throughout the project.

Finally, breaking news articles are exceptionally high quality when compared with the median Wikipedia article: they tended to be longer; have
more links to other Wikipedia articles; have more references and citations;
and have more images, maps, and multimedia. Recent events make more
"raw" material available in the form of reporting and social media content
than historical events requiring archival research skills, providing a richer set
of inputs to generate better articles. But breaking news articles also benefit
from "Linus's Law"[15] where a large number of diverse editors can accomplish
tasks that would seem only possible for a small group of experts to accomplish. These articles also have a complex life cycle of different cohorts of editors cycling through the collaboration over the course of days, weeks, and
years. Biographical articles about the recently deceased often go through a
major rewrite to incorporate information from obituaries as well as a general reappraisal and standardization of structure and style rather than simply changing verb tenses and adding in the relevant information about the
subject's death. Anniversaries have also become occasions for readers and
editors to revisit an article and make new contributions. Wikipedia articles
about current events provide a unique commons for emergent communities
to gather, not only to document and reappraise our understanding of the
causes, contexts, and consequences of major and often traumatic events but
also to support others' information seeking and sensemaking as well.

All of these patterns reinforce the idiom that "Wikipedia works in practice, not in theory." Who are these editors that rapidly self-select and
self-organize themselves in the absence of any formal coordination or del-
egation? Why have breaking news collaborations continued to employ gen-
eralists rather than develop a class of specialists? How did dozens of users
synchronously edit a shared document using an asynchronous tool with
none of features we take for granted in something like Google Docs? These
remain open and vital questions for researchers twenty years after Wikipedia's launch.

Wikipedia in the Age of Disinformation

Despite being the "encyclopedia that anyone can edit" and one of the
most trafficked websites in the world, Wikipedia did not show the same

susceptibility to the coordinated disinformation campaigns that plagued social platforms like Facebook, YouTube, and Twitter around 2016. Although these platforms have made massive investments in human and automated moderation to improve users' experience, allay advertisers' concerns, and head off regulator scrutiny, disinformation, harassment, and other socio-technical sludge remain endemic.[16] Provocateurs, outrage-mongers, and outright fascists have flocked to these "virality engine" platforms to actively recommend fringe ideas and compensate their creators while distributing them to audiences of millions. Platforms' attempts at commonsense content moderation by removing or "demonetizing" the most egregious examples of hate speech and harassment have in turn led to accusations of their threats to "free speech" and "anti-conservative bias." What explains Wikipedia's apparent resilience to the sociotechnical sludge polluting other platforms?

The most obvious hypothesis is the difference in incentives between the user experience of advertising-driven engagement maximization and commons-based peer-production models. Facebook, YouTube, and other popular social platforms generate billions of dollars in revenue by injecting personalized advertising alongside bottomless recommendations and news feeds managed by expensive engineers and infrastructures to engage users' attention. Every user's Facebook News Feed is personalized in response to their relationships, interests, and behavior. Content featuring novelty, humor, and outrage receives greater "engagement," so publishers and advertisers are locked in an arms race to produce ever more attention-grabbing content and target it for users' personalized feeds. Wikipedia has no news-feed,[17] runs no advertising, and has a comparatively minuscule operating budget. But an overlooked and critical difference between Wikipedia and other social platforms is the absence of personalization in the user experience. Every English Wikipedia user's "Abraham Lincoln" article is the same regardless of their geography, gender, browsing history, or social graph. This common experience concentrates collective scrutiny and deliberative capacity rather than diffusing these accountability mechanisms across inscrutable and incommensurable personalized news feeds. Linus's Law—"given enough eyes, all bugs are shallow"—evidently holds for preserving the integrity of social information feeds.

A second hypothesis explaining Wikipedia's resilience to sociotechnical sludge is the absence of algorithmic amplification. The background above illustrates how Wikipedia articles can "trend" in response to current events and popular culture. However, Wikipedia's editors exercise considerable "human in the loop" editorial discretion over both the substance of trending content as well as its amplification mechanisms, unlike the algorithms driving news-feed-centered platforms like Facebook and YouTube that can be manipulated into privileging viral and outrageous content. The most common user experience of Wikipedia is arriving from a search engine and navigating to related articles via hyperlinks or follow-on searches rather than navigating in from a news feed or home page. To the extent Wikipedia has mechanisms for amplifying content to users, they exist on the homepage as "From today's featured article," "In the news," "Did you know," and "On this day." These mechanisms are all explicitly vetted by human editors following documented public policies and consensus-driven deliberation that still have remarkable alacrity in responding to current events. The responsiveness of Wikipedia editors to current events also provides an important counterfactual to claims from engineering culture that human-in-the-loop systems lack the scalability, speed, and accuracy of automated systems, despite accumulating evidence of automated systems' multiple liabilities. Because the oversight and capacity to intervene in Wikipedia's attention amplification mechanisms is delegated across hundreds of administrators and/or thousands of editors, they are substantially harder to compromise than algorithmic systems operating under "security through obscurity" strategies.

Social platforms confronting the limitations of their current engagement and moderation models are turning to Wikipedia. In October 2017, Facebook announced that it would provide "contextual information" about articles in the news feed that would include links to Wikipedia.[18] In March 2018, YouTube Chief Executive Officer Susan Wojcicki outlined a strategy wherein YouTube would connect videos containing conspiracies to corresponding Wikipedia articles in an effort to combat the spread of disinformation.[19] YouTube's decision, in particular, came as a surprise to the Wikipedia community and the Wikimedia Foundation, who were given no forewarning that they would be indirectly policing YouTube's toxic content. The fundamental risk was that the same dynamics that converted information-seeking Google search users into Wikipedia editors could also convert the conspiracists, ideologues, and culture warriors on these platforms into Wikipedia editors. These decisions to outsource content moderation to

Wikipedia were deeply irresponsible: either YouTube failed to comprehend the obvious risks of swamping the smaller volunteer project with their content moderation problems or they did not care.

Facebook's and YouTube's conduct in this case is a classic problem of governing what economists call "common goods" and its corresponding "tragedy of the commons." The knowledge produced—and more importantly, governed—by Wikipedia is "nonexcludable," which means that it can still be used by people who have not contributed to it. However, the governance of this knowledge exhibits patterns of "rivalrousness" in which consumption by one actor reduces availability for others. In this case, Facebook and YouTube contributed nothing to Wikipedia's governance but could still benefit from the credible content generated and governed by the Wikipedia community (nonexcludability). But in outsourcing content moderation to Wikipedia editors and administrators, Facebook and YouTube were potentially reducing Wikipedia editors' capacity to attend to other content generation and moderation demands (rivalrousness). Facebook and YouTube were effectively "overfishing" the capacity of Wikipedia editors and administrators to handle sociotechnical sludge by requiring the volunteer Wikipedia community to do more of all of this work on behalf of a corporation who profits from not having to moderate its own content. But commons do not inevitably end up as tragedies; the research of Elinor Ostrom (which culminated in her 2009 Nobel Memorial Prize in Economic Sciences) charts out strategies for designing institutions for sustaining commons in the face of threats like overuse. Her 2006 edited volume with Charlotte Hess, *Understanding Knowledge as a Commons*, charts prescient strategies for communities like Wikipedia to pursue to "define, protect, and build the knowledge commons in the digital age."[20]

The case of Wikipedia content being redeployed by unscrupulous platforms for their content moderation needs illustrates the risks associated with the "interoperability" of online platforms: content from Platform A can be plugged into Platform B, but these connections can also cause blowback as the bad behavior from Platform B moves to Platform A. Wikipedia's content is reused in both visible and invisible ways across platforms: Google serves up Wikipedia content alongside its search results, Facebook uses it to populate information for its pages, and Apple's Siri or Amazon's Alexa will read summaries of articles. Wikipedia's content is also used in more invisible ways to train algorithms used for translation, image recognition, and concept similarity. These interoperable connections increase the prominence of Wikipedia's content, recruit new users to contribute, and highlight the need to preserve this commons, but every new interoperable link also introduces new threats. If a malicious actor wanted to undermine trust in these other major platforms, an under-realized vector can subtly compromise the quality of information from the Wikipedia and Wikidata content that they ingest.

Wikipedia's resilience to the strategic disinformation campaigns from 2016 should not be interpreted as intrinsic immunity to information manipulation: Wikipedia's most active editors are not representative of the population at large, which creates both biases in its content and blind spots in its responses, which are then ingested and amplified through the web of interoperable dependencies outlined above. Wikipedia administrators botched its response to the Gamergate controversy in 2015 by acquiescing to a manipulative influence campaign and banning five editors who had been fending off extremist content:[21] this case illustrated how Wikipedia's administrative procedures can be hijacked by bad-faith actors to target good-faith editors. On a lighter note, another illustration of the threats of interoperability is a case from October 2017. When users of Apple Siri asked "What is the national anthem of Bulgaria?," they were served "Despacito," a 2017 reggaeton pop hit, rather than the nineteenth-century hymn "Mila Rodino."[22] Somewhere deep in Apple's knowledge graph, much of which is likely trained on Wikipedia and Wikidata, this erroneous pairing was introduced and never validated before being pushed out to millions of users.

Wikipedia and its increasingly important sister project Wikidata have been able to resist disinformation efforts because of the ability to match its supply of human-in-the-loop governance with demand for information: oversight follows the action. While it might be hard to embed disinformation into articles about candidates for an upcoming election because of this superabundance of editorial attention, it might be trivial to persistently embed disinformation into provincial articles about distant historical events, specialized scientific topics, or marginal trivia about national anthems that lack sustained editorial oversight. While Wikipedia's unique editorial model has shown greater resistance to the disinformation, harassment, and manipulation plaguing other social platforms to the point that its content is serving as a front-line defense, there are nevertheless growing precedents that Wikipedia's content and governance has very real vulnerabilities that could easily and quickly propagate throughout a complex technical stack of interoperable technologies.

Conclusion

Encyclopedists have always struggled with the limitations of synthesizing knowledge into paper documents because when the knowledge changes, so must the paper. Wikipedia was not the first encyclopedia to use the online medium to rapidly and inexpensively revise content in response to changes, but its unique "anyone can edit" model had the effect of entangling current events with the viability of the project.

The September 11 attacks were a critical moment in Wikipedia's history. The events brought in an influx of new editors motivated to document the events, perpetrators, victims, and contexts, and the outpouring of collaborative effort in the aftermath of the September 11 attacks validated an underappreciated strategy for growing the project. By simultaneously tapping into editors' pro-social motivations following traumatic events as well as showcasing the quality and timeliness of the project's content in a time of acute information seeking and sensemaking, Wikipedia could convert the large numbers of information-seeking users into new contributors as well as increase popular trust in its radical editorial model. However, Wikipedia editors' overzealous creation of September 11–related content also required the development of new rules and identities as guardrails that persist today about what the encyclopedia is and is not.

Wikipedia editors continue to invest enormous amounts of effort in covering breaking news and current events within the confines of these guardrails. Articles about the recently deceased, natural disasters, conflicts, and popular culture are sites of large and extremely dynamic collaborations involving dozens of editors making hundreds of revisions within hours. While Wikipedia's MediaWiki software was not designed with this use case in mind, these high-tempo collaborations continue to serve crucial roles in sustaining the health of the broader project, close to twenty years after the early precedent of the September 11 attacks: they bring in new users to the project, provide opportunities to disparate subcommunities to temporarily congregate, disseminate innovations and best practices into the rest of the community, and produce high-quality content hyperlinked to other relevant background.

Wikipedia remains a product of a particular historical moment from the early 2000s, in terms of not only its adorably dated interface but also the absence of advertising and engagement, news feeds and recommendation systems, and virality and polarization as central features that define so much of the user experience on other social platforms. Wikipedia's resilience to the disinformation that plagued Facebook, YouTube, and Google in 2016 would suggest this archaic user experience provided an important defense against actors who weaponized these attention amplification mechanisms on other platforms to malicious ends. But this story overlooks other explanations for Wikipedia's apparent resilience: Wikipedia users and editors' attention is shared around common articles rather than distributed across personalized news feeds.

Does Wikipedia's success in covering breaking news and current events chart a path for other platforms to follow? Information seeking and sensemaking about current events drive enormous flows of online collective attention, which explains why "News feeds" and "Trending" topics are ubiquitous on social platforms. Whether and how Wikipedia can channel this demand for information likewise has been central to its ongoing identity, relevance, and sustainability. Wikipedia remains a valuable counterfactual for the potential of designing around information commons, human-in-the-loop decision making, and strong editorial stances in the face of the Silicon Valley consensus emphasizing content personalization, automated moderation, and editorial indifference. The differences in how Wikipedia handles current event information may have insulated it from manipulation, but as platforms increasingly turn to Wikipedia for providing and moderating content, Wikipedia's very real vulnerabilities risk becoming a target.

Notes

1. Lev Grossman, "You—Yes, You—Are TIME's Person of the Year," *Time*, December 25, 2006, http://content.time.com/time/magazine/article/0,9171,1570810,00.html.

2. Wikipedia, s.v. "Wikipedia: In the News," last modified August 30, 2019, https://en.wikipedia.org/wiki/Wikipedia:In_the_news.

3. Jeff Loveland and Joseph Reagle, "Wikipedia and Encyclopedic Production," *New Media & Society* 15, no. 8 (December 2013): 1294–1311, https://doi.org/10.1177/1461444812470428.

4. Brian C. Keegan, "A History of Newswork on Wikipedia," in *Proceedings of the 9th International Symposium on Open Collaboration* (OpenSym, 2013).

5. Wikipedia, s.v. "September 11, 2001 Terrorist Attack," November 3, 2001, version from the Internet Archive's Wayback Machine, http://web.archive.org/web/20011031162201 /http://www.wikipedia.com/wiki.cgi?September_11,_2001_Terrorist_Attack.

6. Wikipedia, s.v. "Wikipedia Talk: In the News/Archive 1a," last edited April 22, 2013, https://en.wikipedia.org/wiki/Wikipedia_talk:In_the_news/Archive_1a.

7. Wikipedia, s.v. "Wikipedia: What Wikipedia Is Not," last edited January 13, 2020, https://en.wikipedia.org/wiki/Wikipedia:What_Wikipedia_is_not.

8. "Wikipedia: What Wikipedia Is Not."

9. Brian C. Keegan, "Hot off the Wiki: Dynamics, Practices, and Structures in Wikipedia's Coverage of the Tohoku Catastrophes," in *Proceedings of the 7th International Symposium on Wikis and Open Collaboration* (WikiSym, 2011).

10. Zachary M. Seward, "Google News Experimenting with Links to Wikipedia on Its Homepage," Nieman Lab, June 9, 2009, https://www.niemanlab.org/2009 /06/google-news-experimenting-with-links-to-wikipedia-on-its-homepage/.

11. Brian C. Keegan and Jed Brubaker, "'Is' to 'Was': Coordination and Commemoration on Posthumous Wikipedia Biographies," in *Proceedings of the 2015 ACM Conference on Computer-Supported Cooperative Work* (CSCW, 2015); Marlon Twyman, Brian C. Keegan, and Aaron Shaw, "Black Lives Matter in Wikipedia: Collaboration and Collective Memory around Online Social Movements," in *Proceedings of the 2017 ACM Conference on Computer-Supported Cooperative Work* (CSCW, 2017); Brian C. Keegan, "The Dynamics of Peer-Produced Political Information during the 2016 U.S. Presidential Campaign," in *Proceedings of the 2019 ACM Conference on Computer-Supported Cooperative Work* (CSCW, 2019).

12. Brian C. Keegan, Darren Gergle, and Noshir S. Contractor, "Staying in the Loop: Structure and Dynamics of Wikipedia's Breaking News Collaborations," in *Proceedings of the Eighth International Symposium on Wikis and Open Collaboration* (WikiSym, 2012).

13. Rebecca Solnit, *A Paradise Built in Hell: The Extraordinary Communities that Arise in Disaster* (New York: Penguin, 2010).

14. "Wikipedia Statistics English," Wikimedia Foundation, last modified August 31, 2019, https://stats.wikimedia.org/EN/TablesWikipediaEN.htm.

15. Eric S. Raymond, *The Cathedral and the Bazaar* (Sebastopol, CA: O'Reilly Press, 1999).

16. Yochai Benkler, Robert Faris, and Hal Roberts, *Network Propaganda: Manipulation, Disinformation, and Radicalization in American Politics* (Oxford, UK: Oxford University Press, 2018).

17. Active editors might quibble with this distinction since Wikipedia's Watchlist summarizes recent changes to articles they follow. There is also a list of Current Events articles. But neither of these are central to the median Wikipedia user's experience.

18. Josh Constine, "Facebook Tries Fighting Fake News with Publisher Info Button on Links," *TechCrunch*, October 5, 2017, https://techcrunch.com/2017/10/05/facebook-article-information-button/.

19. Louise Matsakis, "YouTube Will Link Directly to Wikipedia to Fight Conspiracy Theories," *Wired*, March 13, 2018, https://www.wired.com/story/youtube-will-link-directly-to-wikipedia-to-fight-conspiracies/.

20. Charlotte Hess and Elinor Ostrom, eds., *Understanding Knowledge as a Commons* (Cambridge, MA: MIT Press, n.d.).

21. Lauren C. Williams, "The 'Five Horsemen' of Wikipedia Paid the Price for Getting Between Trolls and Their Victims," *Think Progress*, March 6, 2015, https://thinkprogress.org/the-five-horsemen-of-wikipedia-paid-the-price-for-getting-between-trolls-and-their-victims-9c835aeafdc8/.

22. Nick Statt, "Why Does Siri Think the National Anthem of Bulgaria is 'Despacito'?" *The Verge*, October 4, 2017, https://www.theverge.com/2017/10/4/16427146/apple-iphone-siri-bulgaria-national-anthem-despacito-incorrect.

5   Paid with Interest: COI Editing and Its Discontents

William Beutler

Financially motivated editing of encyclopedia articles presents a quandary for Wikipedia, which the author explores from personal experience as a paid editor seeking to work within its guidelines. A brief overview of the controversial history and colorful characters involved suggests that the phenomenon of "paid editing" doesn't have to remain inscrutable.

Everyone involved with Wikipedia has some kind of interest in what it says. In the popular conception, its volunteer editors are inspired to empower a global audience by compiling information in an accessible format. Practically speaking, though, most Wikipedians participate because the project appeals to their personality or their sense of justice or because there's an ego boost in deciding what the world knows about their pet subject. Its readers care simply because they want to learn something. Everyone's interests are appropriately served.

Things are rather different when the motivation is financial. Most contributors consider editing Wikipedia to promote a business to be a morally precarious endeavor. The site's readers, too, may be alarmed to learn that some edits are made not to benevolently share knowledge with the world but because the writer has a material stake in how the topic is represented. And yet the structure of Wikipedia makes this tension inevitable. The site's vast influence owes something to the fact that anyone can influence it, so when those described in its virtual pages decide to do exactly that, the result is one of Wikipedia's most challenging existential dilemmas.

Wikipedia's favored terminology for this is "conflict of interest," referred to in shorthand as "COI"—although other terms such as "paid editing" or "paid advocacy" are often used. COI is the subject of an official guideline, numerous information pages giving advice to volunteers and paid editors alike, and a lengthy article in the encyclopedia itself chronicling the historical highlights and lowlights (mostly the latter).[1] However, none of these resources really explain how COI has evolved over Wikipedia's two decades in existence.

Fortunately, this is a topic for which I have a rare insight: in addition to being a volunteer editor of more than a dozen years, I am also the founder and chief executive of a digital marketing agency that helps clients navigate their conflicts of interest on Wikipedia. From this perspective, I will outline the history of COI as I've witnessed it, attempt to classify its disparate participants, and share my own personal story, which intersects at all points.

Wikipedia's approach to COI has been characterized by uncertainty and reluctance, responsiveness only in the face of crisis, and by occasional advancement when personal initiative meets pent-up frustrations. However, it is still conceivable that assertive steps could be made to harness COI motives for the benefit of Wikipedia's editors and readers alike. To this end, I will identify opportunities for research in this field, which to date scarcely exists.

Origin Story

I first became aware of Wikipedia through the American political blogosphere, which I covered for a news service based in Washington, DC, in the early 2000s. Among bloggers on the left and right, the usefulness of linking to Wikipedia had become an uncommon point of agreement. I soon became fascinated with this audacious effort to impose order on the messy world of knowledge, not to mention the opinionated community responsible for it.

But the reason I finally started editing, prophetically enough, was because my boss asked me to. In 2006 I had abandoned journalism to join a digital public affairs firm, where undoubtedly I brought up Wikipedia the most among my colleagues. The company's chief executive officer had become concerned with the negative slant on a friend's biographical article and wanted to know if something could be done about it. I investigated and decided something could indeed. But I didn't merely snip away the offending passage; instead I placed a note on the discussion page saying I would add a qualifying adjective to put the matter in context, and then I did just that. This instinct would come to serve me well in a way I couldn't have imagined at the time.

In the months following, I continued making small edits to articles of personal interest. Eventually, I created my first new entry: a biography of Tom Peterson, a retailer and pitchman whose homespun TV advertisements are cherished memories of Oregonians from the 1970s and 1980s. During this time, I began devouring the many policies, guidelines, and essays that explained how Wikipedia made decisions about acceptable and unacceptable content. I found these statutes to be even more captivating than the articles they regulated—it was like discovering the secret rules governing all the knowledge in the universe.

As I gained confidence, my engagement with Wikipedia evolved along two tracks. First, I started attending offline events and making friends in the movement, eventually launching a blog about the community I had come to consider myself a part of.[2] (Chapter 7 is a portrait of how such relationships can develop.) Second, I recognized the possibilities suggested by my initial experiment. Many of my employer's clients were the subject of Wikipedia entries, and these summaries were seldom faultless. Reading the COI guideline carefully, it was apparent that while self-interested editing was discouraged, it was not outright prohibited. I was aware that others had tried and failed to thread this needle, but I believed my prior experiences with the combative blogging community would help me prevail. In particular, I recognized that "it's better to beg for forgiveness than ask for permission" would not apply here.

So I began carefully: I created a secondary account disclosing my employer and relevant client relationships, posted simple edit requests about client issues on discussion pages, and sought out editors willing to make the changes for me. Some ignored me or said no, though frequently enough they would agree and occasionally thank me for being up-front about my COI. Some even granted me "permission" to make the changes myself, pointing to a section of the COI guideline regarding the acceptability of "making uncontroversial edits."[3] Although I still usually asked first, in some cases I returned to the original arrangement: first explaining my reasoning and then making the change. On the whole, this worked out surprisingly well—every once in a while I would run into an editor who disagreed, but before long another volunteer would come along and help us find a solution.

By early 2010, I was convinced there was a bigger market for this service than my employer understood. That summer, I turned in a letter of resignation and embarked on a tour of DC public relations (PR) firms, offering up my Wikipedia expertise on a contract basis. I built a roster of clients one meeting at a time until I had enough work to bring on my first employee, with two more being hired by the end of 2011.

At this point, I was still reluctant to discuss how I earned a living with fellow Wikipedians, fearing their disapproval. COI editing remained a controversial topic. Even if tenuously allowed, it certainly wasn't respected, and for very good reasons: the history of COI, up to this point, was largely a series of individuals and organizations getting caught doing something when they should have known better.

A Brief History of Paid Editing

This history can be divided into four distinct time periods.

First came the prehistoric era, 2001–2005, before Wikipedia had attained a critical mass of public awareness. In this period, it was not unheard of for contributors to make self-interested edits, but the stakes were low, and the perception was that they would simply write their own autobiography or maybe an article about their friend's band. This is why one of the project's earliest advisories against COI editing was called "Vanity guidelines."[4] The signature event of this era was the public embarrassment of Jimmy Wales, Wikipedia's famous cofounder, for editing his own biography in late 2005.[5] This experience no doubt shaped Wales's views on COI editing, and his pronouncements on the subject soon took on a very disapproving tone, which would last through the following era.

In 2006–2009, as Wikipedia itself became more widely known, its community also realized that COI had far-reaching implications. This era properly begins in early 2006 with the cautionary tale of MyWikiBiz, the first business focused on creating and editing Wikipedia entries for paying clients.[6] Its founder, Greg Kohs, was soon blocked from editing by Wales himself and would go on to become one of Wikipedia's most obsessive critics. Meanwhile, with the help of a software tool called WikiScanner, editors soon learned anonymous edits were being made by governments, corporations, and institutions around the world, demonstrating that the old saying "everybody's doing it" applied to this all-new context as well.

Wikipedia's internal governance responded with varying degrees of success. A new "COI Noticeboard" helped to identify suspicious patterns of edits, though actual policy changes remained elusive.[7] The period concludes with the failure of an effort to prohibit paid editing following a long debate in the summer of 2009.[8] Few Wikipedians were great fans of the practice, but the severity of the harm was not clear to everyone, and concerns about unintended consequences of proposed restrictions prevailed.

Tacit acquiescence and passive avoidance characterized the period covering 2010–2013. Several paid editing controversies arose, only to subside without clear resolution. These included the discoveries of pernicious editing for unsavory clients by the since-shuttered London PR firm Bell Pottinger and the "Gibraltarpedia" scandal, in which prominent editors manipulated site processes to benefit their client, the tourism board of Gibraltar.[9] Yet another dispute happened to focus on my work and, as I will explain later, this crisis arguably led to the era's two major positive developments—the first being Wales's outspoken support for the idea that while COI contributors should not edit articles directly, they should be able to ask for help and receive it, and the second being the development of new community procedures to facilitate and supervise this practice. But the biggest and most consequential event was the discovery of a vast sock-puppet network associated with a company called Wiki-PR, whose shamelessness and scale of fraudulence caused the firm to become a shorthand for unethical COI engagement.[10]

The current era, roughly 2014 to the present, begins with the concurrent though not coordinated public responses to the Wiki-PR controversy by the Wikimedia Foundation (WMF) and concerned members of the PR industry, myself included. In February of that year, I convened a roundtable meeting of Wikipedia editors and digital PR executives at the Donovan House hotel in Washington, DC, and by June we had hammered out an open letter to Wikipedia on behalf of most of the big US agencies. Less than a week later, the WMF announced the first change to its Terms of Use in years, officially requiring editors with a financial COI to disclose these connections. Viewed by the community as a crackdown that banned undisclosed COI editing, it also acknowledged that responsible COI engagement was a thing that could exist. This is not to say COI is no longer controversial—and new efforts to subvert Wikipedia are discovered all the time—however, it has reached a kind of equilibrium. It's a known issue, less existentially threatening than before.

An Interesting Conflict

In late 2011, well into the third era of COI, I became involved in highly contentious disputes on two unrelated client articles that soon became the focus of a weeks-long argument that would become the catalyst for longer lasting changes.

The first client was a well-known regional restaurant chain, one already the subject of a low-quality entry that was excessively focused on corporate wrongdoing—in my view, contravening established guidelines about representing topics in proportion to overall coverage, known as "due and undue weight."[11] The second was an automobile industry trade association having no article at all. In both cases, I proposed completely new drafts which I had researched, written, and posted to my user space, seeking comment from unconflicted editors.

To my great surprise, the restaurant article rewrite was approved almost immediately and moved into place by a volunteer editor. This happened too quickly, it turned out, as another editor soon reinserted material about the company's numerous controversies and slapped the page with a COI warning tag. Meanwhile, my draft for the auto trade association was given a lukewarm approval, so I took it live by myself, but the following day it too was affixed with multiple warning templates, this time by an editor who hadn't previously participated in the discussion. Here, my failure to describe the association as a "lobby group" came in for particular criticism.

I was stunned—with the restaurant chain, I had followed the hands-off protocol exactly. With the auto group, my position was more tenuous, but I had experienced plenty of success in similar circumstances. My first move was to ask for help from a couple of editors who had assisted me on other client pages. Alas, one started edit warring on the auto group page, repeatedly removing the warning template, which was each time restored by my detractors. This breach of decorum inspired a complaint to Jimmy Wales via his talk page, asking him to voice his disapproval of my work and the actions of the editor ostensibly helping me. Meanwhile, editors avowedly hostile to paid editing commandeered both articles, removing positive information they considered "puffery" and amplifying critical information I had tried to make less "undue."

Thus did a three-week period centering around New Year's 2012 become the worst stretch of my Wikipedia career, as fierce debates about my work raged on both Wales's talk page (though he remained largely absent) as well as a related thread on a forum for notifying administrators of wayward contributors. I was an active participant, choosing to engage where I thought I could clarify misrepresentations but erred on the side of letting the two sides go at it. I hit refresh constantly, watching with trepidation as new comments appeared. Some editors supported my position, complimenting my written content and willingness to defend myself, while others accused me of being a terrible threat to Wikipedia's future and asserted their intention to closely inspect every article I had ever worked on. One critic took the step of posting an email address for a third client to Wales's page, inviting incensed editors to give them a piece of their minds.

The tide began to turn toward the end of the first week of January. The uproar, which had initially focused on my actions specifically, inspired the creation of two new WikiProjects focused on this activity in general. The first, named WikiProject Integrity, sought to watchdog paid advocacy, and another, called WikiProject Cooperation, aimed to create a collaborative space for working through COI issues.[12] I kept a close eye on the former while eagerly embracing the latter. Off-wiki, a dauntless PR executive named Phil Gomes joined the fray, publishing a post on his blog called "An Open Letter to Jimmy Wales and Wikipedia" and shortly thereafter created a Facebook group dedicated to the topic Corporate Representatives for Ethical Wikipedia Engagement (CREWE).[13] I signed up on the spot, soon becoming an admin and one of its most active members.

What about my clients? By this time, they weren't any longer. In both cases, our agreements had concluded with the placement of each article. My continued interest was not about specific contractual obligations but about my own sense of responsibility. Fortunately, the initial rancor subsided, and a few editors from the new WikiProject Cooperation helped to reassess both entries. A great deal of work was put into the restaurant article, and eventually it was accorded the highest possible recognition: "Featured Article" status. Meanwhile, I waited for the auto group page to settle down before submitting a compromise draft, which was approved without further acrimony. One month later, a heretofore uninvolved WikiProject Automobiles editor appeared from nowhere and added just two words: "lobby group." Since then, the page has remained virtually unchanged for seven years and counting.

A Field Guide to COI Participants

To fully understand COI activity on Wikipedia, we must identify the different types of participants. These categories are broad and their borders porous since everyone has a potential COI, paid or unpaid, with some topics. After all, volunteers too have their own outside relationships and affinities, be they an employer, an ideological cause, or a sports team. Nevertheless, we can usefully split these participants into two camps: those representing Wikipedia's interests and those representing outside interests.

Let's begin with the editors responsible for preserving Wikipedia's integrity, sorted according to their views on COI and degree of interest in the subject.

1. *COI-Neutral Volunteers.* The vast majority think very little about this topic but might stumble across obvious undisclosed paid editing or be asked by a disclosed COI contributor for assistance. Most stay out of it, while some choose to get involved on a case-by-case basis, only to quickly return to their primary editing interests. The first editor to help me on the restaurant article, who quickly backed away from the controversy, fits into this category.

2. *Anti-COI Volunteers.* A relatively small number of Wikipedians think about COI a lot, usually because they are concerned about the risks to Wikipedia's neutrality posed by outsiders focused exclusively on their own interests or are offended that some editors are compensated for labor they give away freely. The founders of WikiProject Integrity, and those who came after my clients' articles, belong to this category. Ironically, in recent years it is anti-COI editors who are among the most involved in adjudicating edit requests, likely figuring they will have better judgment than a volunteer who doesn't fully grasp the troublesome implications of doing favors for financially motivated contributors.

3. *Pro-COI Volunteers.* Effectively zero Wikipedia editors are proponents of COI editing as such. However, from time to time one will stick their neck

out and offer active assistance, but their involvement tends to have a short shelf life, likely owing to the stresses of working with sometimes pushy private interests, not to mention the disapproval of fellow editors. The brave members of WikiProject Cooperation fit here.

Next, let's consider the outsiders looking to influence Wikipedia's content, whether focused on their own interests or acting on behalf of others.

4. *Single-Purpose Accounts.* The least sophisticated actor, and a bit of an outlier in this list, are those who don't know a lot about the site except that it can be edited by anyone and decide to take Wikipedia up on the offer. They are invariably novices who may genuinely not even know there are COI rules and do not spend much time pondering the ethical implications. After all, they are usually focused on a single page, and it's almost always about themselves or their own business. In many cases, their goal is simply to create a page that does not exist, often on subjects that do not meet Wikipedia's eligibility requirements. For most, their involvement with Wikipedia ends in failure, and that's the end of it. But some are irritatingly persistent, and they can waste a lot of volunteers' time.

5. *Self-Interested Organizations.* Of greater concern to Wikipedia's community are the companies, organizations, institutions, governments, and prominent individuals who are either the subject of a Wikipedia entry or who perceive their interests to be affected by the information contained within them and who then resolve to do something about it. They may start by assigning the task to an employee or hiring an outside entity to handle it for them. Their level of sophistication varies widely: some may not take Wikipedia seriously until their typically undisclosed efforts are rebuffed. It is this category which drives the demand for Wikipedia editing services.

6. *Agencies.* As a first resort, some article subjects will turn to the PR firms they already have on retainer. While these companies do not consider Wikipedia a particular focus, as my former employer did not, they may perform the work if their client demands it. Some may assign employees who might then familiarize themselves with Wikipedia's COI rules to figure it out. Whether they actually follow the COI rules, however, is largely a matter of personal or organizational ethics. Unlike the individual editing on one's own behalf, their zeal may be tempered by the fact that it's only one assignment and they know their limitations. Most

companies, contrary to the fears of anti-COI volunteer editors, will give up if it becomes too great a challenge.

7. *Freelancers.* At the opposite end of the scale are the freelancers who have recognized the opportunity that lies in editing Wikipedia for pay and who are notorious in the community for advertising their services on platforms such as Upwork or Fiverr. Few are particularly sophisticated, and they typically represent shallow-pocketed, less-noteworthy clients compared to the agencies. Those who learn enough to make their articles stick and avoid detection may graduate to the next category—but rarely the one after.

8. *Black Hats.* Savviest of all are the search engine optimization and reputation management companies willing to manipulate Wikipedia for their clients in knowing breach of the site's transparency rules. Black hats are the poster children for bad behavior. When detected, like Wiki-PR and its successor firm Status Labs, their accounts are blocked and their names added to a list of known miscreants.[14] So why do they do it? The downside risk is limited by their use of throwaway accounts and offset by the large demand for their services. Even if a project blows up in their face, someone else will be asking for their help soon.

9. *White Hats.* Finally, by far the smallest category of all are those firms offering Wikipedia assistance as a stand-alone service, who disclose their clients on relevant pages and who often (but not always) propose changes for volunteer review instead of editing directly. White hats tend to be led by veterans of the Wikipedia community, and while this does not shield them from criticism, when disagreements arise they are willing to stand by their work. It is this last category to which my firm belongs.

Bright Ideas

Although the controversies around my clients tapered off by the middle of 2012, the wider discussions continued. Most significantly, Wales finally took steps to clarify his thinking around COI. For years he had merely offered strong reprimands to the guilty, but now he exercised his moral authority in the community to make a proactive recommendation, which he called the "bright line" rule.[15] As he said in an interview around this time,

[the] rule is simply that if you are a paid advocate, you should disclose your conflict of interest and never edit article space directly. You are free to enter into a dialogue with the community on talk pages, and to suggest edits or even complete new articles or versions of articles by posting them in your user space.[16]

This wasn't necessarily a new concept, but it was the first time he had communicated this position so clearly. Attempts were made to standardize it as a policy or guideline, though approving new rules had proven increasingly difficult over the years and this failed just like the efforts to ban paid editing. Nonetheless, wishing the problem away had conclusively failed, and no competing alternative emerged. Still smarting from the fallout of my own altercations, I decided my company would follow the "bright line" forever after, even if the rule never became official.

WikiProject Cooperation was a lively scene in 2012, but the excitement soon faded. The project was viewed by some as too pro-COI and was never made part of the COI guideline, so when the early participants declined through attrition, it atrophied. Yet the "ask for help" model has lived on another way via the "Edit Request" system. Rather than an organized WikiProject, making an edit request is a multistage process whereby a COI editor includes a template with a talk page message that flags the post on an administrative page collecting all such requests into an organized queue and that volunteer editors may review on their own time.[17] While the process remains relatively obscure, the COI guideline encourages its use, and it has become, like Wales's "bright line" itself, a passable solution.

Notwithstanding the improving conditions, it always rankled how PR engagement on Wikipedia only ever made the news in cases like Wiki-PR or Bell Pottinger, with the resulting stories invariably failing to mention the guideline-compliant option. If one only ever hears about companies getting caught editing anonymously, it doesn't automatically follow that one should instead declare a COI and ask for help—it leads one to either declare Wikipedia off-limits, as many agencies have done, or just try harder not to get caught.

While there will always be some who treat Wikipedia as a system to be gamed, I've long believed these actors represent a minority of PR professionals. What everyone else needed was a signal that there was in fact a way to do right by their clients and Wikipedia at the same time. Likewise, volunteer editors needed to see that there were thoughtful individuals in the assumedly reprobate field of public relations work who were capable of taking Wikipedia and its policies seriously. Because I kept a foot in both camps, I was in an ideal position to make this happen. At long last, I was going to overcome my reticence and intentionally draw attention to my work.

This was the genesis for the Donovan House hotel meeting and subsequent open letter that became a major event of the fourth era. In late 2013, I started identifying people from both sides of the Wikipedia–PR divide to participate in an open and frank discussion about COI issues. With help from Wikipedia friends and an assist from the CREWE Facebook group, I received commitments from approximately a dozen individuals in total, counting global PR firms, academic institutions, and individual members of the community. I secured a conference room at the Donovan House hotel in Washington, DC, and we set the meeting for February 7, 2014.

The meeting was uncomfortable at first, given the very different initial assumptions among its participants, but was ultimately a success: having a face-to-face conversation helped everyone see that there were more points of agreement than disagreement and reasons to think the pervasive feeling of mutual distrust could be lessened. The most important thing this group could accomplish, we concluded, was for these agencies to collaborate on a statement to release publicly, acknowledging that the industry had thus far failed to treat Wikipedia with proper respect and pledging to do right in the future.

It took some time to arrive at the specific language. Wikipedians involved in the process felt it was important for the statement to read in part as an apology to the community while agency representatives believed they should not be held responsible for the mistakes of others. Despite these differences, we inched closer to a satisfactory version, until finally on June 10 we released a "Statement on Wikipedia from participating communications firms."[18] It had eleven signatories at launch, including eight of the top ten global PR agencies plus my own much-smaller firm. Word spread quickly via positive news coverage, validating my original aim of changing the conversation, at least for the time being. The WMF made its separate announcement about the updated Terms of Use a week later, which inspired a second round of agencies to join—more than two dozen—over the next few weeks. As of 2019, there are more than forty current signatories to the pledge.

At the time, some concerns were expressed that the statement lacked accountability measures, criticisms I considered reasonable though not discrediting. But like previous efforts on Wikipedia, the moment passed and the urgency along with it. Eventually, the CREWE Facebook page fell into disuse as well, with only intermittent spikes of interest following news-worthy paid editing controversies, which continue to occur, although less frequently. While the statement and its ensuing publicity has not changed the behavior of all PR agencies, it has inspired more to disclose their iden-tity and post requests for community review. These efforts are infrequent and not always effective, but there is no question that more PR agencies and individual COI editors are following the procedure nonetheless.

According to research by independent Wikipedians, activity on the "Edit Request" queue has increased steadily in recent years, with the biggest spike in new requests occurring in 2018.[19] From 2012 through 2018, the number of requested edits posted to the queue rose in every year save one, and as of summer 2019 it appeared to stay on the same pace.[20] The number of open requests has risen and fallen, but sustained efforts have kept the backlog manageable. While this research has been extremely limited and attribut-ing cause and effect may be elusive, I am confident our efforts played an important role.

Conclusion

In the latter eras of Wikipedia's COI history, the volunteer community and WMF have taken great strides toward confronting the challenges presented by self-interested editing. However, the edit request system remains opaque and poorly understood on both sides of the COI divide. The only way for this to meaningfully improve is for independent researchers to examine the current ecosystem to describe how well, or how poorly, the system actually works in practice. This essay has offered anecdotal evidence, but it is neces-sarily limited to my own experience.

Many questions are waiting to be asked, including: How do COI con-tributors find information about how to engage with Wikipedia, and what pathways do they take through the site? Why do volunteer editors choose to get involved with COI topics or to avoid them? What kinds of requests are being made by COI contributors, and what are their outcomes? Are these outcomes consistent with Wikipedia guidelines? How effective is the "Edit Request" system, and the Conflict of Interest Noticeboard for that matter? What opportunities exist to improve these processes? And how much undisclosed paid editing is there? As of this writing, there has never been a systematic effort to find these answers.

COI will never cease to be a matter of controversy so long as what Wikipedia says continues to matter in the public sphere. A comprehensive review of the current situation would be valuable for editors who want to minimize disruptions, readers who want accurate information, and entities with a financial stake in what the encyclopedia says about them. Whatever one's motive for getting involved with Wikipedia, and whatever one's feelings about COI, understanding the role it plays now and may play in the future should be in everyone's interest.

Notes

1. Wikipedia, s.v. "Wikipedia: Conflict of interest," accessed September 9, 2019, https://en.wikipedia.org/wiki/Wikipedia:Conflict_of_interest; Wikipedia, s.v. "Conflict of interest editing on Wikipedia," accessed September 9, 2019, https://en.wikipedia.org/wiki/Conflict-of-interest_editing_on_Wikipedia.

2. William Beutler, "The Wikipedian," accessed September 9, 2019, http://thewikipedian.net.

3. Wikipedia, s.v. "Making uncontroversial edits," Wikipedia: Conflict of interest, accessed September 9, 2019, https://en.wikipedia.org/wiki/Wikipedia:Conflict_of_interest#Making_uncontroversial_edits.

4. Wikipedia, s.v. "Wikipedia: Conflict of interest," revision as of August 13, 2005, https://en.wikipedia.org/w/index.php?title=Wikipedia:Conflict_of_interest&diff=20957254&oldid=20899691.

5. Evan Hansen, "Wikipedia Founder Edits Own Bio," *Wired*, December 19, 2005, https://www.wired.com/2005/12/wikipedia-founder-edits-own-bio/.

6. Michael Snow, "Account Used to Create Paid Corporate Entries Shut Down," *The Signpost*, October 9, 2006, https://en.wikipedia.org/wiki/Wikipedia:Wikipedia_Signpost/2006-10-09/MyWikiBiz.

7. Wikipedia, s.v. "Wikipedia: Conflict of interest/Noticeboard," accessed September 9, 2019, https://en.wikipedia.org/wiki/Wikipedia:Conflict_of_interest/Noticeboard.

8. Wikipedia, s.v. "Wikipedia: Requests for comment/Paid editing," accessed September 9, 2019, https://en.wikipedia.org/wiki/Wikipedia:Requests_for_comment/Paid_editing.

9. Dave Lee, "Wikipedia Investigates PR Firm Bell Pottinger's Edits," *BBC News*, March 8, 2012, htfps://www.bbc.com/news/technology-16084861; Tony1, "UK

Chapter Rocked by Gibraltar Scandal," *The Signpost*, September 24, 2012, https://en .wikipedia.org/wiki/Wikipedia:Wikipedia_Signpost/2012-09-24/News_and_notes.

10. The ed17, "Wiki-PR's Extensive Network of Clandestine Paid Advocacy Exposed," *The Signpost*, October 9, 2013, https://en.wikipedia.org/wiki/Wikipedia:Wikipedia _Signpost/2013-10-09/News_and_notes.

11. Wikipedia, s.v. "Due and undue weight," accessed September 9, 2019, https://en .wikipedia.org/wiki/Wikipedia:Neutral_point_of_view#Due_and_undue_weight.

12. Wikipedia, s.v. "Wikipedia: WikiProject Integrity," accessed September 9, 2019, https://en.wikipedia.org/wiki/Wikipedia:WikiProject_Integrity; Wikipedia, s.v. "Wiki-pedia:WikiProject Cooperation," accessed September 9, 2019, https://en.wikipedia .org/wiki/Wikipedia:WikiProject_Cooperation.

13. Phil Gomes, "An Open Letter to Jimmy Wales and Wikipedia," *Where the Fisher-man Ain't* (blog), January 4, 2012, https://blog.philgomes.com/2012/01/open-letter -to-jimmy-wales-and-wikipedia.html; Corporate Representatives for Ethical Wiki-pedia Engagement (CREWE) (Public group), Facebook, accessed September 9, 2019, https://www.facebook.com/groups/crewe.group/.

14. Wikipedia, s.v. "Wikipedia: List of paid editing companies," accessed September 9, 2019, https://en.wikipedia.org/wiki/Wikipedia:List_of_paid_editing_companies.

15. Jimmy Wales, "Paid Advocacy FAQ," Wikipedia, accessed September 9, 2019, https://en.wikipedia.org/wiki/User:Jimbo_Wales/Paid_Advocacy_FAQ.

16. Ocaasi, "Does Wikipedia Pay? The Founder: Jimmy Wales," *The Signpost*, Octo-ber 1, 2012, https://en.wikipedia.org/wiki/Wikipedia:Wikipedia_Signpost/2012-10 -01/Paid_editing.

17. Wikipedia, s.v. "Template: Request edit," accessed September 9, 2019, https://en .wikipedia.org/wiki/Template:Request_edit; Wikipedia, s.v. "Category: Requested edits," accessed September 9, 2019, https://en.wikipedia.org/wiki/Category:Requested _edits.

18. Wikipedia, s.v. "Wikipedia: Statement on Wikipedia from participating com-munications firms," accessed September 9, 2029, https://en.wikipedia.org/wiki/Wiki pedia:Statement_on_Wikipedia_from_participating_communications_firms.

19. Altamel, "The stats," Administrator's noticeboard, Wikipedia, March 26, 2018, https://en.wikipedia.org/wiki/Wikipedia:Administrators%27_noticeboard/Incident Archive979#The_stats.

20. User:AnomieBOT/EDITREQTable, "Year counts," XTools, accessed September 9, 2019, https://xtools.wmflabs.org/articleinfo/en.wikipedia.org/User:AnomieBOT/EDIT REQTable#year-counts.

II Connection

6 Wikipedia and Libraries

Phoebe Ayers

Wikipedia is pushing the venerable field of librarianship to recognize a lesson of the twenty-first century: making knowledge accessible to all requires Wikipedians, librarians, academics, and citizens to work together in collaboration and community.

I am a librarian and a Wikipedia editor. One identity is professional, the other a late-night hobby, but they are two approaches to the same goal: sharing knowledge with the world. Wikipedia and libraries have similar aspirations and goals. They both exist to help people who are looking for information, and they both help curate our society's memory and community. And despite their different cultures and Wikipedia's upstart nature, today there are hundreds of collaborations between librarians and Wikipedians to build the future of open knowledge.

In the areas in which libraries and librarians have participated in Wikipedia, I see three overriding themes that relate to the future of Wikipedia: quality, inclusiveness, and sustainability. In each of these areas, both institutions and individual librarians have already done tremendous work and have a future role to play. It is not a one-way street, either: the aspirations, idealistic values, and joy of the Wikipedia project can also help make the ancient profession of librarianship better, even as we critique and improve Wikipedia.

My story is about building the future of the world's greatest reference work. It is about libraries and Wikipedia, about what it is like to be an author of an encyclopedia, and about being part of a community, and those three things are, for me, inseparable.

In the Beginning

Where to begin? July 2010—staying up late in Gdańsk, Poland (a seaside industrial town and birthplace of the Polish Solidarity movement): shots of vodka fueling intense discussion in a dozen languages. There, the Wikipedians around the table talked about strategies for involving local people in editing online—and about copyright law, of course. Or what about Egypt, in 2008? There, the librarians of the new Library of Alexandria, the Bibliotheca Alexandrina, showed the Wikipedians who were in town how they were turning hand-written Arabic manuscripts from hundreds of years ago into readable digitized text. We spoke about how to put these manuscripts online and what it would mean for that library—or any library—to collaborate with volunteers from around the world who were only coordinated in the loosest of ways. Or, how about starting with Cambridge, Massachusetts? On a hot summer evening in 2006 Wikipedians from around the world (Venezuela, Taiwan, the Netherlands) sat on the steps of the Harvard Law School library, looking out at one of the world's great universities, and day-dreamed about building websites where people anywhere could learn about any subject—where learning would transcend place and where people from all the places we had come from would contribute.

Perhaps I will just begin at the beginning; that is, my beginning. The first time I ever wrote something online that felt momentous was in August 2003. I was sitting at my kitchen table in Seattle, where I was entering a graduate program in library science. I'd read a newspaper article about Wikipedia and was intrigued, so I visited the site and tried it out. I read a few how-to pages, then clicked the "edit this page" tab, composed a couple sentences, and hit save. After a pause, my text displayed in my web browser, and my breath caught in my throat: I had just edited the encyclopedia.

Partly, my astonishment was about how easy it was to edit, which is something that we tend to forget in today's world of slick apps and instant online shopping. By 2003, I had been using the internet and writing online on various platforms for years, but I was also used to most websites requiring accounts or FTP access to update and perhaps a knowledge of HTML. There was nothing beautiful about Wikipedia's early editing interface (and indeed, there still isn't), but as a type of website—that is, the wiki, which had been invented by Ward Cunningham in 1995—it was straightforward. Write in the browser, hit save. Each change, each save, is recorded as a separate version that you can trace the history of, which makes collaboration and revision between many people possible, even smooth.

And the implication of that technology as applied to an encyclopedia was astounding: online contributors who didn't know each other and who weren't pre-vetted or approved could use this tool to participate in creating the record of *all* knowledge. Together, using the internet, it would be possible to build a perpetually changing and updated site that would capture what we know as a species about every aspect of our world. That implication, that aspiration, still takes my breath away. Today, some twenty thousand edits, dozens of trips around the world to meet with other Wikipedia editors, and uncounted hours of discussion later, I have never forgotten that feeling of wonder.

I have spent the sixteen years or so since my first edit sharing this magical, inspirational, joyful, exasperating, problematic project with others through writing and teaching, trying to open Wikipedia's door to new contributors. I've tried to make the larger Wikimedia community a stronger and more stable place through governance and in-person gatherings. And I've tried to bring together my venerable profession of librarianship with the Wikipedia project, which has more in common with a start-up or an old-fashioned barn raising (all hands on deck, the people who show up make the rules) than with a formal institution. And in so doing, I have thought about the ways we might change each other: how libraries, with their deep collections and community roots, can help Wikipedia and, in turn, how Wikipedia, with its idealism, individual empowerment, and global reach, can help libraries and all the rest of the knowledge ecosystem.

Throughout it all, my life has been changed the most by my friendships and collaborations with other Wikipedia editors. Because Wikipedia, in the end, is about individuals: about the person sitting at their dining table, trying to make an article better because they care about the topic or perhaps just because they care about information being accurate online. It's about photographers organizing group trips to take high-quality free photos of cultural heritage sites to add to Wikimedia Commons, before those sites are lost for good. It's about librarians adding references and citations to articles, tying Wikipedia to published knowledge. It's about translators making Wikipedia accessible in their own tongue, often writing the very first encyclopedia to ever exist in their language. And it's about those warm summer nights around the globe at our annual conference[1] and at other meetups and pub nights and edit-a-thons, when we get together and work and daydream about a better world. Wikipedia is a community made up of individuals, and like all communities, it is full of jokes and arguments, disagreements and compromise. It is full of ordinary human relationships, too, in person as well as online: our community has had weddings and breakups, births and deaths, and we celebrate and mourn like any group of people that depends on each other would.

When I look at a Wikipedia article, what I see in my mind's eye are the people behind it: the student; the retiree; the person who sat down one day and decided to write about a topic; and the person who came after them and tried to make it better; and the person who came after them. What I see are my collaborators, even if I do not know their names, and the people I am privileged to call friends.

Libraries

I became a librarian because I wanted to help people. Specifically, I wanted to help people who wanted to find information on something. Though it is core to our work, helping others research information is just one of the many missions of libraries. In their various types and locations libraries also serve as community centers, as archival institutions, and as places of learning, whether it's teaching college students to dive deep into the historical record or teaching children how to read picture books at story time. Public libraries serve as civic institutions, often the only public places in a community that are open to all. Libraries and archives of all kinds also have a role to play as conservers of memory through community and research archives. Most fundamentally, libraries are institutions that help you interact with, and learn from, other people's stories and work.

In hindsight, it seems obvious that there is a natural congruence between libraries and librarians, with their broad mission of helping connect people to information, and Wikipedia, with its broad mission of collecting information on all the world's topics. But in 2003, when I was beginning to become both a librarian and a Wikipedian, the site was still mostly unknown. When it was known amongst librarians and educators, it was viewed with deserved skepticism along with the rest of the burgeoning, user-created internet. It was clear that a hobbyist website, built by anonymous contributors, was not the same thing as the multivolume encyclopedia sets, written and edited by distinguished scholars, which libraries went to great expense and trouble to collect. It was also clear that Wikipedia could not be, and should not be, recommended as an equivalent source; the idea was insulting to many.

And still today, when librarians and educators like myself recommend Wikipedia to students and researchers, that recommendation comes loaded with caveats: Wikipedia articles are inconsistently written and fact-checked, they might be incomplete or biased, and students should rely more on the references cited than on the article itself. And of course Wikipedia is only good for a certain type of information—it aims to include recorded facts that are scientifically vetted, not anecdotes or the type of storytelling that gives richness to our cultural heritage—and as a consequence and because of mirroring the biases of past sources of knowledge, a vast part of the human experience is left out of Wikipedia entirely.

And yet, despite all this reasonable distrust at the beginning, over the first decade of Wikipedia's life the relationship between librarians and Wikipedia shifted. For one thing, Wikipedia itself grew at a tremendous rate, exceeding all expectations. It soon fast exceeded the ability of any other traditional reference source to keep up with the world, especially around topics like breaking news, as Brian Keegan discusses in chapter 4. This first, fast growth of Wikipedia, from 2002 to 2008 or so, came as online participation in general exploded, leading to new potential readers and writers alike. This meant that a few years into Wikipedia's existence, librarians and educators had to grapple with a simple fact: our students and professors and readers were using it. Wikipedia was handy for them, sometimes both handier and more complete than any other source around. It was good for translations, for helping find obscure facts, and for getting freely licensed images. It was remarkably good for finding information on topics that local library collections did not support, particularly in areas where libraries were working with limited resources.[2] And, it was good for education, providing students a window into the process of information collection and curation like no other.

Libraries and archives around the globe also discovered the tremendous power of Wikipedia and her sister projects—Wikimedia Commons in particular—to share archival collections that had previously been locked away, accessible only to a few. Libraries have also interlinked Wikipedia and other Wikimedia projects, such as Wikidata, into technical systems and catalogs to tie existing information resources to Wikipedia.[3] And librarians have become editors in individual capacities, adding articles and improving them and training others to do so as well.[4]

Lastly, libraries and Wikimedia are similar in their ideals and in their policy goals. Like libraries, the Wikimedia projects exist to promote knowledge availability for all—not a neutral goal. And, both libraries and Wikipedia care deeply about user privacy, about openness and accessibility to all, and about resisting censorship. Wikipedia faces current and future threats from government internet regulations; from national and local censorship; and from laws governing privacy, copyright, and intellectual property. Libraries face the same threats and challenges and should share policy and tactics with the free and open internet movement of which Wikipedia is a part.[5]

Libraries, like Wikipedia, are broadly concerned with issues of information quality, inclusiveness (both in access to get information and to create information), and sustainability of the information ecosystem. These three areas are also crucial to the future of Wikipedia: without continuing to maintain high-quality information in articles, an inclusive and diverse editor base and articles that cover all of the world's knowledge, and a sustainable model for editing and vetting articles, Wikipedia will not continue for another twenty years. These areas, then, are worth digging into for how libraries and Wikipedia can work together.

Quality

Encyclopedias differ from other kinds of nonfiction works and information sources in that they do not report on original discoveries but, rather, on what others report to be true ("no original research" reads the English Wikipedia policy on the subject[6]). This is particularly important for Wikipedia, which is written entirely by an anonymous contributor base—unlike a textbook that relies to some degree on the reputation of the author or a research article that relies on peer review for vetting, it is not easy to tell who wrote any given part of any given Wikipedia article, or what their background is, or whether what has been claimed has been reviewed by anyone else. The Wikipedian who added that sentence might be an award-winning senior scientist, or they might be a particularly bright thirteen-year-old (and in fact, some of the very best Wikipedians I've known have started editing in middle school).

As a consequence, Wikipedia relies on references—citations to reliable published work on a topic. This was not always true. In the early years of Wikipedia, authors wrote largely from personal knowledge, or if they drew from sources, they were inconsistently cited. But it was soon realized that if this global project was going to maintain any kind of quality—and more to the point, keep out conspiracy theories, rumor, fakes, and advertising—we would have to leave the process of peer review and vetting what was "notable" to traditional scholarly and news publishing. Today, in theory, every fact that is in Wikipedia must first be vetted elsewhere and documented in a source, which like a good scholar we will then cite. Over the years, these sourcing guidelines have gotten more rigorous: sources should be published by someone other than the subject of the article; they should be peer reviewed; and they should have multiple confirming sources if possible.

Libraries are, of course, in the business of sources. One project related to libraries and Wikipedia is the #1lib1ref campaign—begun by Jake Orlowitz and Alex Stinson at the Wikimedia Foundation and helped along by dozens of volunteers, "One Lib One Ref" has now taken off into an ongoing project that hundreds of libraries and librarians have participated in.[7] (See Jake Orlowitz's chapter 8.) The idea is that while Wikipedia is missing many citations for existing information, if every librarian with access to a research collection added just one citation—one librarian, one reference—we would begin to make a dent in the backlog of improving Wikipedia's quality.

Why librarians in particular? Of course, as a rule we have a propensity toward sourcing things and looking up information. But we also importantly tend to have access to sources of information, including books and research databases that cost a great deal of money. Improving access to information for all is at the heart of Wikipedia, but this goal is hindered by current systems of scholarly publishing, which restrict access to much of the latest research that is published to subscription journals and databases that are priced out of reach of all but the largest, richest research libraries. This is an issue of social justice as well as economics; only a tiny fraction of the population has access to these university collections. And ironically, most Wikipedia editors—stewards of the single most-read information source in the world—do not have access to these research resources either. For over a decade, libraries globally have addressed this by opening their physical doors to Wikipedians, hosting tours, edit-a-thons, and gatherings for active editors to increase access to collections. Librarians have also hosted Wikipedians-in-residence, volunteers or temporarily paid researchers who affiliate with an institution for the purposes of adding information available in libraries to Wikipedia.[8] Stinson and Orlowitz have also worked to make published scholarly research available to vetted Wikipedia editors online through the Wikipedia library project;[9] but though incredibly helpful to the work of writing an encyclopedia, this doesn't assist readers, who also need to be able to access the citations that Wikipedia is based on.

As we look forward to how to improve Wikipedia's quality, one continuing area will be increasing open access for scholarly publishing and making previously locked-away collections digital and available to all. Here, Wikipedia's goals converge with the cutting-edge work libraries are doing to change publishing business models and open up archives and catalogs, and Wikipedia itself provides one of the best arguments for continuing to do so. Though open access for research has been recognized for well over a decade as an area where libraries and Wikipedia have similar aspirations,[10] as we look to the future libraries are also moving to open up data as well as publications. The librarians and Wikimedians working on this recognize that the underlying infrastructure of library metadata also needs to be made free and open and connected to the open linked data systems that underlie Wikipedia and Wikidata in order to have a truly open scholarly ecosystem.[11]

I personally love adding citations to articles that are missing them. Diving deep into the research literature to ferret out the source of some plausible-sounding but unsourced information on Wikipedia provides the deep satisfaction of connecting the historical record and makes use of professional skills I've gathered. But it is work that needs many hands, and to make research truly accessible will require deep shifts across both libraries and scholarly publishing.

Inclusiveness

To find sources, you need a library collection. And every collection, regardless of what sort of library or archive it is in, is chosen and curated by individuals. Though there are various mechanisms and metrics for how books are selected depending on the size and style of library, with large libraries often getting automatic shipments of all the books on a particular topic—at some point, a person chose every book that sits on a library shelf.

And even the largest libraries have boundaries on their collections; every library is necessarily incomplete. National libraries might collect every book published in a particular country, for instance; the largest research libraries might collect comprehensively in a handful of areas. But most libraries are much, much smaller than that. As librarians, we carefully create collections policies and choose collections related to our many missions: to serve our community, to provide entertainment, to educate, to steward the historical record. Nonetheless, any given library only ever has the slimmest slice of the historical record represented within its physical or digital walls. And as a result, the story told by any given library's books and journals and archival collections is only, and can ever be, an opinionated subset of human knowledge, biased in particular ways toward particular perspectives—as discussed in the essays of part III.

To help rectify this, libraries have become masters of collaboration: using interlibrary loan, cooperative cataloging, and shared collecting, libraries work together to increase what is available to their communities. But it is more difficult to overcome the biases inherent in publishing: that marginalized stories aren't recorded, or if they are recorded, they are not widely distributed. Libraries tend to collect in the languages of their constituents, leaving out published works from the rest of the world. And as an academic, it is far easier to both get funded and published if you are already a well-funded researcher working in a prestigious university than if you are not. Collections are also living and change: a library collection of the nineteenth century is today only relevant to historians. Curation is as important an activity as collection.

Further, most library and archival collections are locked away, restricted to those who can physically access the collection and have privileges to do so. Mass digitization projects have changed this by converting physical objects to digital ones that can be easily shared or viewed from afar. These digital representations still must be shared openly, however, and Wikipedia and Wikimedia Commons provide a way to do this that has a wide reach. One early project to share a huge collection of archival materials via Wikimedia was the US National Archives and Record Administration's project to add hundreds of thousands of public domain historical images to Wikimedia Commons. Now these files, which are freely available for use by all, can be added to appropriate Wikipedia articles, enriching our understanding of those historical topics.[12] Dozens of libraries and archives around the world have followed suit either by adding links to collections in Wikipedia articles or adding the collections themselves to Wikimedia Commons.[13] However, thousands of freely licensed collections are still locked away, leaving gaps in our collective understanding of and Wikipedia's representation of the historical record.

In Wikipedia, issues of inclusiveness center around what is written about and by whom. Wikipedia is created by individuals who write primarily about what they are interested in, which can lead to unevenness. Wikipedians have coined a term for the phenomenon of Wikipedia's article coverage leaving out some areas of human perspective and knowledge and emphasizing others: "systemic bias." Systemic bias, on Wikipedia, is the notion that without an explicit corrective, Wikipedia's coverage will drift toward the biases of its contributors and toward the weight of the historical published record which Wikipedia relies on.[14] We see this bias clearly in, for instance, the geographical distribution of article subjects: Wikipedia (in all languages) has vastly more articles on cities, towns, and institutions in North America and Europe than anywhere else.[15] This is both due to the bias of contributors, who tend to be from those places, and the bias of published sources, which thanks to European and Western colonialism have privileged Western history above all other places for hundreds of years.

We see systematic bias again in topical coverage: there is a dearth of articles about women scientists (again, due to the bias of contributors but also due to the bias of historical sources against writing about women in science), and there is an overabundance of articles about military history topics, a topic perhaps of deeper interest to Wikipedia contributors than to the population at large. And we see this bias more subtly in how articles are actually written: in their focus on colonial history rather than native history, for instance.[16] We see it when articles about technologies only give examples on uses in the United States rather than in a global perspective. And we see it when comparing different language editions of Wikipedia, which take different approaches to covering history, even if subtly so. Wikipedia editors aspire to fill in these gaps and correct these biases, but it is unending and often difficult work, subject to debate and rancor as competing goals (that is, to rely only on reliable published sources and also to add things missing from the historical record) clash.

Wikipedia is not finished. Neither is any library collection, but Wikipedia differs in aspiration: it has a perhaps unattainable goal of all the world's knowledge represented comprehensively and fairly. It is worth asking if this is possible or whether Wikipedia's aspirations should instead grow toward acknowledging the impossibility of ever being neutral and of openly displaying the complications of telling many histories in a single way. As Wikipedians, we have spent the last twenty years demonstrating that the encyclopedia format can be stretched to contain orders of magnitude more multitudes than ever before. In our next few decades we could stretch toward a new aspiration: building an authoritative source that clearly shows there are many possible authorities and stories in parallel and that shows what is missing from the encyclopedia as clearly as we show what is included.

In this way I think Wikipedia both serves as an instructive example and an inspiration not just to other reference works but to libraries in general: to make our biases visible in specific and granular ways. Libraries are not neutral, but we often act as if we are,[17] and we are not particularly skilled at making visible to readers what our carefully curated collections include and do not include and why.

Encyclopedias have existed in one form or another for thousands of years, but Wikipedia differs from past attempts both in scale and coverage.[18] There is no defined audience for Wikipedia, and the only limits in scope are in style rather than in topic (we are not a directory, articles should not be too granular, information should be well sourced).[19] As a result, particularly as the largest language editions of Wikipedia[20] approach some degree of apparent comprehensiveness, we must look again, and again, not just at how we know what we know and at what is missing but at whose stories are told and how.

Sustainability

There's no question that many Wikipedia editors are difficult to work with. Pedantic and focused to the point of obsession, the project attracts those for whom performing precise tasks in the service of writing an encyclopedia is an attractive hobby. Because it is a project that is never finished, to-do lists can stretch over years, which can lead to impatience with new contributors who are starting fresh on the same work. Those who show up make the rules on Wikipedia, and for the better part of two decades those who have shown up are single-minded and argumentative, willing and able to spend hundreds of hours toiling alone online.

And yet, Wikipedia editors are also, by and large, wonderful people. Without exception, every good-faith Wikipedia editor I have encountered (and I have been privileged enough to meet hundreds of editors, at meet-ups across five continents) has been passionate about what they know and about knowledge in general; generous with time, attention, and collaboration; curious about everything; and willing to go to extraordinary lengths to build the project for the good of all.

Without the seventy thousand or so active editors across language editions—and of those, particularly the ten thousand or so who make more than a hundred edits a month, adding articles, removing spam, and generally maintaining the site[21]—there is no Wikipedia. Certainly, there would be static articles—those will be offered up online in perpetuity.[22] But without an active hive of people pruning, updating, and revising, those articles would slowly degrade in quality, go out-of-date, and be prone to intentional or unintentional vandalism and biasing. Wikipedia works the very best at a large scale—when there are many eyes on the problem—and the health and strength of our community will determine Wikipedia's future. As the internet in general changes to a world where there are fewer desktops than mobile users and the Wikipedia site feels dated and complex, acquiring new editors is a real challenge. And, as existing editors leave due to disputes or changing interests, maintaining a large, active editor base is an existential challenge for the long-term viability of Wikipedia.[23]

In addition to needing active editors, Wikipedia needs diversity. To cover the world well, the project needs people of all genders, ethnicities, geographic origins, languages, and socioeconomic backgrounds to participate. In some ways, the Wikipedia project has pioneered diversity online, in valuing contributions from those who speak non-Western languages that are otherwise poorly represented on the internet, for instance. In most respects, however, the contributor base has skewed toward those who have had free time, abundant internet access, and the resources to contribute— mostly men, mostly white people, and mostly contributors located in the Global North, especially North America and Europe.

Libraries aspire to work with and serve people of all kinds, across academic institutions and communities of every description. Like many of my peers in libraries who have worked with Wikipedia, I have taught hundreds of people to understand and edit Wikipedia over the years: from students to professors, both in one-off edit-a-thon events hosted by the library and in longer classes.[24] Librarians offering training can serve as a bridge between an often seemingly impenetrable site and the people that we work with in our communities. This can help increase the diversity and ultimately the sustainability of the Wikipedia editor base. Most people that we train in workshops and classes will never come back to edit the site on their own. But some will; and many more will have a deeper understanding of what it means to create information online and apply that to other situations. As the internet overall changes to become more commercialized and controlled than ever before—where most people have an experience of being online that exists entirely within the walled garden of mobile apps[25]—being conversant with the user-generated open internet that Wikipedia is an exemplar of will be more important than ever before.

Sustainability, as a concept, also applies in a more fundamental way to the notion of an encyclopedia project at all. What is encyclopedic, and what does it mean to collect and summarize knowledge, and in the end—what does it mean to attempt to represent truth? Is the very idea of an encyclopedia one that will hold up in the future, or is it too simplistic and flawed to continue?

Training students to edit means training them to think like an encyclopedia editor. Partly, this means learning to look at information with a reflexively critical eye. As a Wikipedia editor, "citation needed" becomes a way of life, whether it's reading the newspaper or a bus-stop advertisement. How do we know what we know? How do we separate fact from supposition or recognize beliefs created from culture and our surroundings versus what we learn explicitly, versus what we discover from experimentation and measurement?

In the present moment, as a culture we are grappling with the right way to assess information, factualness, and truth. There are no models that we have, in libraries or outside of them, for what reliability and truth means when artificial-intelligence-generated deep-faked images are indistinguishable from real portraits or when social networks are flooded with rumor-passing memes. We live in a world of weaponized misinformation. At the same time, in areas ranging from sexual harassment to indigenous rights, people who have been historically marginalized are telling their own stories and claiming the right to speak for themselves rather than being subsumed in the histories told by others. The idea that one history can definitively speak for what happened has never been right, and we are relearning that idea today over and over. Meanwhile, our rate of technological change is faster than it has ever been before: science and technology, like our climate and natural world, are in a state of constant discovery and vast change.

In libraries, for too long we have taught students that there are definitive works and sources that are eminently reliable and that being critical of information can stop with choosing the right source. Some sources are more reliable than others, certainly: more carefully produced, more based on scientific method, and more completely representing knowledge as it currently stands. But no source is entirely complete or entirely definitive; no method of knowledge production is perfect. Wikipedia, with its explicit assumption of being perpetually incomplete and perpetually in progress, can teach every consumer of information an important lesson: that knowledge shifts and that we rewrite the encyclopedia as we go.

Our Future

As we approach twenty years of the Wikipedia project, I worry about our future. Wikipedia, like libraries, has always been a long-term endeavor. On the surface, Wikipedia seems, like most internet companies and websites, to be a project of the moment. In truth, though no one planned for this at the beginning, the aspirational mission of the project is much more than that: to provide and record our heritage and knowledge in perpetuity for everyone. Thinking about Wikipedia like a library, or a museum, makes sense: it is something that must be continually stewarded; something that will be newly discovered, added to, and changed by each new generation; and something that that gains value from longevity.

But to fulfill this promise, to stick around and remain useful and become better, Wikipedia faces many existential challenges ranging from regulation of intellectual property to participation from new editors to the nature of how we perceive truth itself. They are challenges that must be addressed by all of the participants in the project and also by the many kinds of institutions in society (including libraries, archives, and universities) that have a stake in making free knowledge available. Our solutions to these challenges will range from making works available openly to teaching new generations how to think critically about information.

Over the last twenty years I have seen Wikipedia go from something that was an experiment—something we built simply to see if we could do it!—to something that has become a fundamental part of the internet's information infrastructure; it is difficult to imagine the world without it. Our challenge in our next twenty, fifty, and hundred years is to open Wikipedia's doors wider than they ever have been before—to share the joy of documenting and discovering the curious corners of the world with new editors everywhere. And as Wikipedians and librarians, we must bring Wikipedia together with the institutions that have historically stewarded human knowledge to make Wikipedia more accessible, more open, more complete, and more sustainable than ever before.

Wikipedia, to me, represents a hope: a hope that with the right structures humans can collaborate and cooperate on massive projects without top-down structures or control and a hope that we can see all parts of the world as important and worth documenting. It is an extraordinarily optimistic and idealistic vision, an idea that has its roots in Enlightenment encyclopedic traditions but that in execution has become a type of reference that we have never seen before—a unique creation.

When I look at a Wikipedia article, I see the people behind it—the generous, quirky, enthusiastic souls that write and curate Wikipedia. And I see the weight of accumulated knowledge—what we know and what we do not know yet and what has not yet been recorded in Wikipedia. We are writing the world as it is made and building our future as we go.

Acknowledgments: Dedicated to Ben Yates, Ray Saintonge, and especially, to Austin Hair: Wikipedians, collaborators, and friends. I miss you all.

With deep thanks and respect to all of the wiki-brarians I have learned from and worked with over the years. There are too many to name, but the following have particularly shaped my thinking about how libraries and Wikipedia can work together. In no special order, thanks to Merrilee Proffitt, Meg Wacha, Liam Wyatt, Charles Matthews, Alex Stinson, Jake Orlowitz, S. J. Klein, Andrew Lih, Jessamyn West, Jakob Voss, Andrea Zanni, Andrea Forte, Benjamin Mako Hill, Rob Fernandez, Laura Soito, Jennifer Peterson, Rosie Stephenson-Goodknight, Stacey Allison-Cassin, Amy Carleton, Greta Suiter, Rebecca Thorndike-Breeze, Emily Temple-Wood, Richard Knipel, Lori Byrd-McDevitt, Dominic Byrd-McDevitt, Cristian Consonni, Benoit Rochon, Asaf Bartov, Sara Snyder, Kelly Doyle, Tim Spalding, Lauren Pressley, Kristen Shuyler, Jon Beasley-Murray, Brewster Kahle, Stephen LaPorte, and Aaron Swartz—and so many more. Thanks and love to the many more

Wikipedians I've shared a meal, a conversation, or an article with over the years. And thanks too to friends and colleagues at the University of Washington Information School (iSchool) and at every job I've had since then; they have tolerated and indulged my Wikipedia obsession from day one.

Notes

1. Aptly named Wikimania, the Wikimedia community has been holding an annual conference since 2005: Wikimania, last modified December 30, 2019, http://wikimania.wikimedia.org. This is in addition to the hundreds of more local events and meetups that happen around the world; see Meta-Wiki, s.v. "Events," last modified January 20, 2020, https://meta.wikimedia.org/wiki/Events.

2. The International Federation of Library Associations and Institutions (IFLA) and The Wikipedia Library (TWL), "Opportunities for Public Libraries and Wikipedia" (white paper, December 2016), https://www.ifla.org/files/assets/hq/topics/info-society/iflawikipediaandpubliclibraries.pdf.

3. IFLA and TWL, "Opportunities for Academic and Research Libraries and Wikipedia" (white paper, December 2016), https://www.ifla.org/files/assets/hq/topics/info-society/iflawikipediaopportunitiesforacademicandresearchlibraries.pdf.

4. See Merrilee Proffitt, ed., *Leveraging Wikipedia: Connecting Communities of Knowledge* (Chicago: ALA Editions, 2018) for perspectives on connecting libraries, librarians, and Wikipedia.

5. For a longer argument on this subject, see Stephen LaPorte and Phoebe Ayers "Common Interests: Libraries, the Knowledge Commons, and Public Policy," *I/S: A Journal of Law and Policy for the Information Society* 13, no. 1 (Fall 2016), https://kb.osu.edu/bitstream/handle/1811/81136/ISJLP_V13N1_295.pdf.

6. Wikipedia, s.v. "Wikipedia: No Original Research," last modified December 4, 2019, https://en.wikipedia.org/wiki/Wikipedia:No_original_research.

7. Meta-Wiki, s.v. "The Wikipedia Library/1Lib1Ref," last modified December 10, 2019, https://meta.wikimedia.org/wiki/The_Wikipedia_Library/1Lib1Ref.

8. See also the events associated with the Wikipedia Loves Libraries campaign, which ran as a focused volunteer effort to bring Wikipedians and librarians together from 2011–2016 or so; there have been many independent edit-a-thons and workshops in libraries before and since. See "Wikipedia Loves Libraries/Collaborations," Wikimedia Outreach, last modified January 14, 2019, https://outreach.wikimedia.org/wiki/Wikipedia_Loves_Libraries/Collaborations; of note in particular are the library collaborations run in Italy coordinated by members of Wikimedia Italia. See also the GLAM (Galleries, Libraries, Archives and Museums) projects run at

institutions globally; "GLAM Wiki," Wikimedia Outreach, last modified April 10, 2019, https://outreach.wikimedia.org/wiki/GLAM.

9. Wikipedia, s.v. "Wikipedia: The Wikipedia Library," last modified January 16, 2020, https://en.wikipedia.org/wiki/Wikipedia:The_Wikipedia_Library.

10. See, for example, John Willinsky, "What Open Access Research Can Do for Wikipedia," *First Monday* 12, no. 3 (2007), https://firstmonday.org/article/view/1624 /1539.

11. ARL Task Force on Wikimedia and Linked Open Data, "ARL White Paper on Wiki-data: Opportunities and Recommendations" (white paper, Association of Research Libraries, Washington, DC, 2019), https://www.arl.org/resources/arl-whitepaper-on -wikidata/; see also the WikiCite project: Meta-Wiki, s.v. "WikiCite," last modified December 19, 2019, http://meta.wikimedia.org/wiki/Wikicite.

12. See Ed Erhart, "Wikipedia Signpost News and Notes for June 25, 2014," last modified February 8, 2017, https://en.wikipedia.org/wiki/Wikipedia:Wikipedia_Sign post/2014-06-25/News_and_notes for a report on this from Wikipedia's own internal newspaper.

13. One of the earliest projects around this I am aware of is reported in Ann Lally and Carolyn Dunford, "Using Wikipedia to Extend Digital Collections," *D-Lib Maga- zine* 13, no. 5/6 (May/June 2007): 5–6, http://www.dlib.org/dlib/may07/lally/05lally .html.

14. Wikipedia, s.v. "Wikipedia: Systemic bias," last modified January 22, 2020, https://en.wikipedia.org/wiki/Wikipedia:Systemic_bias.

15. See, for example, the work of Mark Graham and the Oxford Internet Institute: Mark Graham, "Wiki Space: Palimpsests and the Politics of Exclusion," in *Critical Point of View: A Wikipedia Reader*, ed. Geert Lovink and Nathanial Tkacz, 269–282, Inc Reader #7, http://www.networkcultures.org/_uploads/%237reader_Wikipedia.pdf.

16. See the work of Carwil Bjork-James; for example, Carwil Bjork-James, "New Maps for an Inclusive Wikipedia: Plotting Strategies to Counter Systemic Bias," Wikipedia Day 2019 NYC, video, 51:12, January 13, 2019, https://livestream.com /internetsociety/wikidaynyc2019/videos/185803949.

17. See Chris Bourg, "Never Neutral: Libraries, Technology, and Inclusion," *Feral Librarian* (blog), January 28, 2015, https://chrisbourg.wordpress.com/2015/01/28 /never-neutral-libraries-technology-and-inclusion/.

18. See Andrew Brown, *A Brief History of Encyclopedias: From Pliny to Wikipedia* (London, UK: Hesperus Press, 2011).

19. Wikipedia, s.v. "Wikipedia: What Wikipedia Is Not," last modified January 13, 2020, https://en.wikipedia.org/wiki/Wikipedia:What_Wikipedia_is_not.

20. English is the largest Wikipedia edition, with German in second place; currently, Swedish and Cebuano (a language of the Philippines) have more articles than German, but that is due to automatically bot-created articles, a source of much debate in the Wikipedia community. See Meta-Wiki, s.v. "List of Wikipedias," lsat modified January 3, 2020, https://meta.wikimedia.org/wiki/List_of_Wikipedias for a list of all editions.

21. See "Wikimedia Statistics," Wikimedia Foundation, accessed September 1, 2019, http://stats.wikimedia.org.

22. As of 2019, the Wikimedia Foundation is building an endowment with the specific purpose of ensuring long-term access to the Wikimedia projects, regardless of the vagaries of reader donations. See Wikimedia Endowment, accessed January 22, 2020, https://wikimediaendowment.org/ for details.

23. There has been a great deal of research into the shrinking editor base of Wikipedia. Whether the total number of editors is declining, stable, or growing depends on the language version and how participation is measured. A summary of some research into declining editorship is in Tom Simonite, "The Decline of Wikipedia," *MIT Technology Review*, October 22, 2013, https://www.technologyreview.com/s/520446/the-decline-of-wikipedia/.

24. See the work of the Wiki Education Foundation (http://wikiedu.org), which works with classrooms and faculty, often in collaboration with librarians; there have also been hundreds of independent classroom projects. See also Wikipedia Loves Libraries associated events. "Wikipedia Loves Libraries," Wikimedia Outreach, last modified February 27, 2018, https://outreach.wikimedia.org/wiki/Wikipedia_Loves_Libraries.

25. A discussion page on the very first wiki, Ward Cunningham's C2, discusses the danger of walled gardens and how to identify them: WikiWikiWeb (C2 Web), s.v. "Walled Garden," last modified November 3, 2014, http://wiki.c2.com/?Walled Garden.

7 Three Links: Be Bold, Assume Good Faith, and There Are No Firm Rules

Rebecca Thorndike-Breeze, Cecelia A. Musselman, and Amy Carleton

Three members of the Working Wikipedia Collaborative reflect on how three Wikipedia principles manifest in their own collaboration and self-understanding.

Three links in what? Over five years of working closely together, we see these three central Wikipedia values as three links in a virtual chain-mail mesh that protects against despair, fake news, and cynicism. Overstatement? Perhaps. Wikipedia is a utopian project, aiming to be a comprehensive encyclopedia in all branches of knowledge. And we acknowledge that, like all utopias, Wikipedia and working in the Wikipedia community have a dark underside. But the community also shines with a powerful light, one seen in the stories of our lives and the connections we have forged.

The Working Wikipedia Collaborative is a group of scholars, teachers, archivists, and librarians working with Wikipedia in higher education in the Boston area—all women, some rogues, and all convinced of the educational and societal value of the Wikipedia project. Three of us share our stories in this chapter, but these are just a part of the work the collaborative has done together—workshops (local, national, and global), presentations, in-class orientations, cross-institutional visits, publications, edit-a-thons, mentoring circles, and elevator pitches. Collaborative members are active sharers in the participatory and collaborative knowledge-creation movement that some have come to call Wikiworld.

We always write *as* the Working Wikipedia Collaborative, but each of our origin stories is unique and strongly shaped by working with and on Wikipedia. For us, working with the encyclopedia and its community has been a valuable forging ground, shaping each of us into links in a wide-reaching mesh of personal and professional connections. In the stories that follow, we highlight three links in that mesh, showing the origins of our collaborative projects and tracking our experience of how Wikipedia has grown.

Rebecca—Be Bold

I met my best friend Nicole back in 2002 at the university bookstore as we both lined up to buy the assigned texts for our first semester of graduate school. The very first thing I ever said to her was, "I am not really good enough to be here."

OK, that's not what I said, exactly. It was more like, "I was a broadcasting major, so I'm not sure how I got into this MA [master of arts] program in English."

Nicole has reminded me of this moment several times over the last seventeen years—while I earned my PhD in literature, when I struck out in my search for a tenure-track job, and when I carved a place for myself teaching writing, rhetoric, and professional communication at the Massachusetts Institute of Technology (MIT). She brings it up because even after all that, I would still find ways to downplay or undercut my intelligence and abilities, just like I did in 2002. And just like it was then, any time I downplay my worth I always turn out to actually have the goods. "You'd start off in class discussion saying, 'I'm just a broadcasting major....' and then follow that up with a totally on point analysis of the piece we were discussing." Her point is that I am *so* good enough to be here.

Graduate school is a well-documented breeding ground for impostor syndrome, and I had a head start, given my decision to change my career trajectory completely. I have felt like an impostor in many different ways throughout my career, and to this day I am not immune. In fact, since I became a member of the Wikipedia community, I regularly put myself in situations that cause momentary flare-ups of impostor syndrome. I do that because I've come to believe very strongly that despite the vastness of all the things I don't yet know how to do, I can rely on my strengths and those of my collaborators to support me as I learn and to achieve things I never could have alone. Wikipedia itself is evidence of the great benefits of pushing ourselves beyond our comfortable wheelhouses of expertise. My time with the Working Wikipedia Collaborative has made very clear that, beyond my scholarship and teaching, I have valuable leadership skills that can help advance the Wikipedia movement and can make positive contributions elsewhere. My key contribution to the Wikipedia move-ment has been to co-organize a series of live Wikipedia editing events (also known as "edit-a-thons") that are focused on diversifying the content and editorship of Wikipedia by training first-time contributors.[1] Though I expe-rienced some intense impostor syndrome as I learned Wikipedia's guide-lines and tried to teach them to others, doing this work showed me the great value of the other qualities I brought with me—namely, the strong public speaking, project management, and leadership abilities I had been cultivating all my life through years of service-oriented collaborative work. It was easy to overlook these qualities because they permeated all facets of my life, including thirteen years of girl-scouting service projects, my work producing student radio shows in college, and collaborating with fellow grad students to reinvent the graduate student organization in my PhD program. Learning and working alongside my friends in the Working Wiki-pedia Collaborative helped me to see the gifts I'd always had that I'd failed to recognize throughout years of scholarly work. And together we saw the power of Wikipedia's exhortation to "be bold," both at work and in life.

Be bold. It's not a simple direction to follow, especially for women, peo-ple of color, LGBTQIA, and other marginalized groups. That's why it is so inspiring when these folks can be bold in the face of overwhelming yet commonplace resistance and rejection—both insidious and overt. For me, as a woman, "Be bold" means setting aside the lifetime of "what ifs" and "you can'ts" that I've been trained to internalize and transform into a base-line of self-doubt. Not just "What if they reject my work?," but also "what if I annoy the wrong person and they start harassing me? Or worse … ?" The fresh perspective on my strengths that I found with the Working Wikipedia Collaborative helped me to be bold anyway. Here's my story.

In 2014, I quit my national search for a tenure-track job as a literature professor and instead sought full-time, permanent employment in the Boston area. I was fortunate to find a secure, non-tenure-track teaching position in MIT's Comparative Media Studies/Writing department. I was happy to get this job because it meant that I could build on the decade-plus of teaching experience I'd amassed throughout graduate school and as an adjunct instructor on the job market. Many PhDs graduating after the 2008 economic collapse were forced to totally reinvent themselves, sometimes taking near-entry-level positions. I was grateful that I didn't need to hit the reset button at age thirty-five.

But I was also pretty frustrated. I didn't have to totally reset, but I did need to recalibrate. I have great stores of knowledge about realist and modernist literature and humanistic inquiry, but in my new role the material that once comprised the all-consuming focus of my life was relegated to the sidelines. I felt like my literary scholarship was demoted to near-hobby status. Publications or conferences in that field would not count for much in my case for retention and promotion because literary studies was not what I was hired to teach. I began learning how to channel my scholarly impulses in my new field of rhetoric and composition—usually in collaboration with peers. I reached out to fellow instructors and friends from graduate school because moving into a new scholarly arena was too scary to do alone. I had no idea what the culture or expectations were, and my post-PhD experience so far had been one plagued by confusion and insecurity. At that time, I needed friends around me as a buffer, or I wasn't going to get anywhere.

Meanwhile, I found myself drawing strength from the punk-DIY sensibility of drummer Janet Weiss, of the rock bands Quasi, Sleater-Kinney, and Wild Flag. Weiss is one of the most respected drummers in the business, and her collaborations are wide-ranging.[2] Her body of work is informed by her strong "rebellious" sense that the work itself is what matters most, not status or money.[3] As I left traditional academia behind and sought to figure out what my work should be, I was inspired by Weiss's fierce independence and looked for opportunities to put my scholarly abilities to use in a way that was open and free to all. Serendipitously, it was also around this time that I found out about a five-day intensive Wikipedia class that focused on Wikipedia's gender gap to be held at MIT and run by Maia Weinstock—science writer, Wikipedian, and overall badass.

For years in my writing classes, I taught students how to begin their research with Wikipedia, and the previous spring we had a fascinating class discussion about Amanda Filipacchi's *New York Times* piece on how Wikipedia editors had removed some authors who happened to be women, including Filipacchi, from the "authors" category, adding them instead to the "women authors" category.[4] I wanted to know more about this and other issues related to gender in the maintenance of Wikipedia and to see if I could help in some way. That class taught me so much, both about the deep complexities of systemic bias—see part III, especially chapter 21—and concrete strategies for crafting new Wikipedia articles. (My first article was a stub for British comics creator Suzy Varty, which has since been expanded by other contributors.) Once I had a grasp of the diversity gaps in Wikipedia—not just the gender gap but major gaps of information about and related to LGBTQIA people, people of color, topics relevant to the global South, and a broad range of academic topics—I saw the potential of classroom Wikipedia projects, both to invigorate the teaching of writing and to enhance the quality of free knowledge for all. In other words, I realized that working with Wikipedia could be a punk-DIY approach to the field of rhetoric and composition.

I turned to friends and colleagues I knew who were also interested in improving the quality of Wikipedia's diversity of information. Back in 2012, Cecelia Musselman was the first person ever to show me how college-level writing instruction could effectively incorporate Wikipedia writing assignments, and so in April 2015, I more or less cornered her on the subway after a regional conference on engaging practices in the college writing classroom. She had just given a presentation on how she developed a service-learning unit in her class through Wikipedia assignments, and I wanted to collaborate with her somehow. As luck would have it, Cecelia and her frequent collaborator, Northeastern University librarian Amanda Rust, were looking for opportunities to present their educational work with Wikipedia from both an instructor and a librarian's perspective, and Cecelia invited me to get involved. For this new project, I reached out to MIT Collections Archivist Greta Kuriger Suiter, who I had met at Maia Weinstock's Wikipedia intensive class and who was already organizing Wikipedia edit-a-thons that brought participants into the MIT archives. And I also recruited Amy Carleton, a friend from my PhD program, a colleague in my program at MIT, and an innovative thinker and teacher. Together, the five of us formed the Working Wikipedia Collaborative, and my crash course in becoming a Wikipedian began. Since then, our group has explored how university libraries, communities, and classrooms can work together with Wikipedia to enhance understanding of collaborative practices, consensus making, and digital citizenship across institutions while also improving Wikipedia article quality.[5]

This experience was eye-opening. Not only did we observe enhanced collaboration, critical thinking, and productivity in our students, but we experienced a radical shift in the way we work together. For the Working Wikipedia Collaborative itself, this revolution took the form of eighteen workshops and conference presentations in the year 2016—far more academic work than any one of us could have accomplished alone. And since then, this collaborative energy has spread to our individual initiatives, with Wikipedia, our institutions, and our own creative projects. Regardless of whether it's our group's project or an individual one, the Working Wikipedia Collaborative remains a major source of moral and practical support.

Yet throughout this time I struggled with impostor syndrome, anxiety, and stage fright. Every presentation or workshop made me feel as though I barely knew what I was talking about; this feeling also permeated my teaching. In my new role at MIT teaching writing, rhetoric, and professional communication to engineering students, I was almost continuously learning new material as I taught it. The sense of shifting sands this created often left me feeling like a stand-up comic who was dying on stage, complete with flop sweat and a pit in my stomach.

I vividly recall a heart-to-heart I had with Amy Carleton about this unshakable impostor syndrome and lack of confidence, despite frequent feedback from audience members and students that my work and teaching were not just competent but engaging and sometimes even inspiring. Funnily enough, this conversation took place at the Marriott bar, just after we had finished our all-day workshop on teaching college writing with Wikipedia at the 2016 Conference on College Composition and Communication. We'd been working hard to prepare for this event for the better part of a year; it was our big debut as the Working Wikipedia Collaborative. We were energized from the discussions we had with participants and by the projects we helped participants to begin to plan for their upcoming classes. And yet, in waves throughout the day, I was rocked by anxiety.

Amy and I talked about Katty Kay and Claire Shipman's work on confidence disparities between men and women—particularly their reporting of a consensus among a broad range of successful women that, despite years of hard work, they didn't really deserve their success—as well as women's reluctance to speak up and take risks in their lives and careers.[6] As alarming as these findings were to me, I was glad to know that I wasn't alone in my bewildering lack of confidence.

With Amy, Cecelia, and the other Working Wikipedia Collaborative members by my side throughout this crash course in being bold, I have established a persistent sense of confidence as well as a new perspective on impostor syndrome. First, even at my most confident, my anxiety isn't going anywhere. But through the support of my collaborators and the genuine enthusiasm we all bring to every event, I have learned to discern and focus on the excitement I feel about the work, which is embedded in the anxiety. This approach consistently leads to more engaging presentations and lessons. Further, I fully embrace the fact that, for me, it is easier—and it is *better*—to be bold in collaboration with others. Even when I'm flying solo at conferences and teaching classes, I like to leave space for audiences and students to share their existing knowledge. This way, they can let me know what they want from their time with me and how I can match what I've prepared to what they need. And making space for audiences and students to share their knowledge can transform conventional academic spaces into more collaborative ones where audiences and students can enrich each other's learning experiences as well as lend presenters and instructors insight.

My link in the chain is a story about how learning Wikipedia's collaborative culture alongside some badass women has influenced my life in a meaningful way, both within and beyond Wikipedia. This is a story about how learning to be a Wikipedian helped me to heal from the emotional and psychological distress caused by our current state of academic precarity. And it's a story about how lining up to address Wikipedia's gender gap by becoming a Wikipedian helped me overcome my lifelong, socially conditioned insecurities about my worthiness to enter new domains and make contributions.

Cecelia—Assume Good Faith

In October 2006, I was teaching a revamped section of Honors Advanced Writing at Northeastern University (NU). My colleague David had overhauled the course, and we were running an experiment—he teaches one section of the course and I teach another, both using his new assignments. We talked wrinkles and successes while hustling to class one day. I confessed that I was having a problem with our reference document assignment. The only encyclopedia my students had ever used was Wikipedia! How could they write the kind of encyclopedia article our assignment asked for?

David shrugged, "So, have them write Wikipedia articles," and dashed into class.

I'm a bit literal and at the time, David was the director of our Advanced Writing in the Disciplines program; it never occurred to me that he might be kidding. I walked straight into class and offered my students the option to work on Wikipedia articles. One hundred percent of them signed on. And why wouldn't they? At that time, everyone was convinced (despite evidence to the contrary) that the encyclopedia wasn't reliable. Most students had been barred from using it for schoolwork in high school (and most still are—thirteen years later) even though they were active users of the encyclopedia. My NU students had access to a good university library. Surely we could find the information needed to build new articles! Looking back, our mix of blind skepticism and bravado is breathtaking—what was I thinking, adding this sort of new, untested assignment in the middle of a term?

I contacted one of our librarians (Amanda Rust, also a collaborative member) to see what she knew about Wikipedia. We quickly found long talk page threads bemoaning the amateurish efforts of undergraduate students. Some editors advocated banning students from whole topic areas. Other Wikipedians were less polite. But others were feeling their way toward a stance I share—students are early stage content experts with access to paywalled information in scholarly publications in academic libraries across the world. As such, they are a vast and powerful resource.

But behind this was an uneasy situation. I didn't trust Wikipedia with my students and Wikipedia didn't really trust students—or any other sort of academic.

I devised a work-around to distance my students from potentially unwelcoming Wikipedians and preserve student privacy but still have them practice writing in Wikipedia's neutral, carefully sourced, encyclopedic way. Students would choose an article that was not yet in the encyclopedia or an article that only existed in stub form, and they would work on the article *entirely offline* in a word processing document. I encouraged students who really wanted to post their articles to the live encyclopedia to do so for extra credit. Students embraced this method; they avoided having to tackle the editing intricacies and technology of the encyclopedia, their academic work stayed safely private, and Wikipedia didn't seem to notice.

But this felt too limiting exactly because it shielded students from important challenges. And it missed the point of writing for Wikipedia—contributing to this vast collaborative effort. And Wikipedia did notice. Fortunately, my school was changing—experiential education grew from a motivation for the university's cooperative program, in which students spend a semester at a time working outside the university in their major fields, to a major part of the university-wide curriculum. The growing co-op and service-learning programs meant that students were out working in communities and corporations. Their work could not be private, and so classroom-based courses were granted greater latitude for asking students to work publicly as well.

The next term I had students create Wikipedia accounts and set up sandboxes in which to work. It was the best of both worlds! We got access to all of Wikipedia's editing tools, and our work remained in relatively private on our own sandbox pages. This worked well enough for a while. About a third of every group chose to publish their articles to Wikipedia for the public.

In rapid succession, several students found that their articles had been scooped out of their sandboxes by editors who patrolled user pages for particular keywords and then published these articles to the encyclopedia; several other students posted their articles and revealed their university affiliation on their user page; one student ran afoul of the medical editors for using research reports as sources instead of reviews; another student inadvertently committed a copyright violation; the Wikipedia Education Program was formed; and my library contact turned into a Wikipedia Campus Ambassador! As I guided students through the assignment each term, I was growing increasingly uncomfortable that we were using Wikipedia in a rather unequal way—we got more from it than it did from us. Each of these incidents could be expanded to a longer story (or cautionary tale), but here, looking back on Wikipedia's growth over twenty years, the important thing was that this all happened over the course of a single academic year. Wikipedia was changing fast.

My early interactions with Wikipedians were testy and defensive. During these early years, it felt like editors first assumed bad faith on the part of all students and gave some pretty presumptuous directions to me as an instructor ("Copyedit" my students work? No, that's not what writing instructors do). My students and I could see that the encyclopedia was home to a number of bad articles—inaccurate, incomplete, plagiarized—but a number of my students using credible, peer-reviewed research reports were chastised by editors for not using good enough sources. These editors would explain criticisms in a cryptic string of acronyms: NPOV, no OR, MEDPRI. Articles that are near total plagiarisms persist to this day (I keep my favorites a secret because they're great teaching tools). Why did the editors we encountered focus on student "bad" behavior when students were acting according to one of Wikipedia's own core principles—good faith? Wikipedia editors are driven by a great passion to devote their time, energy, and expertise to Wikipedia—a passion that claimed to value neutrality and evidence—but from 2006 to 2010, we seemed to be encountering an irrational stereotyping of all students as bumblers or vandals.

Amanda, our campus ambassador, was patient, kind, and persistent. Over the last ten years, we've developed an "Intro to Wikipedia" class session for all of my courses. We introduce students to article organization, talk pages, revision histories, the location of appropriate sources, and responsible source use—as defined by Wikipedia. Students dig around in the encyclopedia, watching how the community works toward resolving differences and improving articles and discussing infamous edit wars, conduct articles, and article rankings. From 2010 to 2015, more and more students posted their articles and edited existing ones instead of working solely in their sandboxes. One of my courses was designated a service-learning course because students would be contributing to something that the Service-Learning program at NU considered to be a public good—the first time that any course got that designation for contributing to a virtual community. Students frequently characterized their Wikipedia work as "real world writing" on course evaluations. When asked by my colleague Neal Lerner about their most meaningful writing project in college, several students named their Wikipedia project.[7] Seeing these results in teaching evaluations, my colleagues began asking me how to incorporate Wikipedia into their writing courses.

And Wikipedia was changing, too. By creating the Wikipedia Education Program in 2010, the Wikimedia Foundation had taken the clear stance that universities were a source of both new editors and vast amounts of information. I started to see (but not participate in) Wikipedia community discussions where editors were puzzling out how to use student contributions without undermining the quality of the encyclopedia instead of just complaining about them. Even the medical editors started to come around. Many of my students have gotten very patient medical editor help in getting their references right, deciding what new findings might actually be worth putting in the encyclopedia, or figuring out technical problems.

Still, I was a "rogue" instructor, not yet acting in partnership with the Education Program, which had by then become the Wiki Education Foundation ("Wiki Ed," described in chapter 20). I made an account but didn't edit for many of the same reasons Rebecca talks about—fear of other editors, fear of stepping on toes, of not being an expert. Soon after creating my account, editor Davy2000 reached out to welcome me (it was his twenty-first birthday!) and we had a friendly chat about his hometown and my interests and how I could better help students work with the encyclopedia.

In late summer of 2015, Wiki Ed contacted me: Would I be interested in testing the newest version of their Dashboard (course management platform)? Of course! The Dashboard allows me to assign each student an article and peer review partners, follow their work, set a timeline of milestones to meet, and get a statistical overview of what each student and the whole class have done.

The combined charm offensive worked. I've taught with the Dashboard ever since. Does this sound like a "you will be assimilated" Borg narrative? Yes, it feels that way to me, too. When faced with the Dashboard that will tell me every edit a student makes and exactly how much they have contributed (with time stamps down to the second), I feel uneasy. Is that level of surveillance necessary for student learning? Or student contributing? I recognize that it allows me to intervene with the two or three students each term who truly struggle to get work done. This level of student surveillance is for me uncomfortably the norm across many course management platforms. But it feels out of step with the assumption of good faith.

Wikipedia continues to change. By the time Wiki Ed reached out to me, the encyclopedia had a greater overall accuracy than the *Encyclopædia Britannica*. Vandalized articles had an average fix time of thirty minutes, aided by bots and page patrols looking for potential vandalism. The community had begun formulating procedures for managing harassment and bullying but only had mixed success. Many editors—prompted by repeated publications in *The Telegraph*, *MIT Technology Review*, *BBC*, and *The Atlantic*, among others—began to recognize the stark gender imbalances in both the editing community and in article topics. Wikipedia was growing up.

My relationship with Wikipedia has come a long way from its testy beginnings. Today, if I teach a course without a Wikipedia project, I feel that my students are missing out. Students love the "real world writing"—and I love their unshaken view of Wikipedia as "real." Students recognize that their Wikipedia contributions will reach far more readers than anything else they might publish. Wikipedia, Wiki Ed, and I have settled into a partnership that allows students to learn many things: critical thinking, how to evaluate sources, how to summarize for a broad audience, how to step out of US-centric ways of writing and perceiving. Perhaps more importantly, Wikipedia has become a powerful forger of global authors. Every semester produces several students who are bitten by the Wikipedia bug—the promise of a global audience, the opportunity to improve coverage of underrepresented groups of people, the ability to add knowledge that they extract from our university library. From a whole new article on neuromorality to sorting out the taxonomy of a single black coral species, I see my students' good-faith efforts filling gaps in the encyclopedia. The Dashboard tells me that, since Fall 2015, I have taught twenty-four courses with 336 students who have added fifty-two articles, edited 486 articles, and uploaded fifty-seven images to the Wikimedia Commons. These articles have been viewed seventy-two million times. I couldn't provide my students with a wider audience any other way.

And my colleague David? We met at a conference two years ago. I told him I'd taken his advice on having students write for Wikipedia. He looked puzzled. "I was kidding!" he said.

Amy—There Are No Firm Rules

The first semester of my PhD program also coincided with another first: my first experience as an instructor-of-record for a college writing class as part of my scholarship award. I had spent the weeks leading up to the term preparing my syllabus with care; it included a balance of scholarly essays, literary texts, and even a film. In my naïveté, I thought I was prepared for anything. Now, after nearly two decades of teaching experience, I know that nothing is predictable. Exhibit A: that first week, a student raised her hand and when I called on her (expecting a question about that day's reading, an excerpt from Paulo Freire's "The Banking Concept of Education" essay from *Pedagogy of the Oppressed*) she instead cocked her head and asked, "So, we are all wondering: *how old are you anyway?*"

My face flushed and I was more than a bit flustered as I stammered out something akin to "old enough to teach this class," though I was only a few years her senior, a fact that my nerves did not project. Even as I left class that day feeling flutters of insecurity, I also had a firm resolve: from that point forward, I would hold fast to a system of rules to assert some kind of teacherly authority. I wanted my students to recognize me as the one in charge, not as a peer. The fact that I set this intention only moments after discussing this passage from Freire's text, "Leaders who do not act dialogically, but insist on imposing their decisions, do not organize the people—they manipulate them. They do not liberate, nor are they liberated: they oppress," was a bit ironic. But my mind was made up.

So while I espoused the virtues of open learning and the value of democratizing education—something I supported, at least in theory—in practice, I became rigid and more and more inflexible, approaching classroom discussion as if it were a script: posing a question and then waiting for the "right" answer. And if students didn't answer, instead of reframing the question and giving them some time to process, consider, and respond—I would quickly move on to the next question on my list as if I were facilitating a literary quiz bowl for course credit.

My manner of assessing written work was no less formulaic. Grammar, format, citations—I ticked these things off on rubrics and wrote in the margins, working from more of a deficit model of assessment than looking for positives and developing skills such as evidence of flexible, critical thinking, synthesis, and creativity. And though I knew intrinsically that this was wrong, it was the only model I knew. It was how *I* had learned, after all. Teacher imparts "wisdom" and student(s) perform it back through reflection. This purely transactional model was stultifying but it had its affordances—it kept order. Like anything else in life with the appearance of stability, however, it was only a matter of time before my assumptions were challenged—and ultimately upended.

I blame it on The Internet.

That semester marked many firsts—including my first encounter with Wikipedia, an online encyclopedia that was quickly eclipsing the utility of the Microsoft Encarta CD-ROMs that were de rigueur in the early 2000s (and most certainly the vintage multivolume set of *World Book* encyclopedias that I had inherited from my stepfather). About a month into the term, when I realized that students were using the website as a go-to place for information rather than heading to the library per my request, I reprinted my syllabus with the addition of this line: "**WIKIPEDIA IS NOT A VALID SOURCE**." And yes, it was in all caps and bold. Students argued that Wikipedia was accessible and expedient, I countered that it was unstable and unreliable. Period. And for a time, I "won" that debate.

As I grew as a thinker in my graduate work, however, I realized this model of classroom management and intellectual close-mindedness was not sustainable. For starters, my graduate seminars were different—people exchanged ideas and debated long-standing interpretations of canonical texts. Professors, experts who had quite actually "written the book" on x, y, or z, were open and encouraging of these new readings and perspectives. And when I read an essay from Shakespeare scholar Stephen Greenblatt, wherein he asserts that culture "gestures toward what appear to be opposite things: constraint and mobility," I started to think about that within the context of intellectual culture. While there are *some* constraints (or frameworks) that can reinforce certain behaviors and modes of performance, they can also afford access and encourage dialogue—that is, (intellectual) mobility. I would like to say that my shift was as sudden and dramatic, but it happened gradually and in stages. And first, I had to learn a lesson—from one of my students.

When B. came to me complaining that he was unable to find good scholarly sources for a research paper he was writing on Brazilian folk music (including genres like *tropicália* and *sertanejo*), I was skeptical. Of course one could find anything in scholarly academic databases, right? (LOL.) There were some Wikipedia articles, though, that could be useful, he said—though he knew my position on using the encyclopedia. He was right, though—Wikipedia was a place where these genres and subgenres of indigenous music were being discussed, so I agreed. And this actually was a light-bulb moment for me—while scholarly databases may contain multitudes, they often exclude many topics, figures, and conversations that fall below the radar of (largely white male) privilege. This was an important lesson.

The next term I deleted the moratorium on Wikipedia from my syllabi and instead incorporated discussion of the reference source into our classroom conversations about source reliability, veracity, and accessibility. And within a few years, my students had moved beyond performing critical assessments of Wikipedia articles to writing their own articles. To date, these students have contributed nearly two hundred thousand words to the English-language edition, including a diverse range of robust articles, from introduction to electromagnetism, to the Pittsburgh water crisis, to tissue engineering of heart valves, to the international entrepreneur rule, just to mention a few. This work has opened up conversations about everything from racial bias (much of Black History is left out of the encyclopedia due to the dominant demographics of its editor base—largely white, millennial males) to gender bias (less than 15 percent of biographical content on

Wikipedia is focused on women) and information access. My students (and I!) have come to see participating in the Wikipedia community as a form of social justice work where the only prerequisite is open-mindedness. This is a "rule" I can get behind.

A postscript: This March, I arrived in Berlin for Wikimedia Summit 2019, an annual conference event where Wikimedians from around the world convene to discuss holistic strategy initiatives for the organization, a non-profit that oversees multiple open knowledge projects—the most recognizable of these being Wikipedia, the online encyclopedia (and fifth most visited website in the world). The central question with which participants grappled this year was what Wikimedia's knowledge ecosystem will look like in 2030. A tall order, for sure. But for over three days, we talked and planned in working groups tied to diversity, accessibility, and labor equity. Amidst all of the intellectual heavy lifting were moments of laughter, shared meals, an international candy table, and a late-night nightclub dance party where we danced late into the night to a DJ setlist crowdsourced by community members that was as diverse as the conference's attendees.

Now, as an active community member, the uniqueness of the culture is something I confess that I often take for granted. But this time, I saw it through new eyes. My music-industry boyfriend—whose only experience with Wikimedia to date had been as an end user of Wikipedia—could barely contain his amazement at seeing a diverse group of individuals from over one hundred countries united with the sole purpose of improving and diversifying informational content to educate the world's population—for free. Weeks later, back in the United States, we attended a jazz concert with a Grammy-award-winning recording artist, and he introduced me backstage by saying I "worked for Wikipedia." *Not really*, I corrected—*I am a volunteer, part of the community*. The artist and his bandmates were intrigued (though first they wanted me to correct some factual inaccuracies on their respective Wikipedia pages!) by this notion of an open information collective where people collaborate freely simply because they are committed to democratizing knowledge. As I spent the next half hour evangelizing about Wikipedia, I confess that I experienced another lightbulb moment—I had truly become an open education advocate, not just in theory, but finally, in practice.

It may have taken a while, but I'd like to think Paulo Freire would be proud.

The more radical the person is, the more fully he or she enters into reality so that, knowing it better, he or she can transform it. This individual is not afraid to confront, to listen, to see the world unveiled. This person is not afraid to meet the people or to enter into a dialogue with them. This person does not consider himself or herself the proprietor of history or of all people, or the liberator of the oppressed; but he or she does commit himself or herself, within history, to fight at their side.

—Paulo Freire, *Pedagogy of the Oppressed* (1968)

Conclusion

The Working Wikipedia Collaborative now operates in a space easily recognizable as what scholars Juah Suoranta and Tere Vadén call "Wikiworld."[8] We work collaboratively on presentations and publications; we share our work freely among our colleagues. We see our students working to create knowledge in other spaces, particularly in social media spaces, in ways that parallel the collaboration and sharing in Wikipedia. While a drawing of our collaborations and influences might appear chaotic, we are clearly working as links in a worldwide mesh of contributors and users.

When a skeptical student asks, "Why would anyone ever do this (work on Wikipedia)?" we have a nuanced, persuasive answer: we know that Wikipedians do what they do because they are committed to the common goal of free information for all. We've also seen firsthand that people become Wikipedians and continue to work as Wikipedians for their own, sometimes quite personal reasons. And we see that, as Wikipedia continues to grow and to grow up, the community is learning to accommodate some messier motivations, to grapple with matters of representation and access that challenge all knowledge-creation projects, to recognize that acting boldly and in good faith need some tempering with rules, and to recognize that for this global project to continue, the rules must also continue to grow and change. We hope that the Wikipedia community continues to challenge their own preconceptions, to push back against bias and exclusion, and to hold fast to their goal of being a global encyclopedia. Perhaps most importantly, as Wikipedia turns twenty, we see the power of a few idealistic values in creating the largest encyclopedia ever.

Acknowledgments: We are fortunate to work with supportive colleagues at both of our institutions and around Boston—really too many to name. Our very warm thanks to Amanda Rust, Greta Kuriger Suiter, Phoebe Ayers, Jami Mathewson, Helaine Blumenthal, Zach McDowell, Neal Lerner, David Kellogg, Kathleen Kelly, the Working Wikipedia Collaborative, Michael, Tim, and Mitch for encouraging and cheerleading over this long learning process. And our gratitude also goes to MIT, Northeastern University, Boston Rhetoric and Writing Network (BRAWN), and the entire Wiki Ed team for supporting workshops, edit-a-thons, new assignment design, and conference attendance.

Notes

1. Rebecca Thorndike-Breeze and Greta Kuriger Suiter, "Hacking Academic Collaboration with GLAM Edit-a-Thons," *WikiStudies* 1, no. 1 (September 29, 2017): 65–95.

2. Isreal Daramola, "Drummer Janet Weiss Announces Departure from Sleater-Kinney," *Spin* (blog), July 1, 2019, https://www.spin.com/2019/07/janet-weiss-sleater -kinney-departure-statement/.

3. MAGNET Staff, "Quasi: Quality Controllers," *Magnet Magazine* (blog), October 14, 2013, http://magnetmagazine.com/2013/10/14/quasi-quality-controllers/.

4. Amanda Filipacchi, "Wikipedia's Sexism toward Female Novelists," *The New York Times*, April 24, 2013, http://www.nytimes.com/2013/04/28/opinion/sunday /wikipedias-sexism-toward-female-novelists.html.

5. Amy Carleton et al., "Working Wikipedia: A Year of Meaningful Collaboration," *Double Helix* 5, no. 0 (December 31, 2017), http://qudoublehelixjournal.org/dh /index.php/dh/article/view/102; Thorndike-Breeze and Suiter, "Hacking Academic Collaboration with GLAM Edit-a-Thons." See also Alan Bilansky, "Using Wikipedia to Teach Audience, Genre, and Collaboration," *Pedagogy* 16, no. 2 (April 1, 2016): 347–355, https://doi.org/10.1215/15314200-3435996; Robert E. Cummings, *Lazy Virtues: Teaching Writing in the Age of Wikipedia* (Nashville, TN: Vanderbilt University Press, 2009); Carra Leah Hood, "Editing Out Obscenity: Wikipedia and Writing Pedagogy," *Computers and Composition Online* (Spring 2009); James P. Purdy, "When the Tenets of Composition Go Public: A Study of Writing in Wikipedia," *College Composition & Communication* 61, no. 2 (2009): 383; Matthew A. Vetter, "Archive 2.0: What Composition Students and Academic Libraries Can Gain from Digital-Collaborative Pedagogies," *Composition Studies* 42, no. 1 (2014): 35–53.

6. Katty Kay and Claire Shipman, "The Confidence Gap," *The Atlantic*, May 2014, https://www.theatlantic.com/magazine/archive/2014/05/the-confidence-gap /359815/.

7. The Meaningful Writing Project (http://meaningfulwritingproject.net/).

8. Juah Suoranta and Tere Vadén, *Wikiworld* (New York: Pluto Press, 2010).

8   How Wikipedia Drove Professors Crazy, Made Me Sane, and Almost Saved the Internet

Jake Orlowitz

Wikipedia's journey to legitimacy paralleled Jake Orlowitz's own journey with mental health and regaining confidence in himself. With both now stable in positions of influence, it's time for deeper questioning.

"I would rather be a man of paradoxes than a man of prejudices."
—Jean-Jacques Rousseau, *Emile*

In 2007 I sat in my used Subaru outside a Colorado mountain town's Starbucks, borrowing their Wi-Fi, when I decided to find out *what made Wikipedia work*. I had been hearing more about the mysterious, crowdsourced website and had been seeing it pop up in Google search results. I thought the concept of an open encyclopedia was neat, but I wanted to understand something more essential: the theoretical underpinnings, the ideology, and the logic behind the site. I may be the first person who began their journey to becoming a Wikipedian by *wanting* to read its policies.

Three hours of digging through the site's seemingly endless rules, guidelines, and essays convinced me, a political theory major adrift in my twenties, that something significant was afoot. The community had created what the Enlightenment philosophers only dreamed of—its own body of common law, common sense, and common knowledge. As Denis Diderot, editor of the French *Encyclopédie*, wrote in 1755:

> The purpose of an encyclopedia is to collect knowledge disseminated around the globe; to set forth its general system to the men with whom we live, and transmit it to those who will come after us, so that the work of preceding centuries will not become useless to the centuries to come; and so that our offspring, becoming better instructed, will at the same time become more virtuous and

happy, and that we should not die without having rendered a service to the human race.[1]

At this point Wikipedia was still a curiosity at best and more commonly a joke. Looking back, it's clear that is no longer the case. Wikipedia has gained ubiquity, influence, and legitimacy. A growing number of professionals and academics endorse critical use of the site, and those who don't or won't endorse it publicly, privately admit to using it anyway. My favorite retelling of this fairy tale transformation comes from a poetic essay which saw the rapid transformation as early as 2008. "The Charms of Wikipedia" in the *New York Review of Books* describes:

> It was like a giant community leaf-raking project in which everyone was called a groundskeeper. Some brought very fancy professional metal rakes, or even back-mounted leaf-blowing systems, and some were just kids thrashing away with the sides of their feet or stuffing handfuls in the pockets of their sweatshirts, but all the leaves they brought to the pile were appreciated. And the pile grew and everyone jumped up and down in it having a wonderful time. And it grew some more, and it became the biggest leaf pile anyone had ever seen anywhere, a world wonder.[2]

Wikipedia's journey to legitimacy paralleled my own recovery from mental illness and the development of the successful *Wikipedia Library* project. Lacking legitimacy creates a mountain to climb. When we get to the top, we feel like victors. But then, we see the terrain stretches well beyond our previous understanding, and we realize how little we have explored.

With Wikipedia and I now both in stable positions of influence, it's a time for deeper questioning as much as it is for celebration. Wikipedia's journey to legitimacy, as with my recovery, was enabled by boldness. That same boldness, however, has left us only partially capable of fulfilling our mission—for, what, and who we have left out is as significant as what we have built.

"The world of reality has its limits; the world of imagination is boundless."
—Jean-Jacques Rousseau, *The Confessions*

In 2009 I returned sheepishly from my Colorado sedan to my parents' comfortable home in suburban Philadelphia. Despite the support offered, my mental health deteriorated, and my isolation from friends and family became nearly total. I edited Wikipedia most hours of the day or night while sitting in my attic bathtub. Though I was erratic and withdrawn,

Wikipedia remained a constant place of intellectual stimulation, expression, and even combat.

Though I'd lost faith in my own direction and hold on reality, Wikipedia was an anchor for my shifting moods and a beacon of hope in reason and collaboration. The mission of the site made compelling sense, directed thousands of strangers to mutual understanding, and produced something entirely new and as close to real consensus as seemed possible to me. It was there for me the night before I went into the mental hospital, and there for me every day thereafter.

In the weeks after my thirteen-day "retreat," I shied away from the activity of my Wikipedia article watchlist and wrote comics about the internal dialogues I was trying to resolve. My own mind was multifaceted, contradictory, wondrous, and fragile. I felt adrift and unformed; I didn't know where to go next. I knew, however, that when I did get around to logging onto Wikipedia as "Ocaasi" (a pseudonym based on my middle name Isaac), the debates felt tangible, and the progress of creating articles and resolving disputes felt rigorous and concrete. It was a space of freedom and experimentation, autonomy and self-expression, anonymity and community.

I wanted to make Wikipedia better. I wanted to prove that this seemingly anarchic model, this chaos of commentary and ferocious search for reliable sources among well-intentioned anonymous thinkers from every corner of the world, could transform the world. I wasn't yet ready to prove my own worth, but I sensed that on Wikipedia, with a consistent and "clueful" use of one's voice and reason, one could establish a reputation within the community that would generate trust, respect, and recognition.

"It is reason which breeds pride and reflection which fortifies it; reason which turns man inward into himself; reason which separates him from everything which troubles or affects him."
—Jean-Jacques Rousseau, *Discourse on the Origin of Inequality*

Wikipedia was becoming more and more visible by 2011, but it was still deeply misunderstood. People didn't look behind the scenes to glimpse its activity and complexity or even know that they could. Wikipedia's roots and philosophy weren't accessible. Its way of processing facts into knowledge and discerning falsehoods from evidence was opaque.

Having multiple conversations one-on-one with new editors gave me useful scripts for explaining Wikipedia's rationales, dynamics, and core principles. What I saw in Wikipedia was not a threat to knowledge, as many pundits claimed and dismissed, but a deep and evolutionary transformation of the search for knowledge that had driven philosophers for millennia. Wikipedia was not "the *Britannica* killer"; it was the *Encyclopédie* reborn in a digital age.

Wikipedia thrives because of a rigorous commitment to *facts*, understood through the lens of a web of policies as the *proportionate summary of legitimate arguments from sources reliable for each claim*. Achieving this is a deeply human process, the kind that scholars practice for years before achieving mastery. At the core of good information is human discretion. The 2008 book *Digital Culture: Understanding New Media* quotes Clay Shirky's prescient observations:

> In fact what Wikipedia presages is a change in the nature of authority. Prior to Britannica, most encyclopaedias derived their authority from the author. Britannica came along and made the relatively radical assertion that you could vest authority in an institution. You trust Britannica, and then we in turn go out and get the people to write the articles. What Wikipedia suggests is that you can vest authority in a visible process. As long as you can see how Wikipedia's working, and can see that the results are acceptable, you can come over time to trust that. And that is a really profound challenge to our notions of what it means to be an institution, what it means to trust something, what it means to have authority in this society.[3]

In this way, Wikipedia presents an antidote to both the rule of unassailable experts and the tyranny of unaccountable algorithms. On Wikipedia, though there are bots—semi-automated processes—of many types, the critical work of evaluating information is a process of community curation. Wikipedia aggregates human judgment, applies it to published sources, and marries it with computational power.

Wikipedia inspires and executes a commons of public fact-checking. I experienced this under pressure during the 2011 Arab Spring, which sparked the revolution and overthrow of Hosni Mubarak in Egypt. While millions gathered in Egypt's Tahrir Square, I and five other determined and vigilant editors provided a first draft of history as it was unfolding.

The article's talk page was our newsroom to decide when a source was legitimate or how many sources were needed to confirm a claim before it was ready to enter the live article. I took this task as seriously as any other before in my life, and it galvanized me with a faith in Wikipedia's dedication to reliable knowledge. Egyptian Activist Wael Ghonim, on a February 2011 *60 Minutes* broadcast, remarked of his country's triumph:

> I call this Revolution 2.0. Revolution 2.0 is, is—I say that our revolution is like Wikipedia, OK? Everyone is contributing content. You don't know the names of the people contributing the content.... This is exactly what happened.... Everyone was contributing small pieces, bits and pieces. We drew this whole picture. We drew this whole picture of a revolution. And that picture—no one is the hero in that picture.[4]

"Virtue is a state of war, and to live in it we have always to combat with ourselves."
—Jean-Jacques Rousseau, *Julie*

Wikipedia's role in breaking news, political campaigns, and scientific debates has only gained prominence. In addition to the pride I felt over being a part of this amazing project, I developed a new uncertainty about whether the public and media could survive the burgeoning onslaught of misinformation in an online ecosystem.

Founder of the Data & Society Research Institute danah boyd pinpointed my critical worry in her 2018 SXSW Edu Keynote, "What Hath We Wrought?":

> I'm not convinced that we know how to educate people who do not share our epistemological frame.... I believe that we need to develop antibodies to help people not be deceived.... We cannot and should not assert authority over epistemology, but we can encourage our students to be more aware of how interpretation is socially constructed. And to understand how that can be manipulated. Of course, just because you know you're being manipulated doesn't mean that you can resist it.... We live in a world of networks now.... So I would argue that we need to start developing a networked response to this networked landscape. And it starts by understanding different ways of constructing knowledge.[5]

Critical thinking and ample facts aren't sufficient in an environment of weaponized information. We need to promote Wikipedia not as a collection of facts but as a *way of knowing*. Many people think of Wikipedia as the site that "anyone can edit," but far fewer people understand that editing on Wikipedia is like stepping into a gauntlet of both algorithmic and human filtering.

An individual edit must pass through targeted text-rejection filters to even make it on the page. Then neural network machine-learning bots seek out nuanced patterns of vandalism. After that, thousands of human "recent change" patrollers look at every suspicious new edit, like a game of whack-a-mole. Over the next few hours and days, experienced editors are notified of updates to any article on their "watchlist," a feed of changes to articles in their specific areas of interest and expertise. At last, words are left for the eyes of millions of readers, many more of whom fix an error rather than add one. We congratulate people when they say, "I edited Wikipedia!" But the real marker of achievement is being able to say, "I made an edit to Wikipedia—*and it stuck.*"

Wikipedia is unique in the modern internet. It is anti-centralization, anti-monopoly, anti-advertising, anti-propaganda, anti-censorship, and anti-clickbait. The media ecosystem has been under siege from corporatization and disinformation, and Wikipedia has been building a bulwark all along. We are pro-engagement, pro-citizen, pro-free knowledge, and pro-transparency. We are constantly defending against efforts to sway, corrupt, or destabilize the encyclopedia. So why did it take so long for people to trust it?

"Since men cannot create new forces, but merely combine and control those which already exist, the only way in which they can preserve themselves is by uniting their separate powers in a combination strong enough to overcome any resistance, uniting them so that their powers are directed by a single motive and act in concert."
—Jean-Jacques Rousseau, *The Social Contract*

Like other tertiary reference works, an encyclopedia is only as good as the sources it is based on. On Wikipedia, there is a deeply rooted concern for citation reliability. If you imagine Wikipedia as a starting point for deeper research—which it should be—then each article is a comprehensive overview attached to a list of quality sources to explore, validate, and verify. Wikipedia is effectively the largest bibliography in human history.

I couldn't accept being without half of the content I needed to draft good new articles when so much of it was locked behind paywalls where access to information required paying for a subscription. This realization inspired me. I realized that despite all of its commitment to reliable sources, *Wikipedia had no library* to call its own. In 2011, frustrated by an inability to find sources on a biography that I was writing, I called up an online research database called HighBeam, which offered free trials for their $200-per-month service. The paid service was too much for me to sustain with no active income.

When I reached HighBeam's customer service, I identified myself only as a Wikipedia editor. I asked for a free account to improve Wikipedia and perhaps a couple more for some of my editing friends. The response changed my life as the HighBeam representative on the spot said, "How about 1,000?" This was the beginning of *The Wikipedia Library*.

Back when I founded the program, librarians would only whisper to us at conferences that they too used Wikipedia. Stigma was omnipresent, and the running line was that Wikipedia was not reliable because anyone can edit it—just don't use it. Critical scholars viewed Wikipedia as a degradation of academic rigor, competent research, and the authority of experts.

Just as my efforts to inform and change the single minds of new editors weren't enough, it also wasn't sufficient to equip highly active Wikipedians with better digital resources. I needed to look beyond the core community to the pillars of expertise and authority in our society and change *their* minds. This meant overcoming a mountain of skepticism, dismissiveness, and inertia among researchers, scholars, teachers, librarians, and other experts. I relished the task. After all, they just needed to understand Wikipedia like I did: as a repository of information guided by community and reason.

The academic critiques of Wikipedia struck me as curious since some of our earliest and most ardent contributors to Wikipedia were *librarians*. As Phoebe Ayers discusses in chapter 6, Wikipedians and librarians found common interest around a culture that valued reference skills, information literacy, and access to information. It was only through the familiarity of regular exposure to reasonably good experiences that changed minds, transformed denigration into acceptance, and fostered legitimacy.

A boost to the alliance between Wikipedia and libraries came in the form of the #1Lib1Ref campaign. Short for *1 Librarian, 1 Reference*—the viral initiative cooked up by my colleague Alex Stinson and I—the campaign asked every librarian in the world to add one citation to Wikipedia as a gift to improve its reliability. In its fourth year now, #1Lib1Ref has added twenty-five thousand citations and four million words—and on social media, forty countries have shared the campaign with twenty-two million people, forty-four million times. #1Lib1Ref has helped popularize the notion that Wikipedians and librarians have symbiotic, complementary roles to play in the dissemination of reliable information to the public.

Wikipedia is now deeply ingrained in the world's information-gathering workflows. As we like to say, "discovery happens on Wikipedia." The traffic of 1.5 billion unique devices accessing Wikipedia fifteen billion times every month with more than six thousand page views every second is astounding. Wikipedia results are often on the first page on Google, excerpted in the popular "knowledge panel" summarizing the Googled topic, and parroted through Apple's *Siri* and Amazon's *Alexa*. As such, Wikipedia is used by almost everybody looking for information online. It's like the *virtual front page of every library*.

Seven years after starting *The Wikipedia Library*, active editors now have access to one hundred thousand free, high-quality academic journals, a sizable portion of the world's scholarship through our library. The program supports volunteers in their unpaid labor with access to research in a way that any research university worth its salt would do. In the battle against ignorance, I wanted Wikipedians overflowing with reliable sources. The project was initially just a volunteer effort; it expanded under an individual grant by the Wikimedia Foundation; and then it was adopted as a core foundation program. The Wikipedia Library now spans a team on four continents working with dozens of communities and publishers to improve Wikipedia's reliability and research.[6]

At times the signs of Wikipedia's evolution into the mainstream are surprising, even to diehards like me. When I see headlines that Wikipedia is used by over 90 percent of medical students, incorporated into expensive library databases for background information, cited in federal court documents, and relied on by Fortune 100 companies like Facebook, Amazon, Apple, and YouTube, I can't believe how far we have come. Looking back on the journey, I beam inside with the validation of our mission: Wikipedia had made it.

And along with Wikipedia and the Wikipedia Library, I had made it, too. I had a stable regimen of psychiatric support from a quiver of medications and therapists, I had found a life partner—also a Wikipedian—and married her, nearly five years after we first met at Wikimania 2012 in Washington, DC. It took me ten years of wandering around Colorado and living back at home with my parents to get my head on straight. As I stabilized, my network of peers, colleagues, and friends filled with people dedicated to this unending, radical project.[7]

It was a winding path, but at the core was a belief in human potential, the power of collaboration, and social interactions enhanced via technology. Intellectual curiosity was fuel for my reemergence and growth as it was for Wikipedia's emergence.

It was the drive to understand how communities function and how knowledge is created and shared that hooked me on Wikipedia. Even when I was most wayward, I was craving deep puzzles—and Wikipedia was an endless bounty of ideas and questions and challenges. As project chronicler Bill Beutler of *The Wikipedian* put it in his essay, "All I Really Needed to Know I Learned Editing Wikipedia," Wikipedia was a fertile space to learn to live and be in a complex world:

> So, does all this mean Wikipedia is perfect? Heck, no! What I mean is that it's an excellent place not just to soak up the sum of all human knowledge, but also to learn how to conduct oneself in a society riven with conflict and ambiguity, where might sometimes seems to make right and in the end all one can really be certain about having the power to safeguard is one's own integrity. Maybe that's a dim view of the world, but when you consider all the bad things that happen every day, you know, getting into (and out of) an edit war on Wikipedia is a relatively safe and surprisingly practical way to learn some key lessons about life.[8]

As I look around at the new challenges I now face—having moved across the country to Santa Cruz, inherited an intrepid eight-year old stepdaughter, and begun to grapple with what it means to have privilege and influence in the digital ecosystem—it is ever more clear to me that Wikipedia, too, is at a seeming apex that is, in fact, just the beginning of its next needed evolution.

"In truth, laws are always useful to those with possessions and harmful to those who have nothing; from which it follows that the social state is advantageous to men only when all possess something and none has too much."
—Jean-Jacques Rousseau, *The Social Contract*

The pillars and choices that set Wikipedia's legitimacy into motion also imbued it with the roots of its future flaws. Having achieved a high degree of ubiquity and increasingly *legitimacy*, Wikipedia now faces new and deep challenges around equity and inclusion, marginalization and representation, global participation and awareness—systemic bias, in short. Reaching the top of one mountain—whether of public respect or personal recovery—is funny in that way because it makes life richer but definitely not simpler.

While Wikipedia outgrew critics' skepticism of its early and teenage years, the community itself is only beginning to grapple with its entrenched gaps and inequities. In besting *Britannica* at its own game, had we accidentally recreated the same Western-dominant, traditional structures of power and privilege? After all, the Enlightenment period I studied in college was not only a scientific resurgence; it was also a period rife with inequality, enslavement, and domination. Enlightenment as a term now evokes as much shame as pride—for what it cost and for who disproportionately bore that cost.

To keep these issues from seeming too abstract, or *postmodern*, I like to think about Emily Temple-Wood, the fearless English Wikipedia administrator who was profiled in a story called "One Woman's Brilliant Fuck You to Wikipedia Trolls." Temple-Wood, a rare woman editor and even an administrator since the age of twelve, faced a torrent of rape threats, death threats, sexually explicit comments, and derogatory harassing remarks. They intruded on her Wikipedia talk page and her personal email. They intruded on her life.

I remember the day when I was standing with Emily outside a conference room waiting to discuss, of all things, marginalization on Wikipedia. That's when another email hit, and it hit a nerve so deep that Emily threw her cell phone at the wall in anger and disgust that she had been targeted again. Rather than lay victimized by the most recent attack, Emily made a profoundly badass decision: for every threat she received, she would write a new article about a woman scientist. For every violation of her emotional and psychological safety, she would etch another invisible woman into the record of history.[9]

Wikipedia, as much as it is a playground for intellectual discourse, is also a battleground for women, people of color, indigenous people, people living outside North America and Europe, and LGBTQIA people (those once called "minorities" indeed constitute a *majority* of the world). The predominantly white, Western, male editing core is demographically small, and yet this group wields a tremendous amount of power. How did young, isolated, brainy hobbyists—who took refuge in collaborative knowledge production—develop hostile practices of exclusion and abuse? How did meritocracy go so awry?

In his prescient essay "Free as in Sexist," Joseph Reagle posits that meritocracy itself is in no way a valueless orientation. A predisposition toward "openness" is on its face equal, but it is actually a choice on a spectrum that values liberty over something different. A community that chooses *freedom from* individual constraints inevitably blocks off paths of the *freedom to* perform supportive, communal functions.[10]

The distinction between so-called negative (freedom from) and positive freedoms (freedom to) were chronicled in twentieth-century political theory first in intellectual historian Isaiah Berlin's essay "Two Concepts of Liberty."[11] Development economist Amartya Sen's 1999 book *Development as Freedom* went further to include not just freedom to associate and speak or freedom to engage in opportunities but also *protection* from relationships rife with power imbalances and exclusion from choices. Positive freedom requires intervention from group and institutional actors to give more people the likelihood of achieving what they want together.[12]

While a more holistic conception of freedom is helpful, an orientation toward liberty in general ignores its opposite pole, *hospitality*, as elegantly framed by activist and Wikipedian Sumana Harihareswara. In her powerful speech on nurturing learning environments, *Hospitality, Jerks, and What I Learned*, she noted:

> The Wikimedia movement really privileges liberty, way over hospitality. And for many people in the Wikimedia movement, free speech, as John Scalzi put it, is the ability to be a dick in every possible circumstance. Criticize others in any words we like, change each other's words, and do anything that is not legally prohibited. Hospitality, on the other hand, is thinking more about right speech, just speech, useful speech, and compassion. We only say and do things that help each other. The first responsibility of every citizen is to help each other achieve our goals, and make each other happy. I think these two views exist on a spectrum, and we are way over to one side, and moving closer to the middle would help everyone learn better and would help us keep and grow our contributor base.[13]

The Wisdom of Crowds author James Surowiecki posits that in order for a crowd to be *wise* and to match or outperform an expert, not only must there be a sufficient number of people but also they must be *diverse* in point of view, *independent* from one another in thinking and acting, and *decentralized* so they can aggregate many tasks.[14] Wikipedia thrives with great numbers of people who coordinate their behaviors loosely from all around the world—but diversity is an area where we are far behind. Though political articles may balance well between left and right sides of the political spectrum, the broader landscape of volunteers looks a lot like me: white, male, college-educated, middle class, and North American (or West European).

One irony of Wikimedia's ad hoc "do-ocracy" is how many rules it still has and how those rules advantage and disadvantage certain groups. The most stringent of Wikipedia's policies are those around *notability* and *reliable sources*. Put simply, these dictate what can exist on Wikipedia. And for generations past and living, for women of color, African scientists, queer activists, and trans artists, the ability to exist on Wikipedia is tantamount to existing online at all.

One of the most inconsistently applied areas of the notability guideline is with "underrepresented" topics. More than a tautology, these are topic areas on Wikipedia that have less coverage than the sources available about them warrant. This is a natural consequence of editors writing about what they know and deleting what they do not. In a movement with significant demographic imbalances, the result—without intention or malice—is areas that don't receive significant coverage on Wikipedia despite meaningful coverage in other domains. Further, because they are unfamiliar, they receive *more* scrutiny when they are written.

There's a self-fulfilling belief in Wikipedia that people who have been forced to live on the margins of society and social power are of marginal notability. Attempting to right notability's wrongs can make it seem like one wants to overrepresent the marginal, but to achieve encyclopedic completeness, what we need to do is something totally different: *correctly represent the marginalized.*

Sometimes there is simply no information about these subjects available in sources that are reputable by Wikipedia's standards. But very often this is a conflation of how Wikipedians see importance when it intersects with a certain "otherness" and a perceived lack of status. Living on the borderline of society does not equate to being of borderline importance. Very often it is precisely the figures who move from the fringes to influence the mainstream who are shifting the frontier of how humans view themselves and treat others, making an outsized impact on the world.

When we make these judgments, we should not only look to "mainstream" sources for proof; we also need to look specifically to the reliable sources *in these communities* from which these figures emerge to establish their notability. The typical criteria for notability of an article in Wikipedia is when multiple independent reliable sources exist about the subject. Here is a complementary definition: a person who had a noticeable impact on a community as recognized in *that community's* most reputable sources. Call that a "community standard" of notability.[15]

Communities differ in the types of sources that exist about them. Power influences who is covered in "mainstream" written, academic sources. Marginalized groups are often best studied and reported on in sources Wikipedia deems "unreliable."

Wikipedia's definition for reliability in a source means having a "reputation for fact-checking and accuracy." In practice, this subjective rubric for evaluating the prestige of journals and books and newspapers leaves out whole swathes of knowledge, including oral, indigenous, and community knowledge. Sources about marginalized people may be not be "centered," but like trade journals—which are generally accepted as good sources on Wikipedia—they're niche *and* reliable. They locate notability in the context of the relevant community and reflect the myriad ways that knowledge is circulated and verified in the world.

"What wisdom can you find greater than kindness."
—Jean-Jacques Rousseau, *Emile*

In August 2018 I had the privilege of joining a group of queer, indigenous, and anti-caste activists organized by the internet equity campaign "Whose Knowledge?" (described in chapter 16). Our task, in four days, was to write a book. *Our Stories, Our Knowledges* laid out in painful detail how Wikipedia and the broader internet serves the world, but it doesn't yet include or reflect the knowledge and contributions of so many people in it.[16]

In a room where I was, for once, the only white man, I felt honored to be present with people whose lives were touched but not extinguished by oppression. I admired them, as it was clear they had so much knowledge I couldn't yet see or would never have stumbled across on my own. In that privileged position, I wished others like me could witness and participate in the rebalancing of power in the open knowledge community. I hoped that through our writings we could bring in more allies to fight these battles of equity and inclusion.

Our task was not to destroy Wikipedia, but to reconceive of it through new eyes—and to bring new voices to it. The voices in that room were full of anger but also an incandescent yearning to make sure they were not ignored or made invisible again. In spite of the dispiriting state of their worlds and the lack of articles about their cultures, there was pride and laughter—a warmth and care for each other.

I admire what we built in Wikipedia, but as I looked around that room I realized we needed to remake it—as I had done to myself years before—all over again.

Notes

1. Denis Diderot, "Encyclopedia," in *The Encyclopedia of Diderot & d'Alembert Collaborative Translation Project*, trans. Philip Steward (Ann Arbor: Michigan Publishing, University of Michigan Library, 2002) (Translation of "Encyclopédie," *Encyclopédie ou Dictionnaire raisonné des sciences, des arts et des métiers*, vol. 5 [Paris, 1775]), http://hdl.handle.net/2027/spo.did2222.0000.004.

2. Nicholson Baker, "The Charms of Wikipedia," *The New York Review of Books*, March 20, 2008, https://www.nybooks.com/articles/2008/03/20/the-charms-of-wikipedia/.

3. Clay Shirky, interview, *BBC: Imagine,* December 5, 2006 (details available at Stuart Ian Burns, "Annotations: Imagine: Here Comes Everybody," *Feeling Listless* (blog), December 6, 2006, https://feelinglistless.blogspot.com/2006/12/imagine-links.html (quoted in Glen Creeber and Royston Martin, eds., *Digital Cultures: Understanding New Media* [Berkshire, UK: Open University Press, 2009], 42).

4. Wael Ghonim, "Wael Ghonim and Egypt's New Age Revolution," interview by Harry Smith, *60 Minutes*, CBS, February 16, 2011, https://www.cbsnews.com/news/wael-ghonim-and-egypts-new-age-revolution/.

5. SXSW EDU, "dana boyd SXSW Keynote: What Hath We Wrought?" YouTube, video, 59:01, March 7, 2018, https://www.youtube.com/watch?v=0I7FVyQCjNg; text available at dana boyd, "You Think You Want Media Literacy … Do You?" Data & Society: Points, March 9, 2018, https://points.datasociety.net/you-think-you-want-media-literacy-do-you-7cad6af18ec2?gi=c0023a37a80b.

6. Jake Orlowitz, "The Wikipedia Library: The Largest Encyclopedia Needs a Digital Library and We are Building It," in *Leveraging Wikipedia*, ed. Merrilee Proffitt (Chicago: ALA Editions, the American Library Association, 2018); text available at Wikimedia Commons, s.v. "File: The Wikipedia Library-The largest encyclopedia needs a digital library and we are building it By Jake Orlowitz.pdf," September 6, 2017, https://commons.wikimedia.org/wiki/File:The_Wikipedia_Library-The_largest_encyclopedia_needs_a_digital_library_and_we_are_building_it_By_Jake_Orlowitz.pdf.

7. Jake Orlowitz, "Journey of a Wikipedian," *Medium.com: The J Curve*, March 18, 2016, https://medium.com/the-j-curve/journey-of-a-wikipedian-c2890e3a8d0c.

8. William Beutler, "All I Really Needed to Know I Learned Editing Wikipedia," *The Wikipedian*, July 12, 2016, http://thewikipedian.net/2016/07/12/ten-years-editing-wikipedia/.

9. Andrew McMillen, "One Woman's Brilliant 'Fuck You' to Wikipedia Trolls," *Wired*, February 6, 2017, https://www.wired.com/2017/02/one-womans-brilliant-fuck-you-to-wikipedia-trolls/.

10. Joseph Reagle, "Free as in Sexist," *First Monday*, January 7, 2013, https://firstmonday.org/article/view/4291/3381.

11. Isaiah Berlin, "Two Concepts of Liberty," *Four Essays on Liberty (London: Oxford University Press*, 1969); text available at Mr. Green's WebSite, "Political Science 2300: Readings," Dixie State University, last modified July 17, 2012, http://cactus.dixie.edu/green/B_Readings/I_Berlin%20Two%20Concpets%20of%20Liberty.pdf.

12. Amartya Sen, *Development as Freedom* (London: Oxford University Press, 1999); text available at "Courses in Informatics," University of Oslo, https://www.uio.no/studier/emner/matnat/ifi/INF9200/v10/readings/papers/Sen.pdf.

13. Sumana Harihareswara, "Hospitality, Jerks, and What I Learned" (opening keynote address, Wiki Conference USA, New York, NY, May 30, 2014); text available at Wikisource, s.v. "Hospitality, Jerks, and What I Learned," last modified July 24, 2016, https://en.wikisource.org/wiki/Hospitality,_Jerks,_and_What_I_Learned.

14. James Surowiecki, *The Wisdom of Crowds (New York: First Anchor*, 2005); text available at Department of Economic Cybernetics, Bucharest Academy of Economic Studies, http://www.asecib.ase.ro/mps/TheWisdomOfCrowds-JamesSurowiecki.pdf.

15. Peter Meyer (User:Econoterms), direct conversation, Wikimania Montreal, August 11, 2017.

16. "Whose Knowledge?" in Sanghapali Aruna et al., *Our Stories, Our Knowledges* (San Diego: University of San Diego, December 2018), https://whoseknowledge.org/wp-content/uploads/2018/12/OurStoriesOurKnowledges-FullResource.pdf.

9   The First Twenty Years of Teaching with Wikipedia: From Faculty Enemy to Faculty Enabler

Robert E. Cummings

Wikipedia jumbles the faculty roles of teaching, researching, and service by challenging traditional notions of faculty expertise, but a more integrated approach for these roles is also possible.

I have never been able to see Wikipedia without the lens of a faculty member. On the one hand, I subconsciously carry with me perpetual concerns about accuracy and reliability. I am often trying to prove to myself that Wikipedia is legitimate work: it is, after all, the world's largest encyclopedia. Writing to Wikipedia follows a set of complicated rules. So if it is a serious project with rules and enforcers and the world relies on its information, it ought to be universally accepted. And on the other hand? I want Wikipedia to be a lark. I also want Wikipedia to be a place where I wander freely and learn lots and lots of information. A guilty pleasure, not unlike pulling a book off a library shelf and simply reading it.

I suspect that these anxieties I experience might speak to inherent conflict in being a faculty member while engaging Wikipedia. Reading Wikipedia, contributing to Wikipedia, and certainly teaching with Wikipedia jumble and reconfigure the faculty identities of teacher and researcher because they recontextualize our relationships with expertise itself. And as our senses of worth as faculty members are heavily tied to our relationships with expertise, engaging with Wikipedia can be a challenge to our very identities. As an example, Dariusz Jemielniak, in chapter 10, can only make sense of his identities as an academic and a Wikipedian by thinking of editing Wikipedia as a role-playing game.

In this essay, I want to examine the traditional roles of faculty and how they define faculty engagement with Wikipedia. I will argue for a more integrated vision for how the faculty roles of teaching and researching are also connected to the role of creating public knowledge. Wikipedia creates challenges for faculty based on these roles, but it also creates opportunities for growth.

Additionally, over these last twenty years, the roles of faculty have changed. And certainly Wikipedia has changed. These changes have important implications for the work of creating public knowledge. But the key insight I wish to offer is that throughout these twenty years of faculty engaging with Wikipedia, the relationship between faculty and their sense of their own expertise governs both successful and fraught interactions.

What are these faculty roles? Most faculty positions combine aspects of up to three functions: teaching, researching, and service. As a tenured faculty member at an American public research university, I am expected to do all three—teach students, research original knowledge, and provide service to university constituents. University constituents are students, my discipline, the university itself, and/or the public. Some faculty positions might only feature one function. For instance, in a prior position as an adjunct faculty member, I held a contract which only asked me to teach for a semester. No service and no research were expected. And at my campus, we have faculty who only conduct research for the university—no teaching and no service. But typically when we think of the roles of a faculty member, we are thinking of someone who balances teaching, researching, and service functions.

The faculty roles of teaching and researching might seem self-defined. As teachers, faculty are responsible for helping students reach particular learning outcomes which are appropriate for a course (and, depending upon the structure of the particular institution, faculty are also responsible for defining learning outcomes for the student). Faculty researching is defined as producing peer-reviewed knowledge from any field. In practice, the research of a bench scientist will look much different than the work of a poet, but the disciplines themselves define what counts as peer-reviewed research, and institutions assign responsibilities to different levels of research participation depending on how they have defined a faculty position.

In both the researching and teaching roles, the faculty's relationship to their expertise is more easily understood than in service roles. When researching, faculty engage their expertise directly by investigating, applying, and extending research. Regardless of the discipline, faculty research offers the purest connection to expertise by directly engaging with a disciplinary understanding of the world—for example, a chemist talking with other chemists about how the world is defined by chemistry. And in teaching, the faculty relationship with expertise is also central—but never fixed and always redefined by the context of the classroom they are addressing. While teaching, faculty must connect novices with their sense of expertise. Memorable teachers seem to do this effortlessly by helping us understand how our view of the world is broken, and their disciplinary content can fix our brokenness.[1] Less inspiring teaching might overlook the needs of learners to contextualize the content of the classroom or fail to appreciate the fact that faculty experts have mental models built up over years of engaging a subject while novice learners approach the subject without those cognitive connections. But even teaching failures are evidence of the intense relationship faculty have with their expertise: in both of these cases, the perspective of the expert can deny the circumspection needed to introduce others to the discipline.

Definitions of faculty service are much more varied and complicated than either teaching or research. In general, the academy has defined faculty service work for the benefit of an academic discipline, institution, or public, which applies the expertise of the faculty member.[2] Most commonly, though, faculty service is for the institution. In practice this can include a raft of different tasks—from resolving student disciplinary conflicts to reviewing faculty tenure and promotion cases. But this category also includes faculty service for the good of the public.

And we faculty who edit Wikipedia in our discipline see our editing actions in this regard—we are applying our faculty expertise for the benefit of public knowledge. This engagement of experts with a public encyclopedia context provides lots of challenges. Some of those challenges include coming to terms with the prohibition on original knowledge; faculty (and student) editors often struggle with the fact that they cannot directly share their original insights on a topic but must instead report on knowledge from published sources. And at other times, we encounter the same challenges from the classroom when we fail to translate expert knowledge to introductory knowledge.

But engaging with Wikipedia can involve faculty writing to their disciplines or beyond. Engaging Wikipedia allows faculty to engage in these roles of researcher, teacher, and student, all at the same time. As researchers, we are experts in a particular area of knowledge which may or may not have a direct connection to the public. As teachers, we use our connection to our expertise for helping to shape minds, and the world's free encyclopedia cannot help but play a role in knowledge formation at any location and on any topic. And when we read Wikipedia, like everyone else, we become students: we likely have no expertise in the particular topic we are reading.

Faculty have a range of reactions to this experience of setting aside their role as experts when engaging Wikipedia: at one end, we react with outrage, questioning the validity of a project which seems hostile to the very notion of expertise. And at the other end of that range we find engaging Wikipedia exhilarating. It allows us to be novices again or to be students in any field imaginable.

When faculty contribute to Wikipedia, we gain experience with a public facing of our specialized knowledge. We experience the knowledge of other fields, produced by other experts, as novices. And in the journey of resetting ourselves as novices, we are reminded of how different the experience of the novice and the experience of the expert can be when approaching a subject. I am not suggesting that we faculty are always vulnerable when walking in the shoes of the novice. After all, we are members of the public and spend the majority of our time struggling to understand aspects of the contemporary world just like any other citizen. Instead, what I am suggesting is that engaging with Wikipedia puts faculty in touch with the difference between novice and expert roles, an understanding of which is vital to our roles as successful teachers. Effective teaching requires the ability to see a subject through the eyes of a newcomer. And the framework of an encyclopedia, as well as the debates about what content belongs in that encyclopedia, helps faculty keep in touch with a beginner's perspective. In addition, reading and or writing to Wikipedia can call into question the value of the work we do as specialized researchers: even if specialized knowledge is created for different purposes and if Wikipedia is free and useful, what is the value of specialized knowledge? Reading Wikipedia puts faculty in touch with the role of being a student again by triggering our natural curiosity, and working or teaching on Wikipedia invites faculty into collaboration with other people who are not in our faculty community but who share a passion for our subjects. In short, experiencing Wikipedia reconfigures our fixed notions of what it means to be a researcher, a teacher, and a servant of the public good.

But we faculty didn't start our engagements with Wikipedia with a fair-minded and balanced approach. For many of the last twenty years,

Wikipedia was seen as the enemy of the faculty and their engagement with expertise. Many faculty first became aware of Wikipedia when students began citing it as a reference in their papers. Students' use of Wikipedia was often tied to plagiarism. Once faculty began to understand that Wikipedia in and of itself was not a plagiarism mill any more than *Encyclopædia Britannica*, they took aim at its open review policy. Faculty, whose relationship with expertise was defined by a peer-review community with qualified reviewers who were accepted on the basis of their established reputations, were not about to embrace a platform of knowledge produced by unqualified and anonymous editors. The very concept of Wikipedia's knowledge production system was an affront to the principles of peer-reviewed knowledge. So Wikipedia was banned from many classrooms because it seemed to violate the faculty's relationship with expertise: if you were teaching students the premises of information literacy and how to vet sources based on qualified peer review, Wikipedia stood as a clear example of what not to do. Popular reception of Wikipedia, which often characterized it as laughably inaccurate, seemed to back up this faculty rejection.[3]

And yet, gradually, faculty positions changed toward begrudging acceptance of Wikipedia. First, faculty recognized that everyone was using Wikipedia anyway. Many of the faculty who banned Wikipedia from their classrooms were also using it from their offices. As Yochai Benkler reminded us in the *Wealth of Networks*, "Different technologies make different kinds of human action and interaction easier or harder to perform. All other things being equal, things that are easier to do are more likely to be done, and things that are harder to do are less likely to be done. All other things are never equal."[4] As it turned out, we faculty were also willing to trade ease of access to Wikipedia for guaranteed accuracy to printed encyclopedias in many cases. It helped also that the founder of Wikipedia, Jimmy Wales, noted that he felt that as an encyclopedia, Wikipedia was an unacceptable source for student papers. To help document the shift from print to digital information, *Encyclopædia Britannica* ceased printing and shifted to an online version supported by banner ads.

All the while, a small but growing number of faculty were teaching with Wikipedia. These faculty saw Wikipedia not as threat to their sense of expertise but rather as an imperfect statement of knowledge which provided students with a unique opportunity to improve public knowledge. Many of these projects were successful, but just as many ran afoul of many of the basic tenets of Wikipedia, including prohibitions against original research when students posted essays or violations of copyright when they posted plagiarized materials. The Wikimedia Foundation started to engage the higher education community directly when it created a specific team to work with educators. And later, this group was spun off to form Wiki Education, a foundation with the express purpose of connecting higher education and Wikipedia (see chapter 20).[5] As these structured classroom interactions with Wikipedia grow in terms of number and influence, they indicate an increasing shift with how faculty envision Wikipedia. Rather than existing as a threat to their expertise, Wikipedia is seen as a common public resource allied to the purposes of teaching and learning. Over these past twenty years, the faculty role of teacher has thus become more integrated with the purposes of Wikipedia.

During these past two decades faculty have also grown to see the value of Wikipedia as a public statement of their peer-reviewed knowledge. These disciplinary organizations have come to understand that Wikipedia is the "front door" for the knowledge they create, further integrating the faculty roles of research and service. Examples include partnerships established by Wiki Education between the Wikipedia community and the American Chemical Society, the American Sociological Association, the Conference on College Composition and Communication, and the National Women's Studies Association.[6] But faculty are not only seeing Wikipedia as a way to translate their specialized knowledge to a larger public; they are also seeing Wikipedia as a way to translate public experience into data for their research. The monitoring of public access to the Wikipedia pages on influenza to track the spread of the disease serves as a good example of how researchers can utilize the open access principles of Wikipedia to create primary data.[7] In this manner, the integration of the faculty roles of teaching, research, and service on Wikipedia become complete: faculty can teach students by improving the Wikipedia pages on influenza, they can research the disease itself by tracking is spread via Wikipedia, and they can perform a public service by ensuring the accuracy of freely available information about influenza via Wikipedia. Roughly twenty years in, Wikipedia has moved from a perceived threat to higher education to an enabler.

Higher education has changed significantly as well in the past twenty years. These increased partnerships among faculty, their professional organizations, and Wikipedia underscore how the platform mirrors shifts in the production of knowledge. Academic disciplines now see their connections to public knowledge as more central to their missions and have moved (often slowly or unevenly) to embrace the fundamentals of open electronic communication: broader participation in content creation, broader participation in content dissemination, and more transparency in content creation. Open access publishing, preprint circulation, Google Scholar, citation tracking, and even social media platforms for academic endeavors are indicative of how traditional higher education institutions have changed in this same period. And as newer faculty enter the academy, they bring a more current sense of expectations of Wikipedia and information exchange to their roles of teaching, researching, and service.

Where do we see the next twenty years taking Wikipedia and faculty? Though we now see Wikipedia as the "good grown-up of the internet" and perhaps a countermodel for the problems of disinformation perpetuated by social media, Wikipedia is also headed directly to a problem.[8] It might be the adult of the internet, but the children of the internet are about to bring down the tent. Regulation is coming for the social media giants in the United States and has already arrived in Europe. (And in societies with totalitarian governments, there never was anything other than regulation.)

Wikipedia and the children of the internet have thrived in the United States because of a fundamental paradigm shift in how we assign responsibility for publication of ideas. In a print age, presses, newspapers, and publishing houses served as intellectual and fiduciary underwriters for the accuracy and reliability of the content found in their publications. And generally, with some significant qualifications, publishers and authors could be held legally accountable for the impact of their content. With the widespread development of the "World Wide Web" in the 1990s, online publishers were able to shift responsibility for the content they published to the public who posted the content. Known as intermediary liability, the relevant section of US law reads: "No provider or user of an interactive computer service shall be treated as the publisher or speaker of any information provided by another information content provider."[9]

The Wikimedia Foundation's stake in intermediary liability was called into question early in its history during what became known as the "Seigenthaler incident." In 2005, journalist John Seigenthaler was the victim of a hoax article posted anonymously on Wikipedia. The Foundation's response summed up the position of those who benefit from intermediary liability—though new policies were developed to improve how the site handles biographies of living persons, the Wikimedia Foundation was not a publisher but a platform for users who were publishing their ideas.[10] Those authors were responsible for their content—not the platform. That shift has served Wikipedia, Facebook, YouTube, and all of the other online content hosts quite well and has generally allowed them to escape responsibility for the content published on their sites. However, with widespread election interference in the 2016 US presidential campaign, it is clear to legislators of any political bent that continuing down a path of laissez-faire regulation for internet companies threatens their livelihoods. And while they have been comfortable giving the benefit of the doubt to internet platforms for decades to afford them space to grow, they are not comfortable once they might have to pay a professional price for the unaccountability of Facebook and its ilk. If the internet is regulated, it is likely to affect adults and children alike.

As long as we have knowledge, we will have tensions about how that knowledge is created. These include tensions about expertise and tensions about agenda. The academy is the home of tensions about knowledge creation; we are comfortable holding multiple perspectives at the same time. Now we are growing comfortable with incorporating Wikipedia and, consequently, allowing Wikipedia to hold a more visible role with shaping public knowledge into our teaching and research practices. Wikipedia has dramatically improved access for knowledge creation and opened up participation. But the real advantage of our partnership is the memory of Wikipedia. We can study how consensus is built. Wikipedia offers the academy and the public a profound opportunity to reflect how knowledge is made. Yes, we have a literature of peer-reviewed research available to us now. But over the next twenty years, as the Wikipedia editing community and higher education continue to work together to produce publicly accessible knowledge, talk pages will have the opportunity to record even more information about how that knowledge is produced. In the future, as this rhetorical record grows about who is shaping knowledge, it will be an even more valuable meta-resource, detailing who participates in knowledge-creation conversations and who is listened to. The record so far (largely male and Western) is not encouraging. But at least there is a record.

Notes

1. This is a rough restatement of Ken Bain's concept of expectation failure, put forth more eloquently in his book *What the Best College Teachers Do* (Cambridge, MA: Harvard University Press, 2004).

2. The American Association of University Professors further divides service into categories of student-centered work, disciplinary work, and community-centered work. "What Do Faculty Do?" American Association of University Professors, accessed June 11, 2019, https://www.aaup.org/issues/faculty-work-workload/what-do-faculty-do.

3. Much of this popular reception is best summarized through Stephen Colbert's concept "Wikiality." Wikipedia, s.v. "Wikipedia: Wikiality and Other Tripling Elephants," accessed June 11, 2019, https://en.wikipedia.org/wiki/Wikipedia:Wikiality_and_Other_Tripling_Elephants.

4. Yochai Benkler, *The Wealth of Networks* (New Haven, CT: Yale University Press, 2006), 36.

5. The author currently serves on the board of directors for Wiki Education.

6. "Partnerships," Wiki Education, accessed June 11, 2019, https://wikiedu.org/partnerships/.

7. David J. McIver and John S. Brownstein, "Wikipedia Usage Estimates Prevalence of Influenza-Like Illness in the United States in Near Real-Time," *PLOS: Computational Biology*, April 17, 2014, https://doi.org/10.1371/journal.pcbi.1003581.

8. Stephen Harrison, "Happy 18th Birthday, Wikipedia: Let's Celebrate the Internet's Good Grown-up," *Washington Post*, January 14, 2019, https://www.washingtonpost.com/opinions/happy-18th-birthday-wikipedia-lets-celebrate-the-internets-good-grown-up/2019/01/14/.

9. Wikipedia, s.v. "Section 230 of the Communications Decency Act," accessed June 11, 2019, https://en.wikipedia.org/w/index.php?title=Section_230_of_the_Communications_Decency_Act&oldid=901115397.

10. Wikipedia, s.v. "Wikipedia Seigenthaler biography incident," accessed June 11, 2019, https://en.wikipedia.org/w/index.php?title=Wikipedia_Seigenthaler_biography_incident&oldid=901241527.

10 Wikipedia as a Role-Playing Game, or Why Some Academics Do Not Like Wikipedia

Dariusz Jemielniak

The best way to understand the sometimes uneasy relationship between Wikipedia and academics is to conceive of it as a game.

There are many ways to start editing Wikipedia, and not all of them involve making a fool of oneself, but that's the path I took. I was running a popular free online dictionary used by about two hundred thousand Polish users monthly. Polish Wikipedia had an article on the dictionary—which I may have contributed to, a little bit. When I noticed that the article was nominated for deletion, I was puzzled: Wikipedia was a community-driven encyclopedia that anyone could edit, and its storage space was not running out any time soon, right? Right?

I checked the page with a discussion about deleting the article and eagerly joined in, certain that I could persuade the disputants of the article's value. I soon found out that even though I was allowed to discuss it, I could not vote due to my nonexistent edit count. So I decided to start editing so as to defend the page I created, and after a lot of effort, I reached the insanely high (as it seemed then) edit count of one hundred edits, allowing me to participate in deletion discussions.

I was not hiding the fact that I created the website that I was defending, and I was confused that the Wikipedians were politely insisting that I had a conflict of interest (or "COI," as discussed in chapter 5) while at the same time claiming that all arguments must fall or stand on their own merit. Their inconsistency was striking, too: their motion to remove an article about a free dictionary website was moot as there were other similar projects with their own articles on Wikipedia, and I immediately and triumphantly pointed this out. It only had the perverse effect of having those projects then be candidates for deletion, though. Plead as I might, I was not able to save the article from being deleted. A well-written encyclopedic entry about my precious website went into oblivion!

Even after this disappointment, I felt there was a certain logic to my opponents' arguments. Since other online dictionaries lost their coverage, too, at least it was fair. More importantly, I noticed that what I had thought was an entirely spontaneous and disorganized conversation was, in fact, a community of many rules and norms.

It took me a while to realize that I must have initially appeared as a shameless self-promoter. Still, I continued editing out of curiosity and for the fun of it. Within a year I became elected as an administrator on Polish Wikipedia. One more year—a bureaucrat. A little later, a global steward, an ombudsman, a Funds Dissemination Committee member, and eventually a trustee of the Wikimedia Foundation. Somewhere along the way, I realized that I was spending way too much time on Wikipedia and that it was affecting my academic work. Instead of cutting down on my activity, I decided I should make it a primary topic of my research.

In this essay, I am going to show why academics are so reluctant to engage in Wikipedia and explain why editing Wikipedia is a role-playing game. Hear me out.

Wikipedia and Academia

When I was beginning my project, there were no solid academic books that I could find about Wikipedia. Later, quite a few were published that I am fully confident are excellent and to the point,[1] but at the time Wikipedia was still gaining the initial interest of the social researchers doing qualitative studies of organizations.

As I just submitted my associate professorship application and was undergoing a tenure review equivalent, I had to strategize on what topic I should take next so that I could build a solid case for my future full professorship. Many faculty members whom I consulted believed that focusing on Wikipedia was a dead end. They pointed out that, even though the topic had not been fully covered, it was also due to the fact that senior professors perceived online communities as a not entirely serious topic and possibly being a temporary fad. More importantly, as I was more and more open and vocal about my support for Wikipedia, I also faced harsh criticism and hostility. On a number of occasions I was sneered or ridiculed at during conference presentations and repeatedly requested to admit that Wikipedia should not be treated seriously.

One of the lessons learned for me was that, apparently, Wikipedia was perceived as something very, very bad in academia, at least in the social sciences. Even though the perception of Wikipedia among scholars has been changing over time[2] and Wikipedia is more and more welcome in classrooms, the wide divide between these two worlds is still very apparent and may be worth reflecting on a little bit.[3]

Everybody in academia uses Wikipedia. And when I mean "everybody," I mean, well, everyone who has a computer, has internet access, and occasionally has questions outside their expertise that may have answers in the body of human knowledge. Numerous studies have shown that the accuracy of Wikipedia is on par with the "professional" encyclopedias,[4] with minor biases going one way or another.[5] It is also much better referenced by design as one of the ground rules is to only add information with valid sources that a reader may verify for themselves—although this rule is not usually enforced.

I asked myself a question then, and it has puzzled me ever since: why are not all academics actively contributing to Wikipedia and using it for their regular classwork? After all, writing Wikipedia articles is a perfect student homework. A standard essay is typically going to land in a shredder immediately after grading, and virtually no one is going to read it ever again. A Wikipedia article, on the other hand, even if initially quite poorly developed, is likely to be useful for many readers who may also gradually improve it and help it grow. It gives a solid chance to give back to the society as well as support the underprivileged for whom Wikipedia is the main source of knowledge.

Also, writing an encyclopedic article is, arguably, a paragon of an academic effort. It requires the collection of valid, reliable scholarly references; the ability to synthesize them and refer to them accurately; and the ability to write in a neutral language. The outcome serves the general public, and the students know that their output will be widely read, which for many raises the bar and increases their motivation significantly.

There are other benefits, too. Wikipedia submissions are frequently verified for plagiarism by volunteers. Wikipedia editors restlessly point out missing references and correct poorly written phrases, and the wiki engine allows detailed tracking of contributions. As a result, a student assignment can not only be writing an article from scratch but also be improving and expanding an existing article.

Given all that, I have wondered why on earth are professors all around the planet so reluctant (as also discussed by Robert Cummings in chapter 9) to include Wikipedia assignments into university course work? After over a decade of spending time among Wikipedians and among my academic peers, I think I have some clues.

First of all, editing Wikipedia seems difficult. There is a large number of rules for editing and formatting that one has to follow, and any professor who would include Wikipedia writing into their curriculum would have to master these as well, even if only to be able to answer simple questions or, at the very least, not answer them with sufficient confidence.

Second, Wikipedia is perceived as inaccurate. It does not matter that its reliability on average is high, according to most studies published; that it is perceived as a normal, neutral source of information by the regular media; or that the majority of medical students find it useful and use it to learn with good results.[6] The perception is shaped much more by spectacular blunders and hoaxes,[7] which are admittedly much more likely to appear on Wikipedia than in a published book encyclopedia. The fact that the latter is getting obsolete day by day or that hoaxes are regularly weeded out by the Wikipedia community and do not stay long in popular articles does not affect this perception much here.

Third, there is a wider change in the society linked to a major crisis of trust in science, leading to defensive and dismissing reactions of academia. Different sides of this phenomenon manifest through, for example, "alterscience" communities such as climate change deniers, anti-vaxxers, homeopaths, or even more exotic flat Earthers and a generalized anti-intellectualism. There are surely many complex reasons for this change happening, including the spread of fake news and network propaganda, but one of the clear side effects is a rapidly declining authority of science in the general public. Doctor Google has become the practitioner of choice and the first source of information for a majority of patients.[8] Nonexperts have less and less respect for formal academic authority, and there is a strong rise of citizen science—a global movement of amateurs gathering and interpreting data as well as making actual and valid scientific discoveries. Wikipedia fits perfectly into this trend since it aims at democratizing academic knowledge. The fact that Wikipedia reveres science and strictly follows the rules of the scholarly reporting of findings does not change the fact that Wikipedians are perceived as circumventing the traditional knowledge distribution channels. Thus, many scholars may recognize the growing distrust in science and its disastrous consequences as somewhat related to anti-credentialism that is so typical on Wikipedia.

Finally, Wikipedia governance is bizarre, messy, and a-hierarchical.[9] For professors, arguably one of the most traditionally structured professions, it must appear as a nightmare.

However, there clearly is also a very real (and not just misconceived) power struggle there. Wikipedia indeed occupies the niche previously reserved only for those high in the academic hierarchy. Still, if Wikipedia is so widely popular and effective in knowledge dissemination, should not scholars eagerly develop it? When I was trying to understand the apparent paradox, I realized that perceiving Wikimedia as a game is, in fact, a useful metaphor explaining it.

Wikipedia as a Role-Playing Game

Wikipedia is a role-playing game (RPG). It is a widely popular massively multiplayer online role-playing game (MMORPG). It is a massive, collaborative action research experiment (as demonstrated in chapter 11) in creating a knowledge-building social movement[10] torn among the good-faith collaboration and pro-social behaviors and the inevitable political struggles, tensions, and reflections of social biases.[11] Wikipedia RPG participants play the roles of encyclopedia writers. Irrespective of their age or occupation, they are deadly serious about staying in character. They created a plethora of rules about putting their ego on the side, behaving in a civil manner, and so on. The number of behavioral policies and guidelines on Wikipedia is much higher than in most "professional" organizations—there are forty-five thousand words just about proper conduct the last time I checked, and there are over one thousand other regulatory documents about other aspects of Wikipedia editing, with a word count reaching millions in total. It is not a coincidence that geek folklore is definitely well rooted in Wiki-pedic culture.

Seeing Wikipedia as an RPG solves several puzzles at once. For instance, it helps explain why real-life credentials are frowned on there. After all, it is not particularly fair to get an advantage for your Dungeons & Dragons character by insisting that you actually know how sword combat works. It also explains why many Wikipedians are well educated or enrolled in doctoral programs but why not so many actually employed in academia: playing a scientist is so much more fun when you are not one for a living.

The perception of Wikipedia as an RPG explains also the reluctance of the ivory tower inhabitants to participate. When you are a soldier, you do not necessarily spend your free time playing paintball with friends. As a result, editing Wikipedia is perceived as a play for those who are academic would-bes. Granted, Wikipedia is read much more widely than any academic textbook and has a much bigger audience than any professor may dream of, but participating might indicate that one is not an actual academic.

Since academia in all its forms worldwide is also a highly ritualized theater with its own scripts, the fact that Wikipedia has concrete real results in knowledge dissemination is irrelevant. Allowing Wikipedia articles as important contributions that could be used in tenure reviews would be like introducing Star Wars X-wings into a Dungeons & Dragons battle—highly effective but somewhat incompatible.

Even though Wikipedia can be seen as an RPG, its outcomes are very real. As a result, we can also observe quite palpable shifts in knowledge-power distribution threatening the privileged caste of academics, which unsurprisingly definitely adds to the sentiment against Wikipedia. A serious game that results in creating the most popular reliable knowledge source in the world and disrupts existing knowledge hierarchies and authority, all in the time of massive anti-academic attacks—what is there not to hate?

Notes

1. Andrew Lih, *The Wikipedia Revolution: How a Bunch of Nobodies Created the World's Greatest Encyclopedia* (New York: Hyperion, 2009); Joseph M. Reagle, *Good Faith Collaboration: The Culture of Wikipedia* (Cambridge, MA: MIT Press, 2010); Nathaniel Tkacz, *Wikipedia and the Politics of Openness* (Chicago: University of Chicago Press, 2015).

2. Eduard Aibar, Josep Lladós-Masllorens, Antoni Meseguer-Artola, Julià Minguillón, and Maura Lerga, "Wikipedia at University: What Faculty Think and Do About It." *The Electronic Library* 33, no. 4 (2015): 668–683; Aline Soules, "Faculty Perception of Wikipedia in the California State University System." *New Library World* 116, no. 3/4 (2015): 213–226.

3. Piotr Konieczny, "*Teaching with Wikipedia in a 21st-Century Classroom: Perceptions of Wikipedia and Its Educational Benefits,*" *Journal of the Association for Information Science and Technology* 67, no. 7 (2016): 1523–1534; Dariusz Jemielniak and Eduard Aibar, "*Bridging the Gap Between Wikipedia and Academia,*" *Journal of the Association for Information Science and Technology* 67, no. 7 (2016): 1773–1776.

4. Richard James, "WikiProject Medicine: Creating Credibility in Consumer Health," *Journal of Hospital Librarianship* 16, no. 4 (2016): 344–351.

5. Shane Greenstein and Feng Zhu, "Do Experts or Crowd-Based Models Produce More Bias? Evidence from Encyclopedia Britannica and Wikipedia," *MIS Quarterly* 42, no. 3 (2018): 945–959.

6. Marcus Messner and Jeff South, "Legitimizing Wikipedia," *Journalism Practice* 5, no. 2 (2011): 145–160; Amin Azzam, David Bresler, Armando Leon, Lauren Maggio, Evans Whitaker, James Heilman, Jake Orlowitz, Valerie Swisher, Lane Rasberry, Kingsley Otoide, Fred Trotter, Will Ross, and Jack D. McCue, "Why Medical Schools Should Embrace Wikipedia: Final-Year Medical Student Contributions to Wikipedia Articles for Academic Credit at One School," *Academic Medicine: Journal of the Association of American Medical Colleges* 92, no. 2 (2017): 194–200.

7. Giovanni Luca Ciampaglia, "Fighting Fake News: A Role for Computational Social Science in the Fight Against Digital Misinformation," *Journal of Computational Social Science* 1, no. 1 (2018): 147–153.

8. Juliette Astrup, "Doctor Google," *Community Practitioner* 91, no. 1 (2018): 28–29.

9. Dariusz Jemielniak, "Wikimedia Movement Governance: The Limits of A-hierarchical Organization," *Journal of Organizational Change Management* 29, no. 3 (2016): 361–378; Piotr Konieczny, "Decision Making in the Self-Evolved Collegiate Court: Wikipedia's Arbitration Committee and Its Implications for Self-Governance and Judiciary in Cyberspace," *International Sociology* 32, no. 6 (2017): 755–774.

10. Dariusz Jemielniak, "Naturally Emerging Regulation and the Danger of delegitimizing Conventional Leadership: Drawing on the Example of Wikipedia," in *The SAGE Handbook of Action Research*, 3rd ed., ed. Hilary Bradbury (Thousand Oaks, CA: Sage, 2015); Piotr Konieczny, "Wikipedia: Community or Social Movement?" *Interface: A Journal for and about Social Movements* 1, no. 2 (2009): 212–232.

11. Joseph M. Reagle, "'Be Nice': Wikipedia Norms for Supportive Communication," *New Review of Hypermedia and Multimedia* 16, no. 1–2 (2010): 161–180; Emiel Rijshouwer, *Organizing Democracy: Power Concentration and Self-Organization in the Evolution of Wikipedia* (Rotterdam: Erasmus University Press, 2019); Nathaniel Tkacz, *Wikipedia and the Politics of Openness* (Chicago: University of Chicago Press, 2015).

11 The Most Important Laboratory for Social Scientific and Computing Research in History

Benjamin Mako Hill and Aaron Shaw

Wikipedia's founders could not have dreamed they were creating the most important laboratory for social scientific and computing research in history, yet Wikipedia has had an enormous effect on academic research.

Twenty years ago, Wikipedia's founders could not have dreamed they were creating the most important laboratory for social scientific and computing research in history. And yet that is exactly what has happened. Wikipedia and its sister projects have launched a thriving scholarly literature. How thriving? Results from Google Scholar suggest that over six thousand scholarly publications mention Wikipedia in their title and over 1.7 million mention it somewhere in their text. For comparison, the phrase "Catholic church"—an organization with a nearly two-thousand-year head start—returns about the same number of mentions in publication titles. In under twenty years, Wikipedia has become one of the most heavily studied organizations of any kind. To the extent that Wikipedia research is a field of study, what major areas of investigation have been pursued in the field so far? What are the big discoveries? The most striking gaps? This essay addresses these questions and considers some of the most important directions Wikipedia research might take in the future.

The State of Wikimedia Research

In 2008, Mako Hill was about to start his first year as a social science graduate student at the Massachusetts Institute of Technology where he hoped to study, among other things, organizational processes that had driven Wikipedia's success. Mako felt it would behoove him to become better connected to the recent academic scholarship on Wikipedia. He was also looking for a topic for a talk he could give at Wikipedia's annual community conference, called "Wikimania," which was going to be hosted by the Library of Alexandria in Egypt. Attempting to solve both problems at once, Mako submitted a session proposal for Wikimania suggesting that he would summarize all of the academic research about Wikipedia published in the previous year in a talk entitled "The State of Wikimedia Scholarship: 2007–2008."

Happily, the proposal was accepted. Two weeks before Wikimania, Mako did a Google Scholar search to build a list of papers he needed to review. He found himself facing nearly eight hundred publications. When Mako tried to import the papers from the search results into his bibliographic management software, Google Scholar's bot detection software banned his laptop. Presumably, no human could (or should!) read that many papers.

Mako never did read all the papers that year, but he managed to create a talk synthesizing some key themes from the previous year in research. Since then, Mako recruited Aaron Shaw to help create new versions of the talk on a yearly basis. Working together since 2008, the two authors of this chapter have collaborated on a "State of Wikimedia Scholarship" talk nearly every year. With a growing cast of collaborators, we sort through the huge pile of published papers with the term "Wikipedia" in their title or abstracts from the past year. Increasingly, we incorporate papers that analyze other communities supported by the Wikimedia Foundation. Each time around, we select five to eight themes that we think capture major tendencies or innovations in research published in the previous year. For the presentation, we summarize each theme and describe an exemplary paper (one per theme) to the Wikimania audience.

Over the first twenty-years of the project's life, Wikipedia research has connected researchers who have formed a new interdisciplinary field. We have each coordinated the program of the International Symposium on Open Collaboration (OpenSym), a conference started in 2005 as WikiSym. As part of this work, we helped coordinate papers in a track dedicated to "Wikipedia and Wikimedia research." Each year the Web Conference (formerly WWW) hosts a workshop that focuses on Wikipedia and Wikimedia research. Since 2011, volunteers have helped create a monthly "Wikimedia Research Newsletter" which is published in English Wikipedia's newsletter *The Signpost* and provides a sort of monthly version of our annual talk. The Wikimedia Foundation runs a monthly "research showcase" where

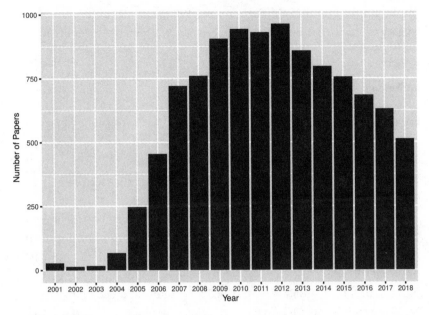

Figure 11.1
Number of items returned for Google Scholar for publications containing "Wikipedia" in the title by year of publication.

researchers from the around the world can present their work. There is an active mailing list for Wikimedia researchers.

As the graph in figure 11.1 suggests, these venues capture only a tiny fraction of Wikimedia research. Our attempt to characterize this body of research in this chapter draws from our experience preparing the annual Wikimania talk each year and from our experience in these other spaces. Like our Wikimania talk, this chapter remains incomplete and aims to provide a brief tour of several important themes. Others have published literature reviews of Wikipedia and Wikimedia research which make attempts to provide more comprehensive—although still limited—approaches.[1] Our experience watching Wikipedia scholarship grow and shift has led to one overarching conclusion: Wikipedia has become part of the mainstream of every social and computational research field we know of. Some areas of study, such as the analysis of human computer interaction, knowledge management, information systems, and online communication, have undergone profound shifts in the past twenty years that have been driven by Wikipedia research. In this process, Wikipedia has acted as a shared object of study that has connected a range of disparate academic fields to each other.

Wikipedia as a Source of Data

Perhaps the most widespread and pervasive form of Wikipedia research is not research "about" Wikipedia at all, but research that uses Wikipedia as a convenient data set to study something else. This was the only theme that showed up every single year during the nine years that we presented the "State of Research" review.

In 2017, Mohamad Mehdi and a team published a systematic literature review of 132 papers that use Wikipedia as a "corpus" of human-generated text.[2] Most of these papers come from the engineering field of information retrieval (IR) where the goal is to devise approaches for calling up particular information from a database. Wikipedia is useful for a wide range of tasks in IR research because it provides a vast database of useful knowledge that is tagged with categories and metadata—but not in the typically "structured" way required by databases.

Another large group of examples comes from the field of natural language processing (NLP), which exists at the intersection of computer science and linguistics. NLP researchers design and evaluate approaches for parsing, understanding, and sometimes generating human-intelligible language. As with IR, Wikipedia presents an opportunity to NLP research because it encompasses an enormous, multilingual data set written and categorized by humans about a wide variety of topics. Wikipedia has proven invaluable as a data set for these applications because it is "natural" in the sense that humans wrote it, because it is made freely available in ways that facilitate computational analysis, and because it exists in hundreds of languages. Nearly half of the papers in Mehdi's review study a version of Wikipedia other than English, and more than a third of the papers look at more than one language edition Wikipedia.

Recently, Wikipedia has spawned a large number of "derivative" data sets and databases that extract data from Wikipedia for studying a wide variety of topics. Similarly, a large body of academic research has focused on building tools to transform data from Wikipedia and to extract specific subsets of data. One of the newest Wikimedia projects, Wikidata, extends these benefits by creating a new layer of structured data that is collaboratively authored and edited like Wikipedia but that formally represents underlying relationships between entities that may be the topics of Wikipedia articles. As Wikipedia and Wikidata continue to grow and render ideas and language more amenable to computational processing, their value as a data set and data source to researchers is also increasing.

The Gender Gap

In 2008, the results of a large opt-in survey of Wikipedia editors suggested that upward of 80 percent of editors of Wikipedia across many language editions were male. The finding sent shockwaves through both the Wikipedia editor and research communities and was widely reported on in the press. Both the Wikimedia Foundation and Wikipedia community have responded by making "the gender gap" a major strategic priority and have poured enormous resources into addressing the disparity. Much of this work has involved research. As a result, issues related to gender have been a theme in our report on Wikipedia research nearly every year since 2012.

One series of papers have aimed to characterize the "gender gap." This work adopted better sampling methods, adjusted for bias in survey response, and in at least one case, commissioned a nationally representative sample of adults in the United States who were asked about their Wikipedia contribution behavior.[3] Some recent projects have also begun to unpack the "gap" by looking at the ways in which it emerges.[4] Although this follow-on work presented a range of different estimates of the scope of the gap in participation between male and female editors, none of the work overturned the basic conclusion that Wikipedia's editor base appears largely, if not overwhelmingly, made up of men.

Another group of studies examines different gender gaps, including gaps in content coverage. For example, research has found that women and people of color are systematically less likely than similarly notable white men to have articles.[5] Other work has shown that Wikipedia's content tends to suffer a range of gender biases and gaps as well—for example, by using terms and images that tend to reflect existing gender bias.[6]

Some work has also connected explanations of the gender gap among contributors to inequality and bias in articles. Existing Wikipedia communities may deter women and others from editing and may define and enforce criteria for article creation in ways that differentially impact articles about or of interest to women.[7]

The work on the gender gap in Wikipedia began with a strong focus on gender inequality within Wikipedia and among Wikipedia editors. More recent work has sought to understand how Wikipedia content may reflect underlying inequalities and patterns of stratification in the world in other ways. This work has shown that, by studying gendered and other types of inequality in Wikipedia, we can learn about some of the mechanisms of social stratification more broadly.

Content Quality and Integrity

Research into content quality and integrity on Wikipedia has also been an enduring focus of Wikipedia research. In a 2005 piece that is one of the most widely discussed examples of Wikipedia research (see chapters 2 and 12), Jim Giles at *Nature* ran an informal study distributing a set of Wikipedia and *Encyclopædia Britannica* articles to experts and asking them to identify errors in each.[8] The expert coders found about the same number of errors in each group, leading to the conclusion—surprising at the time—that Wikipedia articles might be comparable with those produced by professionals and experts. The early *Nature* study has been reproduced in larger samples with results suggesting that, over time, Wikipedia typically surpasses general encyclopedias like *Britannica*.[9] Perhaps more influentially, the template of the Giles study has been repeated over and over again in various knowledge domains that include drug information, mental disorders, and otolaryngology—just to name several topics in medicine.[10]

Of course, quality itself is much more complicated and multidimensional than the sum of factual errors in a sample of articles. A number of studies have tried to assess quality in other terms. Some consider the relative neutrality of articles on contentious topics.[11] Others look for the absence of important information. Wikipedians regularly evaluate the quality of their own articles in terms of comprehensiveness, writing style, the number and reliability of references, and adherence to Wikipedia's own policies. There have been a series of attempts to adapt these types of quality measures quantitatively. This work seems to indicate that although Wikipedia is enormous, many topics are covered in ways that are superficial.[12]

Overall, this body of research has shown the quality of the material that is covered is high.

Some of the most exciting work on these issues has examined the social processes that lead to relatively higher or lower article quality. For example, although quality and viewership of articles are related, a few recent studies have measured the degree to which topics are "underproduced" relative to readers' interest.[13] Another paper shows that articles on contentious topics edited by more ideologically polarized editors tend to become higher quality than those with less diverse editor groups.[14] Other work has sought to understand how readers of Wikipedia perceive quality.[15] In an era where factual information is increasingly contested and polarized, this line of inquiry offers the promise of general insights into the means of producing and sustaining reliable, high quality public knowledge resources.

Wikipedia and Education

Early on in its ascendance, many viewed Wikipedia as a threat to educational authority and a source of dubious information. Initial research on Wikipedia in education documented the ways that students used Wikipedia and, in general, suggested that students were relying on Wikipedia heavily as a first stop for information on a given subject. For many teachers, Wikipedia's open editing policy made its content inherently problematic, if not inherently incompatible, with formal institutions of teaching and learning.

The study of Wikipedia in education has evolved enormously. In part, educators have changed their attitudes about the site, and some studies have attempted to document these shifts.[16] The focus of academic writing about the pedagogical role of Wikipedia is no longer on the questions of *if* students use Wikipedia or how to discourage them from doing so. Instead, researchers of Wikipedia in education now focus on how to engage students in contributing to Wikipedia as part of course work.

Partly, this change seems driven by the success of the Wiki Education Foundation—a spin-off of the Wikimedia Foundation that supports instructors of higher education in incorporating Wikipedia into their classes (see chapter 20). Numerous papers and book chapters now document these experiences. One example from psychology describes the way that ninety-three students in an introductory human development course helped to improve Wikipedia coverage of basic information on human development.[17]

Viewership

The large majority of research on Wikipedia has focused on its content and the social systems that produce it. But Wikipedia isn't only an enormous corpus created by millions, it is also one of the top ten most popular websites on earth—visited by billions of people each year. In 2007, the Wikimedia Foundation started publishing data that summarized what visitors to Wikipedia have looked at. This data has now led to a large body of research on the viewership of the encyclopedia.

Some work on viewership takes advantage of Wikipedia's general usefulness and uses those pages that people visit as an index of how people allocate their attention. For example, the Snowden revelations led to chilling effects where people became systematically less likely to look at certain sensitive topics.[18] Other studies have used Wikipedia viewership data to predict the prevalence of illnesses and influenza, box office revenue, election results in a number of countries, or simply to capture a zeitgeist.[19]

Scholars have also combined data on Wikipedia viewership with editing data to understand the relationship between the consumption and production of knowledge. Some early work in this area considered whether viewership related to participation in editing and content quality.[20] Others have tried to model relatively complex dynamics through which viewers become editors to help produce the encyclopedia.[21]

Organization and Governance

When Wikipedia was first founded, one of the most urgent areas of inquiry focused on the organization and governance of the project. Seminal work by Yochai Benkler, author of chapter 3, suggested that Wikipedia used technology to organize knowledge production in transformative ways. Since then, research on the organization of Wikipedia has grown steadily, often in an attempt to explain its arguably shocking success.[22]

Research has sometimes treated Wikipedia as a community of communities to investigate collaborative processes. For example, both article-level collaborations and organized editing efforts in the form of WikiProjects have attracted extensive research. Perhaps not surprisingly, WikiProjects appear to struggle with many of the same kinds of organizational challenges that affect collaborative efforts elsewhere.[23] Many studies of organization within

Wikipedia have found creative ways to document and describe otherwise familiar patterns and have sometimes revealed distinctions between more familiar organizational practices and those pursued in a large, distributed, online volunteer effort like Wikipedia.

We have been involved in some related work that challenges the "stylized facts" about Wikipedia's organization and that has suggested some of the ways that Wikipedia's mode of organization and governance may be limited.[24] We also advocated for comparative studies that look beyond Wikipedia—and English Wikipedia in particular—to draw more general understandings of the organizational processes involved.[25] Wikipedia includes hundreds of more-or-less completely distinct language communities with different experiences and with different degrees of success. For instance, several papers—ours and others'—undermine the widespread perception that Wikipedia's style of organizing does not entail hierarchies or other patterns of entrenchment among early community leaders.[26] A small number of studies have engaged in comparative work that studies Wikipedia across numerous language editions, illustrating the diversity of collaborative dynamics.[27]

As a large population of organizations, Wikipedia offers a data source of exceptional granularity. Nevertheless, scholars continue to struggle to understand how Wikipedia is like and unlike more traditional organizations. We still know little about when the experience of traditional organizations will be instructive to Wikipedia. For example, in our own work we found that an attempt to import newcomer socialization practices with a long history of success in traditional organizations seemed to have little effect on newcomer retention in Wikipedia.[28] In a related sense, we still know little about when the things we learn about organization in Wikipedia will—or will not—translate into other spaces.

Wikipedia in the World

The metaphor of a laboratory that we used in our introduction depicts Wikipedia as somehow isolated from the rest of the world. However, Wikipedia *affects* the world in important ways as well. Some exciting studies have investigated specific aspects of this relationship.

The earliest versions of this work simply documented the ways that Wikipedia became increasingly integrated into many people's everyday lives. One striking example from 2009 described the growing rate at which legal opinion and published law relied on citations to Wikipedia to establish facts about the world in hundreds of legal opinions in the US district courts and courts of appeals.[29] Other work looks at how Wikipedia content is increasingly syndicated into other places and suggests that an enormous portion of all successful internet searches would be failures if Wikipedia did not exist.[30]

Given its prominence in search engine rankings, a group of scholars—primarily economists—have come to Wikipedia as a platform on which to run experiments *on the world*. For example, one group improved a random set of articles about small European cities and showed that tourism traffic increased relative to a control group whose articles were not improved.[31] Another study showed that improving a randomly selected set of Wikipedia articles about scientific studies tends to increase the citations to the studies mentioned in the articles and tends to shape the language that subsequent research studies use when they describe the cited work.[32]

These studies do more than show that Wikipedia is important, although they certainly do that. They provide important evidence in favor of particular theories of information diffusion, and they document the way that knowledge is created and spreads. In this way, Wikipedia provides not only a laboratory for studying social processes but acts as a key piece of laboratory equipment for studying social behavior "in the wild."

Conclusion

Insights about how the largest volunteer effort in the world have managed to produce the largest encyclopedias in history will continue to advance the frontiers of scientific knowledge. Understanding how Wikipedia and projects like it work can help us organize other parts of social life more effectively.

We conclude with an invocation to researchers to think about Wikipedia even more and in even broader ways. Wikipedia is the most influential and widely accessed free information resource on the internet as well as the most widely used information platform in human history. As such, Wikipedia merits comparisons to other epochal transformations in how humans collect, organize, store, and disseminate ideas. It deserves the scholarly attention it has received. In particular, understanding how and why communities like Wikipedia manage to mobilize vast numbers of volunteers and sustain such high quality, large-scale information resources means looking beyond the boundaries of Wikipedia to conduct comparisons, impact evaluations, and more. That ought to keep us all busy for at least another twenty years.

Acknowledgments: This work was supported by the National Science Foundation (awards IIS-1617129 and IIS-1617468).

Notes

1. Chitu Okoli, Mohamad Mehdi, Mostafa Mesgari, Finn Årup Nielsen, and Arto Lanamäki, "Wikipedia in the Eyes of Its Beholders: A Systematic Review of Scholarly Research on Wikipedia Readers and Readership," *Journal of the Association for Information Science and Technology* 65, no. 12 (2014): 2381–2403, https://doi.org/10.1002/asi.23162; Mohamad Mehdi, Chitu Okoli, Mostafa Mesgari, Finn Årup Nielsen, and Arto Lanamäki, "Excavating the Mother Lode of Human-Generated Text: A Systematic Review of Research That Uses the Wikipedia Corpus," *Information Processing & Management* 53, no. 2 (March 2017): 505–529, https://doi.org/10.1016/j.ipm.2016.07.003.

2. Mehdi et al., "Excavating the Mother Lode of Human-Generated Text."

3. Eszter Hargittai and Aaron Shaw, "Mind the Skills Gap: The Role of Internet Know-How and Gender in Differentiated Contributions to Wikipedia," *Information, Communication & Society* 18, no. 4 (2015): 424–442, https://doi.org/10.1080/1369118X.2014.957711; Benjamin Mako Hill and Aaron Shaw, "The Wikipedia Gender Gap Revisited: Characterizing Survey Response Bias with Propensity Score Estimation," *PLoS ONE* 8, no. 6 (2013): e65782, https://doi.org/10.1371/journal.pone.0065782; Aaron Shaw and Eszter Hargittai, "The Pipeline of Online Participation Inequalities: The Case of Wikipedia Editing." *Journal of Communication* 68, no. 1 (2018): 143–168, https://doi.org/10.1093/joc/jqx003.

4. For example, Shaw and Hargittai, "The Pipeline of Online Participation Inequalities."

5. For example, Joseph Reagle and Lauren Rhue, "Gender Bias in Wikipedia and Britannica," *International Journal of Communication* 5 (2011): 1138–1158, http://ijoc.org/index.php/ijoc/article/view/777; Julia Adams, Hannah Brückner, and Cambria Naslund, "Who Counts as a Notable Sociologist on Wikipedia? Gender, Race, and the 'Professor Test,'" *Socius* 5 (2019), https://doi.org/10.1177/2378023118823946.

6. Max Klein and Piotr Konieczny, "Wikipedia in the World of Global Gender Inequality Indices: What the Biography Gender Gap Is Measuring," in *OpenSym '15: Proceedings of the 11th International Symposium on Open Collaboration*, ed. D. Riehle

(New York: ACM, 2015), 16:1–16:2, https://doi.org/10.1145/2788993.2789849; Claudia Wagner, David Garcia, Mohsen Jadidi, and Markus Strohmaier, "It's a Man's Wikipedia? Assessing Gender Inequality in an Online Encyclopedia," in *Proceedings of the Ninth International AAAI Conference on Web and Social Media (ICWSM '15)* (Palo Alto, CA: AAAI, 2015), 454–463, https://www.aaai.org/ocs/index.php /ICWSM/ICWSM15/paper/view/10585; Olga Zagovora, Fabian Flöck, and Claudia Wagner, "'(Weitergeleitet von Journalistin)': The Gendered Presentation of Professions on Wikipedia," in *WebSci '17: Proceedings of the 2017 ACM on Web Science Conference* (New York: ACM, 2017), 83–92, https://doi.org/10.1145/3091478 .3091488.

7. Julia B. Bear and Benjamin Collier, "Where Are the Women in Wikipedia? Understanding the Different Psychological Experiences of Men and Women in Wikipedia," *Sex Roles* 74, nos. 5–6 (January 4, 2016): 254–265, https://doi.org/10.1007/s11199 -015-0573-y; Amanda Menking, Ingrid Erickson, and Wanda Pratt, "People Who Can Take It: How Women Wikipedians Negotiate and Navigate Safety," in *CHI '19: Proceedings of the 2019 CHI Conference on Human Factors in Computing Systems* (New York: ACM, 2019), https://doi.org/10.1145/3290605.3300702; Heather Ford and Judy Wajcman, "'Anyone Can Edit', Not Everyone Does: Wikipedia's Infrastructure and the Gender Gap," *Social Studies of Science* 47, no. 4 (2017): 511–527, https://doi .org/10.1177/0306312717692172.

8. Jim Giles, "Internet Encyclopaedias Go Head to Head," *Nature* 438, no. 7070 (2005): 900–901, https://doi.org/10.1038/438900a.

9. Fernando Silvério Nifrário Rodrigues, "Colaboração Em Massa Ou Amadorismo Em Massa? Um Estudo Comparativo Da Qualidade Da Informação Científica Produzida Utilizando Os Conceitos E Ferramentas Wiki" (PhD diss., Universidade de Évora, 2012), http://massamateurism.blogspot.co.uk/p/synopsis.html.

10. Kevin A. Clauson, Hyla H. Polen, Maged N. Kamel Boulos, and Joan H. Dzenowagis. "Scope, Completeness, and Accuracy of Drug Information in Wikipedia," *The Annals of Pharmacotherapy* 42, no. 12 (December 2008): 1814–1821, https://doi .org/10.1345/aph.1L474; Thomas J. Hwang, Florence T. Bourgeois, and John D. Seeger, "Drug Safety in the Digital Age," *New England Journal of Medicine* 370, no. 26 (2014): 2460–2462. https://doi.org/10.1056/NEJMp1401767; Jona Kräenbring et al., "Accuracy and Completeness of Drug Information in Wikipedia: A Comparison with Standard Textbooks of Pharmacology," *PLOS ONE* 9, no. 9 (2014): e106930, https://doi.org/10.1371/journal.pone.0106930; N. J. Reavley, A. J. Mackinnon, A. J. Morgan, M. Alvarez-Jimenez, S. E. Hetrick, E. Killackey, B. Nelson, R. Purcell, M. B. H. Yap, and A. F. Jorm, "Quality of Information Sources about Mental Disorders: A Comparison of Wikipedia with Centrally Controlled Web and Printed Sources," *Psychological Medicine* 42, no. 8 (August 2012): 1753–1762, https://doi.org/10.1017 /S003329171100287X; Peter G. Volsky, Cristina M. Baldassari, Sirisha Mushti, and Craig S. Derkay, "Quality of Internet Information in Pediatric Otolaryngology: A

Comparison of Three Most Referenced Websites," *International Journal of Pediatric Otorhinolaryngology* 76, no. 9 (September 2012): 1312–1316, https://doi.org/10.1016 /j.ijporl.2012.05.026.

11. Shane Greenstein and Feng Zhu, "Is Wikipedia Biased?" *American Economic Review* 102, no. 3 (May 2012): 343–348, https://doi.org/10.1257/aer.102.3.343; Shane Greenstein and Feng Zhu, "Do Experts or Crowd-Based Models Produce More Bias? Evidence from Encyclopedia Britannica and Wikipedia," *Management Information Systems Quarterly* 42, no. 3 (2018): 945–959, https://aisel.aisnet.org/misq/vol42/iss3/14.

12. Morten Warncke-Wang, Vivek Ranjan, Loren Terveen, and Brent Hecht, "Misalignment Between Supply and Demand of Quality Content in Peer Production Communities," in *Proceedings of the Ninth International AAAI Conference on Web and Social Media (ICWSM '15)* (Palo Alto, CA: AAAI, 2015), 493–502, https://www.aaai .org/ocs/index.php/ICWSM/ICWSM15/paper/viewFile/10591/10532.

13. Aniket Kittur and Robert E. Kraut, "Harnessing the Wisdom of Crowds in Wikipedia: Quality Through Coordination," in *CSCW '09: Proceedings of the 2008 ACM Conference on Computer Supported Cooperative Work* (New York: ACM, 2008), 37–46, https://doi.org/10.1145/1460563.1460572; Warncke-Wang et al., "Misalignment Between Supply and Demand of Quality Content in Peer Production Communities."

14. Feng Shi, Misha Teplitskiy, Eamon Duede, and James A. Evans, "The Wisdom of Polarized Crowds," *Nature Human Behaviour* 3, no. 4 (April 2019): 329, https://doi .org/10.1038/s41562-019-0541-6.

15. W. Ben Towne, Aniket Kittur, Peter Kinnaird, and James Herblseb, "Your Process Is Showing: Controversy Management and Perceived Quality in Wikipedia," in *CSCW '13: Proceedings of the 2013 Conference on Computer Supported Cooperative Work* (New York: ACM, 2013), 1059–1068, https://doi.org/10.1145/2441776.2441896.

16. Hsin-liang Chen, "The Perspectives of Higher Education Faculty on Wikipedia," *The Electronic Library* 28, no. 3 (J2010): 361–373, https://doi.org/10.1108 /02640471011051954; Aline Soules, "Faculty Perception of Wikipedia in the California State University System," *New Library World* 116, no. 3/4 (2015): 213–226, https://doi.org/10.1108/NLW-08-2014-0096.

17. Christina Shane-Simpson, Elizabeth Che, and Patricia J. Brooks, "Giving Psychology Away: Implementation of Wikipedia Editing in an Introductory Human Development Course," *Psychology Learning & Teaching* 15, no. 3 (2016): 268–293, https://doi.org/10.1177/1475725716653081.

18. Jonathon Penney, "Chilling Effects: Online Surveillance and Wikipedia Use," *Berkeley Technology Law Journal* 31, no. 1 (2016): 117, https://doi.org/10.15779/Z38SS13.

19. David J. McIver and John S. Brownstein, "Wikipedia Usage Estimates Prevalence of Influenza-Like Illness in the United States in Near Real-Time," *PLoS Computational*

Biology 10, no. 4 (2014): e1003581, https://doi.org/10.1371/journal.pcbi.1003581; Márton Mestyán, Taha Yasseri, and János Kertész, "Early Prediction of Movie Box Office Success Based on Wikipedia Activity Big Data," *PLOS ONE* 8, no. 8 (2013): e71226, https://doi.org/10.1371/journal.pone.0071226; Taha Yasseri and Jonathan Bright, "Wikipedia Traffic Data and Electoral Prediction: Towards Theoretically Informed Models," *EPJ Data Science* 5, no. 1 (2016): 22, https://doi.org/10.1140/epjds /s13688-016-0083-3; Benjamin K. Smith and Abel Gustafson, "Using Wikipedia to Predict Election Outcomes: Online Behavior as a Predictor of Voting," *Public Opinion Quarterly* 81, no. 3 (2017): 714–735, https://doi.org/10.1093/poq/nfx007; Gabriele Tolomei et al., "Twitter Anticipates Bursts of Requests for Wikipedia Articles," in *DUBMOD '13: Proceedings of the 2013 Workshop on Data-Driven User Behavioral Modelling and Mining from Social Media* (New York: ACM, 2013), 5–8, https://doi.org/10 .1145/2513577.2538768; Michela Ferron and Paolo Massa, "Beyond the Encyclopedia: Collective Memories in Wikipedia," *Memory Studies* 7, no. 1 (2014): 22–45, https:// doi.org/10.1177/1750698013490590.

20. Reid Priedhorsky, Jilin Chen, Shyong (Tony) K. Lam, Katherine Panciera, Loren Terveen, and John Riedl, "Creating, Destroying, and Restoring Value in Wikipedia," in *GROUP '07: Proceedings of the 2007 International ACM Conference on Supporting Group Work* (New York: ACM, 2007), 259–268, https://doi.org/10.1145/1316624.1316663.

21. Andreea D. Gorbatâi, "The Paradox of Novice Contributions to Collective Production: Evidence from Wikipedia" (working paper, University of California, Berkeley, February 10, 2014), https://papers.ssrn.com/abstract=1949327.

22. Yochai Benkler, *The Wealth of Networks* (New Haven, CT: Yale University Press, 2006); subsequent work includes David A. Hoffman and Salil K. Mehra, "Wikitruth Through Wikiorder," *Emory Law Journal* 59, no. 1 (2009–2010): 151–210, https:// heinonline.org/HOL/P?h=hein.journals/emlj59&i=153; Piotr Konieczny, "Governance, Organization, and Democracy on the Internet: The Iron Law and the Evolution of Wikipedia," *Sociological Forum* 24, no. 1 (2009): 162–192, https://doi.org/10.1111/j .1573-7861.2008.01090.x; Piotr Konieczny, "Adhocratic Governance in the Internet Age: A Case of Wikipedia," *Journal of Information Technology & Politics* 7, no. 4 (2010): 263–283, https://doi.org/10.1080/19331681.2010.489408; Joseph Reagle, *Good Faith Collaboration: The Culture of Wikipedia* (Cambridge, MA: MIT Press, 2010); Dariusz Jemielniak, *Common Knowledge? An Ethnography of Wikipedia* (Stanford, CA: Stanford University, 2014); Emiel Rijshouwer, *Organizing Democracy: Power Concentration and Self-Organization in the Evolution of Wikipedia* (Rotterdam: Erasmus University, 2019), https://repub.eur.nl/pub/113937/.

23. Andrea Forte, Vanesa Larco, and Amy Bruckman, "Decentralization in Wikipedia Governance," *Journal of Management Information Systems* 26, no. 1 (2009): 49–72, https://doi.org/10.2753/MIS0742-1222260103; Loxley Sijia Wang, Jilin Chen, Yuqing Ren, and John Riedl, "Searching for the Goldilocks Zone: Trade-Offs in Managing Online Volunteer Groups," in *CSCW '12: Proceedings of the ACM 2012 Conference*

on Computer Supported Cooperative Work (New York: ACM, 2012), 989–998, https://doi.org/10.1145/2145204.2145351; Haiyi Zhu, Robert E. Kraut, and Aniket Kittur, "Organizing Without Formal Organization: Group Identification, Goal Setting and Social Modeling in Directing Online Production," in *CSCW '12: Proceedings of the ACM 2012 Conference on Computer Supported Cooperative Work* (New York: ACM, 2012), 935–944, https://doi.org/10.1145/2145204.2145344; Jonathan T. Morgan, Michael Gilbert, David W. McDonald, and Mark Zachry, "Project Talk: Coordination Work and Group Membership in WikiProjects," in *WikiSym '13: Proceedings of the 9th International Symposium on Open Collaboration* (New York: ACM, 2013), 3:1–3:10, https://doi.org/10.1145/2491055.2491058.

24. Aaron Shaw and Benjamin Mako Hill, "Laboratories of Oligarchy? How the Iron Law Extends to Peer Production," *Journal of Communication* 64, no. 2 (2014): 215–238, https://doi.org/10.1111/jcom.12082.

25. Benjamin Mako Hill and Aaron Shaw, "Studying Populations of Online Communities," in *The Oxford Handbook of Networked Communication*, ed. Brooke Foucault Welles and Sandra González-Bailón (Oxford, UK: Oxford University Press, 2019), https://doi.org/10.1093/oxfordhb/9780190460518.013.8.

26. Aaron Halfaker, R. Stuart Geiger, Jonathan T. Morgan, and John Riedl, "The Rise and Decline of an Open Collaboration System: How Wikipedia's Reaction to Popularity Is Causing Its Decline," *American Behavioral Scientist* 57, no. 5 (2013): 664–88, https://doi.org/10.1177/0002764212469365; Shaw and Hill, "Laboratories of Oligarchy?"; Nathan TeBlunthuis, Aaron Shaw, and Benjamin Mako Hill, "Revisiting 'The Rise and Decline' in a Population of Peer Production Projects," in *CHI '18: Proceedings of the 2018 CHI Conference on Human Factors in Computing Systems* (New York: ACM, 2018), 355:1–355:7, https://doi.org/10.1145/3173574.3173929.

27. For example, Felipe Ortega, "Wikipedia: A Quantitative Analysis" (PhD diss., Universidad Rey Juan Carlos, Madrid, Spain, 2009), http://libresoft.es/Members/jfelipe/phd-thesis.

28. Sneha Narayan, Jake Orlowitz, Jonathan T. Morgan, Benjamin Mako Hill, and Aaron Shaw, "The Wikipedia Adventure: Field Evaluation of an Interactive Tutorial for New Users," in *CSCW '17: Proceedings of the 2017 ACM Conference on Computer Supported Cooperative Work and Social Computing* (New York: ACM, 2017), 1785–1799, https://doi.org/10.1145/2998181.2998307.

29. Morgan Michelle Stoddard, "Judicial Citation to Wikipedia in Published Federal Court" (master's thesis, University of North Carolina at Chapel Hill, 2009), http://ils.unc.edu/MSpapers/3526.pdf.

30. Nicholas Vincent, Isaac Johnson, and Brent Hecht, "Examining Wikipedia with a Broader Lens: Quantifying the Value of Wikipedia's Relationships with Other Large-Scale Online Communities," in *CHI '18: Proceedings of the 2018 CHI*

Conference on Human Factors in Computing Systems (New York: ACM, 2018), 566:1–566:13, https://doi.org/10.1145/3173574.3174140; Connor McMahon, Isaac L. Johnson, and Brent J. Hecht, "The Substantial Interdependence of Wikipedia and Google: A Case Study on the Relationship Between Peer Production Communities and Information Technologies," in *International AAAI Conference on Web and Social Media (ICWSM 2017)* (Palo Alto, CA: AAAI, 2017), 142–151, http://brenthecht.com/publications/icwsm17_googlewikipedia.pdf.

31. Marit Hinnosaar, Toomas Hinnosaar, M. E. Kummer, and Olga Slivko, "Wikipedia Matters" (working paper, SSRN, Rochester, NY, July 14, 2019), https://papers.ssrn.com/abstract=3046400.

32. Neil Thompson and Douglas Hanley, "Science Is Shaped by Wikipedia: Evidence from a Randomized Control Trial" (MIT Sloan Research Paper No. 5238-17, February 13, 2018), https://papers.ssrn.com/abstract=3039505; Mark Zastrow, "Wikipedia Shapes Language in Science Papers," *Nature News*, September 26, 2017, https://doi.org/10.1038/nature.2017.22656.

12 Collaborating on the Sum of All Knowledge Across Languages

Denny Vrandečić

Wikipedia is available in almost three hundred languages, each with independently developed content and perspectives. By extending lessons learned from Wikipedia and Wikidata toward prose and structured content, more knowledge could be shared across languages and allow each edition to focus on their unique contributions and improve their comprehensiveness and currency.

Every language edition of Wikipedia is written independently of every other language edition. A contributor may consult an existing article in another language edition when writing a new article, or they might even use the content translation tool to help with translating one article to another language, but there is nothing to ensure that articles in different language editions are aligned or kept consistent with each other. This is often regarded as a contribution to knowledge diversity since it allows every language edition to grow independently of all other language editions. So would creating a system that aligns the contents more closely with each other sacrifice that diversity?

Differences Between Wikipedia Language Editions

Wikipedia is often described as a wonder of the modern age. There are more than fifty million articles in almost three hundred languages. The goal of allowing everyone to share in the sum of all knowledge is achieved, right?

Not yet.

The knowledge in Wikipedia is unevenly distributed.[1] Let's take a look at where the first twenty years of editing Wikipedia have taken us.

The number of articles varies between the different language editions of Wikipedia: English, the largest edition, has more than 5.8 million articles; Cebuano—a language spoken in the Philippines—has 5.3 million articles;

Swedish has 3.7 million articles; and German has 2.3 million articles. (Cebuano and Swedish have a large number of machine-generated articles.) In fact, the top nine languages alone hold more than half of all articles across the Wikipedia language editions—and if you take the bottom half of all Wikipedias ranked by size, together they wouldn't have 10 percent of the number of articles in the English Wikipedia.

It is not just the sheer number of articles that differ between editions but their comprehensiveness as well: the English Wikipedia article on Frankfurt has a length of 184,686 characters, a table of contents spanning eighty-seven sections and subsections, ninety-five images, tables and graphs, and ninety-two references—whereas the Hausa Wikipedia article states that it is a city in the German state of Hesse and lists its population and mayor. Hausa is a language spoken natively by forty million people and as a second language by another twenty million.

It is not always the case that the large Wikipedia language editions have more content on a topic. Although readers often consider large Wikipedias to be more comprehensive, local Wikipedias may frequently have more content on topics of local interest: the English Wikipedia knows about the Port of Călărași that it is one of the largest Romanian river ports, located at the Danube near the town of Călărași—and that's it. The Romanian Wikipedia on the other hand offers several paragraphs of content about the port.

The topics covered by the different Wikipedias also overlap less than one would initially assume. English Wikipedia has 5.8 million articles, and German has 2.2 million articles—but only 1.1 million topics are covered by both Wikipedias. A full 1.1 million topics have an article in German—but not in English. The top ten Wikipedias by activity—each of them with more than a million articles—have articles on only one hundred thousand topics in common. In total, the different language Wikipedias cover eighteen million different topics in over fifty million articles—and English only covers 31 percent of the topics.

Besides coverage, there is also the question of how up to date the different language editions are. In June 2018, San Francisco elected London Breed as its new mayor. Nine months later, in March 2019, I conducted an analysis of who the mayor of San Francisco was stated to be according to the different language versions of Wikipedia (see figure 12.1). Of the 292 language editions, a full 165 had a Wikipedia article on San Francisco. Of these, eighty-six named the mayor. The good news is that not a single Wikipedia

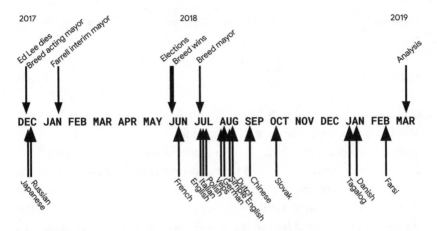

Figure 12.1
The events after the death of Ed Lee until London Breed became mayor on top. On bottom, date that a given Wikipedia was updated to list the new mayor.

lists a wrong mayor—but the vast majority are out of date. English switched the minute London Breed was sworn in. But sixty-two Wikipedia language editions list an out-of-date mayor—and not just the previous mayor Ed Lee, who became mayor in 2011, but also often Gavin Newsom (2004–2011), and his predecessor, Willie Brown (1996–2004). The most out-of-date entry is to be found in the Cebuano Wikipedia, who names Dianne Feinstein as the mayor of San Francisco. She had that role after the assassination of Harvey Milk and George Moscone in 1978 and remained in that position for a decade until 1988—Cebuano was more than thirty years out of date. Only twenty-four language editions had listed the current mayor, London Breed, out of the eighty-six who listed the name at all.

An even more important metric for the success of a Wikipedia are the number of contributors. English has more than thirty-one thousand active contributors—three out of seven active Wikipedians are active, with five or more edits a month, on the English Wikipedia. German, the second most active Wikipedia community, already only has 5,500 active contributors. Only eleven language editions have more than a thousand active contributors—and more than half of all Wikipedias have fewer than ten active contributors. To assume that fewer than ten active contributors can write and maintain a comprehensive encyclopedia in their spare time is optimistic at best. These numbers basically doom the mission of the

Wikimedia movement to realize a world where everyone can contribute to the sum of all knowledge.

Enter Wikidata

Wikidata was launched in 2012 and offers a free, collaborative, multilingual secondary database, collecting structured data to provide support for Wikipedia, Wikimedia Commons, the other wikis of the Wikimedia movement, and for anyone else in the world.[2] Wikidata contains structured information in the form of simple claims, such as "San Francisco—Mayor—London Breed" qualifiers, such as "since—July 11, 2018," and references for these claims—for example, a link to the official election results as published by the city—as shown in figure 12.2.

One of these structured claims would be on the Wikidata page about San Francisco, stating the mayor, as discussed earlier. The individual Wikipedias can then query Wikidata for the current mayor. Of the twenty-four Wikipedias that named the current mayor, eight were current because they were querying Wikidata. I hope to see that number go up. Using Wikidata more extensively can, in the long run, allow for more comprehensive, current, and accessible content while decreasing the maintenance load for contributors.[3]

Figure 12.2
The statement in Wikidata about London Breed being mayor of San Francisco.

Wikidata was developed in the spirit of the Wikipedia's increasing drive to add structure to Wikipedia's articles. Examples of this include the introduction of infoboxes as early as 2002—a quick tabular overview of facts about the topic of the article—and categories in 2004. Over the years, the structured features became increasingly intricate: infoboxes moved to templates; templates started using more sophisticated MediaWiki functions and then later demanded the development of even more powerful MediaWiki features. To maintain the structured data, bots were created—software agents that could read content from Wikipedia or other sources and then perform automatic updates to other parts of Wikipedia. Before the introduction of Wikidata, bots keeping the language links between the different Wikipedias in sync and easily contributed 50 percent and more of all edits in many language editions.

Wikidata allowed for an outlet to many of these activities and relieved the Wikipedias of having to run bots to keep language links in sync or to run massive infobox maintenance tasks. But one lesson I learned from these activities is that I can trust the communities with mastering complex work flows spread out among community members with different capabilities: in fact, a small number of contributors working on intricate template code and developing bots can provide invaluable support to contributors who focus more on maintaining articles and contributors who write the majority of the prose. The community is very heterogeneous, and the different capabilities and backgrounds complement each other to create Wikipedia.

However, Wikidata's structured claims are of a limited expressivity: their subject always must be the topic of the page; every object of a statement must exist as its own item and thus as a page in Wikidata. If it doesn't fit in the rigid data model of Wikidata, it simply cannot be captured in Wikidata— and if it cannot be captured in Wikidata, it cannot be made accessible to the Wikipedias.[4]

For example, let's take a look at the following two sentences from the English Wikipedia article on Ontario, California:

> To impress visitors and potential settlers with the abundance of water in Ontario, a fountain was placed at the Southern Pacific railway station. It was turned on when passenger trains were approaching and frugally turned off again after their departure.

There is no feasible way to express the content of these two sentences in Wikidata—the simple claim and qualifier structure that Wikidata supports cannot capture the subtle situation that is described here.

An Abstract Wikipedia

I suggest that the Wikimedia movement develop an Abstract Wikipedia, a Wikipedia in which the actual textual content is being represented in a language-independent manner. This is an ambitious goal[5]—it requires us to push the current limits of knowledge representation,[6] natural language generation,[7] and collaborative knowledge construction[8] by a significant amount. An Abstract Wikipedia must allow for:

1. relations that connect more than just two participants with heterogeneous roles;
2. composition of items on the fly from values and other items;
3. the expression of knowledge about arbitrary subjects, not just the topic of the page;
4. the ordering of content, to be able to represent a narrative structure; and
5. the expression of redundant information.

Let us explore the last of these requirements: unlike the sentences of a declarative formal knowledge base, human language is usually highly redundant. Formal knowledge bases usually try to avoid redundancy, for good reason. But in a natural language text, redundancy happens frequently. One example is the following sentence:

> Marie Curie is the only person who received two Nobel Prizes in two different sciences.

The sentence is redundant given a list of Nobel Prize award winners and their respective disciplines they have been awarded to—a list that basically every large Wikipedia will contain. But the content of the given sentence nevertheless appears in many of the different language articles on Marie Curie, usually in the first paragraph. So there is obviously something very interesting in this sentence, even though the knowledge expressed in this sentence is already fully contained in most of the Wikipedias it appears in. This form of redundancy is commonplace in natural language—but is usually avoided in formal knowledge bases.

The technical details of the Abstract Wikipedia proposal are presented elsewhere.[9] But the technical architecture is only half of the story. Much more important is the question of whether the communities can meet the challenges of this project.

Wikipedia and Wikidata have shown that the communities are capable of meeting difficult challenges—be it templates in Wikipedia, or constraints in Wikidata, the communities have proven that they can drive comprehensive policy and work-flow changes as well as the necessary technological feature development. Not everyone needs to understand the whole stack to make a feature such as templates a crucial part of Wikipedia.

The Abstract Wikipedia is an ambitious future project. I believe that this is the only way for the Wikimedia movement to achieve its goal, short of developing an artificial intelligence that will make the writing of a comprehensive encyclopedia obsolete anyway.

A Plea for Knowledge Diversity?

When presenting the idea of the Abstract Wikipedia, the first question is usually, "Will this not massively reduce the knowledge diversity of Wikipedia?"[10] By unifying the content between the different language editions, does this not force a single point of view on all languages? Is the Abstract Wikipedia taking away the ability of minority language speakers to maintain their own encyclopedias, to have a space where, for example, indigenous speakers can foster and grow their own point of view, without being forced to unify under the Western US-dominated perspective?

I am sympathetic with the intent of this question. The goal of this question is to ensure that a rich diversity in knowledge is retained and that minority groups have spaces in which they can express themselves and keep their knowledge alive. These are, in my opinion, valuable goals.

The assumption that an Abstract Wikipedia, from which any of the individual language Wikipedias can draw content, will necessarily reduce this diversity is false. In fact, I believe that access to more knowledge and to more perspectives is crucial to achieve an effective knowledge diversity and that the currently perceived knowledge diversity in different language projects is ineffective at best and harmful at worst. In the rest of this essay I will argue why this is the case.

Language Does Not Align with Culture

First, it is wrong to use language as the dimension along which to draw the demarcation line among different content if the Wikimedia movement truly believes that different groups should be able to grow and maintain their own encyclopedias.

In case the Wikimedia movement truly believes that different groups or cultures should have their own Wikipedias, why is there only a single Wikipedia language edition for the English speakers from India, England, Scotland, Australia, the United States, and South Africa? Why is there only one Wikipedia for Brazil and Portugal, leading to much strife? Why aren't there two Wikipedias for US Democrats and Republicans?

The conclusion is that the Wikimedia movement does not believe that language is the right dimension to split knowledge—it is a historical decision, driven by convenience. The core Wikipedia policies, vision, and mission are all geared toward enabling access to the sum of all knowledge to every single reader, no matter what their language, and not toward capturing all knowledge and then subdividing it for consumption based on the languages the reader is comfortable in.

The split along languages leads to the problem that it is much easier for a small language community to go "off the rails"—either to become heavily biased as a whole or to adopt rules and processes which are problematic. The fact that the larger communities have different rules, processes, and outcomes can be beneficial for Wikipedia as a whole since they can experiment with different rules and approaches. But this does not seem to hold true when the communities drop under a certain size and activity level, when there are not enough eyeballs to avoid the development of bad outcomes and traditions. For one example, the article about skirts in the Bavarian Wikipedia features three upskirt pictures—one porn actress, an anime screenshot, and a video showing a drawing of a woman with a skirt getting continuously shorter. The article became like this within a day or two of its creation and, even though it has been edited by a dozen different accounts since then, has remained like this over the last seven years. (This describes the state of the article as of this writing—I hope that with the publication of this chapter, the article will finally be cleaned up).

A Look on Some South Slavic Language Wikipedias

Second, a natural experiment is going on where contributors that are more separated by politics than language differences have separate Wikipedias. There exist individual Wikipedia language editions for Croatian, Serbian,

Bosnian, and Serbo-Croatian. Linguistically, the differences among the dialects of Croatian are often larger than the differences between standard Croatian and standard Serbian. Particularly, the existence of the Serbo-Croatian Wikipedia poses interesting questions about these delineations.

The Croatian Wikipedia has turned to a point of view that has been described as problematic. Certain events and Croat actors during the 1990s independence wars or the 1940s fascist puppet state might be represented more favorably than in most other Wikipedias.[11]

Here are two observations based on my work on south Slavic language Wikipedias.

First, claiming that a more fascist-friendly point of view within a Wikipedia increases the knowledge diversity across all Wikipedias might be technically true but is practically insufficient. Being able to benefit from this diversity requires the reader not only to be comfortable reading several different languages but also to engage deeply enough and spend the time and interest to actually read the article in different languages, which is mostly a profoundly boring exercise since a lot of the content will be overlapping. Finding the juicy differences is anything but easy, especially considering that most readers are reading Wikipedia from mobile devices and are just looking to satisfy a quick information need from a source whose curation they trust.

Most readers will only read a single language version of an article, and thus any diversity that exists across different language editions is practically lost. The sheer existence of this diversity might even be counterproductive as one may argue that the communities should not spend resources on reflecting the true diversity of a topic within each individual language. This would cement the practical uselessness of the knowledge diversity across languages.

Second, many of the same contributors that write the articles with a certain point of view in the Croatian Wikipedia also contribute on the English Wikipedia on the articles about the same topics—but there they suddenly are forced and able to compromise and incorporate a much wider variety of points of view. One might hope the contributors would take the more diverse points of view and migrate them back to their home Wikipedias—but that is often not the case. If contributors harbor a certain point of view (and who doesn't?), it often leads to a situation where they push that point of view as much as they can get away with in each of the projects.

It has to be noted that the most blatant digressions from a neutral point of view in Wikipedias like the Croatian Wikipedia will not be found in the most central articles but in the large periphery of articles surrounding these central articles, which are much harder to keep an eye on.

Abstract Wikipedia and Knowledge Diversity

The Abstract Wikipedia proposal does not require any of the individual language editions to use it. Each language community can decide for each article whether to fall back on the Abstract Wikipedia or whether to create their own article in their language. And even that decision can be more fine-grained: for an individual article, a contributor can decide to incorporate sections or paragraphs from the Abstract Wikipedia.

This allows the individual Wikipedia communities the luxury to entirely concentrate on the differences that are relevant to them. I distinctly remember the situation when I started the Croatian Wikipedia: it felt like I had the burden to first write an article about every country in the world before I could write the articles I cared about, such as my mother's home village—because how could anyone defend a general purpose encyclopedia that might not even have an article on Nigeria, a country with a population of a hundred million, but an article on Donji Humac, a village with a population of 157? Wouldn't you first need an article on all of the chemical elements that make up the world before you can write about a local food?

The Abstract Wikipedia frees a language edition from this burden and allows each community to entirely focus on the parts they care about most—and to simply import the articles from the common source for the topics that are less within their focus. It allows the community to make these decisions. As the communities grow and shift, they can revisit these decisions at any time and adapt them.

At the same time, the Abstract Wikipedia makes these differences more visible since they become explicit. Right now there is no easy way to say whether the fact that Dianne Feinstein is listed as the mayor of San Francisco in the Cebuano Wikipedia is due to cultural particularities of the Cebuano language communities or not. Are the different population numbers of Frankfurt in the different language editions intentional expressions of knowledge diversity? With an Abstract Wikipedia, the individual communities could explicitly choose which articles to create and maintain on their own, and at the same time remove a lot of unintentional differences.

By making these decisions more explicit, it becomes possible to imagine an effective workflow that observes these intentional differences and that sets up a path to integrate them into the common article in the Abstract Wikipedia. Right now, there are 166 different language versions of the article on the chemical element helium—it is basically impossible for a single person to go through all of them and find the content that is intentionally different between them. With an Abstract Wikipedia, which contains commonly shared knowledge, contributors, researchers, and readers can actually take a look at those articles that intentionally have content replacing or adding to the text of the commonly shared one, assess these differences, and see if contributors should integrate the differences in the shared article.

The differences in content may be reflecting difference in policies, particularly in policies of notability and reliability. Whereas on first glance it might seem that the Abstract Wikipedia might require unified notability and reliability requirements across all Wikipedias, this is not the case: due to the fact that local Wikipedias can overlay and suppress content from the Abstract Wikipedia, they can adjust the content displayed on their local Wikipedia based on their own rules. And the increased visibility of such decisions will lead to more easily identified biases and hopefully also to updated rules to reduce said bias.

A New Incentive Infrastructure

The Abstract Wikipedia will evolve the incentive infrastructure of Wikipedia.

Presently, many underrepresented languages are spoken in areas that are multilingual. Often another language spoken in this area is regarded as a high-prestige language and is thus the language of education and literature, whereas the underrepresented language is a low-prestige language. So even though the low-prestige language might have more speakers, the most likely recruits for the Wikipedia communities—people with education who can afford internet access and have enough spare time—will be able to contribute in either of the two languages.

In which language should I contribute? If I write the article about my mother's home town in Croatian, I make it accessible to a few million people. If I write the article about my mother's home town in English, it becomes accessible to more than a hundred times as many people! The work might be the same, but the perceived benefit is orders of magnitude higher: the question becomes, do I teach the world about a local tradition, or do I tell my own people about their tradition? The world is bigger and thus more likely to react, creating a positive feedback loop.

This cannibalizes the communities for local languages by diverting them to the English Wikipedia, which is perceived as the global knowledge community (or to other high-prestige languages, such as Russian or French). This is also reflected in a lot of articles in the press and in academic works about Wikipedia, where the English Wikipedia is being understood as *the* Wikipedia. Whereas it is known that Wikipedia exists in many other languages, journalists and researchers are, often unintentionally, regarding the English Wikipedia as the One True Wikipedia.

Another strong impediment to recruiting contributors to smaller Wikipedia communities is rarely explicitly called out. It is pretty clear that, given the current architecture, these Wikipedias are doomed in achieving their mission. As discussed above, more than half of all Wikipedia language editions have fewer than ten active contributors—and writing a comprehensive, up-to-date Wikipedia is not an achievable goal with so few people writing in their free time. The translation tools offered by the Wikimedia Foundation can considerably help within certain circumstances[12]—but for most of the Wikipedia languages, automatic translation models don't even exist and thus cannot help the languages which would need it the most.

With the Abstract Wikipedia, though, the goal of providing a comprehensive and current encyclopedia in almost any language becomes much more tangible. Instead of taking on the task of creating and maintaining the entire content, only the grammatical and lexical knowledge of a given language needs to be created. This is a far smaller task. Further, this grammatical and lexical knowledge is comparably static—it does not change as much as the encyclopedic content of Wikipedia, thus turning a task that is huge and ongoing into one where the content will grow and be maintained without the need of too much maintenance by the individual language communities.

Yes, the Abstract Wikipedia will require more and different capabilities from a community that has yet to be found, and the challenges will be both novel and big. But the communities of the many Wikimedia projects have repeatedly shown that they can meet complex challenges with ingenious combinations of processes and technological advancements.[13] Wikipedia and Wikidata have both demonstrated the ability to draw on technologically rather simple canvases and create extraordinary rich and complex master-pieces that stand the test of time. The Abstract Wikipedia aims to challenge the communities once again, and the promise this time is nothing else but to finally be able to reap the ultimate goal: to allow every one, no matter what their native language is, to share in the sum of all knowledge.

Acknowledgments: Thanks to the valuable suggestions on improving the article to Jamie Taylor, Daniel Russell, Joseph Reagle, Stephen LaPorte, and Jake Orlowitz.

Notes

1. Patti Bao, Brent J. Hecht, Samuel Carton, Mahmood Quaderi, Michael S. Horn, and Darren Gergle, "Omnipedia: Bridging the Wikipedia Language Gap," in *CHI '12: Proceedings of the Conference on Human Factors in Computing Systems*, ed. Joseph A. Konstan, Ed H. Chi, and Kristina Höök (New York: ACM, 2012), 1075–1084.

2. Denny Vrandečić and Markus Krötzsch, "Wikidata: A Free Collaborative Knowl-edgebase," *Communications of the ACM* 57, no. 10 (October 2014): 78–85, https://doi .org/10.1145/2629489.

3. Lucie-Aimée Kaffee, Hady ElSahar, Pavlos Vougiouklis, Christophe Gravier, Fré-dérique Laforest, Jonathon S. Hare, and Elena Simperl, "Mind the (Language) Gap: Generation of Multilingual Wikipedia Summaries from Wikidata for Article Place-holders," in *Proceedings of the 15th European Semantic Web Conference (ESWC 2018)*, ed. Aldo Gangemi, Roberto Navigli, Marie-Esther Vidal, Pascal Hitzler, Raphaël Troncy, Laura Hollink, Anna Tordai, and Mehwish Alam (Berlin: Springer, 2018), 319–334; Lucie-Aimée Kaffee, Hady ElSahar, Pavlos Vougiouklis, Christophe Gravier, Frédérique Laforest, Jonathon S. Hare, and Elena Simperl, "Learning to Generate Wikipedia Summaries for Underserved Languages from Wikidata," in *Proceedings of the 2018 Conference of the North American Chapter of the Association for Computational Linguistics: Human Language Technologies*, vol. 2, ed. Marilyn Walker, Heng Ji, and Amanda Stent (Stroudsburg, PA: ACL, 2018), 640–645.

4. Denny Vrandečić, "Restricting the World," *Wikimedia Deutschland (blog)*, Febru-ary 22, 2013, https://blog.wikimedia.de/2013/02/22/restricting-the-world/.

5. Umberto Eco, *The Search for the Perfect Language (The Making of Europe)*, trans. James Fentress (Oxford, UK: Blackwell, 1995).

6. Anna Wierzbicka, *Semantics: Primes and Universals* (Oxford, UK: Oxford Univer-sity Press, 1996); Thomas Hoffmann and Graeme Trousdale, "Construction Gram-mar: Introduction," in *The Oxford Handbook of Construction Grammar*, ed. Thomas

Hoffmann and Graeme Trousdale (Oxford, UK: Oxford University Press, 2013), 1–14.

7. Aarne Ranta, *Grammatical Framework: Programming with Multilingual Grammars* (Stanford, CA: CSLI Publications, 2011).

8. Kaarel Kaljurand and Tobias Kuhn, "A Multilingual Semantic Wiki Based on Attempto Controlled English and Grammatical Framework," in *Proceedings of the 10th European Semantic Web Conference (ESWC 2013)*, ed. Philipp Cimiano, Oscar Corcho, Valentina Presutti, Laura Hollink, and Sebastian Rudolph (Berlin: Springer, 2013), 427–441; Wikidata, s.v. "Wikidata: Lexicographical data," accessed June 1, 2019, https://www.wikidata.org/wiki/Wikidata:Lexicographical_data.

9. Denny Vrandečić, "Towards a Multilingual Wikipedia," in *Proceedings of the 31st International Workshop on Description Logics (DL 2018)*, ed. Magdalena Ortiz and Thomas Schneider (Aachen: Ceur-WS, 2018).

10. Mark Graham, "The Problem with Wikidata," *The Atlantic*, April 6, 2012, https://www.theatlantic.com/technology/archive/2012/04/the-problem-with-wikidata/255564/.

11. Sven Milekić, "Croatian-Language Wikipedia: When the Extreme Right Rewrites History," *Osservatorio Balcani e Caucaso*, September 27, 2018, https://www.balcanicaucaso.org/eng/Areas/Croatia/Croatian-language-Wikipedia-when-the-extreme-right-rewrites-history-190081.

12. Ellery Wulczyn, Robert West, Leila Zia, and Jure Leskovec, "Growing Wikipedia Across Languages via Recommendation," in *Proceedings of the 25th International World-Wide Web Conference (WWW 2016)*, ed. Jaqueline Bourdeau, Jim Hendler, Roger Nkambou, Ian Horrocks, and Ben Y. Zhao (New York: ACM, 2016), 975–985.

13. Mathias Schindler and Denny Vrandečić, "Introducing New Features to Wikipedia: Case Studies for Web Science," *IEEE Intelligent Systems* 26, no. 1 (January–February 2011): 56–61.

13　Rise of the Underdog

Heather Ford

Although it is more powerful than it has ever been, Wikipedia is reliant on third parties who are increasingly ingesting its facts and severing them from their source. To survive, Wikipedia needs to initiate a renewed campaign for the right to verifiability.

We all love an underdog. And when *Nature* announced that Wikipedia's quality was almost as good as *Encyclopædia Britannica* for articles about science in 2005, I celebrated. I celebrated because Wikipedia was the David to Big Media's Goliath—the little guy, the people's encyclopedia, the underdog who had succeeded against all odds.

Since then, Wikipedia has moved from the thirty-seventh most visited website in the world into the top ten. Wikipedia is now the top dog for facts as the world's most powerful platforms extract information from Wikipedia articles to fuel the question-and-answer systems that drive search engines like Google and digital assistants including Amazon's Alexa, Apple's Siri, and Google's Assistant.

It is tempting to see Wikipedia in 2020 as the new top dog in the world of facts. The problem is that Wikipedia's status is dependent almost entirely on Google, and the ways in which Wikipedia's content is increasingly represented without credit by major platforms signals Wikipedia's greatest existential threat to date.

Removing links back to Wikipedia as the source of answers to user questions prevents users from visiting Wikipedia to donate or volunteer. More important, however, are the ways in which unattributed facts violate the principle of verifiability on which Wikipedia was founded.

Within the bounds of Wikipedia, users are able to question whether statements are correctly attributed to reliable sources. They are able to contribute to discussions toward consensus and to recognize the traces that signal how unstable or stable statements of fact are. But when those statements are represented without attribution or links back to their messy political and social contexts, they appear as the objective, natural, and stable truth.

In 2020, there are new Goliaths in town in the form of the world's most powerful technology companies, and Wikipedia must rearticulate its foundational principles and highlight its underdog status if it wishes to reinstitute itself as a bastion of justice on the internet.

Once the Underdog

The underdog is a common archetype of some of the most enduring narratives, from the world of sport to politics. Studying the appeal of underdogs over a number of years, Vandello, Goldschmied, and Michniewicz define underdogs as "disadvantaged parties facing advantaged opponents and unlikely to succeed."[1] They write that there are underdog stories from cultures around the world: from the story of David and Goliath, in which the smaller David fights and kills the giant, Goliath, to the Monkey and the Turtle, a Philippine fable in which the patient turtle outwits the physically stronger and selfish monkey.

Underdogs are appealing because they offer an opportunity for redemption—a chance for the weaker individual or group to face a stronger opponent and to beat them, despite the odds leaning significantly against them. Usually, underdogs face off to better resourced competitors in a zero-sum game such as an election or sporting match, but underdogs don't need to win to be appealing. As Vandello, Goldschmied, and Michniewicz state: they just have to *face up* to the bigger, more powerful, better resourced competitor in order to win the hearts of the public.

With the headline "Internet Encyclopaedias Go Head to Head" (see chapter 2), a *Nature* study represented such a competition when it was published in 2005.[2] The study pitted a four-year-old Wikipedia against the centuries-old *Britannica* by asking academic experts to compare forty-two articles relating to science. The verdict? The average science entry in Wikipedia contained around four inaccuracies to *Britannica*'s three, leading *Nature* to announce that "Jimmy Wales' Wikipedia comes close to *Britannica* in terms of the accuracy of its science entries."

The *Nature* study is now the stuff of legend. Although it was criticized for the way that articles were compared and the way that the study was reported, it is mostly used as evidence of the quality of Wikipedia in comparison with traditionally authored reference works.[3] For those of us working in the free and open source software and open content movement, it confirmed what we already thought we knew: that online resources like Wikipedia could attain the same (if not greater) level of quality that traditionally published resources enjoyed because they were open for the public to improve. It gave credence to the idea that content as well as software benefited from openness because, as Eric Raymond famously wrote, "with enough eyes, all bugs are shallow."[4]

In 2005, Wikipedia was being developed on the back of volunteer labor, a handful of paid employees, and a tiny budget. In 2005, I was deep into my tenure as a digital commons activist. As the public lead for Creative Commons South Africa, the executive director of iCommons, and the advisory board of the Wikimedia Foundation, I was in the business of selling openness to the world. In photographs from 2005, I see myself smiling, surrounded by like-minded people from around the world who would meet at the annual iCommons Summit or Wikimania. We would talk about how copyleft was critical to a more innovative internet. For me, freedom and openness via copyleft licenses provided the opportunity for greater access to educational materials critical for countries like my own, burdened by extreme copyright regimes that benefited corporate publishing houses outside of South Africa at the expense of access to knowledge. I believed that open content and free and open source software was in keeping with the sharing of culture emblematic of *Ubuntu*, the Zulu and Xhosa term for "humanity toward others"—the belief in a universal bond that connects people around the world.

Life as an "internet rights activist" wasn't all glamorous. Back home in Johannesburg, it meant countless meetings with anyone who would listen. Talking to funders, academics, lawyers, musicians, publishers, and authors, we would present copyleft as an obvious choice for public knowledge, creativity, education, and creative industries to tiny audiences of skeptical or curious individuals. In my case, it meant tears of frustration when debating intellectual property lawyers about the virtues of the South African Constitutional Court's finding in favor of the trademark dispute between a young T-shirt producer and a multinational beer company. And righteous indignation when hearing about underhanded attempts by large software corporations to stem the tide of open source to protect their hold on public education in Namibia.

I celebrated Wikipedia's success because it was a signal from the establishment that openness was a force to be recognized. I celebrated because Wikipedia had become emblematic of the people of the internet's struggle against Big Media. It signaled success against corporate media giants like the Motion Picture Association of America and its members who were railing aggressively against the ideology and practice of free and open source software and open content because it was considered a significant threat to their business models. In 2005, the peer-to-peer firms Napster, Grokster, and StreamCast had been successfully sued by rights holders, and Lawrence Lessig had lost his case to prevent the US Congress from extending US copyright terms. We all needed a hero, and we needed a few wins under our righteous belts.

When the *Nature* study was published in 2005, Wikipedia represented "the people of the internet" against an old (and sizeable) Big Media who railed against any change that would see them threatened. Ironically, the company behind the *Encyclopædia Britannica* was actually ailing when the *Nature* study drove the final nail into its coffin. But no matter: *Britannica* represented the old and Wikipedia the new. A year later, in 2006, Time Magazine's Person of the Year reinforced this win. Awarding the Person of the Year to "You," the editorial argued that ordinary people now controlled the means of producing information and media because they dissolved the power of the gatekeepers who had previously controlled the public's access to information.

> [The year 2006 is] a story about community and collaboration on a scale never seen before. It's about the cosmic compendium of knowledge Wikipedia and the million-channel people's network YouTube and the online metropolis MySpace. It's about the many wresting power from the few and helping one another for nothing and how that will not only change the world, but also change the way the world changes.[5]

It is this symbolic value that makes underdogs so powerful. Vandello, Goldschmied, and Michniewicz argue that we root for underdogs not only because we want them to succeed but also because we feel "it is right and just for them to do so." We dislike the fact that there is inequality in society—that some individuals or groups face a much more difficult task because they are underresourced. Rooting for the underdog enables us to reconcile or face this injustice (albeit from a distance).

Wikipedia Wars

With few resources and Big Media set against them, Wikipedia was once seen as the underdog to traditional media. As the bastion of openness against the selfishness of proprietary media, its fight was seen as a just one. This was fifteen years ago and now much is changed.

The encyclopedia that was pitted as Wikipedia's competitor, *Britannica*, is now all but dead (the final print version was published in 2010). Wikipedia has moved from the thirty-seventh most visited website in the world when *Nature* published its study in 2005 to within the top ten with many billions of page views a month.

Donations to Wikipedia's host nonprofit, the Wikimedia Foundation, increased dramatically—from about $1.5 million in 2006 to almost $100 million in 2018. From St. Petersburg, Florida, with three employees to corporate headquarters in the heart of San Francisco, California, and a staff of over 250, the Wikimedia Foundation's operating budget and cash reserves are so healthy that some have argued that Wikipedia doesn't need your donations and that the increased budget is turning the Foundation into a corporate behemoth that is unaccountable to its volunteers.[6]

If there is a political battle being fought—between politicians, policies, ideologies or identities—there will be a parallel conflict on Wikipedia. On English Wikipedia, for example, Donald Trump's page is in a constant state of war. In 2018, an edit war ensued about whether to include information about Trump's performance at the 2018 US-Russia summit in Helsinki.[7] On the Brexit article, editors have received death threats and dox attempts when editing information about the impact of Brexit on the United Kingdom and Europe.[8] After Time Magazine published a story by Aatish Tasser that was critical of Indian Prime Minister Narendra Modi, Tasser's English Wikipedia page was vandalized, and screenshots of the vandalized page were distributed over social media as evidence.[9]

The above examples relate to obviously political subjects, but Wikipedia wars are being fought beyond the bounds of politicians' biographies. Representation of current events on Wikipedia is almost always hotly contested. For almost every terrorist attack, natural disaster, or political protest, there will be attempts by competing groups to wrest control over the event narrative on Wikipedia to reflect their version of what happened, to whom it happened, and the reason why it happened. Unexpected events have consequences—for victims, perpetrators, and the governments who distribute resources as a result of such classifications. Wikipedia is therefore regularly the site of battles over what becomes recognized as the neutral point of view, the objective fact, the commonsense perspectives affecting the decisions that ultimately determine who the winners and losers are in the aftermath of an event.

Because of Wikipedia's growing authority, governments now block the site to prevent it from being used to distribute what they deem to be subversive ideas. Wikipedia is currently blocked in China and Turkey, but countries including France, Iran, Pakistan, Russia, Thailand, Tunisia, the United Kingdom, and Venezuela have blocked specific content from a period of a few days to many years.

In 2013, it was found that Iran's censorship of Persian Wikipedia targeted a wide breadth of political, social, religious, and sexual themes, including information related to the Iranian government's human rights record and individuals who have challenged authorities.[10] In the United Kingdom, the Wikipedia article about "Virgin Killer," an album by the German rock band Scorpions, was blacklisted for three days by the Internet Watch Foundation when the album cover image was classified as child pornography. In early 2019, all language editions of Wikipedia were blocked in Venezuela probably because of a Wikipedia article that listed newly appointed National Assembly president Juan Guaidó as "president number 51 of the Bolivarian Republic of Venezuela," thus challenging Nicolás Maduro' s presidency.[11]

How has representation on Wikipedia come to matter so much? The answer is that Wikipedia matters more in the context of the even more powerful third-party platforms that make use of its content than the way it represents subjects on its articles. What matters most is not so much how facts are represented on Wikipedia but how facts that originate on Wikipedia travel to other platforms.

Ask Google who the president of Uganda is or who won MasterChef Australia last year and the results will probably be sourced from (English) Wikipedia in a special "knowledge panel" featured on the right-hand side of the search results and in featured snippets at the top of organic search results. Ask Siri the same questions, and she will probably provide you with an answer that was originally extracted as data from Wikipedia.

Information in Wikipedia articles is being increasingly datafied and extracted by third parties to feed a new generation of question-and-answer machines. If one can control how Wikipedia defines and represents a person, place, event, or thing, then one can control how it is represented not only on Wikipedia but also on Google, Apple, Amazon, and other major platforms. This has not gone unnoticed by the many search engine optimizers, marketers, public relations, and political agents who send their representatives to do battle over facts on Wikipedia.

New Goliaths

From all appearances, then, Wikipedia is now the top dog in the world of facts. Look a little deeper into how Wikipedia arrived at this point and what role it is playing in the new web ecosystem, however, and the picture becomes a little muddier. The printed *Britannica* may be dead and Wikipedia may be the most popular encyclopedia, but Wikipedia is now more than just an encyclopedia, and there are new Goliaths on which Wikipedia is so dependent for its success that they could very easily wipe Wikipedia off the face of the internet.

Google has always prioritized Wikipedia entries in search results, and this is the primary way through which users have discovered Wikipedia content. But in 2012, Google announced a new project that would change how it organized search results. In a blog post entitled "Things, Not Strings," the vice president of engineering for Google, Amit Singhal, wrote that Google was using Wikipedia and other public data sources to seed a Knowledge Graph that would provider "smarter search results" for users.[12] In addition to returning a list of possible results—including Wikipedia articles when a user searched for "Marie Curie," for example—Google would present a "knowledge panel" on the right hand side of the page that would "summarize relevant content around that topic, including key facts you're likely to need for that particular thing."[13]

Soon after Google's announcement, former head of research at the Wikimedia Foundation, Dario Taraborelli, started taking notice of how Google represented information from Wikipedia in its knowledge panels. One of the first iterations featured a prominent backlink to Wikipedia next to each of the facts under the opening paragraph. There was even reference to the

Creative Commons Attribution ShareAlike license that Wikipedia content is licensed under. But, as the panels evolved, blue links to Wikipedia articles started shrinking in size. Over time, the underscore was removed so that the links weren't clickable, and then the links were lightened to a barely visible grey tone. Now, facts under the opening paragraph tend not to be cited at all, and hyperlinked statements refer back to other Google pages.

Taraborelli was concerned at how dependent Wikipedia was on Google and at how changes being made to the way that Wikipedia content was being presented by the search giant could have a significant impact on the sustainability of Wikipedia. If users were being presented with information from Wikipedia without having to visit the site or without even knowing that Wikipedia was the true source, then that would surely affect the numbers of users visiting Wikipedia—as readers, editors, or contributors to the annual fund-raising campaign. These fears were confirmed by research conducted by McMahon, Johnson, and Hecht, who found that facts in the knowledge panels were being predominantly sourced from Wikipedia but that these were "almost never cited" and that this was leading to a significant reduction in traffic to Wikipedia.[14]

Taraborelli was also concerned with a more fundamental principle at issue here: that Google's use of Wikipedia information without credit "undermines people's ability to verify information and, ultimately, to develop well-informed opinions."[15] Verifiability is one of Wikipedia's core content policies. It is defined as the ability for "readers [to be] able to check that any of the information within Wikipedia articles is not just made up."[16]

For editors, verifiability means that "all material must be attributable to reliable, published sources."[17] Wikipedia's verifiability policy, in other words, establishes rights for readers and responsibilities for editors. Readers should have the right to be able to check whether information from Wikipedia is accurately represented by the reliable source from which it originates. Editors should ensure that all information is attributable to reliable sources and that information that is likely to be challenged should be attributed using in-text citations.

It is easy to see Wikipedia as a victim of Google's folly here. The problem is that a project within the Wikimedia stable, Wikidata, has done exactly the same thing—as Andreas Kolbe pointed out in response to the *Washington Post* story about Google's knowledge boxes.[18] As Wikidata's founder, Denny Vrandečić, describes in chapter 12, the project was launched to help efforts just like Google's to better represent Wikipedia's facts by serving as a central storage of structured data for Wikimedia projects. Yet, Wikidata has been populated by millions of statements that are either uncredited to a reliable source or attributed to the entire Wikipedia language version from where they were extracted. The latter does not meet the requirements for verifiability, one of Wikipedia's foundational principles, because it does not enable downstream users the ability to verify or check whether the statements are, indeed, reflective of their source or whether the source itself is reliable.

A number of Wikipedians voiced concern over Wikidata's apparent unconcern with the need for accurate source information for its millions of claims. Andreas Kolbe has contributed multiple articles about the problems with Wikidata. He wrote an op-ed about Wikidata in December 2015 as a counterpoint to the celebratory piece that had been published about the project the month prior.[19]

Kolbe made three observations about the quality of content on Wikidata. The first was the problem of unreferenced or underreferenced claims (more than half of the claims at that time were unreferenced). Second was the fact that Wikidata was extracting facts from Wikipedia and then presenting them under a more permissible copyright license than that of Wikipedia, giving the green light to third-party users like Google to use that content unattributed. And third was that there were problems with the quality of information on Wikidata because of its lack of stringent quality controls.

Kolbe noted a list of "Hoaxes long extinguished on Wikipedia live on, zombie-like, in Wikidata."[20] Wikidata represents a strategic opportunity for search engine optimization specialists and public relations professionals to influence search results. Without stringent quality control mechanisms, however, inaccurate information could be replicated and mirrored on more authoritative platforms which would multiply their detrimental effects.

In the past few years, the list of major platforms making use of Wikipedia information (either directly or via Wikidata) has grown. Now the most important reusers are digital assistants in the form of Amazon's Alexa, Apple's Siri, and Google's Assistant, who answer user questions authoritatively using Wikipedia information. The loss of citations and links back to Wikipedia has grown alongside them as problems of citation loss with Google and Wikidata have been replicated.

The problem, then, is about the process of automated extraction and the logics of knowledge bases more generally than it is about the particular practices by specific companies or organizations. In 2015 and 2016, I wrote a series of articles about this problem with Mark Graham from the Oxford Internet Institute while I was a PhD student there. We argued that the process of automation in the context of the knowledge base had both practical and ethical implications for internet users.[21]

From a practical perspective, we noted that information became less nuanced and its provenance or source obscured. The ethical case involved the loss of agency by users to contest information when that information is transported to third parties like Google. When incorrect information is not linked back to Wikipedia, users are only able to click on a link. There are no clear policies on how information can be changed or who is accountable for that information.

In one case, a journalist whose information was incorrectly appearing in the knowledge panel was informed by Google to submit feedback from multiple internet protocol (IP) addresses—every three or four days, multiple times, using different logins and to "get more people to help you submit feedback."[22] This does not constitute a policy on rectifying false information. Compare Wikipedia's editorial system with its transparent (albeit multitudinous) policies, and one realizes how the datafication of Wikipedia content has removed important rights from internet users.

The Right to Verifiability

Wikipedia was once celebrated because it was seen as the underdog to Big Media. As Wikipedia has become increasingly powerful as a strategic resource for the production of knowledge about the world, battles over representation of its statements have intensified. Wikipedia is strategic today, not only because of how people, places, events, and things are represented in its articles, but also because of the ways in which those articles have become fodder for search engines and digital assistants. From its early prioritization in search results, Wikipedia's facts are now increasingly extracted without credit by artificial intelligence processes that consume its knowledge and present it as objective fact.

As one of most popular websites in the world, it is tempting in 2020 to see Wikipedia as a top dog in the world of facts, but the consumption of Wikipedia's knowledge without credit introduces Wikipedia's greatest existential threat to date. This is not just because of the ways in which third-party actors appropriate Wikipedia content and remove the links that might sustain the community in terms of contributions of donations and volunteer time. More important is that unsourced Wikipedia content threatens the principle of verifiability, one of the fundamental principles on which Wikipedia was built.

Verifiability sets up a series of rights and obligations by readers and editors of Wikipedia to knowledge whose political and social status is transparent. By removing direct links to the Wikipedia article where statements originate from, search engines and digital assistants are removing the clues that readers could use to (a) evaluate the veracity of claims and (b) take active steps to change that information through consensus if they feel that it is false. Without the source of factual statements being attributed to Wikipedia, users will see those facts as solid, incontrovertible truth, when in reality they may have been extracted during a process of consensus building or at the moment in which the article was vandalized.

Until now, platform companies have been asked to contribute to the Wikimedia Foundation's annual fund-raising campaign to "give back" to what they are taking out of the commons.[23] But contributions of cash will not solve what amounts to Wikipedia's greatest existential threat to date. What is needed is a public campaign to reinstate the principle of verifiability in the content that is extracted from Wikipedia by platform companies. Users need to be able to understand (a) exactly where facts originate, (b) how stable or unstable those statements are, (c) how they might become involved in improving the quality of that information, and (d) the rules under which decisions about representation will be made.

Wikipedia was once recognized as the underdog not only because it was underresourced but also, more importantly, because it represented the just fight against more powerful media who sought to limit the possibilities of people around the world to build knowledge products together. Today, the fight is a new one, and Wikipedia must adapt in order to survive.

Sitting back and allowing platform companies to ingest Wikipedia's knowledge and represent it as the incontrovertible truth rather than the messy and variable truths it actually depicts is an injustice. It is an injustice not only for Wikipedians but also for people around the world who use the resource—either directly on Wikimedia servers or indirectly via other platforms like search.

Notes

1. Joseph A. Vandello, Nadav Goldschmied, and Kenneth Michniewicz, "Underdogs as Heroes," in *Handbook of Heroism and Heroic Leadership*, ed. Scott T. Allison, George R. Goethals, and Roderick M. Kramer (New York: Routledge, 2017), 339–355.

2. Jim Giles, "Internet Encyclopaedias Go Head to Head," *Nature* 438 (December 15, 2005): 900–901.

3. Nature Online, "*Encyclopaedia Britannica* and *Nature*: A Response," press release, March 23, 2006; Andrew Orlowski, "Wikipedia Science 31% More Cronky than Britannica's," *The Register*, December 16, 2005, https://www.theregister.co.uk/2005/12/16/wikipedia_britannica_science_comparison.

4. Eric S. Raymond, *The Cathedral and the Bazaar: Musings on Linux and Open Source by an Accidental Revolutionary* (Sebastopol, CA: O'Reilly Media, 2011).

5. Lev Grossman, "You—Yes, You—Are TIME's Person of the Year," *Time Magazine*, December 25, 2006, http://content.time.com/time/magazine/article/0,9171,1570810,00.html.

6. Caitlin Dewey, "Wikipedia Has a Ton of Money. So Why Is It Begging You to Donate Yours?" *Washington Post*, December 2, 2015, https://www.washingtonpost.com/news/the-intersect/wp/2015/12/02/wikipedia-has-a-ton-of-money-so-why-is-it-begging-you-to-donate-yours/; Andrew Orlowski, "Will Wikipedia Honour Jimbo's Promise to STOP Chugging?" *The Register*, December 16, 2016, https://www.theregister.co.uk/2016/12/16/jimmy_wales_wikipedia_fundraising_promise/.

7. Aaron Mak, "Inside the Brutal, Petty War Over Donald Trump's Wikipedia Page," *Slate*, May 28, 2019, https://slate.com/technology/2019/05/donald-trump-wikipedia-page.html.

8. Matt Reynolds, "A Bitter Turf War Is Raging on the Brexit Wikipedia Page," *Wired UK*, April 29, 2019, https://www.wired.co.uk/article/brexit-wikipedia-page-battles.

9. Aria Thaker, "Indian Election Battles Are Being Fought on Wikipedia, Too," *Quartz India*, May 16, 2019, https://qz.com/india/1620023/aatish-taseers-wikipedia-page-isnt-the-only-target-of-modi-fans/.

10. Nima Nazeri and Collin Anderson, *Citation Filtered: Iran's Censorship of Wikipedia* (University of Pennsylvania Scholarly Commons, November 2013), https://repository.upenn.edu/iranmediaprogram/10/.

11. NetBlocks, "Wikipedia Blocked in Venezuela as Internet Controls Tighten," *NetBlocks*, January 28, 2019, https://netblocks.org/reports/wikipedia-blocked-in-venezuela-as-internet-controls-tighten-XaAwR08M.

12. Amit Singhal, "Introducing the Knowledge Graph: Things, Not Strings," *The Keyword*, May 16, 2012, https://www.blog.google/products/search/introducing-knowledge-graph-things-not/.

13. Singhal, "Introducing the Knowledge Graph."

14. Connor McMahon, Isaac Johnson, and Brent Hecht, "The Substantial Interdependence of Wikipedia and Google: A Case Study on the Relationship between Peer Production Communities and Information Technologies," in *Proceedings of the 11th International Conference on Web and Social Media, ICWSM 2017* (AAAI Press, 2017), 142–151.

15. Quoted in Caitlin Dewey, "You Probably Haven't Even Noticed Google's Sketchy Quest to Control the World's Knowledge," *The Washington Post*, May 11, 2016, https://www.washingtonpost.com/news/the-intersect/wp/2016/05/11/you-probably-havent-even-noticed-googles-sketchy-quest-to-control-the-worlds-knowledge/.

16. Wikipedia, s.v. "Wikipedia: Verifiability," last modified January 13, 2010, https://en.wikipedia.org/wiki/Wikipedia:Verifiability.

17. Wikipedia, s.v. "Wikipedia: Verifiability."

18. "In the Media," Wikimedia Signpost, May 28, 2016, https://en.wikipedia.org/wiki/Wikipedia:Wikipedia_Signpost/2016-05-17/In_the_media.

19. Andreas Kolbe, "Whither Wikidata?" *The Signpost*, December 2, 2015, https://en.wikipedia.org/wiki/Wikipedia:Wikipedia_Signpost/2015-12-02/Op-ed.

20. Kolbe, "Whither Wikidata?"

21. Heather Ford and Mark Graham, "Provenance, Power and Place: Linked Data and Opaque Digital Geographies," *Environment and Planning D: Society and Space 34*, no. 6 (2016): 957–970, https://doi.org/10.1177/0263775816668857; Heather Ford and Mark Graham, "Semantic Cities: Coded Geopolitics and the Rise of the Semantic Web," in *Code and the City*, ed. Rob Kitchin and Sung-Yueh Perng (Oxford, UK: Routledge, 2015).

22. Rachel Abrams, "Google Thinks I'm Dead," *The New York Times*, December 16, 2017, https://www.nytimes.com/2017/12/16/business/google-thinks-im-dead.html.

23. Brian Heater, "Are Corporations that Use Wikipedia Giving Back?" *TechCrunch*, March 24, 2018, https://techcrunch.com/2018/03/24/are-corporations-that-use-wikipedia-giving-back/.

III   Vision

14 Why Do I Have Authority to Edit the Page? The Politics of User Agency and Participation on Wikipedia

Alexandria Lockett

What is the power of Wikipedia for users that frequently consume it but don't feel they have the authority to edit it? Wikipedia's potential to represent the full scope of users' knowledge diversity is inhibited by several barriers that suppress inclusive participation.

My first Wikipedia edit was sometime around 2003. I added a cultural reference that was made during a *South Park* episode. However, when I read the entire article, I decided that it was poorly written and needed much narrative improvement. The style seemed choppy, despite the relative accuracy of content. After providing more transitions and vivid action verbs, I felt as if I had done justice to readers by bringing high-quality writing to the article. I checked the page the next day, and my elegant composition had been overridden by clunky prose full of passive voice and simplistic descriptions. My ego was slightly bruised, but I had learned one of the first major lessons of Wikipedia editing: the community judges whether your edits will stand, and you will need to decide if your work is worth fighting for.

Now, almost twenty years later, Wikipedia is older than my first-year college writing students. It has always been part of their digital lives. Meanwhile, I still have distant memories of the *Encyclopædia Britannica's* large volumes occupying the top row of a dusty bookshelf in someone's living room. Nearly all of my current students are completely unfamiliar with the *Britannica*, with the exception of one or two of them who have casually referred to them as "ancient books" at their grandparent's house. In fact, the word encyclopedia itself is not typically part of the contemporary academic vocabulary. Wikipedia, then, has both displaced a brand of encyclopedias that had defined *the* English encyclopedia for over three centuries and endured almost two decades of criticism about its legitimacy. However, despite Wikipedia's widespread use, its potential as a living archive that is capable of representing the full scope of distributed global knowledge remains untapped. Although it is one of the most popular websites online, the vast majority of its users don't edit the page. This chapter examines the implications of this problem by drawing on my experience as a Black Woman editing Wikipedia—both as a first-time user and as a college writing teacher.

Wikipedia Participation Is a Novel Literacy

Wikipedia was very novel in that 2003 postmillennial scene. I was a queer Black Woman sophomore at a predominantly white college in the rural Midwest with all the time in the world to think. The United States was still panicking about September 11. Deployments to Afghanistan were steadily increasing, and George W. Bush was clumsily selling the idea of an Iraq war to the US Congress and the general public. His plan worked since almost everyone was eager to show their patriotism after the fall of the twin towers. The country muted discussions about race, amplifying color-blind slogans like "We are all Americans" to quell and silence a rise in anti-Muslim violence. Further, it was still very taboo to be out of the closet in America. Gay marriage was still illegal; so too was sodomy under the legal precedent of *Bowers v. Hardwick*.[1] The violent deaths of Matthew Shepard and Brandon Teena were part of national headlines that were putting a spotlight on the prevalence of hate crimes against LGBTQ people.[2] Brown wasn't part of the rainbow.[3] Pride celebrations weren't as commercial or joyously attended by straight people. Conversion therapy was a typical response to coming out in the evangelical Christian household. Some of my gay and lesbian friends who waited to come out of the closet until college were being disowned by their families. In this scene, it was unfashionable to be an antiwar, progay, feminist, and/or an environmental activist, but I was highly visible on campus as part of the leadership board of our campus's small but growing LGBTQ organization—PRISM. As I compose this article, a banner boldly celebrating Pride is inscribed in Wikipedia's top-level header alongside a call for editors to develop LGBTQ content. It is a sight to behold because I never imagined that public attitudes toward LGBTQ identities would transform so rapidly. These details matter because my formative experiences with Wikipedia did not include a focus on making it "equitable" or have an awareness that being a Black Woman editor made much difference at all. In other words, Wikipedia's recognition of social issues was simply not part of a general conversation about user participation in 2003. I will return to this point later in the chapter because the issue of editorial authority depends on the extent to which prospective Wikipedia editors feel as if the community recognizes their knowledge as notable enough to be represented in the space.

My best friend at the time, let's call him Dean—a gay white male computer science major—would implore me to join him for his daily ritual of marveling at Wikipedia. In fact, I was looking up information for my mass communications class when he introduced me to the dynamic and free reference site. Astounded by its growth and mesmerized by a clean, organized interface, we found ourselves always using it. We noticed how the uniformity inspired by the graphic user interface (GUI) made any article *seem* true, but we resisted being tricked into believing false information. For example, when we checked Wikipedia for seemingly innocuous stuff like descriptions of a *South Park* or *Queer as Folk* episode, we would notice errors or missing information about intertextual cultural references. So we edited the page! However, neither of us would have identified as Wikipedians. We didn't create usernames to edit or make editing part of everyday life. Yet, we were both children of the Web 1.0 internet where anonymity was valued and deliberation with strangers was part and parcel of most online communication. We probably took for granted that our sociocultural experience with the internet sponsored our willingness to feel free enough to edit Wikipedia. After all, this was a world before the "nerd revolution" and the highly visible dominance of tech giants like Steve Jobs and Mark Zuckerberg. We were social misfits for being into computers and the internet, so editing Wikipedia hardly seemed risky. It was an occasional—highly contextual—thing to do since we were primarily connected to Wikipedia as consumers. We knew others labored there for free, and we appreciated how useful it was.

Nevertheless, contributing to Wikipedia felt satisfyingly subversive because it was easy and meaningful. In the United States, we have been socialized to navigate bureaucracy's mazes of processing requests—which consists of seemingly never-ending streams of forms to fill out, showing and obtaining government and institutional identification, waiting for the "appropriate person" to verify and authorize documents, submitting your inquiry to the other "appropriate persons" before waiting for any number of business days before you obtain a response that confirms or denies the completion of your requests. As Jean Anyon argued almost forty years ago in her widely cited article, "Social Class and the Hidden Curriculum of Work," the education system tacitly prepares us to accept that we will be socialized into similar occupations as our parents and learn how to be managed in ways that perpetuate class inequality.[4] However, Wikipedia afforded users more autonomy than formal education spaces. I didn't need a username; my internet protocol (IP) was sufficient. I didn't need to have endless credentials or degrees to correct records that people would come to rely on, even if my edit(s) were reverted within seconds.

Wikipedia was clearly shaking up the education system back then, and it continues to be taught as a forbidden space. Throughout my undergraduate studies, my peers and I noticed and discussed that our professors were increasingly issuing threats and warnings about using and citing Wikipedia. They feared that their authority could be undermined by anonymous novices mischievously or haphazardly editing pages. But we weren't stupid. We knew that there was a time and place for Wikipedia, and it wasn't in a college research paper.

Instead, Dean and I thought Wikipedia editing illustrated the liberatory potential of the internet. Both of us, also Harry Potter dorks, spent hours discussing MediaWiki's magic. Wikipedia was spell casting for the masses. Anyone could edit the page *quasi-anonymously*. IPs can be tracked and traced back to identifiable users, of course, but these were the pre-Facebook days when internet users cared a lot more about keeping online and offline identities separate. We knew that editing the page meant far more than just tinkering with some text. Back then, no "what you see is what you get" (WYSIWYG) editor existed. From the ability to choose whether to "sign up" with a username to spending numerous days tracking edits to a page, editing meant that you were coding.[5] With MediaWiki, coding was brought down to such an accessible level and made any novice editor feel like a badass. However, we knew more was happening than that, and we did research about how MediaWiki does what it do. The AMP (Apache—MySQL—PhP) stack ensures an archive of your edit. Even if you entered a flame war and got reverted repeatedly, your edit would be part of the site's retrievable history. Moreover, the ability to store those edits on an unprecedented scale and sort through such a vast trove of robust documentation through a navigable interface were novel experiences afforded by these applications. For those of us who grew up taking high school courses like business computer information systems and telecommunications (where Microsoft Windows was your only operating system option, MS Office software was the only way you were taught about data management, and HTML was all it took to make a website), Wikipedia provided access to an entirely different information architecture. As a new type of website, Wikipedia increased our curiosity about the dynamic, distributed possibility of different kinds of code, application systems, and online communities.

Further, the power to tamper with even a millisecond of someone's perception about the truth of any subject could have massive repercussions for education. No longer were generations going to take for granted who or what could count as notable enough to be part of a reference. No longer could educational institutions exclusively centralize student knowledge vis-à-vis textbooks. Wikipedia interrupted the gatekeeping mechanisms of academe, lateralizing who could have a say and opening up a frontier of deliberation that expanded upon the news groups, discussion forums, and Java-powered chat rooms by which Web 1.0 internet users were accustomed. The library's restricted section was now available to any magician seeking to make and break knowledge. Indeed, Wikipedia editing was and continues to be taught as a dark art.

Teaching Wikipedia and Student Resistance

These formative experiences with Wikipedia informed my understanding of writing in the "new digital age." When I started teaching college composition as a first-year graduate student at the University of Oklahoma in 2006, nothing about Wikipedia or the burgeoning Web 2.0 felt that new to me. By that point, we were deep into George W. Bush's war on terror, the recession was about to hit people hard, and uncertainty inspired a lot of us graduate students to avoid the workforce and prolong reckoning with the reality of our further descent into student loan debt. During required teaching assistant workshops and seminars as well as break-room lunches and happy hours, anti-Wikipedia attitudes could inspire long self-righteous conversations about banning this resource in the classroom. Despite their claims to want more social justice in higher ed, nearly every writing teacher I knew—regardless of their political affiliation, gender, religion, and so on—seemed to loathe Wikipedia and take pleasure in talking about their tactics for catching students plagiarizing or even thinking about citing the resource.

Meanwhile, I was hoping my students would have a different experience with Wikipedia. Teaching with digital technology was still not fully institutionalized despite repetitive institutional calls for improving students' digital and information literacy. I took advantage of these pedagogical appeals and started including various opportunities for students to edit Wikipedia. For example, I included a small activity during the first semester I ever taught—when new instructors were discouraged from deviating from the standard curriculum. It was a research assignment, in which I asked students to look at Wikipedia to see if there was an article about their hometown. We utilized government census data as well as state and city websites and print reference entries to update articles with current information. During this process, students noticed when major businesses, educational institutions, places of worship, and traditions (e.g., local festivals) were missing from Wikipedia. Students from rural Oklahoma and those representing different Native American tribes were surprised to discover the absence of their communities.

These knowledge gaps taught them important lessons to transfer to their general academic experience. Everyone in the room had a distinct and valuable experience. Everyone knew something that they could contribute. Everyone should feel free to participate (in editing) because it was mutually beneficial to themselves, to the knowledge they added to the space, and to those who could build on it over time. Some students were excited to edit Wikipedia, but most of them were scared. They didn't want to do it wrong, or they challenged my authority to assign such a forbidden act of knowledge production. My Wikipedia editing assignments caused them to ask many questions about whether what I was doing was acceptable or whether their other instructors were wrong for not including Wikipedia editing in their courses.

To address the depth of their concerns, I weighted Wikipedia assignments as "homework" or "participation" with pass/fail credit. They got an "A" for even attempting to complete it or an "F" for not doing it. With no tutorials available or Wiki Education to provide me with scaffolding materials, I had to teach them how to edit based on my experience. Showing them the site's functions—like the history, talk, and sandbox features—as well as the importance of using a hacker name and drawing on our institutional library resources for secondary research took at least two weeks. Nevertheless, I continued this instruction throughout my teaching at the University of Oklahoma and throughout 2009–2011 when I was obtaining my PhD at the Pennsylvania State University. When teaching at Penn State, I had far less room in the standard syllabus to deviate with my own assignments because instructors were routinely surveilled. I relegated Wikipedia editing to "extra credit" assignments except during summer courses. At that time, I thought that if students learned about the ethics of knowledge production they might be motivated to take responsibility for editing Wikipedia, especially if they understand editing as a civic duty. It wasn't until I started working at Spelman College a few years later that I would be able to more fully understand that race, gender, and social class directly impact students' relationship to editing Wikipedia.

The Liberatory Potential of Wikipedia Editing

From 2011–2014, I took a break from Wikipedia editing in the classroom because I worked in the Writing Center and secured a tenure track position at Spelman College, a small private historically Black college (HBCU) for women. When I started teaching honors composition in 2015, I resumed Wikipedia editing as part of my writing pedagogy. Since my last teaching experience, I was pleasantly surprised to discover that Wikipedia had become a hot topic for those working on the intersections between race, gender, geography, and technology.[6] I learned about FemTechNet, an ambitious collective of academics, artists, and activists dedicated to improving the internet for marginalized communities. Their website taught me about wikistorming and the herstory of Art+Feminism—a distributed global event designed to diversify Wikipedia's coverage of women in the arts (discussed in chapter 15). I also discovered Wiki Education, which offered instructors numerous technical and content resources for teaching Wikipedia editing (discussed in chapter 20). Equipped with Wiki Education's sleek course management system and motivated by the intellectual challenge of representing "notable" knowledge from individuals and communities that are too often invisible in disciplinary sites of scholarship and teaching, I felt considerably more prepared to teach writing Wikipedia than ever before.

However, this time my inspiration for teaching Wikipedia editing was even more complicated. From 2006–2008, I wanted students to be more critical users of technology by understanding that political movements like Free/Libre Open Source Software make sites like Wikipedia possible. In 2015, I was much more aware of the racial and gender politics that affect computing cultures. To be sure, I have deep gratitude for the programmers like Richard Stallman, Linus Torvalds, and Steve Wozniak, who have labored for free to make GNU/Linux/Unix software free and available to all, as well as hacktivists like Aaron Swartz who paid the ultimate price for leaking closed-access scholarship and whistle-blowers like Chelsea Manning who spent years in prison for leaking the Iraq and Afghanistan war logs. However, all Women—regardless of race—face numerous barriers if they attempt to participate in the male-dominated cultures of programming and gaming.

Intersecting the liberatory potential of both open source practice *and* racially diverse gender inclusive participation could be fully realized at Spelman College.

Within this educational space of an HBCU for women, I crafted a syllabus that situated Wikipedia as both capable of preserving and erasing Black Women's intellectual and cultural herstory.[7] By encouraging Black Women students to edit, I strongly believed that they could lead efforts to diversify editor demographics. I also wanted them to understand Wikipedia as far more than an easy, popular place to casually browse for information about entertainment or as a general reference for any topic.

Few, if any, students had actually edited Wikipedia. I underestimated the extent to which these students would resist Wikipedia editing due to several fears that reveal the difficulty of equity work. For instance:

1. Editing Wikipedia to improve content gaps *sounds* good, but editors are often too unfamiliar with the Wikipedia community to fight for the knowledge they seek to represent.

2. Editing Wikipedia involves numerous literacies that present barriers for first-time editors:

   – Deciding whether to be anonymous/choosing a username

   – Gaining technical experience with the Wikipedia website

   – Identifying areas of improvement without being too overwhelmed by the choices available

- Learning how to navigate public and proprietary library resources for secondary sources
- Experimenting with incorporating research into articles within the boundaries of Wikipedia's "neutral style"
- Starting conversations on the talk page with strangers and subjecting oneself to the possibility of harassment or endless dialogue
- Reflecting on the editing experience in a supportive learning community

After teaching with Wikipedia for the first time at Spelman and failing to successfully acclimate most of my first-year honors students to the editing experience, I decided that my efforts would be more successful if I invited more faculty at my institution to participate in this unique teaching endeavor. Few instructors at Spelman teach about Wikipedia in any capacity, only warning students not to ever cite it in a paper. Further, when I introduce Wikipedia to my students, it takes several discussions to encourage them that they will not be penalized for editing Wikipedia since nearly all students' experience with Wikipedia in an educational space has centered on it being an unacceptable resource. This issue is intensified by the fact that they are Black Women students who have made it to the college-level because they have demonstrated their ability to fluently speak and write in standard white English as well as adopt social behaviors that make white people in authority less uncomfortable around Black people. Openly challenging authority is simply not an option for these students because they know that their "success" will be thwarted if they publicly appear to be "too angry" or have a "bad attitude." Their fear of harsh penalties is well justified and needs to be carefully considered when introducing them to Wikipedia editing.

Ultimately, my students became highly motivated to edit Wikipedia when they realized that its content fails to accurately represent significant cultural and intellectual contributions of Black Women, Spelman College, and HBCUs in general. To transform both student and faculty resistance to Wikipedia editing then, they would need the space and opportunity to recognize the importance of editing with **purpose**. Inspired by a Black History month edit-a-thon that Howard University organized in 2015, I began seeking other Atlanta University Center (AUC) instructors interested in the digital humanities and teaching writing with technology.[8] If more instructors taught Wikipedia editing, students would feel more comfortable with the complex and novel experience.

Therefore, in summer 2016, Professor Jamila Lyn—a colleague formerly employed at Morehouse College—and I collaboratively applied for an Associated Colleges of the South (ACS) grant to create an extensive three-day cross-institutional interdisciplinary faculty development event entitled "Integrating Wikipedia into Writing-Intensive Courses."[9] In addition to twelve on-site faculty, we opened select parts of the symposium for free, with remote participation being available to any interested instructor or Galleries, Libraries, Archives, and Museum (GLAM) staff and faculty. All of our on-site attendees were first-time editors and faced similar challenges as students editing for the first time.

Jamila and I decided that both faculty and students in the AUC might decide to engage Wikipedia if they could collaboratively connect over the problem of race and gender content gaps outside the classroom. Thus, we followed up on the 2016 ACS symposium in spring 2017 by co-organizing a Black Women's Herstory Wikipedia Edit-a-thon. Our event took place alongside hundreds of other similar events as part of Art+Feminism. It was, to my knowledge, Spelman's first-ever Art+Feminism Edit-a-thon and culminated in at least fifty new Black Women Wikipedia editors.[10] As previously discussed, the vast majority (at least 85 percent) of Wikipedia's editors are (white) males.[11] We were determined to change that, recognizing that Wikipedia offered a rich educational and activist opportunity for students and faculty in the AUC. We wanted to harness the power of discovery, debate, and documentation to diversify Wikipedia coverage. Our objective was to more broadly conceive of the word "Art" in Art+Feminism. By adding more articles about notable Black Women in the arts, media, and advocacy, we aimed to show that Black Women's fight for representation and control over our own individual and collective images has been both an artistic and political struggle. The 2017 Spelman Art+Feminism Meetup Wikipedia Page provides more details about the event, editing approaches for making herstory, and selected articles for development.

Moreover, I used the edit-a-thon as an opportunity to strengthen my efforts to teach Wikipedia editing in both introductory and advanced writing courses. I also used the event to strengthen partnerships in and across campus. We acquired significant financial support from Morehouse Academic Affairs ($1,000), Spelman Honors ($500), the Spelman English

Department ($300), Art+Feminism ($100), and the Wikipedia Foundation ($500 worth of swag). In addition, the Spelman Comprehensive Writing Program offered us space to hold the event inside our campus writing center, and the AUC Robert W. Woodruff Library offered a few librarians to help staff the event. Aleta Turner, a local Wikimedian and circulation supervisor at Athens-Clark County Library, also attended and assisted. Additionally, several on-campus units and organizations helped actively promote the event. These included the African Diaspora & the World Program, the Bonner Office of Civic Engagement, the Office of the Provost, the Office of Undergraduate Studies, and the Women's Research and Resource Center.

On the date of the event, March 5, 2017, we conducted a two-hour training session with approximately forty mostly young Black Women students in attendance with a few Black Women faculty and several librarians representing various genders and ethnicities (white, Black, Latinx, etc.). Early in the session, several students asked, "Why do I have the authority to change the page?" This question about whether one ought to be editing Wikipedia on the grounds of ability and/or agency highlights one of the core problems that affects human potential for knowledge production along every boundary of teaching and learning across media, geographies, and institutions. Surely, as these suspicious students recognized, Wikipedia editing (especially as a Black Woman) comes with some kind of risk. Online harassment is one well-known challenge, but to willingly publicly expose the reality of the limits and sum of one's own knowledge also comes with a considerable psychological burden within the sociopolitical context of a patriarchal adversarial culture that incentivizes proclamations of certainty over truth.[12] I bore witness to this problem during my prior experience teaching Wikipedia editing, but the problem was spelled out with brutal clarity among prospective Black Women editors. When I bring this chapter to conclusion, I will continue to contemplate how racial and gender politics affects new editors' sense of authority and, thus, how I interpret Wikipedia's impact at its twentieth anniversary.

The issue of authority always deeply unsettles Spelman students, whether they are writing with pen, voice, and/or computer. These Black Women bravely engaged Wikipedia—the website that anyone can edit—as often as any user but with little sense of duty to contribute to the space—even when they see poorly written or inaccurate information. As we know, Wikipedia is frequently used and relied on as a reference, despite many teachers' typical ominous warning: don't use Wikipedia as a source. Nevertheless, Wikipedia is easier to use than many traditionally educational materials. The free platform continues to work its way into formal education through Google's algorithmic power as a major broker in the knowledge economy—its powerful search engine juts Wikipedia entries to the top of results, obtaining automatic trust from users through its familiar and well-organized GUI.[13]

Further, Wikipedia serves as a subtle but powerful form of information warfare against colonized populations. The colonial act of erasing cultures includes the psychological condition of feeling as if you cannot and should not "disrupt" the information architecture. The dominance of white male editors correlates with a severe lack of participation and coverage about people representing historically disadvantaged groups, especially women of all races and ethnicities.[14]

Fortunately, Wikipedia's homogeneity is not destiny. Due to its radically open platform design, *anyone* can technically edit. Even if a user's change is overridden or reverted, the wiki architecture enables the archiving of any and all user activity. We also need to continue to critically analyze the extent to which we can accurately determine the cultural backgrounds of editors. In fact, some studies critique estimates of user demographics.[15] What appears on Wikipedia depends on the knowledge users choose to represent there. Editors, regardless of experience, must be willing to engage the community and make compelling arguments in defense of one's edits.

Nevertheless, participants' anxiety about editing Wikipedia funks up the how-to tutorial approach or the idea that attending a single edit-a-thon could sustain their motivation to continue editing Wikipedia. During Spelman's first Art+Feminism edit-a-thon, students conversed about editors' authority throughout the entire event. One of the most memorable discussions was about how students did not feel the classroom space alone would be capable of enabling them to edit Wikipedia with confidence. They admitted that their fear of failing and the instructor's watchful eye was hardly the kind of environment that sponsors meaningful digital activism. In fact, students would need to *feel free* to edit Wikipedia—not as a required class assignment and not being unprepared to handle a hostile response from entering a digital space dominated by white males. Their concerns revealed that our communities need to take radical action to reckon with the historical and present problem of Black Women recovering and documenting our intellectual and cultural history. Certainly, a distributed global event designed to diversify Wikipedia's coverage of (Black) women in the arts can provide the context for recruiting new editors, but more opportunities for engagement are necessary. The prospect of increasing Black Women editors on Wikipedia will be more likely with structural support from social movements that connect digital activism and higher education (like #CiteBlackWomen), campus and community support for edit-a-thons focused on knowledge equity, and Wikipedia instruction in writing-intensive courses across the disciplines. Toward this end, I strategically connected the Art+Feminism edit-a-thon to three writing courses, collaborated with our office of civic engagement to get Wikipedia editing to count as an activity that students could use to fulfill their service requirement at the college, and provided faculty development for instructors willing and able to teach Wikipedia editing.[16] This approach required exhaustive effort, but if educators are committed to social justice, they will encourage students to edit Wikipedia as a practical method for learning how to be leaders that advocate for equitable knowledge production in the twenty-first century.

Wikipedia, Inclusion, and Digital Citizenship

As Wikipedia turns twenty, nearly all of my students, regardless of their classification, have been trained to believe that Wikipedia editing is not a possibility available to them. However, since 2006, one of the major shifts in attitudes toward Wikipedia is that it has become an object of critique for reproducing social inequality. In particular, grand narratives about Wikipedia's unreliability have expanded to include the issue of editor demographics and social justice. One of the dominant arguments against Wikipedia's legitimacy was that it would be prone to misinformation because user anonymity would encourage deceit. Although this continues to be a popular critique of Wikipedia, the problems of diversity and inclusion has increasingly drawn global attention from artists, scientists, activists, librarians, curators, and educators. WikiProjects like *Women in Red* and the *African Diaspora* focus on expanding race and gendered content. Feminists like Adrienne Wadewitz increased public awareness about the problem of gender inequity on Wikipedia. Jacqueline Mabey, Siân Evans, Michael Mandiberg, and Laurel Ptak founded the first Art+Feminism in 2014.[17] These initiatives, led by experienced Wikipedians, have globally expanded through the growth of both Art+Feminism and Wiki Education, which are both officially non-profit organizations with staff and structured program support.

Wikipedia as a site of social justice work redefines its potential uses in formal education. Directly involving students in knowledge production actualizes the bedrock of their freedom to participate in our contemporary information economy—can they be motivated to use Wikipedia to learn how to fill gaps in knowledge that our communities know (or what we ought to know), do credible research, sort through the data dumps, and mark their authorship in a public collaborative writing space?

Indeed, one of my major motivations for teaching Wikipedia editing since 2006 is that I have observed its vast potential for deeply engaging our students with twenty-first-century knowledge production and intellectual service. Wikipedia editing can align student, faculty, and staff goals in a distinctly womanist method—through edit-a-thons, for example, everyone was invited to participate, regardless of "expertise," because we all know something. By coming together to share our knowledge, we all benefited from the exchange. The social aspect of knowledge production and learning strengthens our spirit and our will to seek wisdom in the honor of both our individual excellence and our ancestors—to whom a great cognitive and emotional debt must be paid for our ability to tell the "herstory" of Black Women's intellectual and cultural legacies.[18]

Notes

1. *Bowers v. Hardwick*, 478 US 186, 106 S. Ct. 2841, 92 L. Ed. 2d 140 (1986); see also Yvonne L. Tharpes, "Bowers v. Hardwick and the Legitimization of Homophobia in America," *Howard Law Journal* 30 (1987): 829.

2. David Artavia, "Matt Shepard, Tyler Oakley: Lives Separated by Two Decades of Change," *The Advocate*, September 24, 2018, https://www.advocate.com/youth/2018/9/24/matt-shepard-tyler-oakley-lives-separated-two-decades-change.

3. Alex Abad-Santos, "Philadelphia's New, Inclusive Gay Pride Flag Is Making Gay White Men Angry," *Vox*, June 20, 2017, https://www.vox.com/culture/2017/6/20/15821858/gay-pride-flag-philadelphia-fight-explained.

4. Jean Anyon, "Social Class and the Hidden Curriculum of Work," *Journal of Education* 162, no. 1 (1980): 67–92, https://doi.org/10.1177/002205748016200106.

5. Kevin Brooks and Chris Lindgren, "Responding to the Coding Crisis: From Code Year to Computational Literacy," in *Strategic Discourse: The Politics of (New) Literacy*

Crises, ed. Lynn Lewis (Logan, UT: Composition Digital Press/Utah State University Press, 2015): 1–22; see also Annette Vee, *Coding Literacy: How Computer Programming Is Changing Writing* (Cambridge, MA: MIT Press, 2017).

6. Ari Schlesinger, W. Keith Edwards, and Rebecca E. Grinter, "Intersectional HCI: Engaging Identity through Gender, Race, and Class," in *Proceedings of the 2017 CHI Conference on Human Factors in Computing Systems* (New York: ACM, 2017): 5415, http://dx.doi.org/10.1145/3025453.3025766.

7. Alexandria Lockett, "Wikis, Wikipedia and Writing Syllabus," accessed October 14, 2019, http://www.alexandrialockett.com/customizable-syllabus-for-wikis-writing-and -wikipedia-an-honors-first-year-composition-course/.

8. Taylor Gordon, "Howard Students and Professors Among Many Helping to Add More Black History to Wikipedia's Predominantly White Database," *Atlanta Blackstar*, February 22, 2015, https://atlantablackstar.com/2015/02/22/howard-students -professors-among-many-helping-add-black-history-wikipedias-predominantly -white-database/.

9. For more information and resources, see: Alexandria Lockett, "Teaching with Wikipedia (Open Resources)," Google Drive, accessed October 14, 2019, https://docs.google.com /document/d/1uNnzqiWmGMneEeDi-F0FT7BdIZ785DxKIOk_FIJAGMI/mobilebasic, and the "ACS Symposium Webinar Packet," Google Drive, accessed October 14, 2019, https://issuu.com/alexandrialockett/docs/webinar_copy_of_2016_acs_symposium_

10. Tyler Stephens, "Spreading Black Girl Magic to Wikipedia," *The Blueprint*, May 2017, https://issuu.com/spelmanbp/docs/spelman_college_blueprint_may_2017_; see also "Spelman's Art+Womanism 2017 Photo Gallery," AlexandriaLockett.com, accessed October 14, 2019, http://www.alexandrialockett.com/artfeminism-wikipedia -edit-a-thon-at-spelman-college-a-photo-gallery/; "Spelman's Art+Womanism 2017 Reflections and Press," AlexandriaLockett.com, accessed October 14, 2019, http:// www.alexandrialockett.com/black-womens-herstory-artfeminism-edit-a-thon-at -spelman-college-reflections-and-press/; our total "Contributions" in Atlanta Spelman ArtAndFeminism 2017, accessed October 14, 2019, https://outreachdashboard .wmflabs.org/courses/Spelman_College/Atlanta_Spelman_ArtAndFeminism_2017.

11. Gráinne Ní Aodha, "Wikipedia's Community Is 85% Male, and Founder Jimmy Wales Isn't Sure How to Fix It," *TheJournal.ie*, October 29, 2017, https://www.thejournal .ie/wikipedia-founder-gender-imbalance-3668767-Oct2017/; see also Heather Ford and Judy Wajcman, "'Anyone Can Edit,' Not Everyone Does: Wikipedia's Infrastructure and the Gender Gap," *Social Studies of Science* 47, no. 4 (2017): 511–527, https://doi.org /10.1177/0306312717692172.

12. Emily Dreyfuss, "Twitter is Indeed Toxic for Women, Amnesty Report Says," *Wired*, December 18, 2018, https://www.wired.com/story/amnesty-report-twitter-abuse -women/.

13. Alamir Novin and Eric Meyers, "Making Sense of Conflicting Science Information: Exploring Bias in the Search Engine Result Page," in *Proceedings of the 2017 Conference Human Information Interaction and Retrieval* (New York: ACM, 2017), 175–184, https://doi.org/10.1145/3020165.3020185; see also Lee Rainie and Bill Tancer, "Wikipedia: When in Doubt, Multitudes Seek It Out," *Pew Research Center Publications*, April 24, 2007, http://www.tony-silva.com/download/wiki-pew.pdf.

14. Benjamin Collier and Julia Bear, "Conflict, Criticism, or Confidence: An Empirical Examination of the Gender Gap in Wikipedia Contributions," in *Proceedings of the ACM 2012 Conference on Computer Supported Cooperative Work* (New York: ACM, 2017): 383–392, https://doi.org/10.1145/2145204.2145265; see also Aaron Shaw and Eszter Hargittai, "The Pipeline of Online Participation Inequalities: The Case of Wikipedia Editing," *Journal of Communication* 68, no. 1 (2018): 143–168, https://doi.org/10.1093/joc/jqx003; Jennifer C. Edwards, "Wiki Women: Bringing Women into Wikipedia through Activism and Pedagogy," *The History Teacher* 48, no. 3 (2015): 409–436; Kat Stoeffel, "Closing Wikipedia's Gender Gap—Reluctantly," *The Cut*, February 11, 2014, https://www.thecut.com/2014/02/closing-wikipedias-gender-gap-reluctantly.html; Adrienne Wadewitz, "Wikipedia Is Pushing the Boundaries of Scholarly Practice but the Gender Gap Must Be Addressed," *LSE Impact Blog* (blog), April 9, 2013, https://blogs.lse.ac.uk/impactofsocialsciences/2013/04/09/change-the-world-edit-wikipedia/; Claudia Wagner, David Garcia, Mohsen Jadidi, and Markus Strohmaier, "It's a Man's Wikipedia? Assessing Gender Inequality in an Online Encyclopedia," in *Proceedings of the Ninth International Conference on Web and Social Media* (Palo Alto, CA: The AAAI Press, 2015): 454–463; Jodi L. Wilson, "Proceed with Extreme Caution: Citation to Wikipedia in Light of Contributor Demographics and Content Policies," *Vanderbilt Journal of Entertainment & Technology Law* 16 (2013): 857.

15. Benjamin Mako Hill and Aaron Shaw, "The Wikipedia Gender Gap Revisited: Characterizing Survey Response Bias with Propensity Score Estimation," *PloS One* 8, no. 6 (2013), https://doi.org/10.1371/journal.pone.0065782.

16. At Spelman, first- and second-year students are required to complete ten hours of service per week through our Bonner Office of Civic Engagement. Convincing its director to authorize the edit-a-thon as a service event significantly increased Art+Feminism Edit-a-thon participation and radically transformed the institutions understanding of service.

17. Robin Cembalest, "101 Women Artists Who Got Wikipedia Pages This Week," *ARTnews*, February 6, 2014, http://www.artnews.com/2014/02/06/art-and-feminism-wikipedia-editathon-creates-pages-for-women-artists/.

18. See Wikipedia, s.v. "Herstorical Womanist Research Methods," s.v. "Wikipedia: Meetup/Spelman College/Art+Womanism 2017," accessed October 14, 2019, https://en.wikipedia.org/wiki/Wikipedia:Meetup/Spelman_College/Art%2BWomanism_2017#Herstorical_Womanist_Research_Methods_for_Improving_Articles.

15　What We Talk About When We Talk About Community

Siân Evans, Jacqueline Mabey, Michael Mandiberg, and Melissa Tamani

Four members of Art+Feminism speak to the challenges and invisible work of organizing community from an intersectional feminist perspective within the larger Wikipedia community.

As Wikipedia enters its third decade, an honest conversation about community—how we build it, who is included, and how we care for it—is urgently needed. In engaging with Wikipedia through a feminist lens, we, the lead co-organizers of Art+Feminism, continually reflect on what it means to build and participate in communities, online and in person, within the Wikimedia movement and outside of it. A key insight for us is that when we talk about "community," we cannot assume that we are speaking of the same thing. In doing our work, conflict has emerged when we run up against the unspoken presuppositions about what kind of participation counts and who can edit the encyclopedia that "anybody can edit." Using Art+Feminism as a case study, we will explore the work of information activism and community building in open source communities like Wikipedia with an eye toward building more inclusive, diverse, and equitable communities.

Art+Feminism is a do-it-yourself and do-it-with-others campaign to improve Wikipedia's content on gender, feminism, and the arts. We train editors of all gender identities and expressions how to edit in response to the gaps in participation and content on the most important popular free culture project. The Art+Feminism model was, from the beginning, a radical reworking of how edit-a-thons are organized. Art+Feminism was catalyzed by two separate conversations that took place in fall 2013 between the four cofounders, Siân Evans, Jacqueline Mabey, Michael Mandiberg, and Laurel Ptak. Evans was sharing her ideas about how to reboot the Women and Art Special Interest Group (SIG) associated with the Art Libraries Society of North America with Mabey. They discussed the Ada Lovelace Day Wikipedia edit-a-thons, which had recently been in the news; the goal of these events is to write about the work of women in STEM (Science, Technology, Engineering, and Math).[1] Evans thought a similar event focusing on women in the arts might breathe life into the dormant SIG. Mabey later relayed this information to Michael Mandiberg, an artist and educator, who had used Wikipedia in teaching, assigning students stub articles to expand instead of term papers. Coincidentally, that same day Mandiberg engaged curator Laurel Ptak in a similar conversation. At the time, Ptak was a fellow at Eyebeam, a center for art and technology in New York, researching cyberfeminism. Mandiberg encouraged her to organize an edit-a-thon focused on art, technology, and feminism as a part of her fellowship. With so many simultaneous conversations, it seemed like the project was meant to be.

Art+Feminism emerged during a period of growing public awareness of the varied ways structural inequality plays out on Wikipedia. In 2011, the *New York Times* published a debate on the topic of Wikipedia's gender gap, opening up a public discourse on open culture and the ways in which it can be, at best, "clubby" and, at worst, toxic for women.[2] Two years later, writer Amanda Filipacchi authored an opinion piece for the *Times*, in response to a Wikipedian who was removing women from the "American novelists" category and moving these articles into a subcategory for "American women novelists"[3] in an attempt to improve the layout of a lengthy page. The result was a category purged of women, who had been moved elsewhere. Filipacchi's article generated several other think pieces on the topic as well as a flood of commentary, tagged #AmericanWomenNovelists, on social media platforms like Facebook and Twitter.[4] However, at the same time, Wikipedians were discussing this practice on Wikipedia's talk pages.[5] While the issues were the same, these conversations were worlds apart. We wanted to draw attention to the ability of individuals to engage with these debates on Wikipedia. But, as soon as we brought some people into this debate on Wikipedia, their votes were considered campaigning and thus were struck by experienced Wikipedians. From the start, Art+Feminism was shaped by this insider-outsider dynamic that would continue to play out in our six years working on the project.

The cofounders met via video conference on November 2013 to discuss the possibility of collaboration. We agreed to hold an event at Eyebeam and widely distribute a call for participation among our personal and professional networks. The call to participation quickly went viral: that first year, thirty-one edit-a-thons took place in locations across six countries with approximately six hundred participants creating 101 new articles and improving at least ninety articles.[6] The response to the call for participation was no doubt fueled by a desire to correct the historical record. Organizers and participants wanted to see themselves reflected in Wikipedia and for Wikipedia to more accurately represent our histories.

We have argued elsewhere that the success of our outreach is due to our method of communicating and organizing primarily off-wiki,[7] as opposed to on Wikipedia meetup pages. We sent out our call for participation via email, professional list serves, and social media. We theorized that the steep learning curve for Wikipedia editing (especially before the advent of the VisualEditor in 2015) was disincentivizing for organizers. First of all, how were new editors supposed to find events that only existed on a platform they were unfamiliar with and which was never designed for discoverability? And, second, organizing on-wiki required the event organizers to be comfortable both in Wikitext and the Wikimedia community. Of course, many women already felt unwelcome in the community, so how were they to be expected to organize solely on its platform?

The topic touched a nerve. People and organizations that we had no direct relationship with were quickly reaching out. We kept an eye on the Facebook event page, the Wikipedia meetup page, and our communal email address; whenever anyone posted about wanting to start their own event, we immediately reached out with assistance. The event at Portland State University came together via a discussion on the Facebook event page in a matter of minutes.[8] We supported each node in different ways. For some locations we organized all of the key elements (location, subject area expert, Wikipedians) while some of the venues approached us with all elements assembled; most of the events were somewhere in between. This organizational strategy continues to be true, six years later. As our community has grown, however, we have come to wonder: what is Art+Feminism's place within the larger Wikipedia community?

Who Gets to Decide Who Belongs on a Platform for "Everyone"?

Community is a complex term because while it implies inclusion, it can often entail exclusion as well. As an adjective, it is often used to suggest uncomplicated goodness, but we must remember that exclusion is what creates the conceptual coherence of a community. This is, unfortunately, particularly true of open source communities, such as Open Source Software or Free/Libre Open Source Software. Wikipedia's gender gap is certainly not unique. An analysis of the 2017 GitHub Open Source Survey showed that 90 percent of survey respondents identified as male, with only 3 percent identifying as women and 1 percent as nonbinary. Less than 1 percent identified as transgender. Further, only 14 percent of respondents identified as a minority in their country of residence.[9] Because these projects are open with few barriers to entry, one would assume that there should be no problem for new participants. However, for at least a decade, female developers have complained of the "unfriendly atmosphere both online and offline."[10] Open source communities are complex social worlds whose "flame wars" can be discouraging for new participants, especially women and members of other marginalized communities.

Perhaps the most obvious example of how a culture of online harassment plays out on Wikipedia was the conduct on pages related to Gamergate. The controversy known as "Gamergate" itself became public in 2014 when several women involved in the video game industry became the victims of a series of online and offline misogynistic attacks. Although it had its roots in video game culture, Gamergate became a flashpoint for discussion about gendered online harassment, including on platforms like Wikipedia. In the end, the Wikipedia Arbitration Committee (Arbcom) sanctioned several editors on both sides over edits to the "Gamergate controversy" article—a contentious decision within the community. Public statements were issued by the Wikimedia Foundation, by two of the editors who were brought before the Arbcom, and in an unusual instance, by the Arbcom itself. As Michael Mandiberg wrote in *Social Text*,

> what's frustrating is that Wikipedia's ArbCom is structured to act in the letter of the law but maybe not the spirit, and as such, is ripe for abuse by the kind of process we've seen take place. The principles on which Wikipedia is founded assume everyone is acting in good faith, and seem unprepared for the Men's Rights Activism spawned from Reddit, 4chan, and 8chan. It's an example of what Astra Taylor says, that "open" in no way means "equal."[11]

Wikipedia's idealistic community guidelines—"be bold" and "assume good faith"—do not take into account the pervasiveness of online harassment and how it plays out in the lives of women, people of color, people with disabilities, LGBTQIA people, and folks from other marginalized communities.

Harassment often bleeds from one platform to another, from online to "in real life," and Wikipedia is no exception.[12] According to a 2017 Pew poll, 41 percent of Americans claim they've been harassed online while nearly one-in-five "have been subjected to particularly severe forms of harassment online, such as physical threats, harassment over a sustained period, sexual harassment or stalking." Further, one in ten note having been targeted due to their physical appearance, race, or gender, and "although most people believe harassment is often facilitated by the anonymity that the internet provides, these experiences can involve acquaintances, friends or even family members."[13]

We have experienced several forms of harassment since founding Art+Feminism from both within and outside the Wikipedia community. The largest targeted Twitter campaign of harassment came after the Museum of Modern Art created a Facebook event page for the live stream of our 2017 edit-a-thon opening panel about internet activism, featuring writer Joanne McNeil, Data & Society Research Institute Fellow Zara Rahman, and Kimberly Drew, curator and creator of the Black Contemporary Art Tumblr.[14] This was largely the result of men's rights activists (MRAs) bandwagoning on an initial comment by an influential MRA activist.[15] We, as individuals, luckily remained largely unscathed because we operate all our social media under the collective identity of Art+Feminism. But, as is often the case with online harassment, no one was held accountable for the tweetstorm.

We have been subject to personal attacks and individual harassment from within the Wikipedia community, however. The most notable case involved an editor with whom we had previously worked.[16] Over two years, this individual posted hostile comments on various Art+Feminism pages, including comments on grant proposals which elicited formal warnings of "uncivil" behavior. They attacked Art+Feminism and individuals involved with the project on Twitter, repeatedly misgendering team members and, in some cases, making claims about people in ways that were potentially harmful to their employment. They also actively interfered with our organizational efforts, including nominating training materials for deletion on procedural grounds days before our campaign was set to start and sabotaging other efforts across Wikimedia platforms, including Wikidata. They were eventually banned, but only after multiple reports over the course of two years from both within and outside the Art+Feminism collective. This was the culmination of two exhausting years of documentation and repeated reports on top of the usual affective labor of organizing.

The amount of labor it takes to report these types of experiences, in addition to the harm of the abuse itself, can be a major reason people do not continue to work on Wikipedia projects. A recent *New York Times* article highlighted the abuse experienced by LGBTQIA-identified individuals on Wikipedia. One interviewee, Pax Ahimsa Gethen, a trans male Wikipedian who was harassed for several months, reported their harasser posting their deadname as well as telling them they were "unloved" and belonged in an internment camp. Gethen is quoted as saying, "I'm not getting paid for this. Why should I volunteer my time to be abused?"[17]

Further, we've experienced verbal or physical harassment at every national or global Wikipedia-related event we have attended. We have reported these incidents to the conference organizer and/or to the Wikimedia Foundation's Trust and Safety team if they are present. With one exception, these complaints did not result in action taken during these conferences. We found it particularly galling at Wikimania 2017 that, during his keynote address, Jimmy Wales claimed that Wikipedia was great at dealing with harassment.[18]

Partially in response to these experiences, we created our own more inclusive and specific Safe Space/Brave Space Policy to hold all of our organizers accountable to our shared values.[19] This policy was a collective effort based on our informed experiences across various intersections of identity. It was created in collaboration with organizers around the world, and we wish to acknowledge that we do this work in solidarity with a wide-reaching feminist network. One of the key components of our Safe Space/Brave Space policy is to "confront harassment and reduce harm." This, in and of itself, is labor that often results in further alienation or "outsider status." As the #metoo movement and Black Lives Matter has shown, the silence around discrimination and violence against marginalized communities is the status quo. What does it mean to speak out? In many cases, it means making yourself vulnerable to further harassment as well as alienation from communities you participate in.

In the process of writing this book chapter, Art+Feminism (along with some other Wikipedia-related organizations) called out an alleged instance of personal and physical abuse that others in the community had brought to our attention. Our process of calling out was both intentional and careful, with the primary goal of causing less harm to everyone involved. Necessarily, this kind of work requires hours of discussion and negotiation that is both exhausting and invisible. We reached out to other community members who, we thought, might have similar reservations about participating in a project with someone accused of abuse, and some chose to join in solidarity. This work was exhausting and potentially harmful to a project we all cared deeply for but was a necessary move to "confront harassment and reduce harm" in our community.

Lam et al.'s presentation at the 7th International Symposium on Wikis and Open Collaboration was aptly titled "WP:Clubhouse?" using Wikipedia's policy language to suggest that community is, perhaps, the wrong term to describe a group that polices its boundaries often along race and gender lines.[20] To echo their question: are we talking about community, or are we talking about a clubhouse? This brings us back to the title of this chapter: "what we talk about when we talk about community." How is Wikipedia "open" if there are so many barriers to entry for women, LGBTQIA-identified folks, and people of color?

Whose Labor Is Recognized as Labor? Can a Community Focus on Content Creation Recognize the Gendered Labor Required to Reproduce Community?

Wikipedia is a community that focuses on numbers: number of articles created, number of citations, and so on. While as of 2019, the Wikimedia Foundation counts 36,421,998 Wikipedia accounts, only 130,136 are considered "active editors."[21] When Larry Sanger and Jimmy Wales founded Wikipedia in 2001, its growth was rapid, with over twenty thousand articles in its first year and a growing community of "Wikipedians" who worked collectively to write and edit the content. In the mid-2000s, however, the site's popularity boomed and criticism of vandalism on Wikipedia became a mainstream debate.[22] Established editors responded by creating an elaborate set of policies and guidelines for participation as well as automated bots to handle routine checks for grammar and citations, among other things. As Tom Simonite has noted, "But those tougher rules and the more suspicious atmosphere that came along with them had an unintended consequence. Newcomers to Wikipedia making their first, tentative edits—and the inevitable mistakes—became less likely to stick around. Being steam-rollered by the newly efficient, impersonal editing machine was no fun."[23]

Indeed, a comprehensive study of the longevity of newcomers to Wikipedia has found that new editors are far more likely to have their initial edits rejected and leave than their predecessors in the early days of Wikipedia were.[24] And, another study has shown that women are even more likely to have their edits reverted than men and less likely to come back.[25] This suggests that helping new users feel comfortable editing on Wikipedia will require a huge effort to change these norms.

What counts as labor on Wikipedia is a fraught question. The creation of the encyclopedia itself and its various offshoots (Wikimedia Commons, Wikidata, etc.) all rely on volunteer labor. Drawing on the research of Tiziana Terranova, who has argued that social media and crowdsourcing platforms are for all intents and purposes "digital sweatshops," Dorothy Howard, lead co-organizer for the 2015 campaign, has argued that Wikipedia's reliance on unpaid labor blurs the line between information activism and digital labor.[26] But it is clear that in the eyes of the on-wiki community, the labor of love that is Wikipedia is one that is based on content creation, not on community building.

In 2016, the Wikipedia community was asked to weigh in on global metrics, which included the active editor counts. We argued that these events do not accurately measure the success of individuals or projects because they relied solely on Wikipedia edit counts, negating the other community-building work of catalyzing other important Wiki projects like AfroCROWD and holding edit-a-thons with a global reach. It is worth quoting our feedback at length here:

> We would like to reconsider the definition of a retained active editor. At present, a retained active editor is defined as a user that has made at least 5 edits per month in article space, for a period of 6 or 12 months. All three of the lead organizers for Art+Feminism do not qualify as "retained active editors" over a 12 or 6 month period in its current definition. *Think about that.* We are metapedians who spend much/most of our time in meta, AfD [articles for deletion], meetup and talk pages; we compose longer texts (like this) collaboratively in a word doc or make all our edits in our sandbox like good Wikipedians, then paste them into articles space and only get credit for one edit; we spend many hours a week organizing off-wiki; we go to Wikicon and give presentations that demonstrate leadership and which others learn from. None of this "counts." Furthermore, the annual schedules of academia and the NY art world means that two out of the three of us take much

of August off from as much responsibility as we can, Wikipedia included. It strikes us that this resembles a re-inscription of a traditional hierarchy of gendered labor. This facilitation is the invisible labor of "making of the home"—we are enabling the legible work of other people. This work is erased as legitimate labor. The historical campaign Wages for Housework argued that housework was not understood as legitimate work or labor because it is not remunerated.[27]

In response to our feedback, the Wikimedia Foundation eventually changed its global metrics, removing the retained active editor requirement.[28]

Both Howard and Mandiberg have alluded to the emotional or affective labor of community organizing on Wikipedia, with Mandiberg specifically referring to it as "the labor of being afraid."[29] As we've made clear in our discussions of harassment on Wikipedia, organizing a feminist editing collective requires a lot of emotional labor. But that labor is also on top of other kinds of immaterial labor—such as community organizing, peer education, social media production, event organizing, and so forth—that are involved in organizing a month of edit-a-thons each year that, on average, includes around three hundred events all over the world, with over four thousand participants editing or creating twenty-five thousand articles on Wikipedia.[30] Producing social media posts, managing volunteers and staff, and securing grant funding to pay for childcare, coffee, and snacks and then processing those reimbursement payments for events in countries all over the world (with their varied banking requirements) is the labor of organizing that so often keeps the Art+Feminism team from the labor of editing. And this labor is gendered.[31]

What Happens When Thousands of New Contributors Contribute Tens of Thousands of New Articles? How Does the Community React?

As researchers have shown, the Wikipedia community has grown increasingly inhospitable to new editors.[32] This has had a great impact on the Art+Feminism project which, from its genesis, relied heavily on the openness of Wikipedia. Our approach has always been to encourage users to "be bold" and participate in the world's largest online encyclopedia, a tool we all use daily. And, as we stated earlier, this mantle was taken seriously. With over six years, 1,100 events, fourteen thousand participants, and fifty-eight thousand articles, we are one of the longest-running and largest edit-a-thons in Wikipedia history. And it is also true that much of this work is not being done by what we traditionally refer to as Wikipedians, although we encourage all of the artists, activists, writers, educators, and librarians who are organizing and editing to see themselves as "Wikipedians," even if the community doesn't necessarily see them as such.

Because we encourage new editors to participate in Wikipedia, we understand that this will necessarily mean good faith errors. Anyone who teaches knows that learning requires mistakes. Over the years we've implemented a rigorous monitoring process to help new editors ensure that their articles don't get deleted or help explain why a particular article isn't considered notable within Wikipedia's guidelines. We encourage first time editors to improve one of the five thousand pages we track via Wikidata[33] and specifically direct them to the seven hundred English and fifty Spanish articles from this set which also have key article improvement alert templates, indicating they need further citations or links or have questionable notability; we direct people who want to make new pages to the Art+Feminism Draft Template;[34] and we encourage event organizers to vet articles before moving them from Draft to Article space. We use the Programs and Events Dashboard to track the alerts on all of the articles edited at our events; we post articles that have been proposed for deletion—through PROD (proposed deletion) or AfD (article for deletion)—to a Slack channel called #firebrigade where experienced editors can review these articles and either improve them or support their deletion when warranted. During the 2018 campaign, we tracked these deleted articles and determined that only 0.67 percent of our new articles were deleted. This is quite different from the 80 percent deletion rate that is often discussed as the percentage of new articles deleted in "New pages patrol."[35]

Despite all of this, our articles are challenged, our grant reports questioned, and worse. In one instance early on, an organizer in Australia didn't heed our recommendation to seek out an experienced Wikipedian. We found out via an experienced editor who posted a skeptical email to a large Wikimedia mailing list; we handled the situation, and within twenty-four hours had found an editor to help with the edit-a-thon. This should have ended there, but instead editors went on to comment on organizers' personal social media pages about the "mess" we had made in Australia, and a number of event organizers canceled their events due to what they felt was abusive behavior from these Wikipedians; later these same Wikipedians made similar comments on our meta pages. Again, we ask: who is the

Wikipedia community for? If it's only for those who *already* understand the Byzantine system of guidelines, policies, and social hierarchies, how can it possibly be welcoming to newcomers?

What Are the Challenges of Building Communities That Traverse Geographies and Languages?

The global nature of a campaign like Art+Feminism is one of its greatest strengths and greatest challenges. For example, the dynamics of managing a gender-gap-related edit-a-thon are radically different in a context where there are no experienced Wikipedians available to attend events in person, where there are no "reliable" published sources on women artists' lives and works, and where there is a considerable digital literacy gap or where it is unsafe for people to gather in public places. All of these are or have been factors in organizing events in Latin America, for example.

Siko Bouterse and Anasuya Sengupta have spoken eloquently on how the Wikipedia community is, at best, not prepared and, at worst, hostile to the concept of local and indigenous knowledge(s):

> Wikipedians—particularly on the English Wikipedia—have found it hard to accept sources that are local publications in non-familiar languages, and certainly, to accept and accommodate the fact that the majority of the world's knowledge (especially but not only in the global South) is oral, not written in published material. Google estimated a few years ago that the total number of published books in the world is about 130 million in 480 languages, but there are over 7000 languages and dialects in the world. "Oral citations"—a concept first explored by Achal Prabhala and his team in a fascinating 2011 film called People Are Knowledge—are not yet given credence within the community of editors.[36]

Early on in Art+Feminism's development, we established a Regional Ambassador program so that we could adopt a more localized and decentralized model of organizing. The Regional Ambassador program consists of a network of activists, academics, and art workers who are familiar with the Wikipedia environment and who enable fluid and close dialogue between the campaign and the hundreds of organizers around the world. Currently, the program includes both an informal network of volunteers as well as a more formal network of organizers in Africa, Latin America, the United States, Canada, Europe, and Asia who coordinate directly with the core leadership team. These organizers typically participate in or contribute to the creation of support networks among art workers, art institutions, feminist activists, and Wikipedians that are either regional or based on a shared language or culture, such as Lusophone or Latin America and Spain.

Working globally introduces variables of geography and language as well as the challenge of negotiating the dynamics and tensions between the Global North and the Global South. The hundreds of organizers and participants come from diverse cultural, geographic, economic, and educational backgrounds. We are well aware of this diversity and have tried to adapt to it to the best of our abilities. For example, we have spent significant time rewriting and redesigning training materials to make the content more accessible, and this includes integrating translation to multiple languages into our workflow as a permanent practice.[37] Further, bringing voices from the Global South directly into the leadership collective has greatly affected the way that we organize.[38] Early on in Art+Feminism's organizing, we realized that our leadership collective and materials weren't speaking directly to all the communities we were working with. So, in response, we commissioned a diversity audit and have based much of our work since then on the recommendations.[39]

Earlier we mentioned how the Wikipedia community values the number of edits made by users above all and that users who create content develop clout within the community. Given that the research that indicates that the average active editor of Wikipedia is an educated white cisgender man living in the Global North, this means that the editors with the most clout tend to be educated white cisgender men living in the Global North.[40] This is particularly relevant because it makes it difficult to increase the presence of people from the Global South, especially those facing structural violence or segregation. This brings up the question: when thousands of women and other marginalized communities take on the challenge of participating in a voluntary platform, how can we support and do justice to their work?

We've already talked about the harassment the core team has experienced in our work, but this is made exponentially more complicated in other geographical and language Wikipedia contexts. Art+Feminism organizers have had multiple run-ins with Italian Wikipedians, for example. One of our organizers and a seasoned Wikipedian, Camelia Boban, recently told the *New York Times* that a user once publicly insinuated that she was a prostitute.[41] Another organizer has written extensively about her negative experience working on Italian Wikipedia for Italian *VICE*.[42] In this instance, the organizer curated a list of well-known video game and digital media artists whose pages were all subsequently deleted on notability grounds, despite the artists having work shown in the Whitney Biennial, among other major exhibitions, and works in major permanent collections.[43] These deletions included nitpicking language typical of Wikipedians wielding guidelines and policies to dissuade new editors from participating, also known as "wikilawyering."[44] And when these editors were asked in good faith to help edit the article instead of deleting it, they declined.[45] In this case, it was clear that the editors recommending the deletion had far less knowledge about the subject matter than the original editors.

We have observed this type of behavior on talk and AfD pages across multiple language Wikipedias; we've experienced similar arguments on English and Spanish Wikipedia, for example. We would argue that this kind of behavior speaks volumes to the ways the insider knowledge of Wikipedia communities and discourses can be used to create boundaries that are inaccessible to women and other marginalized communities. In instances of harassment on other language Wikipedias, unfortunately, the onus is almost entirely on our Regional Ambassador to do all the editing and affective labor involved as our core organizing committee usually cannot intervene due to language barriers. Where possible, we have also relied on informal translations and interventions by other members of our collective with the requisite language skills.

Unfortunately, truly building out a support and safety net for our organizers in local disputes is something that will require greater bandwidth and capacity than we currently have. More importantly, it is work that would require major structural changes within the larger Wikipedia community. It would require a community that is not so white and male. It would require safe and brave space guidelines and avenues for applying them. It would require diversity and equity work from both the Wikipedia Foundation and the community. As long as editors are suspicious of new users, women, people of color, LGBTQIA people, and editors from the Global South will continue to feel unwelcome. In the words of our former director, McKensie Mack, on the experience of working on a Wikipedia-related project as someone who identifies as queer, black, and nonbinary: "It's really important to note that the community is transphobic and homophobic. It's also extremely closed to race and gender equity. Going to conferences and being treated like a doll was terrible. The Art+Feminism collective made me feel welcome, but it was basically you all and nobody else. And that was definitely a huge problem."[46]

Conclusion

In this chapter, we've mapped out a veritable hellscape of microaggressions within the Wikipedia community. However, it's important to note that we—along with thousands of others—continue to participate in the Wikipedia project and community because we believe in it. We're critical because we are, above all, invested. Indeed, we have always believed and continue to believe that Wikipedia has radical feminist potential. In the words of Diana Maffia,

> the Wikipedia initiative is in perfect harmony with the critical feminist project: to take knowledge out of the cloisters, to encourage a collective form of knowledge production, to equate voices to give an opportunity to all proposals, to establish collective forms of correction and not under the undisputed authority of an expert, to install new themes, to influence the agendas of knowledge, to establish links between science, technology and society, to democratize access to knowledge and to allow the public appropriation of its results.[47]

We have seen this ethic modeled within the community as well. We've received wonderful support from the Wikimedia Foundation's Community Resources Team, both financially and emotionally. Art+Feminism would not have been successful without their mentorship. We've also received incredible support from amazing Wikipedians in New York, across the United States, and around the world, without whom the expansion of this project wouldn't have been possible. Many of these people have been with us since day one and continue to attend events and help organize every year.

As Art+Feminism looks forward, the project will bring more voices into our leadership collective in the same way we've tried to bring more voices into Wikipedia at large. As the leadership collective necessarily becomes more diverse, it will better support our regional organizers and also model Wikipedia's radical intersectional feminist potential. As organizers, we do this for a particular moment: that instance where a new editor realizes that their knowledge counts and that they can shape the way other people learn. Watching women, people of color, LGBTQIA folks, and people from varied other marginalized identities feel empowered to share their research and skills is always rewarding. We strongly believe that Wikimedia's future depends on becoming a place where *all* members of the community are recognized and valued.

Notes

1. See, for example, Andrea Peterson, "Happy Ada Lovelace Day! Go Add Some Nerdy Ladies to Wikipedia," *The Washington Post*, October 15, 2013, https://www .washingtonpost.com/news/the-switch/wp/2013/10/15/happy-ada-lovelace-day-go -add-some-nerdy-ladies-to-wikipedia/.

2. "Room for Debate: Where Are the Women in Wikipedia," *The New York Times*, February 2, 2011, https://www.nytimes.com/roomfordebate/2011/02/02/where-are -the-women-in-wikipedia.

3. Amanda Filipacchi, "Wikipedia's Sexism Toward Female Novelists," *The New York Times*, April 24, 2013, https://www.nytimes.com/2013/04/28/opinion/sunday /wikipedias-sexism-toward-female-novelists.html

4. For example, see: G.F., "The Economist Explains: Who Really Runs Wikipedia," *The Economist*, May 6, 2013, https://www.economist.com/the-economist-explains /2013/05/05/who-really-runs-wikipedia; Amanda Filipacchi, "Sexism on Wikipedia Is Not the Work of a 'Single Misguided Editor': It's a Widespread Problem," *The Atlantic*, April 30, 2013, https://www.theatlantic.com/sexes/archive/2013/04/sexism -on-wikipedia-is-not-the-work-of-a-single-misguided-editor/275405/; Deanna Zandt, "Yes, Wikipedia is Sexist—That's Why It Needs You," *Forbes*, April 26, 2013, https:// www.forbes.com/sites/deannazandt/2013/04/26/yes-wikipedia-is-sexist-thats-why-it -needs-you/#541c49b364bf.

5. See Wikipedia, s.v. "Category: American Women Novelists," s.v. "Categories for Discussion: Log April 24. 2013," last modified December 4, 2013, https://en .wikipedia.org/wiki/Wikipedia:Categories_for_discussion/Log/2013_April_24 #Category:American_women_novelists; Wikipedia, s.v. "Category Talk: American Women Novelists," last modified December 27, 2015, https://en.wikipedia.org/wiki /Category_talk:American_women_novelists.

6. We should note here that, before the release of the Programs and Events Dashboard (https://meta.wikimedia.org/wiki/Programs_%26_Events_Dashboard), tracking numbers of articles created and editors attending relied on self-reporting which, for new editors and organizers, was not always a given.

7. Jacqueline Mabey and Michael Mandiberg, "How we organized a 1500 person meetup (and you could too)" (lecture, WikiConference North America, Washington, DC, October 10, 2015), https://commons.wikimedia.org/wiki/File:How_we_organ ized_a_1500_person_meetup_(and_you_could_too)_at_WikiConference_USA_2015 .webm.

8. View the Facebook post and the discussion thread here: Julie Perini, "Portland pals: let's talk," Facebook, January 8, 2014, https://www.facebook.com/events/139163 2164423119/permalink/1393456370907365/.

9. R. Stuart Geiger, "Summary Analysis of the 2017 GitHub Open Source Survey," *arXiv*, June 8 2017, https://arxiv.org/abs/1706.02777.

10. Whitney E. Powell, D. Scott Hunsinger, B. Dawn Medlin, "Gender Differences within the Open Source Community: An Exploratory Study," *Journal of Information Technology Management* 21, no. 4, (2010): 31.

11. Michael Mandiberg, "The Affective Labor of Wikipedia: GamerGate, Harassment, and Peer Production," *SocialText Online*, February 1, 2015, http://socialtextjournal .org/affective-labor-of-wikipedia-gamergate; Astra Taylor, "The Internet's Destructive Gender Gap: Why the Web Can't Abandon Its Misogyny," *Salon*, April 10, 2014, https://www.salon.com/2014/04/10/the_internets_destructive_gender_gap_why _the_web_cant_abandon_its_misogyny_partner/.

12. The Wikimedia Foundation Support & Safety Team, *Harassment Survey 2015 Results Report* (San Francisco, CA: Wikimedia Foundation, 2015), 15, https://upload .wikimedia.org/wikipedia/commons/5/52/Harassment_Survey_2015_-_Results _Report.pdf.

13. Duggan Maeve, *Online Harassment 2017* (Washington, DC: Pew Research Center, July 11, 2017), https://www.pewinternet.org/2017/07/11/online-harassment-2017/.

14. Kimberly Drew, Joanne McNeil, and Zara Rahman, "2018 Wikipedia Edit-a-thon: Art+Feminism | MoMA LIVE," YouTube, video, 1:05:26, March 11, 2017, https://www.youtube.com/watch?v=d-ADrn3UzHk.

15. View the Twitter discussion thread here: MoMA, The Museum of Modern Art (@MuseumModernArt), "Join us 3/11 for Wikipedia Edit-a-thon: Art+Feminism! Begins 10am w/@jomc, @zararah & @museummammy. Info & RSVP: http://mo.ma /wikipedia_rsvp," Twitter, March 8, 2017, 12:14 p.m., https://twitter.com/Museum ModernArt/status/839524754038075393.

16. It is important to note that we use gender neutral pronouns throughout this chapter but it should be acknowledged that abuse within the Wikipedia community (and online in general) is often cast as being gendered, but in many cases it can also cross gender lines.

17. Julia Jacobs, "Wikipedia Isn't Officially a Social Network. But the Harassment Can Get Ugly," *The New York Times*, April 8, 2019, https://www.nytimes.com/2019 /04/08/us/wikipedia-harassment-wikimedia-foundation.html.

18. For our immediate response see Art+Feminism (@artandfeminism), "To @ jimmy_wales it was an #artandfeminism editathon at MoMA & no, Wikipedia is not great at dealing with harassment," Twitter, August 13, 2017, 4:42p.m., https:// twitter.com/artandfeminism/status/896849435879247872/photo/1.

19. Wikipedia, s.v. "Wikipedia: Meetup Page: Art+Feminism Safe Space/Brave Space Policy," last modified December 27, 2015, https://en.wikipedia.org/wiki/Wikipedia: Meetup/ArtandFeminism/Safespacepolicy.

20. Shyong (Tony) K. Lam, Anuradha Uduwage, Zhenhua Dong, Shilad Sen, David R. Musicant, Loren Terveen, and John Riedl, "WP:Clubhouse? An Exploration of Wikipedia's Gender Imbalance," in *WikiSym '11: Proceedings of the 7th International Symposium on Wikis and Open Collaboration* (New York: ACM, 2011), 1–10.

21. Wikipedia, s.v. "Wikipedia: Wikipedians," last modified May 9, 2019, https://en .wikipedia.org/wiki/Wikipedia:Wikipedians.

22. Tom Simonite, "The Decline of Wikipedia," *MIT Technology Review*, October 23, 2013, https://www.technologyreview.com/s/520446/the-decline-of-wikipedia/.

23. Simonite, "The Decline of Wikipedia."

24. A. Halfaker, R. S. Gieger, J. Morgan, and J. Riedl, "The Rise and Decline of an Open Collaboration System: How Wikipedia's Reaction to Sudden Popularity Is Causing Its Decline," *American Behavioral Scientist* 57, no. 5 (2013): 664–688, https:// doi.org/10.1177/0002764212469365.

25. Lam et al., "WP:Clubhouse?"

26. Dorothy Howard, "Labor and the New Encyclopedia," *Dis Magazine*, March 2015.

27. Meta-Wiki, s.v. "Talk: Global Metrics/Review," last modified August 2, 2016, https://meta.wikimedia.org/wiki/Talk:Global_metrics/Review.

28. See Meta-Wiki, s.v. "Talk: Global Metrics/Review"; Wikimedia, s.v. "Grant Metrics Instead of Global Metrics," s.v. "Grants: IdeaLab: Redesigning Global Metrics and Its Support," last modified September 14, 2016, https://meta.wikimedia .org/wiki/Grants:IdeaLab/Redesigning_Global_Metrics_%26_its_support/Outcome #Grant_metrics_instead_of_Global_Metrics.

29. Mandiberg, "The Affective Labor of Wikipedia."

30. Meta-Wiki, s.v. "Art+Feminism Simple Annual Planning Grant Midpoint Report 2018–2019," last modified June 3, 2019, https://meta.wikimedia.org/wiki /Art%2BFeminism_User_Group/Reporting/MidpointReport2018-2019.

31. See Brooke Erin Duffy, *(Not) Getting Paid to Do What You Love: Gender, Social Media, and Aspirational Work* (New Haven, CT: Yale University Press, 2017) for an analysis of how the labor of social media production is gendered; see Silvia Federici, *Caliban and the Witch: Women, the Body and Primitive Accumulation* (New York: Autonomedia, 2014) for essential writing on the gendering of reproductive labor.

32. Halfaker et al., "The Rise and Decline of an Open Collaboration System."

33. Wikidata Query Service, query for all items with "on focus list of Wikimedia project (P5008)" of "Art+Feminism (Q24909800)," https://w.wiki/4mA.

34. Wikipedia, s.v. "Use the Draft Template," s.v. "Wikipedia: Meetup/ArtAndFeminism," last modified April 4, 2019, https://en.wikipedia.org/wiki/Wikipedia:Meetup/ArtAndFeminism#Use_the_Draft_Template.

35. Meta-Wiki, s.v. "Less than 1% of All Articles Were Deleted," s.v. "Art+Feminism User Group/Reporting/MidpointReport2017-2018," last modified June 3, 2019, https://meta.wikimedia.org/wiki/Art%2BFeminism_User_Group/Reporting/MidpointReport2017-2018#Less_than_1%_of_all_articles_were_Deleted.

36. Flavia Fascendi, "Reshaping the Internet for Women," *Association for Progressive Communication*, January 9, 2017, https://www.apc.org/en/news/reshaping-internet-women.

37. Meta-Wiki, s.v. "Translated Materials," s.v. "Art+Feminism User Group/Reporting/MidpointReport2018-2019," last modified June 3, 2019, https://meta.wikimedia.org/wiki/Art%2BFeminism_User_Group/Reporting/MidpointReport2018-2019#Translated_materials.

38. Meta-Wiki, s.v. "Art+Feminism User Group/Planning/Staffing2018," last modified August 14, 2018, https://meta.wikimedia.org/w/index.php?title=Art%2BFeminism_User_Group/Planning/Staffing2018.

39. Alice Backer, Sheetal Prajapati, and Marin Watts, *Art+Feminism Diversity Audit* (2016), https://upload.wikimedia.org/wikipedia/commons/0/07/2016ArtAndFeminismDiversityReview.pdf.

40. Mani Pande, "Wikipedia Editors Do It for Fun: First Results of Our 2011 Editor Survey," *Wikimedia Foundation* (blog), June 10, 2011, https://blog.wikimedia.org/2011/06/10/wikipedia-editors-do-it-for-fun-first-results-of-our-2011-editor-survey/.

41. Jacobs, "Wikipedia Isn't Officially a Social Network."

42. Annamaria Andrea Vitali, "Come ho cercato di combattere il sessismo su Wikipedia in italiano," *VICE: Motherboard*, June 27, 2017, https://www.vice.com/it/article/7xz5vq/come-ho-cercato-di-combattere-il-sessismo-di-wikipedia-italia.

43. Vitali, "Come ho cercato di combattere il sessismo su Wikipedia in italiano."

44. Wikipedia, s.v. "Wikipedia: Wikilawyering," last modified May 11, 2019, https://en.wikipedia.org/wiki/Wikipedia:Wikilawyering.

45. Vitali, "Come ho cercato di combattere il sessismo su Wikipedia in italiano."

46. McKensie Mack, personal interview by Siân Evans, June 7, 2019.

47. Diana Maffia, "Género y lengua. Dos brechas clave en el ámbito de la ciencia y la tecnología," in *La cuestión de género en el mundo digital. Wikipedia y otras comunidades. Conferencia Wikigénero*, ed. Juan Nadalini (Buenos Aires: Wikimedia Argentina, 2014), 8, https://upload.wikimedia.org/wikipedia/commons/1/1d/La_cuesti%C3%B3n_de_g%C3%A9nero_en_el_mundo_digital._Wikipedia_y_otras_comunidades..pdf.

16   Toward a Wikipedia For and From Us All

Adele Godoy Vrana, Anasuya Sengupta, and Siko Bouterse

To build a Wikipedia that reflects the full breadth and depth of humanity, we must deconstruct the myths that allow misogyny, racism, colonialism, and other forms of oppression to flourish in our communities and build new practices for the next twenty years. As Whose Knowledge? cofounders, we draw on our experiences to offer paths forward.

We love Wikipedia. As readers, and as contributors. But we also hate what it can do to many of us from marginalized communities around the world. Most Wikipedians find it hard to accept that a truly inspiring model of peer production can sit alongside misogyny, racism, and colonialism, but this has indeed been our experience of Wikipedia's first twenty years.

Don't get us wrong; we do love Wikipedia. But for us, our passion for the projects translates into tough love. We believe in speaking up about some of the critical issues of marginalization that have been lurking, invisible, or silenced over the past twenty years. And we believe that acting to change this status quo will make Wikipedia and the Wikimedia movement more powerful and relevant over the next twenty.

We were initially drawn to the encyclopedia and the movement several years ago as feminists, scholars, organizers, and people who are curious about the many worlds we inhabit.

Siko Bouterse is an online community organizer, digital activist, feminist, and mother of a feminist. She grew up in the United States with family spread across three continents in both the Global North and Global South, and her interest in the internet began as a way to connect people across languages, cultures, and spaces. She joined the Wikimedia Foundation in 2011 and became both director of community resources (a temporary state) and a Wikipedian (something she'll probably never get over).

Feeling marginalized and missing from history as a woman, she was first drawn to working on Wikipedia's gender gap. Today Siko continues to use her cisgender white privilege to challenge injustice and inequality of many forms online.

Anasuya Sengupta is an Indian feminist activist and scholar who lives and works across multiple continents and online as a Wikipedian. Having stopped editing after a couple of anonymous improvements in 2006, she joined the Wikimedia Foundation in 2012, became chief grantmaking officer, and then began in earnest to edit and amplify marginalized knowledges on Wikipedia as a volunteer (there's no stopping her now). She's led and supported social justice initiatives in India and the United States, particularly against caste- and sexuality-based discriminations, religious fundamentalisms, and gender-based violence. She acknowledges the multiple and simultaneous positions of power and disempowerment she holds and experiences, especially as an "upper caste" or savarna brown woman from the Global South.

Adele Godoy Vrana is an Afro-Brazilian feminist and social justice activist who joined the Wikimedia movement in 2012. As the former director of strategic partnerships at the Wikimedia Foundation, she led partnership initiatives to help increase access to Wikipedia in the Global South. A Wikimedian against all odds, she decided to stick around to make the point that black women belong everywhere, with or without an edit count. As a marginalized Global South student, she first learned of Wikipedia in her mid-twenties when she could not afford to buy books. She has been grateful to Wikipedia since then while also determined to make the knowledges of people like her visible, heard, and affirmed as part of this movement.

As we became part of the Wikimedia movement, all three of us saw the potential in this huge multilingual, global, online community and project to collect and curate the many textures and layers of human knowledge. Yet we also knew that this potential was far from being met. At the time we joined the Wikimedia Foundation, Wikipedia's gender and Global South gaps were already documented, but very few were actively and collaboratively working to address these gaps. It was still contentious to even mention these gaps in polite Wikipedian society. Much of our time at the Foundation was spent making these issues central to the Wikimedia movement and supporting new initiatives to address them. But perhaps because innovation so rarely comes from an institutional core, by 2015 we'd begun to see that we would be able to make more joyful and transformative progress in some of these areas from the outside, and eventually each of us left the Wikimedia Foundation to cofound Whose Knowledge?.

Increasingly over the past eight years, many new initiatives, groups, and collaborations have begun to address some of these content and contributor gaps. Today, working to address the gender gap has become a regular part of many Wikimedia chapters' annual programming. Wikimedian user groups have been growing across the Global South. Initiatives like AfroCROWD, Black Lunch Table (chapter 17), Art+Feminism (chapter 15), Wikimujeres, Dalit History Month, and Women in Red are working to create new content and inspire new editors from marginalized communities.

We've been happy to collaborate with a growing number of these groups and initiatives in our shared aim to improve Wikipedia. We began Whose Knowledge? in 2016 to center the knowledge of marginalized communities on the internet. We work as a global campaign with women, people of color, LGBTQIA communities, indigenous peoples, and others from the Global South to build and represent more of all of our knowledge online, including on Wikimedia projects.

We've supported marginalized communities like the Dalits, those formerly and pejoratively known as the "untouchables" in India; Native Americans in the United States; and queer feminists in Bosnia and Herzegovina to add their knowledge to Wikipedia.[1] We've partnered with Wikimedians and feminist organizations around the world to add images of women to Wikimedia Commons and Wikipedia in our annual #VisibleWikiWomen campaign.[2] And we organized our first "Decolonizing the Internet," convening at Wikimania 2018 in Cape Town, where we brought together activists, artists, scholars, technologists, and Wikipedians.[3] Most were women and transgender folks, people of color and people from the Global South, and many were attending a Wikipedia event for the very first time.

Despite these collective efforts, Wikipedia is not yet the Wikipedia the world deserves. Wikipedia's five pillars of free knowledge include that it's written from "a neutral point of view," that people should be treated with "respect and civility," and that it's an "encyclopedia."[4] These have helped Wikipedia—impossible in theory—be possible in practice. Yet bringing marginalized knowledges to Wikipedia will mean shaking these pillars without destroying its foundations. It will mean challenging Wikipedians to be reflexive about whether the norms, rules, and bureaucracy that made Wikipedia flourish in the last twenty years might kill it over the next twenty.

To do this, we also need to start naming and deconstructing some of the significant myths that are getting in our way and keeping us from building collective bodies of knowledge that truly reflect the full breadth and depth of the world. By naming these myths and sharing ideas for practices to move forward in different ways, we hope to reimagine and redesign Wikipedia as a more equitable, thriving source of knowledge for and from us all.

We begin by sharing the data that shows how urgently we need to examine these myths and by describing the frames that help us understand why they exist and are perpetuated in the first place.

The Data and Frames That Inspire Us

Over half of the world is now online. Nearly half of all women are now online.[5] Three-fourths of those online today are from the Global South—from Asia, Latin America, Africa, the Caribbean and Pacific Islands.[6]

Yet the internet and Wikipedia—the encyclopedia of the world—don't reflect this reality in either content or contribution. The largest open and free knowledge platform online was begun by white men from North America and Europe as a digital encyclopedia, extending a long enlightenment-driven tradition into cyberspace—as recounted in chapter 19. Today, a relatively privileged minority of the world is still writing about the majority on Wikipedia.

Only 20 percent of the world, primarily white male editors from North America and Europe, edits 80 percent of Wikipedia.[7] Because who you are impacts what you create, this lack of diversity in contributors leads to lack of diversity in content. Researchers at Oxford Internet Institute recently found that, although Africa has nearly twice the population of Europe, it has only 15 percent the amount of Wikipedia articles.[8] There are more articles written about Antarctica than most countries in Africa and many in Latin America and Asia. Less than one-fourth of all Wikipedia biographies today represent women in nearly every language version of Wikipedia.[9]

Wikipedia is still missing so much knowledge from marginalized communities around the world, and we don't yet have useful data or research about LGBTQIA, indigenous, or black and brown contributors and content. It may be because we don't often ask these critical questions of who and what is missing or consider the responses to these questions as central to the future of Wikipedia.

Bringing people of color, women, LGBTQIA, indigenous, and Global South folks to Wikipedia and the Wikimedia movement is not only ethical, it is also strategically necessary for survival because that mythical "next billion" readers and potential content creators is already online (and they're nearly three billion!).[10] An encyclopedia that intends to grow and truly be the sum of all human knowledge needs locally relevant content that connects the majority of the world, not only the minority.

Yet it is not surprising that this is the status quo. Wikipedia reflects the realities of the worlds we live in and the ways in which power and privilege operate today and have operated historically.

This is what feminist activist and scholar Srilatha Batliwala calls direct, indirect, and agenda-setting power.[11] *Direct power* is often easily visible and shows who wields control over different resources, spaces, and assets—like the Wikimedia Foundation, which operates the websites. *Agenda-setting power* is often hidden and behind the scenes: it determines who sets the agenda and how; what issues, perspectives, and approaches are amplified, and which are undermined or ignored; what is considered important and what is not. Examples of this might include Wikipedia or Wikimedia Commons admins, who ultimately determine which articles should be kept and which should be deleted or which online campaigns should be promoted and which shouldn't. Finally, the most insidious power—which operates through the others—is *indirect* or invisible power, which molds the way we think about ourselves and the attitudes and biases we have. Many of these invisible biases are experienced as we argue over what does or does not belong in an encyclopedia.

Power often feels invisible until you begin to see it everywhere. Abuse of power happens when we don't call it out or talk about what concerns us, including on Wikipedia. As we've said elsewhere, we all hold different structures and positions of power and privilege in different contexts. In some situations, we can hold power "over" others in the room or space, and in some contexts, we are the ones who feel disempowered.[12]

Everyone is, or can be, an ally to someone else. We can build a better Wikipedia in solidarity with each other. But the first step is to recognize the myths that are keeping us from working together in productive ways—and then to build new, welcoming, and inclusive practices that will make this happen.

Myths of Wikipedia

Myth: The Eighteenth-Century Enlightenment Invented Science, Technology, and Knowledge at Large

When we talk about the history of science and technology, where do you begin? When someone talks about knowledge, what do you think about? For many white male Wikipedians, science, technology, and knowledge were created in the eighteenth century. The "Enlightenment" era originates the notion of the "encyclopedia" as the repository of all knowledge.

Yet, if you ask these same questions to the three of us, we wouldn't start there. Anasuya will probably tell you about the ways in which writing and number systems evolved in Sumeria and Akkadia (present day Iran and Iraq), how the representation of the zero traveled from the Indian subcontinent and into the Arab world, and how Aryabhata measured time in the fifth century. Siko is likely to talk about Native American and women's deep knowledge of the land, plants, animals, and human bodies, which has existed for millennia, as well as the vast knowledge of astronomy, geography, architecture, and horticulture that medieval travelers from North Africa, the Arabian peninsula, and eastern Mediterranean brought to Europe. Adele might tell you that when she thinks about knowledge, she thinks about her grandmother, who had indigenous origins and knew about the native Brazilian plants that could cure many kinds of illness.

All these histories and definitions of knowledge are true. But not all of them are created and known equally. When we think about Wikipedia, the deeper and broader set of histories and knowledges that the three of us represent—the histories and knowledges of the majority of the world—don't make the cut. They are not considered neutral, notable, or citable enough to be part of the world's biggest online encyclopedia.

After twenty years of great accomplishments, if Wikipedia truly wants to celebrate, collect, and curate all the knowledge of the world, here's the place to start: science, technology, and knowledge at large are not an eighteenth-century European creation. Nor is the effort primarily male. The first farmers—most of whom were, as they continue to be, women—were scientists. Ancient African villages were constructed in complex fractal mathematical patterns.[13] And the oldest existing university in the world was set up in 859 ce by the Arab Muslim woman scholar Fatima Al-Fihri in Morocco.[14]

Why do we forget these far richer, broader, more diverse histories of our world and its knowledges? Because the age of "Enlightenment" for Europe was the age of "Empire" for the rest of us: from the eighteenth century onward (and a little earlier for Latin America), the Global South—Africa, Asia, Latin America, and the Pacific and Caribbean islands—was assaulted and attacked by European colonizers. With the collusion and cooperation of some of our own people, Global South histories and knowledges, our ways of knowing and being, were either destroyed, marginalized, or made completely invisible to others.

Even unintentionally, have Wikipedians assumed that the only worthwhile histories of science and technology are European and North American? That knowledge itself can only be understood through an eighteenth-century construction of the encyclopedia? If so, are we willing to change our assumptions, policies, and structures to expand the histories and knowledges we once left out? As we celebrate the last twenty years, now seems to be the right time to make the changes that will make Wikipedia a truly global knowledge repository for many more years to come.

Practices to Move Forward

Let's agree that context matters. Everyone has a point of view, and only by bringing many perspectives and interests together can we work toward any form of collective "neutrality." It's time to stop assuming that white men's knowledge from the Global North is "neutral" while knowledge from marginalized communities is pushing a "point of view." Your understanding of science, technology, and knowledge depends on who you are, where you come from, and what you look like. And the content you choose to create reflects who is creating it. It's time to consider campaigns like Wiki Loves Pride and Dalit History Month to be just as relevant to building "the sum of all human knowledge" as Wiki Loves Monuments and collaboration drives about railway stations. Each of these reflects the worldviews, interests, and expertise of people who choose to focus on these topics. Wikipedia's ongoing relevance as the largest online repository of knowledge will depend on whether we allow these plural worldviews to coexist or to continue to allow one group to dominate.

Let's expand our understanding of knowledge. So much of the world's knowledge and histories are oral, embodied, and unpublished. What would Wikipedia look like if it made significant space for oral knowledge? If citing oral testimony from indigenous grandmothers was as normal to Wikipedians as citing the *New York Times*? If we looked at the expertise of a dancer in the same way we understood the expertise of a physicist? Unless we want Wikipedia to continue representing only a very small fraction of the world's knowledge, it's time to develop new strategies and actions to incorporate multiple forms of knowledge.

Let's rethink notability policies. Biographies of people who are women, transgender, black, brown, indigenous, queer, or from the Global South are more likely to be considered not "notable" and thus not included on Wikipedia because marginalized communities are vastly underrepresented in the kinds of published sources that Wikipedians consider "reliable." Marielle Franco, a queer Black woman from Brazil, was an important politician and human rights activist who had to die to become notable enough for Wikipedia.[15] Going forward, we need to stop applying the same set of norms and rules that keep out your uncle's latest garage band or pyramid scheme to black and brown women and other marginalized communities on Wikipedia. To do this, we need to build collective understanding that systemic bias, marginalization, and oppression is reinforced through Wikipedia's current understanding of reliable sources and notability and make policy changes.

Myth: The Gender Gap Is the Main or Only Diversity Problem to Solve on Wikipedia

Over the past ten years, the Wikimedia movement has begun to recognize the lack of diversity among Wikipedia editors and to discuss it as a challenge for Wikipedia's future.

When we first joined Wikipedia, there were already startling stats that documented the encyclopedia's abysmal gender gap, finding that only one in ten Wikipedians identified as women.[16] Thanks to volunteers, activists, researchers, and allies from around the world, a lot has been done to address this issue.

Fixing the gender gap, however, became the proxy for fixing Wikipedia's diversity problem. While gender is no longer a taboo topic, Wikipedians are often still too uncomfortable to talk openly about racism, decolonization, indigeneity, and homophobia or transphobia.

In practical terms, addressing Wikipedia's diversity problem has meant to create more seats at the table for white women. And strategies that work to bring more cisgender white women and Global North content to the encyclopedia will not necessarily work for other marginalized communities or for folks who are marginalized in multiple, intersecting ways. The strategies that help a white, able-bodied, cisgendered woman speaking English are unlikely to be as supportive for a queer black woman who is visually impaired and reads Portuguese braille.

The sad reality is that despite all the efforts to address the gender gap, women continue to face the same problems that have been documented for the past decade, including hostile cultures, unwritten or confusingly written rules, and unfair policies that send clear signals for women to stay away. But this should not prevent Wikipedians from embracing complex conversations about intersectional identities and other forms of marginalization. Instead, it should encourage Wikipedians to tackle these systemic issues together.

Wikipedia and other open knowledge spaces need to understand that systems of power and privilege are so hard to dismantle precisely because they encompass multiple forms of oppression and subjugation. Patriarchy, racism, colonization, homophobia, transphobia, and xenophobia reinforce and feed off each other. You can't fix your diversity problem while having a single-issue agenda where patriarchy is called out but other systems of power and privilege remain intact.

As we reimagine the Wikipedia we want to build for the future, we'll need to stop compartmentalizing and instead consider how the intersections of race, gender, sexuality, indigeneity, class, language, Global North/ Global South differences, and so on act together to influence both participation and content. Equity, rather than a simple understanding of diversity, should be our true goal.

Practices to Move Forward

Let's make sure the conversation about equity and diversity keeps expanding. The Wikimedia movement needs to be talking about race, decolonization, indigeneity, and LGBTQIA issues because ignoring these is not an option. In 2019, Art+Feminism (discussed in chapter 15) expanded their focus to explicitly include gender nonbinary people.[17] That same year, our #VisibleWikiWomen campaign added an explicit focus on #WomenofColors, encouraging participants to especially add images of black, brown, and indigenous cis and transgender women.

Let's deepen and expand Wikipedia research. Research on the gender gap is important, and we're glad to have the data that exists on this topic so far.

Data can help catalyze actions. It would also be very useful to have data about content and contributors from other marginalized communities to help everyone better understand Wikipedia's race gaps, Global South gaps, LGBTQIA gaps, and more.

Let's make sure we're supporting action by resourcing it. Much has been said about the gender gap, but there needs to be substantial investment of resources going toward addressing this gap as well as many other equity issues. The actions of the Wikimedia movement should be at least as loud and strong as its words. The amount of people, money, and time we spend on activities aimed at addressing these gaps and supporting marginalized communities speaks volumes about how much we actually care and how much we'll likely achieve.

Let's make equitable power sharing and resource mobilization our goal instead of just a few diverse seats at the table. In our time at the Wikimedia Foundation, Anasuya and Adele were the only women of color from the Global South in executive positions, while there were a handful of people who looked like Siko in leadership. Numbers are necessary but woefully insufficient. Having a few seats like these did not mean the Foundation was openly discussing and addressing systemic bias and oppression or that we had the power or resources to drive the agenda and change the status quo. Without critical mass, having a few marginalized folks amid a majority who retains power and privilege can work as an excuse to avoid real changes. Inviting marginalized communities in and creating seats at the table is just the beginning. Next, we need to make sure everyone is safe, seen, heard, empowered, and resourced to make significant changes.

Let's work together as allies across multiple intersections. White men, we want you on our side! Our Decolonizing the Internet 2018 conference included people from so many different backgrounds and identities, including white men as allies, precisely because we know that big complex problems require lots of people with different skills and experiences to work together on multiple solutions.

Myth: Violence Is Only Physical. And It's Only Abuse If It's Been Repeated Many Times

People from marginalized communities experience violence every day as they participate in Wikipedia. Sometimes it's so overt and obvious that it does get labeled as harassment, and occasionally the perpetrator of the harassment is held to some account. However, in most cases, abuse and violence occur more subtly and with different forms of power: verbal, sexual, economic, and so on.[18] Because patriarchy has socialized so many of us around the world today to believe that it's not violence unless a man has punched his wife in the face, many forms of daily violence, including emotional and verbal abuse, are ignored—including on Wikipedia. Over the many years we've lived and worked on Wikipedia, we've seen far too many examples of this.

Deadnaming, a practice of saying or writing a transgender person's old name from before they transitioned, and refusing to use a transgender or nonbinary person's chosen pronouns is a form of violence that happens to trans and nonbinary editors on Wikipedia on a regular basis. It's kept many good trans and nonbinary encyclopedians from coming in and sticking around. When you're already fighting for the right to exist in the larger world, why would you also want to do it as an online hobby?

In 2018 we worked with an LGBTQIA group in Bosnia and Herzegovina who were writing Wikipedia articles about notable queer feminists from the region. When participants went to add six well-sourced biographies of notable writers, artists, historians, and activists to Bosnian Wikipedia, the articles were immediately nominated for deletion. When one article's creator politely asked for a rationale, a deleting administrator suggested that all they needed to do was remove the person's "personal sexual affiliation" from the biography. It's still not OK to be queer in Bosnia, and LGBTQIA folks experience daily violence in the streets of their cities. This violence is perpetuated online by telling a queer person that their article about another queer person (who clearly meets the notability guidelines) can live on Wikipedia if they just don't mention their sexuality.

We have seen a Wikipedia gender gap organizer lose her job because of the actions of a troll who stalked her personal life, looking for ways to bring her down. She stepped away from Wikipedia for a long time as a result. This, too, is a form of violence.

We have seen Dalit women's contributions to Wikipedia being contested at every turn, not because they're vandalizing Wikipedia but because they upset the status quo of how European and upper-caste Wikipedians choose to represent caste on Wikipedia. Because of their status at the bottom of the caste pyramid, Dalits experience daily harassment and violence in real life as well as online.[19] On Wikipedia, a long-time Wikipedian has doggedly rolled back thoughtfully sourced contributions from Dalit editors and belittled their edits. He has also aggressively asked Dalit History Month organizers to personally identify themselves, despite the common norm of anonymity on Wikipedia. When the harassment was reported to the Wikimedia Foundation's Trust and Safety team, we read an all-too-familiar response that harassment has to be "egregious" in order for action to be taken, and nothing was done.

But what counts as "egregious"? Who decides? Without shared clarity and the centering of marginalized communities in defining the scope and consequences of different forms of violence, everyday forms of violence add up. They add up to an encyclopedia where those with the most privilege, tolerance for aggression, and leisure time continue being seen as our most valued editors while others are made to feel unwelcome in different ways.

So how can we ever hope to address Wikipedia's gender gap or systemic bias issues if we're unwilling to address acts of violence that permeate our online and offline worlds every day?

Practices to Move Forward

Let's speak up, even if it's difficult. Let's call out violence and abuse of all kinds. Let's call in our friends who might not realize they're complicit in perpetuating violence. We need to "call out" violence and abuse by their names. Even if it's not slapping, even if it's not hitting. Even if it's not explicit rape threats. Even if it's "just" once or twice. Let's stop minimizing the everyday violence that folks from marginalized communities experience in our movement and start by recognizing that every time any form of violence happens, it has a cost to the Wikipedia we're trying to build together. We should "call in" folks who may not even realize they are part of perpetuating this violence: all of us bear responsibility to reach out to people with understanding and generosity while challenging them to break the cycles of violence. We can do this quietly; it doesn't always have to be in public, but these conversations need to happen.

If we don't speak up, we're part of the system. If we don't call in our friends who might be adding to the problem, even unintentionally, we're not really being good friends.

In particular, as Wikipedians, we need to recognize that "virtual" violence is still violence. We need to admit that the sometimes hostile, often confrontational nature of on-wiki conversations feel painful and abusive to newbies, to women and trans folks, to people who speak a different language, to marginalized communities of different kinds. And we know that this nature of violent argumentation can be the starting point for far more disturbing ad hominem attacks, sexist or racist slurs, and various forms of digital doxxing and harassment. At the same time, as Wikipedians, we need to accept that violence in any sphere of our lives needs to be condemned, not condoned, whether it's on a talk page, on a street, at a Wikimedia event, or at home.

Even in the course of writing this chapter, we spoke up about instances of abuse and violence that hadn't occurred on Wikipedia but that we understood to have been perpetrated by a member of the Wikipedia community. We knew that if we chose to consider the abuse as "just personal" and considered it our role to focus on "egregious" incidents that happened only on-wiki or at formal Wikipedia events, our day-to-day lives would be easier. But we know all too well that the personal is deeply political, and spills over into the professional. These artificial separations of "personal," "professional," and "political" hide many forms of silence, especially around abuse and discrimination. We could not dismiss a woman's story of domestic abuse—and continue to be part of building the perpetrator's career within our community—without reflection, recognition, and discussion. So we joined with a larger group of concerned wiki-folks and raised the issue—as thoughtfully as we could—of who we would and would not work with going forward and what behaviors are acceptable in our communities.

Let's do it together. Let's not have those being harassed, abused, or discriminated against be the sole voices challenging violence. We've learned that it's both unfair and ineffective to expect that the person or people who are most affected by violence should be the only ones who speak up, including on Wikipedia. We need others—allies—to step up and support those impacted, especially those who have some privilege themselves. In both the Bosnian and Dalit cases above, having long-time Wikipedians as allies helped content remain on Wikipedia. When well-known editors step up to vote to retain content, improve articles, and support newer editors in crafting arguments using Wikipedia's coded language, this helps to break the cycle of violence.

Myth: A Wikipedian Is Born, Not Made

This saying is particularly brutalizing for someone like Anasuya and her Dalit friends, who come from South Asia, and have to contend with an oppressive caste system that believes that manual scavengers—those who clean toilets and handle corpses—are born, not made. This is brutalizing for someone like Adele and her Afro-Brazilian friends, whose ancestors were once enslaved and who still need campaigns to prove their lives matter. Or for Siko and her indigenous friends, who grew up in California with narratives of history that dismissed women and portrayed indigenous people as born savages rather than those who resisted brutal colonization.

No, Wikipedians are not born from immaculate conception. Wikipedians and Wikimedians are also a social construct. Yes, editing Wikipedia does need a certain interest in knowledge, a curiosity about the world, and a generosity with sharing it—but those traits are in significant swathes of populations across the world, not simply in the eighty thousand incredible volunteers who currently edit Wikipedia. And yes, organizing Wikimedia events and projects online and offline needs some interest in organizing communities and a generosity in holding them together, but those traits are also in significant groups of people, not just those who currently are at the center of our movement.

Wikipedia volunteers have had to learn how to enter, to participate, and to behave a certain way to be part of our communities and movement. But what happens when you don't know where to start, what to learn, and whom to ask for support? Not everyone even realizes that they *can* edit Wikipedia if they're not already part of a group who know they can. Everyone— particularly those of us who come from marginalized communities—likes and sometimes needs to be invited to join a space or a community to feel welcome and at ease there.

Once you understand you actually can edit, many other barriers remain, including confusing rules, requirements that may not make any sense in the context of your culture's knowledge, and unfriendly editors who will come yell at you on-wiki if you do it wrong.

If you do manage to overcome these barriers and stay for a while, you will then learn that the way other Wikipedians recognize you is solely based on your "edit count," the number of times you publish a change to content. But when you're from a marginalized community, you'll learn that your articles will face extra scrutiny, so you can't publish half-finished things. So women, for example, publish more words in fewer edits than men do.[20] Many from the Global South who have unpredictable internet and electricity connections write entire articles offline and upload each article with a single edit. In other words, if you're sitting in the middle of Maharashtra, you may have created five amazing new articles and organized an offline event to support other new editors to do the same, but you have an edit count of five and will still not be counted as a "real" Wikipedian.

These are not simple hoops one can easily jump through. These are significant foundational barriers for anyone who wants to edit Wikipedia or to become a Wikipedian, especially those marginalized folks who may need extra support to justify spending their limited free time and resources on-wiki.

Practices to Move Forward

Let's move beyond the edit count as a way to honor and acknowledge contributions in the Wikimedia movement. Wikipedia, its sister projects, and our movement needs people who fulfill many different kinds of roles and responsibilities. And if we continue to ask the question (even in our heads) of "what is your edit count?" as the only credible way to assess a person's legitimacy in the movement, we deny significant parts of our movement the respect they deserve for organizing events, managing communities, ensuring local partnerships, and so on. We also shut down the possibility of these people becoming editors, even if their entry points to the movement were not through editing.

Let's translate interest and generosity into practical ways in which people can contribute to Wikipedia. In 2014, African Wikimedians held their first ever gathering, called Wiki Indaba, in Cape Town. At the time, most people, including in our movement, thought that they could never get a significant community together like the Europeans had. In 2018, just four years later, that same group hosted a major global Wikimania in Cape Town, with a clear clarion call for Ubuntu—the southern African philosophy and practice of connected humanity, "I am because we are"—as a way to collectively challenge the knowledge gaps in our projects and communities.

Let's offer help instead of criticism when new editors make mistakes. The best edit-a-thons have experienced editors warmly helping newbies to improve. Rather than showing people all the ways and places they've gone wrong or making them "prove" why their article should not be deleted, what if we jumped in to fix mistakes, add sources, and show them how to make those improvements themselves next time? What if before deciding they were wrong and going onto their talk pages to yell or argue, we stopped to consider if perhaps they too have experience and expertise we can learn from?

Myth: Ignoring Uncomfortable Things Makes Them Disappear

When we first joined the Wikimedia movement, no one talked about race. No one talked about transgender editors, either. Folks had only just started talking about how Wikipedia was missing women. They had barely started talking about how it was missing contributions from the Global South.

Not talking about race has not fixed racism on Wikipedia. When we joined the Wikimedia Foundation in San Francisco, we were met with puzzled looks when we asked who the African American, indigenous, black, or Latinx editors were in the US Wikipedian community. We didn't encounter them at meetups or conferences; we didn't know their names. Yet we were told over and over again that the North American Wikipedian community was flourishing, possibly even at saturation. How could this be true when significant slices of the US population were not represented as editors or in content?

Ignoring gender-based violence in the Wikimedia movement has also not made it go away. Wikimedia chapters have been brought to a standstill by instances of violence against women from long-time male editors. Women organizers have been discouraged from continuing to lead projects that improve Wikipedia because of harassment and abuse. Trans and nonbinary people don't often stay long on Wikipedia because of the everyday violence they face. Often we become aware of these stories only because we're listening for the whispers and following up with our trusted colleagues to gather more information. All too often nothing happens because silence is considered safest. But when we do nothing, these problems don't go away. They grow bigger, and they happen again, in the same or different contexts.

Practices for Moving Forward

Let's talk about these uncomfortable things together. Through discomfort and a genuine willingness to engage with it comes improvement and transformation. Let's talk about how racism manifests on Wikipedia in obvious and subtle ways. Let's talk about gender-based violence. About transphobia. About different kinds of systemic biases that cause underrepresentation in Wikipedia and its sister projects in both contributors and content. If our projects are truly to be the largest and most useful open knowledge ecosystem, we need to be willing to have the tough conversations about whose knowledge is currently missing and why.

Let's support groups and efforts working on specific knowledge gaps, not troll them. What has helped address gaps in content written by and about black communities on Wikipedia? Projects like AfroCROWD and Black Lunch Table that specifically focus on calling out these gaps and inviting and supporting more black editors to help fill them. Whose Knowledge's #VisibleWikiWomen campaign—in partnership with these groups and others like Women in Red, Wikimujeres, and similar groups across the world—has been able to add the images of nearly five thousand important women to Wikimedia Commons in two years. Yet even as we all get support from a number of Wikimedians, we also receive condemnation, backlash, and threats as we do this work. And even if this form of trolling is by a vocal minority, the fact that the majority doesn't push back explicitly makes this feel like lonely, dangerous, and unacknowledged work. Let's all start speaking up and pushing back in solidarity.

Building For and From Us All

Wikipedia can survive and thrive over the next twenty years and grow into something even more amazing than it already is. It will need us to deconstruct the myths that exclude people and content and limit our potential. It will require us to expand the definitions of who and what belongs on Wikipedia, to work together in mutual respect and solidarity, and to build and share new practices to become the fullest online knowledge repository that we aspire to be. We're looking forward to learning, developing, and exchanging more of these practices with everyone who wishes to be a part of this journey of Ubuntu, of connected humanity. Let's build this together: a Wikipedia for and from us all.

Notes

1. "Knowledge Sharing," Whose Knowledge?, accessed August 1, 2019, https://whoseknowledge.org/initiatives/community-knowledge-sharing/.

2. "#VisibleWikiWomen 2019," Whose Knowledge?, accessed August 1, 2019, https://whoseknowledge.org/initiatives/visiblewikiwomen-2019/.

3. "Decolonizing the Internet: Whose Knowledge? Summary Report 2018," Whose Knowledge?, accessed August 1, 2019, https://whoseknowledge.org/wp-content/uploads/2018/11/DTI-2018-Summary-Report.pdf.

4. Wikipedia, s.v. "Wikipedia: Five pillars," last modified January 26, 2020, https://en.wikipedia.org/wiki/Wikipedia:Five_pillars.

5. International Telecommunication Union, *ICT Facts and Figures 2017* (Geneva: ITU, July 2017), https://www.itu.int/en/ITU-D/Statistics/Documents/facts/ICTFacts Figures2017.pdf.

6. "Internet World Stats," Internet World Stats, accessed August 1, 2019, https:// www.internetworldstats.com/stats.htm.

7. Anasuya Sengupta, Siko Bouterse, and Kira Allmann, "Build an Internet For, and From, Us All," *Nature*, November 28, 2018, https://www.nature.com/articles/d41586 -018-07506-7.

8. Martin Dittus, "The Uneven Geography of Wikipedia," Oxford Internet Institute, October 16, 2018, https://geography.oii.ox.ac.uk/the-uneven-geography-of-wikipedia/.

9. "Gender by Language," Wikimedia Labs, accessed August 1, 2019, http://whgi .wmflabs.org/gender-by-language.html.

10. "Internet World Stats," Internet World Stats, accessed August 1, 2019, https:// www.internetworldstats.com/stats.htm.

11. Srilatha Batliwala, *Feminist Leadership in Social Transformation: A Conceptual Cloud* (New Delhi/New York: CREA, 2011), https://www.uc.edu/content/dam/uc /ucwc/docs/CREA.pdf.

12. S. Aruna et al., "How to Ally and Be a Good Guest," in *Our Stories, Our Knowledges* (San Diego, CA: University of San Diego, November 2018), https://whoseknowledge .org/wp-content/uploads/2018/11/OurstoriesOurknowledges-Part4-1.pdf.

13. Ron Eglash, *African Fractals: Modern Computing and Indigenous Design* (New Brunswick, NJ: Rutgers University Press, 1999).

14. Wikipedia, s.v. "Fatima al-Fihri," accessed August 1, 2019, https://en.wikipedia .org/wiki/Fatima_al-Fihri.

15. Adele Vrana, "The Life and Death of Marielle Franco on Wikipedia," Whose Knowledge?, March 26, 2018, https://whoseknowledge.org/the-life-and-death-of-mari elle-franco-on-wikipedia/.

16. Ayush Khanna, "Nine out of Ten Wikipedians Continue to Be Men: Editor Survey," Wikimedia Foundation, April 27, 2012, https://blog.wikimedia.org/2012 /04/27/nine-out-of-ten-wikipedians-continue-to-be-men/.

17. Art+Feminism, "2019 Wikipedia Edit- a-Thon Saturday, March 2 at the Museum of Modern Art," press release, February 14, 2019, accessed August 1, 2019, https:// artandfeminism.tumblr.com/post/182804392150/2019-wikipedia-edit-a-thon -saturday-march-2-at.

18. Etienne G. Krug, Linda L. Dahlberg, James A. Mercy, Anthony B. Zwi, and Rafael Lozano, eds., *World Report on Violence and Health* (Geneva: World Health

Organization, 2002), 5, https://apps.who.int/iris/bitstream/handle/10665/42495/924
1545615_eng.pdf.

19. Thenmozhi Soundararajan, "Twitter's Caste Problem," *New York Times*, December 3, 2018, https://www.nytimes.com/2018/12/03/opinion/twitter-india-caste-trolls
.html.

20. Judd Antin et al., "Gender Differences in Wikipedia Editing," in *WikiSym '11:
Proceedings of the 7th International Symposium on Wikis and Open Collaboration* (New
York: ACM, 2011), http://people.ischool.berkeley.edu/~coye/Pubs/Articles/Gender
WikiSym2011.pdf.

17 The Myth of the Comprehensive Historical Archive

Jina Valentine, Eliza Myrie, and Heather Hart

Wikipedia is an undertaking of mythic proportions, as is addressing its deficits. The Black Lunch Table project is inspired by the myth, the potential possibility, and works to increase the conversation around resource equity, gender and racial bias, and knowledge gaps within and beyond Wikipedia.

From the outset, Wikipedia has espoused the ideals of free and open knowledge, catalyzing a mass authorship of cultural history worldwide. As the site on which narratives are drafted, contested, revised, and cited, Wikipedia attempts a hopeful and earnest approximation of a comprehensive and democratically authored history. This is of course an impossible goal. Realizing an archive that is both complete and democratic is a task of a mythic proportion. It would require establishing technological, educational, and cultural resource equity worldwide, and the deprioritizing of Eurocentric historical narratives and English-language Wikipedia. Nonetheless, Wikipedians are collectively invested in constructing an archive of infinite scope and complexity. We are enamored of this mythic, utopian vision.

Myths as metaphors for infinite tasks of unfathomable scope abound throughout culture. Perhaps the most well-known is that of Sisyphus eternally pushing a boulder uphill and of Penelope's endless weaving and unweaving her tapestry. The interminable tasks themselves are generally not the focus when we speak of them. Rather, they are metaphors for present or past situations and offer propositions for imagining the future. As with other myths, the quest for a comprehensive encyclopedia is itself significant, but the various discourses it catalyzes and contributes to are just as important. These discourses are Wikipedia-specific, but they relate to issues symptomatic of local and international sociopolitical conditions.

The Black Lunch Table Wikipedia project is inspired by the myth, the potential possibility. The work we do contributes to discourse around resource equity, gender and racial bias, and knowledge gaps within and beyond Wikipedia. Our work both directly and indirectly affects change around those issues. While we don't imagine our project will be able to solve all of its own goals, we do hope that our engagement with Wikipedia will affect how folks conceive of historical authorship more broadly and that they will come to share our belief that histories are neither static nor linear. Through educating the public about our project as it works to identify knowledge gaps on Wikipedia, we hope that everyone will feel they can and should contribute to historical authorship as we all have something at stake in how our histories are told.

Mythic Being: Who Is Black Lunch Table?

The Black Lunch Table (BLT) is an ongoing collaboration founded by artists Jina Valentine and Heather Hart that intends to fill holes in the documentation of contemporary art history. Our project is inspired by questions related to authorship: *Who writes the record? What is omitted from the record?* Those who have access to knowledge and its production determine what is included in the historical record. Authoring the dominant historical narrative means determining who is other and the terms by which they are treated as such. BLT is a critical gesture to disrupt that narrative. Our project mobilizes a democratic rewriting of contemporary art and cultural history, with the overall aim of filling gaps in and decentralizing authorship of the dominant historical record.

BLT began in 2005 at the Skowhegan School of Painting and Sculpture in Maine. Organized around literal and metaphorical lunch tables, BLT takes the school lunchroom phenomenon as its starting point. It has existed in numerous forms since then and is presently comprised of a series of community roundtables, an online oral history archive, and Wikipedia project.

As we researched models for the BLT archive and noted those artists omitted from the larger art historical archives, we wondered what artists had also been omitted from the world's most widely referenced encyclopedia. We were surprised by how many there were. Our Wikipedia project redresses these omissions. The BLT Wikipedia project mobilizes a collective authoring of articles on the lives and works of Black artists. When we began our Wikipedia project in 2014, important figures such as Fred Moten, Hamza Walker, Meschac Gaba, Peggy Cooper Cafritz, and Valerie Cassel Oliver were all without pages. Five years later, each has a page that began as a BLT target. We are inspired to continue this work as we note what artists, curators, and art historians remain underdocumented on Wikipedia.

Access to Knowledge and Its Production

We are descended of ancestors whose histories have been largely erased or altogether left undocumented. Of the little genealogical information that ties us to our African and indigenous heritages, inaccuracies abound, and the stories are incomplete. We have made efforts to fill these holes with the family lore, oral histories, and traditions we are bequeathed. We know that those who witnessed our ancestors' histories lacked fora to offer testimony of it. And that absent a voice to account for those stories, that testimony is forever lost. Meanwhile, as we witness the continued underdocumentation of Black and brown people, we wish to testify, to make record of it.

We both pursued graduate art degrees but were left with lingering questions about the art histories we'd been taught. We imagine these questions were not unique to our experiences: *Why are there so few Black Artists included in the canon of Western Art History? Is "Black Art History" a topic to be segregated out of the rest of contemporary art history, as a parallel and unequal timeline? Why? And where, as young, aspiring artists do we fit into this already unfolding discourse?*

BLT's original task list of notable Black artists with missing or incomplete articles was several hundred names long. As of this writing, this focus list for our edit-a-thons has grown to over thirteen hundred names and remains incomplete. This is not due to inattention to the task of authoring or editing these articles but rather that we are continuously discovering names, movements, and artworks that are otherwise significant but have been omitted from Wikipedia. And many of these artists are still living, creating, exhibiting, and producing material, requiring their articles to be continually updated.

The length of the list plainly illustrates the magnitude of our task—it is one of Sisyphean proportions. The task list is also a clear manifestation of systemic bias. As it enumerates historical omissions on Wikipedia, it points to larger failings in the documentation of cultural production. What is missing on Wikipedia is most certainly missing from other popular archives.

The task list is an accounting of so much of what was missing from the histories we were taught. The task list, as an aggregation of missing articles, both illustrates a void in our collective history and demands for its resolution. We actively name that which we sought in order to determine our places within this history.

Potential Possibilities: Inclusion + Omission

In the twenty years since Wikipedia's founding, how it is accessed and who is able to access it along with the internet as its supportive interface have all changed dramatically. It is crucial to note these changes when considering how and where researchers, students, and various other netizens access information. It is useful to examine what information was available on Wikipedia in the early days. In 2007, there were two million articles total in 161 languages;[1] a dozen years later, there are approximately six million English-language articles and forty million articles in 293 non-English languages.[2]

Consider that in 1998 only 26 percent of Americans had regular access to the internet versus 2018 where 81percent of US households have broadband access to the internet and 76 percent of those households have smartphones.[3] In 1998 (before smartphones were widely available), access to information most often required consulting physical, printed media. In 2019, it's likely that information sought can be found through a quick Google search (on a smartphone), one that often includes a link to a Wikipedia article as the first result. As the amount of information documented on the platform grew exponentially over those years, so did users' expectation of finding the information they sought. There is a general perception that Wikipedia hosts a comprehensive collection of knowledge—that everything worth documentation exists in some form on the platform.

The vast majority of Google searches and, by a slim majority, the number of Wikipedia queries are conducted via smartphone. Because of *how* we search for information in 2019, first-page Google results wield enormous intellectual capital, social capital, and financial capital. In this era wherein *Googling* is often conflated with *researching*, offering easy access to answers and info, folks generally trust the first page of Google results. That first-page real estate is most often populated by an infobox, a link to Wikipedia, a link to Amazon—links to the most (algorithmically) "relevant" result.[4]

In particular, internet users give the *Knowledge Panel* (that box that appears in the top of the Google search with basic information about a subject) our full faith. The Knowledge Panel sources data from several sites, including Wikipedia and Wikidata, and presents a tidy summation of the pertinent (basic) facts about a person, place, or thing. There's much debate and criticism over the value, potential inaccuracy, and bias in coverage related to the Knowledge Panel.[5] And tracing the varied and entangled systems of bias at play in Knowledge Panel production is complicated. Perhaps the most problematic issue is that the Knowledge Panel shows *the most important information* on a given subject. Nuanced information is depreciated by that which can be presented as unquestionable and uncomplicated and sans context.

Search subjects bolstered by Knowledge Panels attain greater visibility, credibility, and notability. Those Wikipedia subjects that have received sufficient authoring, citation, and development *and* an infobox will be most visible in a simple search. This structure reinforces existing knowledge and notability hierarchies. A subject with an infobox included in their Wikipedia article (and therefore a Knowledge Panel on Google) will accumulate additional validation, further establishing that subject as most important or *most relevant*. Stunningly, approximately two-thirds of Wikipedia articles lack an infobox. Our concern here is for the two-thirds of articles whose most essential information cannot be tidily summed up into an infobox, whose most essential information is difficult to cite due to systemic bias in media and academic focus, or whose article hasn't received the attention due because it falls outside the interest areas of most Wiki contributors.

What Does It Matter Who Is Speaking?

Considering *how* we access information and *who* accesses it is only part of the story.[6] The ratio of regular contributors to Wikipedia to the rate of access to articles is astounding. As of 2016, a mere 1 percent of Wikipedia users are also regular contributors, authoring more than half of the content. Another way to illustrate that is approximately thirteen hundred people regularly contribute to creating over three-quarters of the six hundred new articles posted to Wikipedia every day; and every day there are approximately 13.9 million unique page views. Following that calculus, we can say: ±99 percent of folks access Wikipedia as read-only, expecting the platform to offer the information they seek. Most never question, *who is this 1 percent writing articles?*

As the French theorist Michel Foucault noted, *"Everything is said in every age."*[7] Theories relating to semiotics discuss how languages are formed out of necessity. New words are born to describe phenomena and culture specific to an era.[8] This idea also suggests that which is left unsaid can be seen to describe what was lacking in that culture. In other words, if there's no language to describe it, either it didn't exist or wasn't noteworthy. It's not inaccurate to apply this logic in considering what histories remain underdocumented on Wikipedia. Those topics or figures lacking sufficient documentation indeed transpired, existed, and certainly many were noteworthy. The gaps in coverage are the result of an era's systemic biases. Presently, those gaps evidence the values of a dominant Western culture and the determinations regarding what is historicized and what's omitted from the record.

The Future Is Self-Organized

As Wikipedians, we are invested in the mythic and utopian ideals of open source knowledge creation and open access to information. Our investment in this myth of democratic authorship is cautious and critically aware of the inherent flaws of crowdsourced content. Chief among those is that open source authorship results in glorifying some aspects of culture while ignoring others. Contributions to Wikipedia establish the difference between the legendary and the stuff of lore. That which is included in the larger record becomes part of the canon: cited sources, verified content, and notability are proof that a thing should be widely known, duly documented, and canonized.

Wikipedia relies on crowdsourced research, writing, editing, license-free photo contribution, coding, and community organization. This idealistic approach is intended to eliminate prioritization of subjects backed by capital and to avoid the influence of funders or special interests, any language that supports persuasive ideologies or viewpoints,[9] and the monetization of contributions (e.g., paid editing). As such, Wikipedia articles afford a reprieve from the incessant barrage of consumerist language intended to peddle wares, values, and experiences.

This approach intends to promote the formation of a lateral organization and a self-governed community, encouraging a diversity of interests to be reflected on the platform. As we edit what we are interested in or find affinity with, that diversity should be reflected on Wikipedia. And it is, relatively speaking. But this strategy assumes that for each knowledge area (language, country, issue) there are people with equal resources (time, knowledge, authority) to write, edit, code, organize, and teach/share ideas and work flows. It also assumes equal access to technology, research materials, and free time, globally.

While the language common to an era reflects its values and that which is unarticulated remains unaccounted for, we must also consider that which is seen as *notable* is also determined through the circulation of ideas and meaning making by consensus.[10] The influence of capital is visible in paid search engine prioritization as it quite literally creates links between queries and subjects with institutions and their interests. In terms of Wikipedia, the effects of capital on notability are somewhat more complex, but they result in the same propping up of well-documented subjects and the diminution of lesser known subjects. Notability standards on Wikipedia encourage article creation about those subjects that are most critical to human knowledge. However, they are based on the assumption that all culturally or historically significant subjects have been documented *and* published by credible sources.

Why We Wiki

BLT's engagement with Wikipedia includes contributing to the ongoing discourse around notability. Many otherwise significant Black artists are omitted from dominant art historical narratives and receive insufficient attention from the cultural media, making it difficult or impossible to prove they're notable enough for inclusion on Wikipedia. Although we agree that establishing a verifiable standard for an encyclopedic entry is necessary, such policies as "Wikipedia notability standards" fail to adequately take into account systemic and implicit biases that exist in art exhibition, art criticism, and art historical writing. Wikipedia risks mimicking the same system it was built to disrupt.

When we first began our Wikipedia project, the notability standards for visual artists were so high that they excluded the majority of artists considered notable by contemporary arts and cultural institutions. An artist must have had at least two major museum exhibitions and received multiple reviews in credible journals. This standard was created through a flawed peer-review system drafted by Wikipedians who may not have had any familiarity with the art world or its measures. These notability standards as they are defined could not take into account the potential for systemic bias that precludes many significant artists from achieving that specific formulation of professional achievement.

In order to find those artists elided by the systemic bias inherent in such notability guidelines, BLT considers the following:

- the lingering effects of slavery, segregation, redlining, and busing as they relate to current issues around resource and knowledge equity: *Who gets to be an artist? Who has access to cultural resources in their communities?*

- the demographic of under/graduate arts programs, gallery rosters, major museum group exhibitions, and major museum solo exhibitions in the United States

- museum boards memberships and their influence in determining exhibition seasons; the demographic of curators at major museums in the United States; the collectorship of artworks and how this intersects with board composition

- both the demographic and aesthetic biases of art critics, art historians, academicians, scholars: *Whose work is seen, discussed, canonized?*

- the demographic and knowledge base of Wikipedia admins who establish notability standards for artists and other specialized professions; while peer-reviewed articles are recommended for article citation, does Wiki governance include such industry-specific peership models?

- the dearth of citable sources and historical and critical writing about Black artists

From these deficits we grow our task list. The majority of us do not meet the notability standards Wikipedia has set. Nevertheless, we start new articles. Some are flagged for deletion, many remain. We must be bold.

In the past few years, notability standards for visual artists have become less restrictive, yet the potential for systemic bias to influence notability remains. There are many Black artists whose mentorship and effect on later generations of Black artists is difficult or impossible to cite, not for a lack of artistic production on the artists' part, but for a general lack of published secondary source material about their lives and work and insufficient exhibition records. Additionally, the editorship—which includes Wikipedia administrators, arbitration and governance committees, safe-space committees, and diversity-related committees—is predominantly composed of middle class, college-educated white men who can afford to volunteer their time and efforts. We tend to author, edit, and advocate for subjects with which we find affinity. So again, we ask, *who is this 1 percent?* The myth of a democratically and globally authored encyclopedia is of course beautifully compelling, but we remain far from achieving this goal.

Who Is the 1 Percent? The Demographics of Wikipedia Editors

While Wikipedia is an open source platform where anyone can have a voice in writing and editing historical records, a Wikimedia Foundation survey showed that about 91 percent of Wikipedia editors are male and 77 percent are white.[11] The statistic of race however has not been an official study of the Foundation. When we investigated the origins of this statistic, we were told by multiple editors that it was an unofficial *visual assessment*. The problematics of assessing another's racial identification based on visual appearance aside, this statistic only accounts for the demographics at select social gatherings and workshops. We imagine it includes an international population, and that the non-white 33 percent is predominantly not of the African Diaspora. So we imagine, based on our own assessment, that Wikipedia editors that identify as Black fall well below 15 percent.

The methodology and resultant metrics for the gender survey were far more rigorous. Despite the various critiques related to accuracy, that survey at least provided sound evidence of a substantial gender gap among editors. The gender gap article on Wikipedia further examines its successes and shortcomings, including accounting for editors who opted out of participating. More recent articles include discussion of the fact that this data is eight years old and should be afforded a time line for updating.

Our critique of these surveys and the implementation of the findings is that they fail to examine diversity-related issues as intersectional. And moreso, addressing gender disparity with a critical study and analysis and race disparity with undocumented visual assessment (the methodology and metrics of which are nowhere to be found online) prioritizes one issue over the other. This naturally sets up a space for gender inclusion that overshadows the work of race and ethnic diversity.[12]

Considering diversity-related issues through the lens of intersectionality also enables the Foundation (and editors, including Wikipedia project managers) to address related concerns in the more nuanced and critical manner they are due. For example, resource and knowledge equity intersects with race and gender parity and ought to be studied and addressed as interrelated. Studies on the distribution of cultural resources and access to technology by geographic region[13] could offer context or insights into the gender and race gaps in specific communities and provide clues for how to address them.

Wikipedia does need more editors of color and women editors and more quality articles on notable Black artists to reflect a more true and inclusive history. Our project intends to decentralize Wikipedia editing about Black visual artists, bringing the movement to communities and sites that would normally not host an editing event. Participants have a hand in directly authoring stories for future generations and in impacting systems that may not have been built for them.

We are actively cultivating a more diverse editorship, in addition to encouraging editors in the majority demographic to focus on marginalized or omitted subject matter. BLT creates spaces that encourage people of color and women to join the Wikipedia movement by hosting events focused on improving or creating pages for Black visual artists while also encouraging white male editors to focus on gaps in coverage on Wikipedia.

Infinite Possibilities for Engagement

We describe the BLT project as *nomadic*, as one that seeks to meet the people where they are, both physically and metaphorically. We travel to spaces in order to connect with people who would normally not have the initiative or confidence to approach Wikipedia editing on their own and to introduce focus of marginalized communities on Wikipedia to more experienced editors.

We are presently working to decentralize our engagements away from larger institutions by exploring strategies for hosting with smaller cultural and community institutions. Our intention is to bring our events to spaces that are community-run and perhaps underserved. In order to democratize the authoring of cultural history, we need to address access to and the unequal distribution of cultural resources. To democratize the authoring of cultural history, we need to bring our project to the people.

By taking our project out to the potential editors we are able to witness the moment when historians, laymen, and academics alike realize that Wikipedia is a useful, vetted, reliable resource and that editing is empowering, gratifying, and fun. To do this, our project creates space for editors that is focused on one-on-one attention to lessen the sense of intimidation felt by those new to the platform.

Meeting the people where they are demystifies the process of contributing to Wikipedia and helps to illustrate the many possibilities for engagement on the platform. Above all else, we hope that our efforts serve to increase the ethnic diversity among the editorship and provide affirmation that these new editor's voices are not only welcome but critically necessary.

Our project has raised awareness about the importance of this work, particularly as it pertains to the often unrecorded history of Black visual artists. We are constantly receiving emails, Facebook messages, and so forth from cultural workers who have noticed that this info or that person is missing or needs editing on Wikipedia. Most often they are interested in learning how to fix the error or omission themselves and are seeking guidance.

Because the levels of completeness and quality among the articles on our task list vary so widely, there are in fact endless possibilities for new editors to engage: we encourage grammarians and punctuation police, source-material researchers, biography updaters, fact citers, and photo contributors to find their place.

In the past year, our WikiCommons Photo Initiative (a pop-up photo booth) has become a highlight of our work. The primary objective of the photo initiative is to quite literally increase the visibility of Black visual artists on Wikimedia. The process is simple: we invite a local Black photographer to host a pop-up portrait studio at our edit-a-thon; we invite local artists on our Wikipedia list to have their photo taken; the photographer releases all portraits to WikiCommons for use (eventual use, if the artist still lacks a page; or immediate if they have one) on the artists' Wikipedia article. Thus far we have uploaded nine hundred photos to the Commons, dozens of which have been incorporated into artists' Wikipedia articles.

The photo initiative is an opportunity for everyone to contribute in a small but incredibly impactful way. Those articles with photos and infoboxes appear in Google searches with a prominent Knowledge Panel, which informs folks about the basic facts related to the subject *and* presents them as noteworthy and included in the ever-growing record of human knowledge.

Art + the Archival Impulse

Why is it important that BLT is an artist project? What does it mean that we are asking artists to write our own art history? We are challenging the status quo. BLT is engaged in radical archiving and institutional critique. We are pushing the structures of cultural, historical, and social institutions to change. Our Wikipedia project intends to rewrite the record and make right the systemic biases that have led to historical omissions.

Self-aware in our involvement as Wikipedians, we question whether Wikipedia is indeed a "movement" or simply another institution. Its utopian mission of Sisyphean proportions requires would-be Wikipedians to believe that their investments are for a just and worthy cause: *together we can create a free and comprehensive record of all human knowledge.* BLT is inspired in our engagement with this possibility, with the myth. We acknowledge that our investment in this mythic goal is more of a salve than a solution. As artists, we don't imagine we are saving the world.

"*'What does it matter who is speaking,' someone said.*" Artists are already speaking. We are perhaps the best positioned to empower those without a soapbox or the confidence to speak, to add their voice and their historical perspective to the record.

Artworks like BLT intend to shift the lens by which folks view the world, challenge institutions to do better to reflect the interests of the publics they purport to represent, invite the uninvited to the table, and redraw the lines within linear narratives, elucidating their complexity and amplifying the multivocality extant in a peoples' history. Artists imagine new structures for the organization of archives and new points at which to access them. We find value where others find none. We imagine our work is a product of the times we live in; the communities we build together; and the ideas, resources, and knowledge we inherit, impart to others, and leave as our legacies.

We imagine our biographies, our articles, are valuable in context and connection to others. Those connections illustrate a complex cartography of conversations, aesthetics, and ideas; the brilliance of individuals at each point is revealed as their stories are recounted. We imagine the story of human knowledge as one that is infinitely complex, multivocal, and interconnected. Attempting to illustrate even an approximate likeness of it requires tracing as many connections as possible and engaging as many voices as possible. We imagine the scope of our project, and the project of Wikipedia, is infinite. We are enamored of the infinite potentialities present in this endeavor.

Notes

1. Wikipedia, s.v. "Wikipedia," accessed April 25, 2019, https://en.wikipedia.org /wiki/Wikipedia#Launch_and_early_growth.

2. Wikipedia, s.v. "Wikipedia: Size comparisons," accessed April 25, 2019, https://en .wikipedia.org/wiki/Wikipedia:Size_comparisons.

3. It's unfortunately outside the scope of this essay to dive into how these statistics vary among socioeconomic, race, and education-level classifications. Kurt Bauman, "More Than Two-Thirds Access Internet on Mobile Devices," US Census Bureau, August 8, 2018, https://www.census.gov/library/stories/2018/08/internet-access.html.

4. In-depth discussion of algorithmic bias is unfortunately beyond the scope of this article. But check out Algorithmic Justice League (https://www.ajlunited.org) for resources on the subject.

5. Caitlin Dewey, "You Probably Haven't Even Noticed Google's Sketchy Quest to Control the World's Knowledge," *The Washington Post*, May 11, 2016, https://www .washingtonpost.com/news/the-intersect/wp/2016/05/11/you-probably-havent -even-noticed-googles-sketchy-quest-to-control-the-worlds-knowledge/.

6. The quote "What does it matter who is speaking?," attributed to Samuel Beckett, can be found in Michel Foucault, "What Is an Author?" in *The Foucault Reader: An Introduction to Foucault's Thought*, ed. Paul Rainbow (New York: Penguin, 1991), 101.

7. While language expresses that which is communicable and relevant in each era, it also identifies that which is omitted and inarticulable. In Foucault's concise formulation, "everything is said in every age." The factors conditioning an age—giving every era its style, its trends, and its values—direct the formation of the language used in that era. That which is socio-temporally relevant in each age is visible and productive of the language describing it. As a result, what remains unsaid illustrates the negative spaces within a culture.

8. "Updates to the OED," Oxford English Dictionary, accessed August 9, 2019, https://public.oed.com/updates/.

9. Such language is flagged as in this article for example: Wikipedia, s.v. "Theaster Gates," accessed November 1, 2019, https://en.wikipedia.org/wiki/Theaster_Gates.

10. *The spectacle is capital accumulated to the point that it becomes images.*" The Situationist Internationale (SI) was a group of artists whose films, texts, and interventions in everyday life intended to change the world by making the public aware of and empowered to change the conditions of their realities. The theory of the "spectacle" is central to their work and basically asks people to question popular ideologies, imagery, political systems, and aesthetics. Guy Debord, in *Society of the Spectacle*, trans. K. Knabb (London, UK: Rebel Press, 2005), states that capitalist mechanisms want the public to believe that *all that is good appears and all that appears is good.* We should question what monies promote which ideologies and challenge popular beliefs.

11. Wikipedia, s.v. "Wikipedia: Wikipedians/Demographics," accessed March 15, 2018. https://en.wikipedia.org/wiki/Wikipedia:Wikipedians/Demographics.

12. The article on systemic bias among Wikipedia editors only gives passing reference to racial bias: Wikipedia, s.v. "Wikipedia: Systemic_bias," accessed November 1, 2019, https://en.wikipedia.org/wiki/Wikipedia:Systemic_bias#The_average_Wikipedian.

13. "Chicago Heat Maps," The Field Foundation of Illinois, August 1, 2017, https://fieldfoundation.org/wp-content/uploads/2019/03/Field-Foundation-Heat-Maps-THazel-Edits.pdf.

18 No Internet, No Problem

Stéphane Coillet-Matillon

While much has been said about Wikipedia's editors and how they work and interact, we seldom think of those who cannot easily access it—because of poor connectivity, high data costs, or outright censorship—yet still do.

It was on a Monday afternoon that I realized I could change the lives of four billion people. As a Wikipedian, this was a rather interesting proposition: almost fifteen years after the encyclopedia's launch, these represented the bottom half of the world—those we could not reach because they had no internet access—and yet we had made it our fundamental objective to bring knowledge to. We are now closer to the twenty-year mark, and though there has been some progress, the Wikimedia movement as a whole still hardly acknowledges offline access as a fundamental issue.

There are many reasons for this—starting with the fact that the Wikimedia movement has always been a movement of writers (and curators) rather than readers. In fact, I fully expect that at least one other contributor to this volume will raise the fact that Wikipedia's design and general user experience has hardly changed since it went live in late 2001. The website has pretty much become the Rolling Stones of the internet: yes, they're old, but they're still around, unlike these one-hit-wonder punks that were supposed to replace them. So why try to fix something that nobody notices is broken?

Fair enough. At least that's what one would say if they shared the general dogma that we are in the best of all possible worlds, and therefore, progress must be on the horizon. Conventional wisdom has it that we shall wake up one day and find it on our doorstep. Yet, if the past few years have taught me anything, it is that this kind of thing only happens because a couple of outliers took it upon themselves to make that delivery happen.

Twenty years ago, much of the internet was on dial-up connections. Then came broadband. But for those who could not afford the former, the latter is not much help. The same goes for those facing increased censorship. For them and countless others, the solution has been found in the offline distribution and consumption of Wikipedia. The demand is enormous and has largely been ignored by the broader Wikimedia movement because it is, quite literally, disconnected from it. And for the foreseeable future at least, the issue is here to stay.

New World Hoarders

In 2016, I was sitting in my office at Wikimedia Switzerland, preparing the dreaded annual Funds Dissemination Committee (FDC) grant proposal for the Swiss Wikimedia Chapter. An FDC grant request is an interesting process in and of itself as chapters plan their activities for the coming year and request the corresponding funding from the Foundation. The committee itself was until recently made up of volunteers from the editor community, but its decision making is pretty opaque; anyone concerned with governance would probably raise an eyebrow at the prospect of having random strangers with no specific qualification distribute several million dollars of donors' money. But like Wikipedia itself, the process works much better in reality than in theory.

Quite a few of these programmatic activities rest on the shoulders and goodwill of Wikimedia volunteers. A good example are edit-a-thons, events where Wikipedians will teach wannabe Wikipedians (or the general public, depending on how the event is framed) how to channel their nerd potential for the common encyclopedic good. The chapter helps with booking rooms; provides an institutional point of contact for the host institution; and makes sure that snacks, drinks, and a friendly space policy are available (as well as the inevitable drum beating to publicize the event). But since the show will in the end be run by volunteers who sometimes have to prioritize their own life over evangelizing, each chapter is essentially promising things it is not entirely sure it can deliver. In spite of this, and yet again, something that does not make sense on paper does, in fact, prove itself to work remarkably well day after day after day (almost 7,300 of them and counting).

The key here is to promise things that are ambitious yet manageable (*"We will teach people how to edit!"*), are reasonably cost effective (*"with volunteers* *to train them and $50 worth of cookies to lure them in"*), and, what may be the hardest part, have an impact (*"We'll end up with more Wikipedians than we started with"*). As things often turn out, if everyone uses Wikipedia and finds it a fairly reliable encyclopedic resource, editor retention is a much, much harder task. I found out over time that people either have it in them or not. And if they do, they probably will learn to edit on their own, which can be complicated but not any more than, say, learning to ski; simply be aware that if you start to like it, your (social) life is likely to go dangerously downhill from there. Some will come and realize that there is no magic; that editing articles takes time, dedication, and potentially the willingness to argue over minute details for days or weeks at length.[1]

Chapters need to justify their existence, and organizing edit-a-thons is probably one of the lowest hanging fruits of community building. Another much touted example is GLAM (Galleries, Libraries, Archives, and Museums) relationship building—trying to convince institutions to share their art with the public—a much harder task than what one would expect. Many still find the prospect of sharing digital copies of their collections with the masses to be something that goes against their primary mission of telling said masses what to look at and in what order. Overall, every chapter and user group around the world offers some variant of these two avenues: either to bring new Wikipedians into the fold or to bring material that average Wikimedians couldn't produce themselves. For the past twenty years, the Wikimedia movement has considered that to "[give] free access to the sum of all human knowledge," it first had to accumulate it.

And then comes a black swan event, a game-changing opportunity so big, so unique, that you know that whatever metric is normally thrown at you has become irrelevant. Rather than scrounge for a couple of new editors here and there, rather than "freeing" images few would ever look at, this event told me that I should stop looking for content and content producers and instead start considering those in need of this content.

This black swan, in my case, turned out to be a small, wingless kiwi.

One Child, Two Fathers

Kiwix (with an "x") was born in 2006–2007, from two fathers who did not know each other at the time but had pretty much had the same idea—or rather, had made the same observation—at the same time: Wikipedia is a great resource, but not everyone can access it. The reasons are many but in the end boil down to the fact that there may not be any connectivity where the reader sits. They will not, therefore, be able to connect to and query the Wikimedia servers from their device. In the Wikimedia world, this simple statement is almost a conceptual breakthrough as most editors, by definition, are connected to the internet and enjoy a fairly decent level of connectivity.

When one is happily amassing the sum of all human knowledge, seeing it take shape and hearing increasingly positive feedback from people discussing it every day around them or in the news, life is a bubble of unending progress. The Wikimedia movement is infused with an infallible West Coast optimism that technology will ultimately catch up and solve everything: it is easy, almost natural, to be blinded to those who are not around or cannot interact and therefore have no voice. Wikipedia editors are not particularly strong on readers' experiences, but as far as addressing connectivity issues go, discussing these within the movement has often felt similar to discussing famine with people whose only lunch option is an all-you-can-eat buffet: it's a terrible thing, yes, please do keep talking while I get myself a second serving of Netflix.

The first "father" of Kiwix, therefore, had to be Renaud Gaudin, a French expatriate who had made himself a new life in Bamako, Mali. For him, and for Mali in general, the lack of connectivity in 2006 was almost a given (and to a great extent still is nowadays). But five years after its inception Wikipedia was picking up fame and volume, and Gaudin knew of it. His solution to bring the sum of all human knowledge to his fellow Malians was called Moulinwiki (from Moulin Rouge; every coder wants to be a provocateur, and in his rather conservative, barren environment, the idea of Parisian sophistication and decadence had quite a bit of appeal). The software acted as an offline reader for the Wikipedia article dumps, and most of the encyclopedia could be stored as a series of zip files on a DVD. Gaudin and his team initially caught the eye of the local US Agency for International Development office, who promptly decided to share a basic desktop version with the local Peace Corps members. The reception was good, but no systematic effort to update the content was made, and so the project never really went anywhere (or almost: a Syrian refugee—who certainly had never set foot in West Africa—reached out in 2019 to tell us how much of an avid user he was). But Gaudin had anyway moved on to the next iteration of the idea, thanks to a chance contact with Emmanuel Engelhart.

Engelhart is the other creator of Kiwix and also a French expat, living at the time between Germany and Switzerland (he would later move to Switzerland for good). The problem was somewhat different on his end; there was no immediate intention of helping poor kids get a better education, no international partner to work with, but something much closer to home as Engelhart's mother was living in the French countryside where connectivity was excruciatingly poor. He could not share with her the wonders of Wikipedia, which he had already started editing in 2003. And so he set out to work, almost at the same time as Renaud Gaudin did more than four thousand kilometers away, on a portable, offline version of Wikipedia. The technology, in his case, quickly came to rest on a novel compression system called openZIM, an improved and open source version of the proprietary (and deprecated) zeno format. The Kiwix name, for its part, was born out of a wiki-based play on words: wiki/kiwi, with an x at the end for good measure.

Like its African counterpart, Kiwix quickly started to attract interest—first in the free software community, then from more commercially minded folks. Paris-based search engine company Linterweb saw this as an opportunity to showcase its service to the Wikimedia community and agreed to help with the hosting and development. Five thousand DVDs, each with a selection of two thousand articles in English, were prepared. Only 250 had been sold after a year. The relationship quickly soured as Engelhart wanted to keep the Kiwix project as the free open source software project he had imagined; for him, any commercial offer had to be entirely separate. The partnership was formally terminated in a December 2008 announcement. Linterweb subsequently tried to launch a clone called Okawix (a name based on the almost eponymous Congolese giraffe; why such a fascination with exotic animals, no one knows), but without its main developer to give it direction, the project never really took off.

Things weren't so bad for Engelhart as before parting ways the owner of Linterweb had put him in touch with Renaud Gaudin. The two coders got along very well, so much so that Moulinwiki and Kiwix merged shortly thereafter. The project continued, now twice as strong at the core and attracting more volunteer developers from around the world. But as its popularity grew, so did its costs. Working as a Wikimedian in Residence at the Swiss National Library, Engelhart reached out to Wikimedia Switzerland asking for support (as converting Wikipedia dumps to a single openZIM file does take quite a bit more computing power than a personal computer can offer). Meanwhile, Wikipedia had kept its impressive growth, leaving DVDs unable to cope with the amount of information it presented, and so universities from around the world started to step in to provide free mirroring services for the increasing bandwidth load created by the ever-expanding size of ZIM files. In an ironic turn of events, the offline Wikipedia could now only be accessed by first downloading it (and therefore being online). The software was put in repositories and remained free as in speech as well as free as in beer. The project trudged along, pretty much like any other freeware, except that its main audience was offline and had almost no way of making it known that they enjoyed it. Almost.

Elephant, Meet Room

Then, around 2015, with the encyclopedia's fifteenth anniversary around the corner, things started to become interesting for everyone. Wikimedia Switzerland (or WMCH as shorthands go in the wiki world) had gone through a period of sustained expansion and had only recently in 2013 started to professionalize. It was still fragile and understaffed, and all hell nearly broke loose when the previous executive director quit almost overnight after personal tragedy struck. The Foundation was supportive— building personal relationships and having the squeaky-cleanest (dare I say Swiss) accounting books helped a lot to foster an understanding that things were under control—but San Francisco still needed to know what the impact of its previous grants was and had already started to reduce the amounts it allocated to its larger, older affiliates. With its already absurdly high quality of life, Switzerland's costs were compounded by WMCH's multilingual setup. The default option until then had been that every effort had to be duplicated in at least three, if not four, language versions (despite the fact that Italian speakers, for instance, only represent less than 5 percent of the country's population and even less of the local Wikimedia contributors). In the end, with new management in place (me), it was as good a time as any to sit back, find out what Wikimedia Switzerland was really good at, and where it wanted to go. The encyclopedia was turning fifteen; the chapter, ten—technically both teenagers, even if barely. Adolescence, we are told, comes from Latin *adolescere*—to grow up.

Which programs worked, which did not? We knew we probably would have to cut some activities and that others could be improved. One can wonder why these questions had not been addressed earlier, but it is important to remember that back then nobody really knew how to recruit and grow contributors for a globe-spanning encyclopedia. It took five to seven years for chapters to professionalize—meaning that until then, the Foundation was relying on the same volunteers who offered and ran the programs to evaluate their impact. For free. In their spare time.

Interestingly, among all the activities the chapter supported, no one on either side of the pond had ever really questioned the value of Kiwix. Both San Francisco and Switzerland were hubs of ultra-connectivity, so maybe people felt a kind of guilt about it and figured they ought to provide at least token support for those around the world that did not have the "chance" to edit. Elsewhere, and in spite of growing evidence to the contrary, everyone in the movement was still assuming that it was every human being's ultimate destiny to be able to contribute to the sum of human knowledge. What *really* mattered, therefore, was how many community managers were needed to run edit-a-thons; how many partnerships could be signed with museums to transfer their collections to Wikimedia Commons; and how local chapters could help curate, improve, and feed the Wikimedia projects. Compared with all of these, supporting volunteer-run Kiwix with server costs only was a real bargain.

But the times, they were a-changin', and considering that several thousand dollars were nevertheless spent each year on a poorly understood project, we had to know what offline access really meant. Wikimedia Switzerland was paying to bring content to people we weren't sure existed. And if they existed and could connect to our servers, then why on earth would they need an offline Wikipedia?

Hello, World

The answer was only a phone call away placed one fateful Monday. According to Engelhart (and, more importantly, the server logs), there had been a little over eight hundred thousand (!) downloads of Kiwix over the year—and we were in September, meaning that there was almost a full quarter's worth of additional downloads still ahead of us. These numbers were for the desktop version alone; the Android and iOS versions of Kiwix hadn't been released yet, and a bulky hotspot was only starting to be distributed. Yet at the same time, Wikimedia Switzerland could consider itself successful if it had twenty or thirty participants coming to the edit-a-thons it organized at the National Library. The numbers simply could not be compared. It felt like we were in nineteenth-century California, digging for editor gold when the actual riches and impact had been all along in selling nails.

For someone with such success, Engelhart was pretty humble—or simply more interested in technical challenges than usage metrics, a common occurrence among free software enthusiasts. He had been in touch with a few organizations. But it did not take much digging around to realize that there was, indeed, a much broader demand for an offline version of Wikipedia. With a bit of hindsight, it is not particularly hard to understand why it would have the same appeal in unconnected areas as it had elsewhere. Because poor connectivity usually correlates with poor educational resources, it only makes sense that the appeal of a free encyclopedia should be even greater than in areas where there was at least some competition for pupils' attention. Whereas in the United States and Europe the project had to prove its value against venerable competitors such as *Britannica* and other established works,[2] in most of the world the comparison was literally between Wikipedia and ... nothing.

And so Kiwix had users in sub-Saharan Africa—not only Mali, the early adopter; but also in Madagascar, with the Alliance Française; in Botswana, again with the ubiquitous Peace Corps; and in the Democratic Republic of the Congo, on the University of Kinshasa's internal network. The list goes on, and all of this happened without any sort of advertising or communication, just like Wikipedia never really had to advertise itself. We could make sense of these use cases as they broadly fit the initial idea—bringing knowledge to those in need and at minimal cost. In spite of all the reluctance, schools and libraries are logical partners and distributors for an encyclopedic project while international development organizations constitute a great vector and bring an additional veneer of respectability. Seeing them distribute Wikipedia, therefore, was a huge success but not an unbelievable surprise. It simply made sense. But then things got really interesting when we stumbled upon other use cases whose schooling was entirely different from anything we had envisioned.

The Yalu River acts as a natural border between China and North Korea. Because most of its finite resources are aimed at making sure that the demilitarized zone with South Korea is effectively impassable, North Korea's northern border is surprisingly porous. In fact, while official exchanges do happen between the two communist states, the region is also bustling with informal trade. Food, clothes, appliances; wherever there is demand, an offer will materialize. This includes material goods, of course, but also cultural ones such as movies, TV shows ... and encyclopedias.[3]

Because it was free for the taking and redistributing, a few defector groups had started repurposing Kiwix for an entirely new mission—they would put the Korean Wikipedia, K-Pop songs, and South Korean movies onto flash drives, swim across the river (they later purchased a small carrier drone), and "lose" said flash drives on the streets. Curiosity would do the rest—who would not want to try to sneak peek at someone else's data? In a country where everything is propaganda, it appears that the best counter-propaganda simply is to present people with facts and let them figure it out for themselves.[4] Say what you will about reader friendliness, but Wikipedia is good with facts.

At the other end of the spectrum—and, quite literally, the other side of the world—the Cuban government has also been very officially using Kiwix to distribute its own version of Wikipedia, EcuRed. Because connectivity is a major issue across the country, every city and municipality on the island has its own state-sponsored Joven Club de Computación (Youth Computer Club), and every one of them is mandated to provide locals with a copy of the equally state-sponsored encyclopedia. But for its tone and editorial choices, it is very much a clone of Wikipedia (whose least neutral part, EcuRed notes drily, relates to "the revolutionary processes happening in South America").[5] Yet Kiwix is distributed without alteration, and accessing the free (as in speech) encyclopedia is only a click away, which people seem to happily do. To boot, an informal network called Paquete Semanal also circulates hard drives loaded with movies and offline copies of Wikipedia, which people can then transfer onto their own computer or phone for personal—and discrete—consumption.[6]

The list of unexpected deployments goes on and on and on. For example, a German merchant sailor who updates Wikipedia every couple of years when going home; Andean communities refurbishing discarded cathode-ray tube (CRT) screens for the local library to use as makeshift computers; Eritreans buying offline copies of the encyclopedia for a dollar from their local cybercafé so they can prepare their classes; and on, and on.

Off We Go

Once we knew about these uses, it was hard to continue seeing Kiwix as a mere side project; a namesake organization was formally incorporated at the beginning of 2017 with the support of both the Wikimedia Foundation and Wikimedia Switzerland. The ambition is clearly to develop the software (now born a second time) a lot more aggressively: we estimate our current user base to three million—80 percent of which are in the Global South as opposed to more than 70 percent of Wikipedia's users in the Global North[7]—and we aim to double that number every year, hoping to approach one hundred million by 2023.

The connected, "developed" world is so well ordered and so increasingly online (as shown by the growth of cloud-based services) that we forget that the real world is still full of cracks where necessity is the mother of invention. Twenty years after the birth of Wikipedia, we are not so much living in a world of *have* and *have-nots* than in a world of *have it easy* and *have it harder*. I believe that Kiwix helps us move to this new paradigm and brings us closer to the idea of knowledge for all.

Four billion people—the bottom half of the world—still have no reliable access to the internet. While connectivity is improving, so are its challenges. Censorship is generally on the rise, and a neutral, independent encyclopedia is as much of a chance for some as it is a threat for others as Turkey and China's clampdowns on Wikipedia show. Simple economics will also always make it so that there will be places that are not worth being connected to the wider world; after all, it took nearly twenty years for Wikipedia to reach the richest, most connected half of our world. One way or another, and at least for the foreseeable future, offline access to Wikimedia content is here to stay.

Acknowledgments: Many thanks to François Hirt and Alice Nichols for their comments and proofreading.

Notes

1. David McCandless, "Wikipedia's Lamest Edit Wars," Information Is Beautiful, accessed 27 August 2019, https://informationisbeautiful.net/visualizations/wikipedia-lamest-edit-wars/.

2. Lucy Holman Rector, "Comparison of Wikipedia and Other Encyclopedias for Accuracy, Breadth, and Depth in Historical Articles," *Reference Services Review* 36, no. 1 (2008): 7–22, https://doi.org/10.1108/00907320810851998.

3. Roland Bleiker, "North Korea's Hidden Revolution: How the Information Underground Is Transforming a Closed Society," *Cambridge Review of International Affairs* 31, no. 2 (2018): 239–241, https://doi.org/10.1080/09557571.2018.1446708.

4. Adele Peters, "The Dangerous Mission to Undermine North Korea With Flash Drives," *Fast Company*, May 8, 2017, https://www.fastcompany.com/40418835/the -dangerous-mission-to-undermine-north-korea-with-flash-drives.

5. EcuRed, s.v. "Wikipedia," accessed August 27, 2019, https://www.ecured.cu/index .php?title=Wikipedia&oldid=3369975.

6. Michaelanne Dye, David Nemer, Josiah Mangiameli, Amy S. Bruckman, and Neha Kumar, "El Paquete Semanal: The Week's Internet in Cuba," in *CHI '18: Proceedings of the 2018 CHI Conference on Human Factors in Computing Systems* (New York: ACM, 2018), https://doi.org/10.1145/3173574.3174213.

7. Erik Zachte, "Just How Many People Are Reading Wikipedia in Your Country, and What Language Are They Using?" Wikimedia Foundation, October 27, 2017, https://blog.wikimedia.org/2017/10/27/new-interactive-visualization-wikipedia/.

19 Possible Enlightenments: Wikipedia's Encyclopedic Promise and Epistemological Failure

Matthew A. Vetter

Wikipedia challenges traditional notions of expertise, authorship, access, and transparency. It also conserves features of the genre that characterize its emergence from Western Enlightenment logic. Given Wikipedia's maturity, how can we understand this contradiction?

Twenty years ago, I was an undergraduate at the University of Kentucky. Wikipedia was there, too, of course, but very much in the background. It wasn't until ten years later, around 2011, that I began to actually attend to and reflect on the project as a collaborative and technologically mediated system and philosophy for knowledge creation, curation, and distribution. Throughout this essay, I use the term *epistemology* to describe this system as well as its related philosophy. I came to Wikipedia through English composition as scholars in that field discovered the encyclopedia's adaptability for teaching writing and research.[1] Some of these scholars were also asking their college students to actively participate in the (English version) of Wikipedia. This was an exciting prospect and one that I jumped on in my own teaching.

Yet my initial attraction to Wikipedia was always its ambitions regarding knowledge sharing and the rhetoric surrounding those ambitions. In an often-quoted interview in 2004, Wales asked us to "imagine a world in which every single person on the planet is given free access to the sum of all human knowledge."[2] Like many others, I found myself drawn to the enormity of this idea and drawn to the prospect of how I might motivate students by both challenging previous academic receptions of Wikipedia and giving them access to Wales's idealism.

Looking back, it has always been this optimism that was so attractive, but that attraction mutated as I continued to teach, edit, and study Wikipedia over the last decade. I wrote my doctoral dissertation, which I defended in 2015, on Wikipedia, and that document also demonstrated the evolution of my thinking about the encyclopedia. What began as a strictly educational application of the ways in which Wikipedia could be used to teach writing (especially in terms of how participating in the encyclopedia could help students accomplish traditional learning outcomes), by the end, became something else.

I began focusing more and more on the complicated reality of Wikipedia's biases toward Western, rational, and print-centric knowledge-making practices: especially its well-documented gender gap and marginalization of indigenous knowledges. Wikipedia's optimistic rhetoric never ceased to amaze me, but it became more complex as I began to consider how it both challenged and conserved the boundaries of the encyclopedic genre. Wikipedia challenges traditional notions of expertise, authorship, access, and transparency, among other constructs. At the same time, it conserves features of the genre that characterize its emergence from Western Enlightenment logic—especially practices and policies related to verifiability and reliability that are rooted in print-centric notions of knowledge curation. Going forward, now that the encyclopedia is essentially a young adult, how should we understand Wikipedia as a project that promises possible enlightenment? How should we understand Wikipedia as an encyclopedia that fails to fully represent global and multicultural diversity? Can we understand both of these possibilities simultaneously?

In this chapter, I reveal the ways in which, despite postmodern critiques,[3] Wikipedia continues to promise enlightenment, and we (the Wikipedia community as well as academics engaged in Wikipedia-based education) continue to be pulled toward that promise. I have structured my contribution as an aporia, or riddle, in order to consider Wikipedia's encyclopedic promise as both a rhetorical strategy and state of puzzlement or impasse: an impossible question. Wikipedia's page on "aporia" was the first mainspace article I edited in March 2011.[4] As such, it serves as a touchstone regarding my original entry into the Wikipedia community as well as a philosophical analogy for my own evolving understanding of the encyclopedia's promise and failure. Ultimately, I argue that the reconciliation of these competing claims becomes possible by calling attention to Wikipedia's transparent and dynamic properties. Such properties can help us understand the encyclopedia as an epistemology that is constantly in process, one that is always evolving and striving toward a universal circle of knowledge.

Wikipedia's Encyclopedic Promise

In "What Is an Encyclopedia? A Brief Overview from Pliny to Wikipedia," Dan O'Sullivan charts a succinct history of the genre, noting its major ambition for universal knowledge as well as how the genre has emerged as both a conservative and radical textual enterprise. Moving quickly through history, O'Sullivan traces a Western encyclopedic tradition by examining Pliny's *Natural History* (first century), Vincent de Beauvais's *Speculum Maius* (thirteenth century), Francis Bacon's *Novum Organum* (seventeenth century), Ephraim Chambers's *Cyclopaedia* (eighteenth century), Denis Diderot and Jean le Rond d'Alembert's *Encyclopédie* (eighteenth century), the *Encyclopædia Britannica* (nineteenth century), and finally Wikipedia (twenty-first century). O'Sullivan places particular emphasis on the Enlightenment period as crucial to the genre's major development and growth.[5] Further, while all of these experiments share common goals of gathering and organizing human knowledge, instantiations of the genre in the Enlightenment period mirror more closely some of Wikipedia's (and indeed modern encyclopedias in general) most basic motivations. In brief, the scientific rationalism of the Enlightenment insisted on the possibility of the collection and curation of all human knowledge and its benefit to society. My purpose here is not to trace the history of the genre, however. Instead, I hope to introduce the first element of this essay's aporia, Wikipedia's promise, as historically situated—emerging directly from an Enlightenment positioning of the genre. Compare, for instance, Jimmy Wales (2004) description of the project of Wikipedia—"Imagine a world in which every single person is given free access to the sum of all human knowledge. That's what we're doing"[6]—with Denis Diderot's in 1775:

> Indeed, the purpose of an encyclopedia is to collect knowledge disseminated around the globe; to set forth its general system to the men with whom we live, and transmit it to those who will come after us, so that the work of preceding centuries will not become useless to the centuries to come; and so that our offspring, becoming better instructed, will at the same time become more virtuous and happy, and that we should not die without having rendered a service to the human race.[7]

Both definitions appear in the Wikipedia information page on Wikipedia's purpose, which also includes statements such as "Wikipedia has a lofty goal: a comprehensive collection of all of the knowledge in the world" and the more subtle "Wikipedia's purpose is to benefit readers by acting as an encyclopedia, a comprehensive written compendium that contains information on all branches of knowledge."[8] In both definitions of their respective encyclopedia projects, Wales and Diderot draw on an ambitious, Enlightenment-era understanding of knowledge as a tangible commodity, something that can be collected and distributed. In this rationalistic positioning, knowledge is something to be tracked down, recorded, and shared with the world. We might forgive Diderot's idealism, given his historical milieu. For Wales and the wider Wikipedia community, however, such a view of epistemology is in direct conflict with postmodern notions of knowledge emerging in the twentieth century. Such a conflict also constitutes the most problematic aspects of Wikipedia's failure to live up to its own ambitions for universal knowledge, which I reveal in the following discussion of the encyclopedia's neglect of indigenous knowledge.

Wikipedia's Epistemological Failure

Like Diderot's *Encyclopédie*, Wikipedia is an enormously ambitious project in that it insists that the encyclopedic endeavor itself (the gathering of all human knowledge) is at all possible. Further, Wikipedia's adherence to print culture, especially in terms of how it verifies factual claims,[9] both signals and reinforces the rational and modern insistence on the primacy of the written word as dominant medium for the communication of knowledge. As asserted by Peter Gallert and Maja van der Velden,

> Wikipedia as an encyclopedia is rooted in a culture of writing—not simply in the usage of a writing system to express and conserve thoughts, but in the almost exclusive usage of written sources for the body of its content. In its endeavor to systemize and codify the knowledge of mankind it voluntarily restricts itself to facts that are supported by reliable, published, third-party sources, as defined by its editor community.[10]

Ultimately, this allegiance to print discourse—which has become central to the encyclopedic genre itself since the invention of the printing press—also limits the genre from accomplishing its ambitions for creating and maintaining a universal "circle of knowledge." Instead of encouraging a diversity of knowledge-making practices beyond those rooted in print, Wikipedia excludes editors who practice or only have access to marginalized knowledge-making practices (e.g., oral histories). Because of this, Wikipedia presents an epistemological condition that is essentially paradoxical—an aporia. As Noopur Raval argues, making a platform open access does not automatically translate to equality of participation, ease of access, or cultural acceptance of the medium.

> The question remains: where does one start? Does one wait for these thousands of un-become (those who cannot participate and cannot be recognized) digital citizens standing in the shadows to gradually emerge and adopt new technologies or does one rework the project's imagination to make space for various stakeholders who may not speak/write and document in the same way?[11]

Wikipedia's adherence to the practice and tradition of print places it firmly in the encyclopedic tradition, yet it is also this placement that prevents it from accomplishing its encyclopedic goal of becoming a global human knowledge source. This adherence manifests in three specific policies that maintain traditional Western textual practices: the policies of verifiability, no original research, and notability. All three policies, it's important to state, play a significant role in the creation of reliable content, and yet, all three also serve to limit Wikipedia's universality. The principle of verifiability requires that articles are sourced with reliable content that can be easily verified, that is published and widely available either in digital or print form.[12] "No original research," as applied to article mainspace, prohibits the use of "material—such as facts, allegations, and ideas—for which no reliable, published sources exist."[13] Finally, the principle of notability requires that topics (to be represented in Wikipedia) have significant coverage from reliable (usually printed) sources independent of the subject.[14] These three policies significantly define the encyclopedia's knowledge-making practices, especially in terms of what is represented and who is writing those representations.

The dominance of print culture plays a significant role in the marginalization of indigenous knowledge cultures, especially when their knowledge is stored and transmitted orally. Peter Gallert and Maja van der Velden further explain what happens to these cultures in Wikipedia:

> For many aspects of the culture, tradition, and knowledge of indigenous people, there exist no or insufficient written records. This puts indigenous knowledge in Wikipedia, particularly on its largest language edition, the English Wikipedia,

into a disadvantageous situation. Oral information transmission is not regarded as a way of publishing by the online encyclopedia, knowledge keepers are often believed to be too close to their narrative's subjects to follow a neutral point of view, and passing on songs and stories is not seen as a reliable way of preserving knowledge.[15]

Wikipedia's failure to represent and engage indigenous and/or oral knowledge practices is only one example of the systemic biases at work in the encyclopedia. Researchers, academics, and Wikimedians alike have also addressed problems related to the encyclopedia's gender gap as inherently systemic.[16] The indigenous knowledge problem, however, does help to illustrate the ways in which the Wikipedia's encyclopedic promise falls short.

These are not new issues. Nor are they unacknowledged by the Wikimedia community. The Oral Citations Project, for instance, an initiative and research project led by Indian Wikimedian Achal Prabhala to validate alternative verifiability practices and engage oral epistemologies, was completed in 2011. The project was funded by Wikimedia itself, and garnered attention from several media outlets. It did not, however, drastically or significantly change Wikipedia's print-centric verifiability policy. In a response to a question on a talk page about the project's outcome, for example, Asaf Bartov, a Wikimedia grant officer, wrote the following: "[The project] has not gained adoption or significant attention from the editing community; it remains a possible direction, and may be picked up in the future, if and when the editing community shows interest in tackling this formidable challenge."[17]

This poor representation of indigenous knowledge prompts the question: Why and how does enlightenment rhetoric persist in and about Wikipedia? I direct this question to the Wikipedia community. But I also ask a similar question of myself. Given what I have learned in the last decade about the impossibility of universal knowledge, why do I continue to be enthralled and excited by Wikipedia's enlightenment potential? This is the aporia, the riddle, that I attempt to answer in the final section.

Possible and Impossible Answers: Wikipedia as Game, or Blind Man's Bluff

Toward the end of his brief essay "What Is an Encyclopedia? An Historical Overview from Pliny to Wikipedia," Dan O'Sullivan further describes this impossibility of universal coverage in the following passage:

The illusion of a totalizing drive for universal knowledge—a project that is manifestly impossible to achieve, even with the most advanced technology and the enthusiastic cooperation of thousands—is also quite inappropriate in the emergent postmodern, skeptical, and multicultural world of today. Indeed, knowledge cannot be exhaustively collected and stored in this manner but is always tied to the local time and situation in which it was developed and deployed, constantly in a state of flux.[18]

While he does not cite specific theorists, his critique is consistent with philosophical advances of the twentieth century. More specifically, post-structuralist theorists such as Jacques Derrida and Michel Foucault have interrogated traditional notions of knowledge by acknowledging their logocentrism (the faulty assumption that knowledge exists independent of language) and their historicity (the notion that knowledge is always created and characterized by historical context.)[19] Bruno Latour continues such deconstruction by charting the social construction of scientific knowledge; while Friedrich Nietzsche challenges the possibility of empirical objectivity itself.[20] Here I would make a distinction between, on the one hand, Derrida and Latour, who critique the transparency of language and empiricism respectively, and on the other, Foucault and Nietzsche, who critique the ethics and intent of those engaged in knowledge-making processes.

In Nietzsche's cynical philosophy especially, humankind has neither the capacity or desire for truth, and takes up instead,

deception, flattering, lying, and cheating ... the constant fluttering around the single flame of vanity ... deeply immersed in illusions and dream images; their eye only glides over the surface of things ... their feeling nowhere leads into truth, but contents itself with the reception of stimuli, playing, as it were, a game of blind man's bluff.[21]

For Nietzsche, the game of blind man's bluff is an apt analogy for the ways in which the desire for power, self-interest, ignorance, and language motivate and inform human philosophy. In such an analogy, truth becomes a game in which the main player is blindfolded—incapable of seeing the alternative motivations that drive their search for knowledge. In contrast to Nietzsche's cynicism, I would like to place Wikipedia's more optimistic rhetoric regarding its self-stated purpose: "Wikipedia has a lofty goal: a comprehensive collection of all of the knowledge in the world."[22] Not only does this ambition assume the possibility of a commodifiable and stable mass of knowledge (that only needs to be collected and made available);

it also assumes that Wikipedians will go about collecting that knowledge through a procedure that is both altruistic and methodologically balanced.

In other words, the ambitious and lofty rhetoric of Wikipedia's encyclopedic project often neglects to consider its editors' self-interests or ulterior motives. And yet, of course volunteer editors are motivated by their own interests to improve and create encyclopedic content. Further, there will always be paid and political editing in Wikipedia. Self-interest can even help to explain Wikipedia's content gaps—as the homogeneity of editorial demographics creates a homogeneity of well-covered subject areas and subject coverage gaps—as policy makers in Wikipedia reify knowledge practices that reflect their own cultures and cultural values.

It's important to pause here to make a note about my own motives in writing this essay. I wrote in the introduction that Wikipedia's optimistic rhetoric never ceased to amaze me but only became more complex as I began to realize how it both challenges and conserves the boundaries of the encyclopedic genre. This remains true, even as I wade into Nietzsche's cynical vision. Wikipedia remains the most comprehensive and equitable knowledge project we have known. And while I challenge its failure to represent universal knowledge, I also hold in my mind contesting arguments regarding what the community has accomplished. To put it another way, it is always my admiration for the project of Wikipedia that compels me to reflect and critique it as an epistemological project.

Perhaps if we soften Nietzsche's philosophy slightly—remove its cynicism and misanthropic critique—we might better understand how self-interest works both in opposition to and in support of Wikipedia's ambitious goals. Yes, self-interested editing leads to imbalances of content and biases among representations of genders, topics, and even geographies.[23] But self-interest also means that editors focus on the development of articles and topics they would like to see improved; it encourages participation and enables the altruistic volunteering of time and effort that have made this and other peer production projects so successful.

Further, while Nietzsche's description of knowledge as game is a useful analogy for understanding the curation of knowledge in Wikipedia, I would also revise the rules of such a game. In particular, I would argue that Wikipedia has, in many ways, removed the blindfold from "blind man's bluff." Indeed, it is Wikipedia's radical transparency and dynamism that ultimately allows a resolution of the conflict between its encyclopedic promise and epistemological failure. Unlike encyclopedias before it, Wikipedia is not a stable object. Rather, it remains perpetually unfinished. It is a performance or experience in epistemology, and its processes are available (to those who choose to play the game) on countless pages devoted to discussion, history, policy, and governance of the encyclopedia.

Wikipedia as Epistemology in Process

Because of its innovative application of the wiki platform for large-scale peer production, Wikipedia represent an epistemology in process: one that is always evolving alongside social, cultural, and technological influences. Further, it is this unfinished and in-process state that helps to reconcile the tension between the encyclopedia's ambition and its failure to fully carry out that ambition. Reconciliation of Wikipedia's failures to represent multiple forms and methods of knowledge curation requires that we see opportunity in its unfinished form. Moreover, it requires that we be more attentive to those spaces in the encyclopedia that allow and enact the recursive and collaborative process of knowledge production and curation: history pages which show us multiple iterations of an article in development and talk pages where editors negotiate an article in development. It is this flux and negotiation, ultimately, that demonstrates the encyclopedia's capability to exist within rationalist *and* postmodern realities, to value the enlightenment ambitions of the encyclopedic genre (via Diderot) *and* the complicated postmodern reality of knowledge as socially constructed.

Notes

1. Robert E. Cummings, *Lazy Virtues: Teaching Writing in the Age of Wikipedia* (Nashville, TN: Vanderbilt University Press, 2009); Carra L. Hood, "Editing out Obscenity: Wikipedia and Writing Pedagogy," *Computers and Composition Online* (Spring 2009), https://www2.bgsu.edu/departments/english/cconline/wiki_hood/index.html; James P. Purdy, "When the Tenets of Composition Go Public: A Study of Writing in Wikipedia," *College Composition and Communication* 61, no. 2 (December 2009): 351–373.

2. Jimmy Wales, "Wikipedia Founder Jimmy Wales Responds," *Slashdot*, July 28, 2004, https://slashdot.org/story/04/07/28/1351230/wikipedia-founder-jimmy-wales -responds.

3. Jacques Derrida, *Of Grammatology* (Baltimore, MD: Johns Hopkins University Press, 1998); Michel Foucault, *The Courage of the Truth (The Government of Self and*

Others II): Lectures at the College De France, 1983–1984 (London, UK: Palgrave Mac-Millan, 2011); Bruno Latour, Steve Woolgar, and Jonas Salk, *Laboratory Life: The Construction of Scientific Facts* (Princeton, NJ: Princeton University Press, 2013); Friedrich Nietzsche, *On Truth and Lies in a Nonmoral Sense* (Chicago: Aristeus Books, 2012).

4. Wikipedia, s.v. "Aporia: Difference between Revisions," last modified March 8, 2011, https://en.wikipedia.org/w/index.php?title=Aporia&type=revision&diff=417869078 &oldid=398840873.

5. Dan O'Sullivan, "What Is an Encyclopedia? A Brief Overview from Pliny to Wikipedia," in *Critical Point of View: A Wikipedia Reader*, ed. Geert Lovink and Nathaniel Tkacz (Amsterdam: Institute of Network Cultures, 2011), 34–49.

6. Wales, "Wikipedia Founder Jimmy Wales Responds."

7. Denis Diderot, *Rameau's Nephew, and Other Works* (Garden City, NY: Doubleday, 1956).

8. Wikipedia, s.v. *"Wikipedia: Purpose,"* last modified July 3, 2019, https://en.wikipedia .org/wiki/Wikipedia:Purpose.

9. Wikipedia, s.v. "Wikipedia: Verifiability," last modified August 21, 2019, https://en .wikipedia.org/wiki/Wikipedia:Verifiability.

10. Peter Gallert and Maja Van der Velden, "Reliable Sources for Indigenous Knowledge: Dissecting Wikipedia's Catch-22," in *Embracing Indigenous Knowledge in a New Technology Design Paradigm*, ed. Nicola J. Bidwell and Heike Winschiers-Theophilus (Indigenous Knowledge Technology Conference, 2013).

11. Raval Noopur, "The Encyclopedia Must Fail!—Notes on Queering Wikipedia," *ADA: A Journal of Gender, New Media, & Technology*, no. 5 (July 2014).

12. Wikipedia, s.v. "Wikipedia: Verifiability," last modified August 21, 2019, https://en .wikipedia.org/wiki/Wikipedia:Verifiability.

13. Wikipedia, s.v. "Wikipedia: No Original Research" last modified August 21, 2019, https://en.wikipedia.org/wiki/Wikipedia:No_original_research.

14. Wikipedia, s.v. "Wikipedia: Notability" Wikipedia, last modified August 22, 2019, https://en.wikipedia.org/wiki/Wikipedia:Notability.

15. Gallert and Van der Velden, "Reliable Sources for Indigenous Knowledge," 2.

16. Benjamin Collier and Julia Bear, "Conflict, Criticism, Or Confidence: An Empirical Examination of The Gender Gap in Wikipedia Contributions," in *CSCW '12: Proceedings of the ACM 2012 conference on Computer Supported Cooperative Work* (New York: ACM, 2012), https://doi.org/10.1145/2145204.2145265; Ruediger Glott, Philipp Schmidt, and Rishab Ghosh, *Wikipedia Survey Overview* (Maastricht: UNU-MERIT, March 2010), http://www.ris.org/uploadi/editor/1305050082Wikipedia_Overview_15March2010

-FINAL.pdf; Leigh Gruwell, "Wikipedia's Politics of Exclusion: Gender, Epistemology, and Feminist Rhetorical (In)action." *Computers and Composition*, 37, (September 2015): 117–131; Adrianne Wadewitz, "Wikipedia's Gender Gap and the Complicated Reality of Systemic Gender Bias," *Hastac*, July 26, 2013, https://www.hastac.org/blogs /wadewitz/2013/07/26/wikipedias-gender-gap-and-complicated-reality-systemic -gender-bias.

17. Meta-Wiki, s.v. "Research Talk: Oral Citations," last modified June 28, 2016, https://meta.wikimedia.org/wiki/Research_talk:Oral_Citations.

18. O'Sullivan, "What Is an Encyclopedia?" 48.

19. Derrida, *Of Grammatology*; Foucault, *The Courage of the Truth*.

20. Latour, Woolgar, and Salk, *Laboratory Life*; Nietzsche, *On Truth and Lies in a Non-moral Sense*.

21. Ibid.

22. Wikipedia, s.v. "Wikipedia: Purpose."

23. Mark Graham, "Wiki Space: Palimpsests and the Politics of Exclusion," in *Critical Point of View: A Wikipedia Reader*, ed. Geert Lovink and Nathaniel Tkacz (Amsterdam: Institute of Network Cultures, 2011): 269–282.

20 Equity, Policy, and Newcomers: Five Journeys from Wiki Education

Ian A. Ramjohn and LiAnna L. Davis

We tell the story of Wikipedia's engagement with equity and policy by weaving together five stories of individuals who became Wikipedians—and who all work for Wiki Education to envision a future where Wikipedia has more diverse content and contributors.

When you edit Wikipedia, you step into a great human endeavor, the largest collective project ever. In this essay, we weave together five stories of becoming Wikipedians into a narrative that tells a part of Wikipedia's story around equity and policy in a way that no single narrative could tell—and leads to a future in which Wikipedia has more diverse content and contributors through Wiki Education's programs.

Ian Ramjohn first edited Wikipedia in 2004 after seeing a segment about it on a BBC magazine program then known as *Click Online*. Sage Ross joined in 2005 as a more interesting use of his time in graduate school than writing a term paper. Ryan McGrady created his account in 2007 but spent his first few years learning about the community—for him, Wikipedia was primarily an academic object for study. LiAnna Davis became a Wikipedian in 2010 when she worked to launch the education program for the Wikimedia Foundation. Elysia Webb joined Wikipedia in 2017 as a participant in Wiki Education's Student Program.

Our experiences tell us that what built Wikipedia in the first decade led it to plateau in the second decade—and won't enable Wikipedia to survive the coming decades. The "if you build it, they will come" philosophy leads to a certain type of contributor—the naturally engaged Wikipedian. Naturally engaged Wikipedians are people like us: we came to Wikipedia because we believe in the vision of the sum of all human knowledge, and we have the privilege of education, the tenacity to engage in sometimes challenging online spaces, and the time to devote to volunteering in service of Wikipedia. We filled its editor ranks in the first decade. Over time we developed policies designed to codify quality standards. But in our single-minded pursuit of quality, we ended up creating a labyrinth of rules and guidelines that keeps all but the most dedicated newcomers out. We naturally engaged Wikipedians, a relatively homogeneous group, also failed to spend enough time considering how all our rules reified systemic bias. That led to Wikipedia's plateau in its second decade as active editor numbers flatlined after an initial spurt of growth.

Why is this problematic? Because the sum of all human knowledge isn't just in the hands of people like us. It requires more diverse content and more diverse contributors, people who have knowledge to share but don't find Wikipedia's structure conducive to sharing that knowledge. The policies developed by well-meaning early Wikipedians have led to the inequities that exist today in English Wikipedia's content and contributors. And if we don't fix our problems, thereby enabling new voices and new content, Wikipedia will cease to be the world's go-to resource for quality information.

We can solve these issues by systematically bringing new contributors to Wikipedia at scale through structured programs like those we run at Wiki Education. Our individual backgrounds with Wikipedia have led us to understand and reflect on Wikipedia's equity issues and how policy has reinforced them. And through our programs, we see a path forward to ensure open knowledge is even more representative, accurate, and complete in the coming decades.

Telling Our Stories

For Ian Ramjohn, what hooked him in Wikipedia from the start was the sense of empowerment. Traditionally, knowledge creation was a top-down process that was centered in the developed world. Knowledge creation was—and still is, in many ways—an imperialist venture. The fact that Ian was able to fix incorrect and out-of-date information about Trinidad and Tobago (his home country) changed the way he related to the world.

"When you come from a small, relatively unimportant developing country, what gets written about you is what other people have to say," Ian explains. "Maybe there's the occasional interested scholar who can change 'harmless' to '*mostly* harmless' in the entry about you, but you're always, at best, a bug under the microscope."

Sage Ross joined Wikipedia in 2005. His first efforts were driven by a desire to fill gaps: "I basically dumped a term paper into a new article about the history of atomism." Six months later, he returned because he had another term paper to write but one he had lost all interest in. "That's when I actually became a Wikipedian, primarily to avoid writing a term paper."

His initial writing was linked to his field of doctoral work—he wrote about the history of science, he curated articles, and he organized a Wiki-Project around the topic. Around this time, Sage also grew interested in *The Signpost*, Wikipedia's community newspaper, first as a reader, then as a contributor, focusing on what academics were saying about Wikipedia. A gap in the production of *The Signpost* led Sage to take over as temporary editor and, eventually, as editor in chief.

Ryan McGrady created his Wikipedia account in 2007. Initially he mostly lurked, trying to understand how Wikipedia worked. He spent a lot of time digging through policy talk pages, notice boards, and their archives. He saw Wikipedia primarily as an academic object for research. Over time, he became an evangelist for Wikipedia, talking about it in classes and working to promote understanding of it. In 2012, he used Wikipedia as a teaching tool in his classes and had his students contribute content. It was only after he started teaching with Wikipedia that he felt the need to jump in and become a full-fledged Wikipedia contributor.

The English Wikipedia saw its greatest growth in 2005–2007, and after that growth it entered a period of sharp decline. As Joseph Reagle recounts in chapter 1, the demise of Wikipedia had been predicted pretty much from the beginning of the project, but the post-2007 period was one of real decline. The number of active editors fell precipitously, and academics, journalists, and Wikipedians themselves started questioning the viability of the project. In an effort to counter this decline, the Wikimedia Foundation started engaging in programmatic work. Frank Schulenburg, who at the time was head of public outreach, had noticed a trend: Wikipedia editors who were also university instructors were assigning students to edit Wikipedia as a class assignment, and this was a successful way of bringing more high-quality content from new contributors to Wikipedia. But it was challenging to use Wikipedia as a teaching tool unless you had deep Wikipedia expertise as a contributor yourself. Frank assembled a team to provide that expertise so teaching with Wikipedia could be expanded to non-Wikipedian faculty.

Sage, the graduate student turned *Signpost* editor, was recruited to join the team. So was LiAnna Davis, who had studied Wikipedia academically but hadn't made many contributions. Her role was to do communications for the pilot of this new program, and she spent time speaking to the media about it, communicating with existing Wikipedians, and creating help resources for student editors in the program.

"The best way to really learn how to do something yourself is to train others to do it," LiAnna says. "I quickly learned the ins and outs of Wikipedia, so I could distill the most important elements down for our program participants."

By 2012, the program LiAnna and Sage worked on had reached a plateau within the Wikimedia Foundation, but it still had unfulfilled potential. In 2013, the Wikimedia Foundation spun off the program into an independent organization called Wiki Education. LiAnna and Sage became staff of the new organization and, within a year, brought Ian and Ryan on board too.

Elysia Webb's introduction to Wikipedia was different. For her, Wikipedia had always been around—it was just another part of the infrastructure of the internet. She was introduced to the idea of editing Wikipedia as part of a Wiki Education–supported class she took as a graduate student in 2017. While this was an assignment she was doing for class, she was also motivated because she was writing about something she really cared about—the bat species she was studying for her master's degree. This experience demystified the editing process.

She came to Wikipedia believing that it was a fairly complete work but soon realized that there were large gaps in the coverage of bats. This changed her perception from "I can edit" to "I *should* edit." The size of the task was daunting: 75 percent of bat articles were stubs, meaning more than one thousand articles on bats needed improvement. But, she thought, "if I don't do it, who will?" Elysia started actively contributing content during her free time, quickly racking up thousands of edits. In 2018, Elysia also joined Wiki Education's staff.

Comparing and Contrasting Our Experiences

The five of us have similarities in our motivation and evolution as editors and some notable differences.

We all identified gaps in Wikipedia's coverage and saw ourselves as having the tools to help fill those gaps. Sage, Elysia, and Ian were all motivated to become Wikipedians because of this—they saw gaps in coverage, recognized that they each had the skills to fill those gaps, and felt an obligation to fill those gaps. Ryan came to that realization along the way by finding things that were missing and that he wanted to write about. LiAnna, on the other hand, has always worked at scale to fill content gaps. She was hired by the Wikimedia Foundation to recruit people in academia to work to fill these gaps.

Our integration into the community came in different ways. Sage, Ryan, and LiAnna were drawn into the community by getting to know other Wikimedians at events and meetups. Getting to know the people behind the accounts, getting to know people in real life, were major factors in drawing them into the community. As Sage notes, "Meetups helped solidify me feeling like I had a place in the community."

Elysia's integration into the community came through content collaboration and WikiProjects and later through her experiences with colleagues at Wiki Education. Like LiAnna, Elysia's professional life intersected with Wikipedia quite early on in her Wikipedia career.

Ian's integration into the community sits in contrast to these—he built his sense of community by editing controversial topics. He edited the race article, and he also edited articles in the areas of US politics, evolution, intelligent design, and climate change. On the race article, both his ally and his opponent became on-wiki friends of his. He formed friendships with like-minded editors in the other areas as well. Many of these friendships were formed "in the trenches," trying to serve as a bulwark against editors who were organized off-wiki.

Wikipedia is a global community, but for Sage, Ryan, and Elysia, the global experience came later. Ian, on the other hand, found himself editing alongside a mixture of editors from the United States, the United Kingdom, Australia, India, and continental Europe. The editor who nominated him for adminship is Czech. National varieties of English were important to him from the beginning because he preferred not to use American spelling for articles about Trinidad and Tobago. While LiAnna's first year was spent focusing primarily on supporting programs in the United States, by 2011 she had moved into a global role, working to grow education programs in

India, Brazil, Egypt, Jordan, Algeria, and Saudi Arabia while also supporting affiliate-led efforts in a dozen additional countries globally.

By 2018, however, all five of us were staff of Wiki Education, united in our professional mission to improve English Wikipedia content at scale by empowering subject matter experts to fill content gaps.

Thinking About Equity

When Ian joined Wikipedia, the opportunities seemed vast. In 2004 the "write what you know" ethos still prevailed in Wikipedia. The content on Wikipedia should be verifiable, certainly, but few people expected references to be right there in the article. For Ian, equity was the reason he was on Wikipedia—here was an opportunity to present the developing world on similar footing to the developed world to ensure that just as every town in the United States had a Wikipedia article, so too might every town in the developing world. He wanted to build up the corpus of articles that were about places and people that probably wouldn't matter to most readers in the developed world but that *would* matter if the goal of Wikipedia really was to gather the sum-total of human knowledge.

At the same time, Ian encountered racism from the beginning. An early interaction with a neo-Nazi led him to find an administrator (admin) to ask for help. The neo-Nazi was blocked from editing Wikipedia, but other less disruptive people still existed, people who followed the rules but who promoted "racial realism" or who spoke of "white pride." One of Ian's on-wiki friends, an African American woman, received nonstop harassment that included having pictures of lynchings regularly posted to her user page. While the community blocked these harassers on sight, it was obvious that dealing with these people was a major impediment to her ability to contribute to Wikipedia.

For Ian, recognition of the problem of gender equity came slowly. In a world where "male" is the default normal and people edit behind pseudonyms, it's easy to slip into acceptance that things are the way they are on Wikipedia. The presence of a few prominent women among the community of editors made it easy to miss the scarcity of women in general. But it became impossible to miss the fact that the people who were targeted for harassment, the people who were driven out, tended to be women.

Sage was attracted to the project because of the vision of a world where everyone had access to the sum total of human knowledge; his academic background gave an excellent context for understanding the role that sourcing could play. "As a historian of science, I was keenly aware of the idea of knowledge as a socially embedded process because that was pretty central to my daily intellectual work," Sage says. "I understood the reasons behind the unevenness of topic areas, the massive privilege-based coverage of what's on Wikipedia, the root problems with sourcing being embedded in a broader cultural issue of how rules and norms reify those things."

Working on *The Signpost* strengthened his understanding of the problem of systemic bias on Wikipedia. Reading what others were writing about Wikipedia and looking at the project itself with a journalistic eye brought this issue to the forefront. But it wasn't until he attended his first few meetups that the issue of gender imbalance in the Wikipedia community became "viscerally obvious."

Sage gave a lightning talk at a New York conference about the egregious examples of gender bias present in Wikimedia Commons, the image repository for Wikipedia. Off-wiki, he bonded with the handful of influential women in the US editing community and spent hours discussing gender bias on Wikipedia with them.

Wikipedia's systemic bias was a key factor in LiAnna's ongoing work with Wikipedia. When she joined, survey results had just shown more than 90 percent of Wikipedia's editors identified as male.

"As a woman, I clearly can help fix the gender bias simply by being an active community member," LiAnna says. "But I took a different approach to devoting my time to Wikipedia. I set out to see how I could—at scale—empower others who don't identify as male to contribute."

Colleges and universities turned out to be a great place to start as the higher education population in the United States is around 60 percent female. As director of programs for Wiki Education, LiAnna oversaw work to target academic faculty related to race, gender, and sexuality, bringing more and more diverse contributors to Wikipedia through class assignments. (See chapter 14 for Alexandria Lockett's experiences with this as a teacher.) LiAnna occasionally contributes content herself, but she sees her biggest achievement as overseeing the scaling of a program that now supports sixteen thousand students in editing Wikipedia each year. The program as a whole does way more to improve Wikipedia's coverage of systemic bias topic areas and bringing new contributor voices than any one volunteer editing individually could.

This focus on equity has been a driving force of our work at Wiki Education. Even staff who didn't previously appreciate how prevalent the content gaps are on Wikipedia are now fully dedicated to reducing systemic bias.

For Ryan, the importance of equity and the issue of systemic bias came to the forefront through involvement in both Wiki Education and the Wikimedia New York chapter. His initial academic interest in Wikipedia had focused on accuracy, but over time, he slowly came to realize the real challenge facing Wikipedia was in equity issues.

"My whole concept of criticism of Wikipedia moved from reliability and accuracy to systemic bias," Ryan says. "I realized reliability had been resolved, our understanding of that is well established, but equity is both important and interesting. I have a much more heightened awareness of how who has written Wikipedia influences it."

Elysia, as a female scientist by education, was taken aback when she first learned of Wikipedia's gender bias.

"I'm in the biological sciences, which has a male slant, but it's really pretty even, especially in the field of bats. There are many women bat scientists," Elysia explains. "So I didn't really think about equity when I was just writing content. I kept being misgendered, people would assume I was a man, which was a little odd. Since I started this position with Wiki Education, I've started seeing editing Wikipedia as more of a revolutionary act in terms of equity and representation. I've identified there are a lot of systemic biases to why people don't contribute."

Thinking About Policies

Attracting Wikipedians who don't look like or think like the typical Wikipedian is an important tool for adding content that would otherwise not get added because the existing community members haven't prioritized these issues. But having more diverse voices among the editing community is also important for discussions around interpreting notability and reliable source guidelines.

Wikipedia reflects the biases of the wider world. Scientists are more difficult to write about than athletes because more news articles are written about athletes. But "reliable sourcing" is culturally determined—the decision to accept a source as "reliable" or "not reliable" depends on the people who choose to become involved in the decision. Sometimes it's just a matter of trusting the word of a Wikipedian you've come to believe is knowledgeable. A discussion about the reliability of the *Daily Mail* in 2017 attracted more than seventy informed participants. A similar discussion about a Zimbabwean publication would likely attract few participants.

Policies and guidelines like "reliable sources" and "notability" are where many of Wikipedia's systemic bias conflicts emerge. To understand the issue, it's important to look back at the history of policy development on Wikipedia.

Wikipedia entered a time of dramatic change between late 2005 and early 2007. The editing community grew explosively, and culture was less likely to be passed from established editors to new editors. Newcomers were more likely to interact with other newcomers. Written policies became more important because it wasn't possible to just follow what the established editors were doing. Policies became harder to change as they no longer just described how the community did things—increasingly they described how the community should do things.

"In the early days, thanks to its sourcing policies, Wikipedia was a breakwater that the waves of propaganda crashed against," Ian recalls. "Policies are important. But as Wikipedia got more complete, as its policies have ossified, it's harder to make change."

One of the biggest social markers in the community is becoming an administrator. As policies solidified, it became harder and harder to go through the adminship process. Sage tried to make a stand with his own request for adminship (RfA), one of the myriad complex Wikipedia processes.

"In reporting for *The Signpost*, looking at trends in how editors were joining the community, active editor trends, adminship trends, and other broader discussions going on at the time, I decided the bar was ratcheting up too much," Sage says. "I wanted to get back to the idea that adminship is no big deal, and I decided that I was probably about as active and dedicated to Wikipedia as I was ever likely to be, so I may as well test it, make a point, push back in whatever way I could to the ratcheting up of the bureaucracy. So I said I wasn't going to answer any of the supposedly optional questions. And I passed anyway."

Sage's stand gave him the admin rights—but sadly didn't result in the culture change he was hoping for. And the bureaucracy has only gotten more ossified over the years.

"By the time I started paying attention, the rules were already in a state where they were hard to change," Ryan says. "They've only gotten more so over time. When I started, you could still make bold changes. For a major change, you'd get pushback, and it would go to an RfC [request for comment]. But you could still make a bold change and it might stick—now, those days seem to be gone."

Coming Together at Wiki Education

If an experienced editor like Ryan can't make bold changes stick, imagine how challenging it is for a newcomer to Wikipedia, twenty years into the project. If they attempt to do more than fix a typo, newcomers are met with welcome messages that point them to hundreds of policy and guideline pages, and running the gauntlet of "new pages patrol" or "articles for creation" tends to make them abandon Wikipedia quickly.

"As the community grows inward-looking, it's harder to add fresh blood," Ian says. "So we need new ways, like bringing students in, like training subject matter experts. We fight new battles because we can—equity matters because Wikipedia matters. When Wikipedia was mostly porn stars and Pokémon, it wasn't important, so people didn't care what percentage of biographies of scientists were of women—we were happy to have a few articles on Nobel laureates. But because no one cared about equity early on, it's a huge hill to climb."

Against this backdrop, the five of us—along with our exceptional colleagues—are climbing that hill. We have managed to enable tens of thousands of new editors to effectively contribute content to Wikipedia, especially in content areas previously undercovered because of systemic bias issues. Using our own experiences and histories, we've actively worked within the ossified policies of Wikipedia to overcome systemic bias challenges and bring more equitable content to the project.

Only a tiny fraction of the students, like Elysia, contribute in a sustained, ongoing fashion, mirroring the retention challenge of other outreach projects. Some have posited that Wikipedia isn't retaining new editors because of technical challenges with the editing interface, or talk pages being too outdated, or grumpy community members. These are admittedly challenges newcomers face, but Wiki Education has shown that it's possible, with the right training and support, for almost anyone to make a meaningful contribution to Wikipedia. Being a Wikipedian is more than just one engagement with the encyclopedia: it entails ongoing work of writing content, participating in discussions, and editing others' work. Our experience successfully onboarding tens of thousands of new editors who move on after writing one article leads us to the conclusion that anyone can make a meaningful contribution, but only a small fraction will feel the calling to stay engaged as Wikipedians. Most Wikipedians were Wikipedians before they ever hit the edit button.

"Potential Wikipedians are extremely rare. The people who become people like us, for the most part, show up on Wikipedia and feel like they've come home," Ian says. "They feel like this is what they 'need' to do with their lives."

That's why we see large-scale programs like the ones we run at Wiki Education to be so critical for the future of Wikipedia. To survive, Wikipedia needs to nurture the existing community while simultaneously offering programs at scale to attract more equitable content and contributors. And if those contributors simply fill one content gap and move on, that's okay: not everyone is a naturally engaged Wikipedian. But Wikipedia still needs their voice. And that's why programs like ours are so important.

We haven't always gotten the model right. When the program started in 2010, Sage was in charge of recruiting expert Wikipedians who would volunteer to help onboard new student editors into the ways of the community. We originally envisioned the process would work through volunteer energy, just as many of us had joined the community.

"At the time I joined the staff, I didn't have an acute sense of the ways that the potential of the idea of Wikipedia was being actively constrained by the scale of the community," Sage says. "It became clear that the sort of volunteer energy, capacity, and flexibility to turn their collective energy to a big task is actually quite small. Individually, we can do tons of stuff. But in a time where Featured Article nominations are closed not because they had flaws but because there wasn't enough reviewer interest, Wikipedia as a process and entity on its own is severely constrained by the scale of its core community."

Our experience has taught us that the idea that volunteers have the energy and ability to grow the community only works to a certain point—the point

English Wikipedia reached within the first decade. And it only attracts the type of person who is willing to navigate the labyrinth of Wikipedia policies and guidelines to share knowledge. But not everybody whose knowledge we want is participating or even can participate. That's why organizations like Wiki Education are so critical to Wikipedia's future.

LiAnna and Sage—along with other original Wiki Education colleagues—set out to overcome the constraint of volunteer energy by developing a program model that doesn't rely on volunteers. LiAnna led program development to scale, from supporting three thousand students a year when Wiki Education spun off from the Wikimedia Foundation to supporting sixteen thousand students a year, without growing the staff dedicated to that program. We accomplished this in part because Sage has led the technical development of a suite of software tools called the Dashboard that have enabled us to streamline our processes. Ian and Elysia joined staff to serve in a role we call "Wikipedia Experts," who provide human support for when our automated systems aren't enough to answer program participants' questions.

"Through our Dashboard software and our process-driven approach to staff time allocation, we were able to eliminate many of the bottlenecks to scaling," LiAnna explains. "Our online trainings explain to newcomers exactly what they need to know in language they can understand—and our Wikipedia Experts are exceptional at jumping in as a friendly helper to resolve cases where challenges arise."

While the Student Program is our flagship, we also offer other programs targeted at different audiences. Ryan, for example, works on our Wiki Scholars & Scientists Program, where we lead subject matter experts through a twelve-week course on editing Wikipedia and provide certification on successful completion of the course. An interesting finding so far in this program has been that many of our course participants had existing Wikipedia accounts. They'd tried to edit on their own—and failed. But doing so in a structured course environment overseen by professional staff like those of us at Wiki Education gives them the opportunity to share their knowledge with the world—and to have it stick on Wikipedia.

"I've gained appreciation for the potential of programs for bringing people to Wikipedia for the improvement of public knowledge," Ryan says. "It's meaningful not just for oneself to contribute, but also to bring people to Wikipedia."

By working together, the five of us and our colleagues at Wiki Education have been able to create something more than the sum of its parts. The individual efforts the five of us as Wikipedians could have had on Wikipedia's content is far eclipsed by the sixty million words of content that has been added by the program participants we've brought to Wikipedia and supported as they successfully added their voices to the world's largest collaborative project. And the content is more equitable than anything we could've produced as individuals because it brings in diverse voices to the editing community.

Looking Into the Future

So what made us remain Wikipedians? What kept us around? Elysia's observations probably hold true for all of us: "I saw a very clear, urgent, and unmistakable need for someone like me. I am the person who has the skills and knowledge to fix this. I realized: Wikipedia needs me. As a graduate student, I had a faith and belief in my knowledge. I felt like not quite an expert but certainly more qualified than most people to fill in this content gap."

We all saw that we had the skills to make a contribution, we had confidence in our skills, and we saw gaps that, if we didn't fill them, wouldn't get filled. We felt like we were home when we edited Wikipedia. Naturally engaged Wikipedians like us are a rare but vital breed. But to collect the sum of all human knowledge, we need more than just the natural Wikipedians. We need diverse voices to help close content gaps through structured, scalable programs designed to empower one-time contributions.

That's the role organizations like Wiki Education can play in Wikipedia's future. Funded primarily by grants from large foundations, we're able to offer newcomer training programs at scale. By identifying equity gaps, explaining complex policies, and providing friendly faces from the community to our program participants, Wiki Education is tackling Wikipedia's challenges head-on—and succeeding. In 2019, 20 percent of all of English Wikipedia's new active editors came from our program.

As we continue to scale our work, we will continue to have a massive impact on the quality of content, the diversity of contributors, and hopefully in the future the inequities in policies. Large-scale operations to bring new content, new contributors, and new knowledge to Wikipedia—or Wikidata, or whatever the next frontier of open knowledge is—are critically important for us to achieve that vision we all were initially motivated by: creating the sum of all human knowledge.

"It's been empowering to say, how can we remove these barriers, how can we make Wikipedia more equitable and diverse?" Elysia says. "I became a wildlife biologist because I wanted to save the world, but I changed fields to Wikipedia because I want to save the world."

Acknowledgments: The authors would like to extend special gratitude to Sage Ross, Ryan McGrady, and Elysia Webb, for candidly and graciously sharing their stories with us, and by extension, with you. Thanks also to our Wiki Education colleagues, including Sage, Ryan, and Elysia, as well as T. J. Bliss, Helaine Blumenthal, Will Kent, Frank Schulenburg, Shalor Toncray, Cassidy Villeneuve, and Samantha Weald, who offered feedback on an earlier version of this chapter. And of course, we appreciate the tens of thousands of people who have edited Wikipedia through our programs, whose contributions inspire us every day.

21   Wikipedia Has a Bias Problem

Jackie Koerner

The leader of free knowledge has a bias problem. Wikipedia contributors strive for neutrality, but the reality is they are distorting knowledge equity. It's all their fault. But that doesn't mean they can't be the solution.

Wikipedia started my love affair with free knowledge and open education. Like any relationship, it had its problems. Over the years, I felt hurt, inspired, embarrassed, hopeful, and unsafe. First, in 2001, I found a new way to discover information. In 2008, I received harassment on-wiki for the first time. In 2009, the dean resented my passion for open education, and as a result, my graduate degree sat in limbo. In 2014, I used Wikipedia as a springboard for my research. In 2017, thousands of academics laughed at me as I stood on stage and said, "I edit Wikipedia." The uncertainty fed doubts I held about Wikipedia. This caused me to stop and reflect on what Wikipedia meant to me.

Initially, I knew nothing about educational inequities.[1] I grew up in a privileged part of the United States. My school received sufficient funding enabling it to easily meet the educational needs of students.[2] I only knew what I experienced. That changed in 2001 when I became acquainted with Wikipedia. I learned what free knowledge means. I admit I initially consumed content and contributed nothing in return. That changed in 2016 when Wikipedia helped me when I needed it the most. It gave me a purpose when I felt I had none. Quickly, I realized how much Wikipedia needed me too.

Working with Wikipedia is tricky. Working with my peers to improve access to knowledge brings me joy. But it pains me to see denigration. For example, to make more room in the category "American novelists," contributors removed women novelists from the category.[3] The women novelists were placed in a subcategory named "American women novelists." The people moving women from one category to the other thought they solved a problem but they exacerbated another. They didn't consider why they moved the women and not the men nor the marginalization they were perpetuating. This example illuminates how our actions affect Wikipedia in subtle ways.

These subtle ways affecting Wikipedia are bias. Bias creates an unwelcoming environment for people and content on Wikipedia. Our biases influence societal structures, practices, and principles. It's no different for Wikipedia. After twenty years of development, Wikipedia still prevents the very thing it set out to change.

What Is Knowledge Equity?

In 1948, the Universal Declaration of Human Rights listed education as a human right.[4] Despite the simplicity of this notion of *equity meaning everyone*, its realization remains out of reach: more than 262 million youth do not attend school, with six out of ten youths struggling to obtain basic literacy—leading to 750 million illiterate adults.[5]

Wikipedia has been a radical force in providing material for education. Examples include Wiki Education and their work on improving student learning outcomes using Wikipedia in the United States (chapter 20); the Wikipedia Library, provisioning access to paywalled databases for Wikipedia contributors (chapter 8); and the Wikipedia + Libraries: Better Together program, strengthening the relationship between public libraries and Wikipedia (chapter 6).[6]

Yet Wikipedia's aspiration of sharing the "sum of all human knowledge" falls short. While Wikipedia has dramatically increased the accessibility of knowledge, the type of knowledge available remains incomplete.

The Wikimedia 2030 project envisions free knowledge as truly representative of human diversity. Nine teams with over a hundred community members, including myself, work to outline the services and structures necessary for greater participation and representation. The Wikimedia 2030 project declared that

> as a social movement, we will focus our efforts on the knowledge and communities that have been left out by structures of power and privilege. We will welcome people from every background to build strong and diverse communities. We will break down the social, political, and technical barriers preventing people from accessing and contributing to free knowledge.[7]

This is knowledge equity—the participation and presence of all people is the only way we can achieve equity in the knowledge presented on Wikipedia.

Where Wikipedia Fails Knowledge Equity

Uneven participation and representation on Wikipedia reproduce knowledge inequality. These structures of power and privilege survive without intentional efforts to disrupt them. The community structures of power and privilege perpetuated by bias act to interrupt Wikipedia's potential knowledge equity. Not challenging bias is worse than ignorance. We know it exists and choose to do nothing. Bias disrupts everything, and allowing it to spread uncontrollably will lead to Wikipedia's demise.

The Wikimedia 2030 commitment describes what Wikipedia hopes to achieve for knowledge equity. The action to achieve such, however, has not yet been defined. Wikipedia is the platform to support knowledge equity, and of course, a provider of free knowledge should practice knowledge equity. The people building the encyclopedia need to practice it too.

What Is Bias?

Bias consists of the thoughts and beliefs we have about society. We learn these biased thoughts and beliefs from family, friends, and the media. Bias is not based on facts, and it is socially constructed. Learning bias is not conscious or deliberate.

We all have biases. People are not bad for having biases. Bias influences our actions, beliefs, relationships, and even our work. The most common biases people think about when they hear the word bias are gender, sexual orientation, and racism. People feel if they are not acting in overtly sexist or racist ways, they are not biased. Acting on our biases is completely unconscious. Just like the example of the contributors moving women novelists, we generally do not intend to act in biased ways. It's often completely unintended, but that does not mean the result is any less harmful.

Learning bias is unavoidable and completely unconscious, but this does not mean we get to absolve all responsibility. Recognizing our own biases is hard work. It's easier to identify bias in others than it is in ourselves. We tend to join groups and seek information that confirms our thoughts and beliefs.

There is much work being done regarding gender bias on Wikipedia. While the gender bias does largely imbalance Wikipedia, this is not the only bias working to misrepresent knowledge.

Bias Is a Problem for Wikipedia

While we try to be neutral, our work on Wikipedia will always involve bias. Bias can appear in many areas, like Wikipedia's policies, practices, content, and participation.

Bias leads to barriers to inclusion. These barriers mean imbalanced participation and distorted knowledge. The most recognizable barriers relate to contributor retention, emerging communities, and content exclusion.

Disruption of bias is hard. The most common example is demonstrated by the harried response that proposed changes to policy or practice receive. Contributors who unquestioningly defend policy or practice make it difficult to implement inclusive changes. This happens because they are not seeking to understand but rather to be heard.

Confirmation bias occurs when people feel reaffirmed in their beliefs due to their interpretation of information. This happens when contributors read other discussion comments that support their perspective or see how often the policy works rather than considering where it does not work. This behavior maintains the problematic power dynamics within Wikipedia's community and prevents the project from encompassing underrepresented knowledge.

Examining one's own bias is difficult. Here is an example. At Wikimania 2017, I presented a session about bias.[8] When I completed my presentation and asked for questions, one person stood up. They asked, how you tell someone they are wrong when they tell you that you acted in a biased manner? I was delighted when the room filled with chatter and murmurs.

When a person is called out for bias, it's usually warranted. This person felt they were wronged when someone brought their bias to their attention. I invited people from the audience to answer the question. Many responded with content from the session, and some even shared personal stories of how bias tormented them and disrupted their work.

After thoughtful responses, encouragement, and honest vulnerability, the person still refused the possibility that they could be biased. This frustrated them so terribly that for the remainder of the multi-day event they tried to convince me of my faulty assumption.

This resistance to addressing personal bias still haunts the contributor, as they posted about the interaction nearly two years later. They wrote a post in a discussion on Wikipedia explaining their experience, expressing the feeling the audience in the room that day judged them unfairly. The person went on to ask a similar question: how to tell someone from a "minority group" they are wrong about encyclopedia writing, without them thinking it is a white man abusing his power privilege. Unfortunately, this is a white man abusing his power privilege. They choose to remain moored in their ways about encyclopedia development, knowledge curation, and equity instead of asking questions like, "How are we excluding people and their knowledge by doing things this way?" Asking this question might end up being a real eye-opener for a lot of people and could advance Wikipedia toward achieving knowledge equity.

Acknowledging bias is hard, and while it is painful work, it is critical. Wikipedia grapples with bias, and we need to be honest about our role in it. We all need to be aware of the problem and take action to reduce the influence of bias.

Where Bias Shows Up in Policy and Practice

Wikipedia policies and practices largely follow Westernized traditions of knowledge sharing and information publishing. More inclusive changes to the policies and practices are difficult to undertake. This sends the message that quality means Westernized practices and excludes anything and anyone not following these arbitrary principles.

Wikipedia was built in the early 2000s. The internet was very different back then. People published anything they wanted on their websites. Making online purchases seemed risky. Teachers laughed when students suggested doing online research. Policies and practices developed on Wikipedia responded to the problems the internet dealt with at the time. These problems still exist, but we have learned a lot considering the internet is so integrated into our lives. Although the internet has changed over the past twenty years, the policies and practices on Wikipedia have kept their same rigid beginnings.

Wikipedia materialized through predominantly Westernized cisgender male voices, opinions, and biases. The awareness in the community at that time illustrated a rather singular point of view and developed policies and practices accordingly. This foundation is difficult to break. Preference on Wikipedia concerning changes or inclusion is still very singular and causes diverse participants to have to work within the dominant culture.[9]

In the example I gave in the previous section, I feel the contributor was telling themselves the story of: "This is the policy. They are not following the policy. I will educate them about this policy." I hoped the Wikipedia contributor would have listened and reflected on the information and vulnerability being given in that room. We knew this contributor meant no ill will but saw they were stuck viewing the world through their perspective and their bias.

If they had reflected on the interaction, what they would have taken away from the session would have been very different. Perhaps they would see how, while not meaning to do so, they were applying their biased perspective on the situation and telling others in the community how things should be done.

We are all victims of the stories we tell ourselves. The response in situations like this should not be holding our policies so tightly that we cannot figure out how to listen to concerns. We should adapt our policies to a more inclusive and equitable world.

This narrow and inflexible behavior functions within the Wikipedia community to oppress and exclude. Simply because experience and history have been traditionally told from white, cisgender, male perspectives, these voices and perspectives within society are taken as fact when often they are opinions or interpretations. We all experience life from our lived experiences; the Wikipedia community is no different.[10]

By infusing homogeneous points of view into policies and practices of a community, a disservice is being done. Content and people are being removed and excluded if they do not fit into the policies and practices designed by the existing cohort of contributors.

How Reliable Sources Are a Bad Thing

One important policy is a good example of a well-intended bias perpetuating knowledge inequity. The reliable sources policy limits the sources and forms of information used on Wikipedia. This policy developed out of a need to keep people from posting unsubstantiated claims to the encyclopedia. Requiring reliable sources is a good thing, but the implementation on Wikipedia is the opposite.

Defining materials to fit the policy means limitations. As of this publication, knowledge from published, written materials with a preference toward academic and peer-reviewed publications epitomizes reliability. The reliable sources policy limits knowledge equity by ignoring knowledge that falls outside of the rules.

The knowledge available in published, written materials is biased. People and knowledge published in written materials are largely white and male. The way the current reliable sources policy is written and followed leads to an information imbalance on Wikipedia. There is far less content about women on Wikipedia than there is about men: as of October 2019, only 18 percent of biographies on Wikipedia are about women.[11]

The bias toward Westernized publications and knowledge-sharing practices exaggerates the lack of diverse content on Wikipedia. If there is no source about a person (or a topic) to meet the standards of the Wikipedia community, then no article will be written. That person is excluded from history. By following policies like reliable sources, contributors are replicating and magnifying the bias already depicted by published sources.

Contributors use their personal beliefs to determine, design, and follow policies. The dilemma grows when those in power within the Wikipedia community deny agency to those challenging the policies and practices of the Wikipedia community.

The policies around reliability are often applied in a way that removes anything varied or diverse. We should aim for balance in content. We should provide knowledge from diverse sources. Instead, we are refusing to listen to one another. This has to stop. Information is not accurately represented. Contributors are pushed away. Knowledge is lost.

What Went Wrong?

In the Wikipedia community, people are not listening to each other. Collaboration devolves into combative discourse. Discussions surrounding knowledge equity, reliability, verifiability, and neutrality draw their energy from bias. Communities and knowledge remain excluded.

The community often reacts to questions about the policies, practices, and community norms in a defensive way. Notable people cannot be documented because nothing about them exists in an acceptable published format.[12] Information is discredited, even when quoted from the subject in an oral history.[13] Women scientists only become notable because of an award while their male colleagues were notable before any such acknowledgment.[14]

Although social groups with power possess the privilege to address imbalances caused by bias, the responsibility for abolishing ignorance unfairly lies with the excluded or oppressed. This emotional labor taxes an already overtaxed individual and community. This is no different on Wikipedia. "Be bold!" But being bold can be risky. Anyone has the power to enact change, but power structures privilege long-time contributors, administrators, and policy writers. Within the Wikipedia community, these groups work together to deny change.

For example, when discussing information gatekeeping as a worrisome practice, another contributor disagreed with me. Instead of engaging in the discussion and trying to create a solution, they chose to "read all forty-eight pages" of my website and sent me a message about being "great enemies" if I disagreed with them. The person justified this behavior by mentioning the countless hours and thousands of dollars they contributed to Wikipedia.

This uncomfortable experience was mild compared with that of others, but they all have the same intentions: to silence diverse voices. The rampantly unchecked power dynamics within the community function to silence the voices aiming to address bias in content and policy on Wikipedia.

The Wikipedia we need must eliminate narrow policies and practices and elevate the culture to become inclusive. If we are not reaching the people who need our service, we are practicing inequity.[15]

There Is Hope

Education serves as a great tool for social mobility and stability. Wikipedia paints an illustration of daily acts of human decency. Here the Wikipedia community works tirelessly for societal good via an unmatched source of volunteerism. Festering imbalances exist due to the rather homogeneous composition of the contributor pool, the restrictive policies they created, and the inconsistent way in which the policies are practiced. The sum of all human knowledge cannot be built under these conditions where logic is designed out of the illogical. But there is hope. Wikipedia is just turning twenty.

How to initiate this change is for no one person or homogeneous group to undertake. The curation of knowledge, development of policies, and denial of change decided in such groups stunts the growth of Wikipedia. It serves no purpose or benefit to the longevity or growth of Wikipedia. Continuing to accept community consensus developed through homogeneous groups will keep Wikipedia in a perpetually sophomoric state. We should be concerned about quality sources, and we need to listen to what quality sources mean across the world. We should volunteer, and we should make space at the table for more people to volunteer too. There is not a limited amount of equity.

Equity comes from actions people take against oppressive and imbalanced policies and practices in society. We can change the world if we choose to enact equitable policies and practices on Wikipedia, refuse to manipulate discourse to squash diverse perspectives, and acknowledge that change is not scary but rather impressive. Without change, we continue to inflict and deepen wounds opened by oppression, exclusion, and continued ignorance.

What Can Be Done

The content in this chapter might sound familiar to you, but it might also be different in many ways. By listening to each other's lived experiences, we change together as a community. We must not only accept what we find acceptable for ourselves but accept what is needed for knowledge equity.[16]

In addressing knowledge equity and implementing these changes to reduce the effect of societal challenges on Wikipedia, we must proceed with care. Some areas need more structured support than others—such as setting stronger cultural norms and being empowered to act on bad behavior.[17] We should encourage growth through methods of listening, witnessing, and advocating. Growth this way can change the environment for Wikipedia and knowledge equity.

Wikipedia as a community and an encyclopedia has accomplished some amazing things in the first twenty years of its life. We learned what it means to collaborate online to build an encyclopedia. Much information has been developed about online communities, online collaboration, and information sharing. Educators and knowledge professionals began using Wikipedia to teach information literacy, regardless of the concerns and issues colleagues expressed. The Wikipedia community has come so far, but there is so much more to be done. If there is any hope for truly achieving the sum of all human knowledge, the next chapter in Wikipedia's life needs to meaningfully address the inequities perpetuated by bias. Although unfinished, rather progressive in some circles, and a little rough around the edges, even at twenty Wikipedia is the experimental educational equalizer and the solution to knowledge equity. We just have to stop preventing its success.

Notes

1. UNESCO Institute for Statistics, *Reducing Global Poverty through Universal Primary and Secondary Education*, (Policy Paper 32/Fact Sheet 44, UNESCO, June 2017), https://unesdoc.unesco.org/ark:/48223/pf0000250392.

2. Cory Turner, "Why America's Schools Have a Money Problem," *Morning Edition*, NPR, April 18, 2016, https://www.npr.org/2016/04/18/474256366/why-americas-schools-have-a-money-problem.

3. Alison Flood, "Wikipedia Bumps Women from 'American Novelists' Category," *The Guardian*, April 25, 2013, accessed July 20, 2019, https://www.theguardian.com/books/2013/apr/25/wikipedia-women-american-novelists.

4. Wikimedia, s.v. "File:The Universal Declaration of Human Rights 10 December 1948 .jpg" (United Nations), last modified March 12, 2019, https://commons.wikimedia.org/wiki/File:The_universal_declaration_of_human_rights_10_December_1948.jpg.

5. "Leading SDG4—Education 2030," UNESCO, n.d., accessed July 29, 2019, https://en.unesco.org/themes/education2030-sdg4.

6. Wikimedia Commons, s.v. "File:Student Learning Outcomes using Wikipedia-based Assignments Fall 2016 Research Report.pdf," June 1, 2017, accessed June 10, 2019, https://commons.m.wikimedia.org/wiki/File:Student_Learning_Outcomes_using_Wikipedia-based_Assignments_Fall_2016_Research_Report.pdf.

7. Meta-Wiki, s.v. "Knowledge Equity," s.v. "Strategy/Wikimedia Movement/2017/ Direction," accessed June 16, 2019, https://meta.wikimedia.org/wiki/Strategy/Wikimedia_movement/2017/Direction#Knowledge_equity:_Knowledge_and_communities_that_have_been_left_out_by_structures_of_power_and_privilege.

8. Wikimedia Commons, s.v. "File:Koerner Implicit Bias Wikimania 2017.pdf" (Jackie Koerner), accessed on June 10, 2019, https://commons.wikimedia.org/wiki/File:Koerner_Implicit_Bias_Wikimania_2017.pdf.

9. Amanda Menking, Ingrid Erickson, and Wanda Pratt, "People Who Can Take It: How Women Wikipedians Negotiate and Nagivate Safely," in *CHI '19: Proceedings of the 2019 CHI Conference on Human Factors in Computing Systems* (New York: ACM, 2019), https://dl.acm.org/doi/10.1145/3290605.3300702.

10. Marti Johnson and Alex Wang, "Wikimedia Foundation Releases Gender Equity Report," Wikimedia Foundation, September 21, 2018, https://wikimediafoundation.org/2018/09/21/advancing-gender-equity-conversations-with-movement-leaders/.

11. Wikipedia, s.v. "Wikipedia: WikiProject Women in Red," accessed October 26, 2019, https://en.wikipedia.org/wiki/Wikipedia:WikiProject_Women_in_Red.

12. Wikipedia, s.v. "Notability Is Geared towards the White Male Perspective," s.v. "Wikipedia talk: Notability/Archive 63," accessed June 10, 2019, https://en.wikipedia.org/wiki/Wikipedia_talk:Notability/Archive_63.

13. Wikipedia, s.v. "Wikipedia: Oral History," accessed on June 10, 2019, https://en.wikipedia.org/wiki/Wikipedia:Oral_history.

14. Dawn Bazely, "Why Nobel Winner Donna Strickland Didn't Have a Wikipedia Page," *The Washington Post*, October 8, 2018, https://www.washingtonpost.com/outlook/2018/10/08/why-nobel-winner-donna-strickland-didnt-have-wikipedia-page/?utm_term=.f0c748d01376.

15. Miranda Fricker, *Epistemic Injustice: Power and the Ethics of Knowing* (New York: Oxford University Press, 2007).

16. Walter Frick, "Wikipedia Is More Biased Than Britannica, but Don't Blame the Crowd," *Harvard Business Review*, December 3, 2014, https://hbr.org/2014/12/wikipedia-is-more-biased-than-britannica-but-dont-blame-the-crowd.

17. "Your Code of Conduct," Open Source Guides, n.d., accessed June 10, 2019, https://opensource.guide/code-of-conduct/.

IV Capstone

22 Capstone: Making History, Building the Future Together

Katherine Maher

The Wikimedia Foundation's executive director reflects on the past, present, and future of Wikipedia, informed by Wikimedia 2030, the vision and strategy project by the global Wikimedia movement and free knowledge partners.

Wikipedia turned fifteen years old on January 11, 2016. Later that same year, in a time of concern about "fake news" and disinformation, I attended an event focused on the future of the news media. Wikipedia isn't a news organization, so I was an outlier in the room. I seated myself at a small roundtable on the topic of trust with some hesitation: after all, journalists are frequently skeptical about Wikipedia's reliability. One by one, the attendees went around the room, introducing themselves and the reason they'd joined the session.

When it was my turn, I said: "Wikipedia has gone from being a punch line about the unreliability of people on the internet to becoming one of the most trusted sites online. I'm here to see what we can learn from one another." To my surprise, there were nodding heads around the table. It was a moment that would have been difficult to imagine even a few years ago.

As Wikipedia and the Wikimedia movement and projects enter our third decade, my expectation is that we'll continue to confound expectations. Today, Wikipedia includes fifty million articles across three hundred languages, ranging in size from six million articles on English Wikipedia to just over one thousand articles on Tulu Wikipedia. It is joined by a number of other successful free knowledge projects, including Wikidata, Wikimedia Commons, and Wikisource. Every single month, we estimate that around one billion people spend a collective sixty thousand years reading

Wikipedia. Together, the Wikimedia projects constitute one of the top ten most visited digital platforms on the planet.

Much more than an encyclopedia that anyone can edit, Wikipedia has fundamentally and irrevocably transformed models for how people and communities can experience and create knowledge, within and far beyond the various Wikimedia projects. It is a resource to people around the globe seeking information about history, politics, and pop culture. It is a project in nation building through language, a tool for cultural preservation, and a platform for debates over representation and truth. It is a database used by researchers, universities, and cultural institutions to share and publicize their data and collections.

It is one of the world's most widely used sources for training machine-learning applications. It is a trove of insight about humanity: our interests, our predilections, our biases. It is a byword for collaborative participation, a definitive oracle (has that celebrity really died?), a pop-culture signifier (see Stephen Colbert, elephants[1]), and an abbreviated verb for information seeking ("let me wiki that"). Each year, as Wikipedia has grown, it has become more integral, more important, and more irreplaceable to our shared cultural consciousness. Far more than an internet encyclopedia, it is a living compendium of our knowledge.

Wikimedia's Future

As this volume of reflections on the first twenty years of Wikipedia goes to press, the Wikimedia movement has recently completed a global, collaborative process to build a vision for the Wikipedia of 2030. Launched shortly after Wikipedia's fifteenth birthday, this "movement strategy" was an opportunity to consider what the Wikimedia community had accomplished and what was still to come. It was a chance to look at the distance between "the encyclopedia anyone can edit" and "a world in which every single person can freely share in the sum of all knowledge"—and ask ourselves how the Wikimedia movement might set about closing that gap. What would it take to reach more people? What would it mean if the whole world really could participate? What does "all knowledge" even mean?

To try to answer these questions, members of the Wikimedia movement spent a year talking to each other and others around the globe. They worked to reinterpret our vision—"Imagine a world in which every single

> "Imagine a world in which every single human being can freely share in the sum of all knowledge. That's our commitment."
>
> The vision of the Wikimedia movement is more than an aspirational statement. It offers us principles for how we approach our work.
>
> **Explicit**
>
> - *"Every single human being."* Everyone should be able to participate in knowledge, regardless of origin, ability, nationality, geography, language, culture, or other identifying factors.
> - *"Freely share."* Engagement with knowledge should not be subject to barriers or limits, whether economic, political, social, or otherwise. Knowledge should be participatory, easily read, reused, remixed, or revised—not merely consumed.
> - *"Sum of all knowledge."* Knowledge is vast, mutable, and continuously in evolution. "The sum" of knowledge should be inclusive and representative of the diversity of the world at large, unlike many canonical representations which suffer from implicit biases.
>
> **Implicit**
>
> - *We cannot do this alone.* An aspirational vision of this magnitude cannot be achieved by only Wikimedia. This paradigm shift requires many partners and allies.
> - *We are still far from this world.* Representations of knowledge are imperfect and often heavily biased. Many barriers and limitations preclude access and participation.
> - *A better world.* Our vision has a purpose beyond collection. A world of greater understanding is a world better equipped to address our collective challenges.

human being can freely share in the sum of all knowledge"—and to make plans for what we should be doing to realize it.

We hosted gatherings and discussions with people from seventy countries and consultations in more than twenty languages. We spoke with current Wikimedia movement members and partners as well as people learning about Wikimedia for the first time. We commissioned research into the state of the world today and the state of the world to come. We interviewed 150 experts from the worlds of academia, arts and culture, epistemology, education, open science, and technology.

As a community of collaborators and information enthusiasts, we took the values and practices honed over years of creating Wikipedia and used them to explore, examine, and propose a direction for our future, together. One thing quickly became evident in our conversations about the future—the world the Wikimedia projects emerged from is no longer the world in which we operate today.

Some of these changes are promising and positive, offering us new opportunities to interpret our vision, connect with people, and expand free knowledge in the world. However, just as many are concerning changes with potential negative implications for the long-term health of the global Wikimedia community, our projects, and our ability to pursue our vision of a world of international cooperation, constructive discourse, and collaboration in the service of our global knowledge commons.

We see a world that's more connected than ever before, with bandwidth costs decreasing, making it easier for everyone to get online. Primary and secondary education enrollment rates are rising, as are global literacy rates. We're seeing a growing population of young, engaged, and online youth eager to effect change in their communities and on a global scale. But alongside these positive changes, we're also seeing new challenges and threats.

The world is becoming less open as authoritarian governments close spaces for dissent and debate. Democracies are struggling with increased polarization and decreased trust in institutions. The internet, once a relatively open and creative space, has become increasingly consolidated, centralized, and homogenized, perpetuating power and control within a handful of corporations. Data gathering and tracking has enabled a "public-private surveillance" economy that seeks to know everything about everyone.

The Wikimedia 2030 consultation put these changes at the center of the conversation, recognizing the need for our projects and communities to continue to adapt and evolve in order to meet the opportunities and challenges ahead.

Wikimedia 2030

We synthesized the collective thoughts, feedback, and hopes from hundreds of conversations about the future into a shared direction.

By 2030, Wikimedia will become the essential infrastructure of the ecosystem of free knowledge, and anyone who shares our vision will be able to join us.

We, the Wikimedia contributors, communities, and organizations, will advance our world by collecting knowledge that fully represents human diversity, and by building the services and structures that enable others to do the same. We will carry on our mission of developing content as we have done in the past, and we will go further.

Knowledge as a service: To serve our users, we will become a platform that serves open knowledge to the world across interfaces and communities. We will build tools for allies and partners to organize and exchange free knowledge beyond Wikimedia. Our infrastructure will enable us and others to collect and use different forms of free, trusted knowledge.

Knowledge equity: As a social movement, we will focus our efforts on the knowledge and communities that have been left out by structures of power and privilege. We will welcome people from every background to build strong and diverse communities. We will break down the social, political, and technical barriers preventing people from accessing and contributing to free knowledge.[2]

The final language of the strategic direction adopted by the Wikimedia community acknowledges a world in which free knowledge is potentially plentiful but in need of critical support. It maintains the spirit of openness to all but recognizes the importance of building communities with shared purpose and good faith. We committed to undertaking this ambition informed by the guiding perspectives of "knowledge equity" and "knowledge as a service" as we seek to engage and include more perspectives from around the globe while ensuring Wikipedia is as dynamic and useful in the future as it is today.

It means that the popular idea of "Wikipedia" should be expansive and inclusive. When people hear "Wikipedia," it should conjure up endless knowledge—one in which the articles of the encyclopedia are a point of entry into a rich, multilingual ecosystem of discovery; one which integrates rich annotations and citations, augmented and multimedia experiences, connections to external resources, complex insights, and robust linked open data structures. Wikipedia should be both a destination for learning and a network of exploration, connecting concepts, collections, and institutions, elevating and interconnecting disparate resources of open knowledge, making all knowledge more accessible and discoverable.

This is Wikipedia the encyclopedia, of course, but also so much more. Neither the Wikimedia vision statement nor the 2030 strategic direction mention anything about a website or Wikipedia specifically. Instead, we recognize a goal whose intention is to enrich all of humanity and we cannot reach that alone.

Beyond the Encyclopedia

What does it mean to be the essential infrastructure of free knowledge? While "infrastructure" conjures up rigid and impersonal features, it is better understood as building the critical social, technical, and political support systems necessary to bear the ambition of a world in which free knowledge is produced and shared, not only in the Wikimedia ecosystem but also across many different communities, projects, and institutions.

It means supporting the people and institutions that produce free knowledge and championing the conditions that enable its production and dissemination. It is knowledge as a platform and also a community of creators, curators, advocates, donors, and allies around the globe. It is a body of knowledge and also a powerful voice that stands for the importance of free and open information, standards, policies, and practices in service of our public knowledge commons. It is a website and a movement which believes in the importance of the integrity of information and the fundamental right to inquire, learn, and seek answers.

Together, the people, technology, and voice of a movement make up the essential support system for free knowledge. Together, we will enable the collection, curation, and dissemination of free knowledge across the planet. Together, we can build the tools and infrastructure to host, catalog, tag, revise, and share knowledge, both in the Wikimedia ecosystem and far beyond. Together, we can extend the public domain and grow openly licensed content, advocate on behalf of knowledge-enabling policies and standards, and defend our essential rights to inquiry and information.

If this sounds radical, consider how far Wikipedia has already changed our conception of the encyclopedia: no longer a hardbound, finite, alphabetized collection of books but an infinite exploration of interconnected discovery and learning. The future of Wikipedia is an opportunity to extend this evolution even further. It means embracing *encyclopedic* in an etymological sense, a circular, looping, endless education.

To realize this future, we will not only need to reconceive the encyclopedia (again) but also be open to the evolution of the Wikimedia projects and communities, perhaps in transformational ways.

Our global communities, well established in wealthy, northern countries, must grow to more fully represent the diversity of the world's languages, cultures, and contexts. Our underlying technology platform will need to be open and dynamic, able to integrate emerging and augmentative technologies and respond to as-yet unknown evolutions in devices, interfaces, and user experiences. The act of writing the encyclopedia may remain core to our identity but will need to be supplemented by other acts of collaboration, curation, and creation as well as new form factors for consuming and sharing knowledge.

Fortunately, the seeds of many of these changes have already taken root in the Wikimedia movement of today. In this sense, the 2030 strategic direction is less a radical re-envisioning of Wikimedia than a codification of emergent trends: growth of new communities in previously underrepresented languages and geographies, successful new projects focused on original sources and structured data, experiments in augmented machine-learning experiences, and new partners and allies in the movement for free culture.

The Experience

The next billion people to come online will come to Wikipedia through many devices and channels, so we must consider what it means to build beyond the desktop or mobile browser and anticipate a future in which people can access information across a host of devices and interfaces. For anyone to be able to join us in the work or exploration of free knowledge, we have to revisit the idea of what makes the Wikimedia experience meaningful, relevant, and useful as technology and the world change around us.

This is not only about the emergent needs of tomorrow but also the changing needs of users today who have different expectations for form factors, interactions, and user experiences. To stay relevant and relatable, Wikimedia must find a balance between retaining our identity and evolving to meet the world where it is and where it's going.

"Editing" Wikipedia

One of the most identifiable values of Wikimedia is the "read/write" nature of our projects. Anyone can be an editor, and any aspect of the projects is open to change. This has been core to Wikipedia's model over the years, ensuring that as both knowledge and technology have changed, Wikipedia has been changing, too. It allows for articles to be quickly created, for editors to continuously refine and add nuance to complex concepts, for new ideas and new voices to challenge bias or add fresh perspective. It is a "consent or contest" paradigm, inviting everyone to be a critical reader and active participant in Wikipedia's knowledge.

When this "open to change" model launched, it was at the cutting edge of participation on the internet. Today, people have very different expectations about the interfaces, tools, and experiences that they use to create content on the internet. For our open, participatory model to remain compelling, the experience of contributing to Wikipedia should evolve to feel as fresh, contemporary, and full of possibility to the next generation of contributors as it was to the very first Wikipedians.

There are many straightforward but important changes that could significantly improve the experience of contributing to the Wikimedia projects today. In 2018–2019, the Wikimedia Foundation's Product department published an important series of essays on these changes, "Product Perspectives" on the subject of Wikipedia reader and editor experiences, as well as culture, scale, trust, augmentation, and tooling.[3] These user experience essays explored the possibilities for new form factors, rich content, the needs of contributors, customized experiences, and improving how people discover and explore knowledge across the projects.

Many small evolutions to the Wikimedia interface could have a dramatic impact on the user experience and overall enjoyment of participating in the Wikimedia projects. Welcoming language, customized wayfinding, instructional onboarding, familiar contribution and consumption interfaces, suggested actions, and explicit gratitude and feedback are all areas where small changes could make significant improvements in the Wikimedia experience—and potentially improve the quality of new editor contributions and overall retention.

Wikipedia came to be in an era of desktop computing, and its long-form, detail-oriented knowledge production process has worked well in this context. The mechanical keyboard and screen setups of desktops and laptops are designed for word processing and managing complex, long-lead tasks. A commitment to this form factor may have contributed to an initial reluctance and delay in embracing mobile devices as a possible new form factor for productive contributions. Yet despite some initial uncertainty about demand, improvements in Wikimedia's mobile editing interfaces and the introduction of more powerful mobile editing tools have proven very popular. In a world of mobile ubiquity, we see significant opportunities ahead, particularly for smaller, discrete "micro-contribution" tasks such as adding citations or image and data tagging.

Evolving the on-site editing experience and introducing new forms of contribution will require time, consideration, and care. But all of these actions are within a fairly well-understood cycle of "read, edit, publish, read," all of which take place directly on the Wikipedia websites. But what about editing Wikipedia content out in the wild, off the main websites? What would it mean to make an edit to Wikipedia-sourced information directly through Google's Knowledge Panel search result interface? How does an editable voice assistant interface sound and interact? What about navigating a contribution through an augmented or mixed-reality experience? The "editability promise," of being able to improve and update nearly any knowledge, nearly any time, is an essential part of who we are. For Wikipedia's future to stay true to Wikipedia's origins, we'll need to answer these questions.

"Reading" Wikipedia

Today Wikipedia takes the form of articles. Articles are primarily text with a smattering of images and data, and the way people interact with the information within them is by reading the text for insight. But is reading the only or even the best way to engage with the sum of the world's knowledge? What learning experiences will users seek on the Wikipedia of the future? In what ways will people "read" or interact with Wikipedia, off the Wikipedia projects? As the devices, interfaces, and demographics of internet users continue to evolve, we're already seeing changes toward multiplatform, multimodal knowledge-seeking behaviors.

Web searches for video content increasingly rival searches for text and image content. Younger users are more video forward, and newer users of the web are often navigating in second languages. Demand for digital services is also increasing among more nontraditional internet users, such as the 750 million illiterate adults[4] and many more millions of lower literacy individuals seeking access to opportunity and entertainment. Video can offer immersive learning experiences that may be more engaging than text, whether for reasons of accessibility, literacy, or practical demonstration.

For some time now, Wikipedia editors have been proposing the introduction of video and other rich media experiences to Wikipedia. While Wikimedia Commons has seen recent renewed growth as a freely licensed media repository, its usability lags behind other media hosting sites, and it remains primarily a service for images rather than rich media. And multimedia poses interesting questions for Wikimedia editors: What does it mean to collaborate on a video? What constitutes a neutral point of view in photography? To be successful, the projects will have to address practical issues of hosting, discoverability, and usability as well as more philosophical questions around neutrality and editorial voice.

Whether on the web, through talking to your phone's digital assistant, or in an augmented reality headset, people increasingly expect digital experiences to anticipate their needs and interests. Wikipedia is unlikely to ever embrace "personalization," in which the platform collects private data and uses it to make opaque algorithmic recommendations. This would be against our values of privacy as well as be counter to Wikipedia's spirit of discovery and serendipity. However, we could embrace "customization," empowering people with tools to curate their experiences. Integrated alongside increasingly powerful tools for knowledge discovery, the Wikipedia of the future is one that informs, delights, and compels.

While the questions of video and other multimedia experiences, personalization, or discovery are largely related to what happens on the Wikimedia projects, Wikimedia's knowledge experiences are rapidly evolving off-projects as other platforms and brands repurpose and customize Wikimedia's content to meet the needs of their users.

Recent years have seen a major increase in the utility and adoption of voice assistants, interfaces which combine voice recognition, natural language processing, and speech synthesis to produce a conversational query service. Some researchers anticipate that voice-based search queries could overtake text-based queries by 2020.[5] Already, Wikipedia results populate the major voice assistant services, answering contextual and factual questions on the phone or around the kitchen table. Voice-based search creates opportunities for new ambient learning behaviors, giving people the ability to seek information as they go about their lives, expanding augmentative information-seeking behaviors.

Voice search gives us a preview of more sophisticated voice services, with the potential to address major accessibility, literacy, and other structural barriers. Voice services can increase usability and availability of key services for those with visual impairments. Natural language voice interactions can help low familiarity or fluency speakers quickly clarify search queries and adjust results. For languages that are primarily spoken rather than written, that are not widely digitized, or that lack localized product and user experiences, verbal services offer a "leapfrog" opportunity to surpass existing limitations and address previously underserved groups.

Voice reuse of Wikipedia is just one of the ways in which Wikipedia content may be explored or "read" in the future. Already, artists, engineers, and innovators use Wikimedia's content, data, and media to build augmented and mixed-reality experiences, annotate and enrich mapping platforms, and build virtual galaxies of knowledge.[6] It is impossible to predict the other ways in which interfaces, devices, and experiences may yet evolve. Instead, the Wikipedia of the future should anticipate new ways in which people will experience and contribute knowledge. It should serve knowledge to the world across interfaces and communities and enable everyone to collect, organize, and exchange knowledge that fully represents human diversity. To do this, we'll want to retool the technical platform to be more open and flexible—a process that is already underway.

The Platform

Wikipedia is best known to people through its content and interfaces, but to embrace an expansive and inclusive future of knowledge, we should also look to the underlying technical platform that supports how we collect, curate, and share knowledge. The stability, resiliency, and flexibility of the technical "stack" sets the parameters for the possibilities of what we can build: how fast, how flexible, how dynamic, how accessible, how secure. Today we have an opportunity to be intentional about how this platform can itself be a tool in advancing the 2030 vision.

Wikimedia's technical stack has been affectionately described by the Wikimedia Foundation's technical staff as having a "just-in-time" architecture, one which evolved in response to Wikipedia's growth in content and popularity. While this refers to the sometimes ad hoc nature of solutions which emerge when running a major global website with relatively limited resources, it also nicely captures how Wikimedia content principles have informed the technical systems on which it runs: many small workable hacks have proven more practical and serviceable than elegant but impractical perfection.

This approach has allowed volunteer and paid developers to solve emergent problems, adapt to new use cases, and introduce increasingly sophisticated tools and services, all while (mostly) keeping the projects up and running. However, the core of the platform very much reflects its origins in the static HTML internet of the mid-2000s. For the future of Wikimedia and the future of free knowledge, the platform needs some intentional updates. From multidevice and multimedia capabilities to support new forms of knowledge, to more complex integrations of machine learning and distributed security, there is an opportunity to more fundamentally reimagine our stack to integrate the innovations of the last decade.

New technologies around censorship resistance, privacy, and availability need to be integrated to protect our users and content in the more hostile internet of today. As governments and malicious actors increase pressure on free knowledge, improved performance, security, and resiliency of the technical stack help serve as a bulwark to protect the integrity of the knowledge and data within the Wikimedia ecosystem, the privacy of editors and readers, and the availability of the sites themselves.

The way in which the platform stores, updates, and serves knowledge today works well for the article model of Wikipedia, but it introduces some limitations on more dynamic reuse of knowledge. Currently, edits are saved and presented as a single body of unstructured text. This works well for reading and editing whole articles, but it makes it difficult to isolate specific data or insights. Imagine if we were instead able to deconstruct the information in articles or attributes of a media file and store them in structured and semantically understandable units. These would not only be meaningful within Wikipedia, they would also have meaningful value as independent, parsable units of knowledge within the broader digital knowledge ecosystem.

Building structured units of knowledge addresses part of this future: they would be more easily reused and remixed into new experiences and interfaces, more easily syndicated by other knowledge services, and more easily updated in more modular fashions. Alongside this more modular content, we have the opportunity to evolve structured citations accordingly—enabling structured, rich knowledge that can present information in context and, sometimes, in conflict. Presenting multiple claims and highlighting conflict and congruence while incorporating modular verification information can enrich our understanding of topics and the authorities that give them weight.

The transition from unstructured to structured knowledge is directly connected to another goal of platform evolution: the move to a more service-oriented architecture. Ideally, the openness of the platform should mirror the openness of the content—a platform that makes it easy for anyone, from community members to external knowledge partners to the Wikimedia Foundation itself, to easily build and create new experiences and services on top of Wikimedia.

Today, building something off of Wikipedia's knowledge base requires immersing oneself in mailing lists and documentation and navigating the full stack or bringing a brute-force application of computational and engineering power to scrape sense from the wilderness. Imagine an alternative: still a fully open stack with a structured knowledge corpus and architectural coherence, built with contemporary libraries and languages, offering an accessible, usable, and well-documented service layer. Sophisticated technical contributors could continue to participate in governance and development of the platform's architecture, performance, security, database schemas, and other technical matters. Major reusers could access the "firehose" of dynamic database updates. Individual creators and companies could build new services and insights.

Of the many possibilities for platform evolution, another significant evolution is the growing use of machine learning and artificial intelligence on the Wikimedia projects. Wikimedia has relied on machine augmentation since our beginnings—there are dozens of bots that operate on Wikipedia, performing various routine functions so that humans don't have to. Machine intelligence already assists editors in evaluating edit and article quality and providing rough translations of articles between various languages. We anticipate that this use of machine learning and artificial intelligence will continue to grow, although in ways that may remain largely invisible to a casual user.

In the future, we expect machine learning to help readers and editors alike. It could enable communities to grow the projects even more ambitiously, synthesizing and syncing knowledge across languages, highlighting content gaps and bias, identifying under-loved articles, automatically translating between Wikipedia language versions, or using natural language generation to create "stubs" or rough drafts of articles from collections of secondary sources. For readers, it could assemble customized reading lists, propose contextual article groups for deeper learning, recommend related images and media, and more.

In addition to growing Wikimedia's quality and quantity, machine learning may also prove to be a valuable tool addressing an area of great concern on the internet of 2020: misinformation and manipulation. Tools that assist Wikipedia editors in recognizing suspicious clusters of contributions, networks of editors, spikes in editing activity, or patterns of words and linguistic signifiers could be possible applications. Of course, the best tools would be additive to the existing approaches Wikipedia editors use to maintain knowledge quality and identify bad-faith activity. They should build on existing efforts, supporting the work and intentions of the people who contribute to Wikipedia.

The function, development, and deployment of machine learning on the Wikimedia projects should abide by what Wikimedia researchers and engineers have adopted as the principles of ethical Wikimedia artificial intelligence: fairness, transparency, and accountability.[7] Volunteers and staff working on these efforts today envision a future where Wikipedia offers both tools and a learning environment for contributors to "train the machines" so that our artificial intelligences are as distributed, accessible, and open as any other part of the Wikimedia ecosystem.

The Wikimedia technical platform of today is already a remarkable achievement. With limited resources and developer time, it reliably serves hundreds of millions of users and billions of page views every single month to all corners of the planet. The future of Wikimedia offers this platform an opportunity to evolve from a supporting function to a strategic one, offering new knowledge formats, structured knowledge, new service layers, federated knowledge hosting, and augmented intelligence—an indispensable piece of infrastructure for the essential support system for free knowledge.

The People

As much as the technology and user experiences of the Wikimedia platforms shape our work, the volunteer community is what truly differentiates the Wikimedia movement and mission. In survey after survey, we find that Wikimedians contribute to Wikipedia and the other Wikimedia projects because they are animated by the promise of the mission of free and open knowledge for the world.

The community that sustains Wikipedia today has built something remarkable and unprecedented in the world, and they deserve celebration and continued support and recognition. And if we believe that the world is better when more people can share in free knowledge and that this can only happen when more people openly collaborate with one another, we must recognize who is still missing from the picture.

We find a stark example of the unevenness of the Wikimedia community in looking at Wikipedia contributions around the globe. More people from the country of the Netherlands, with a population of around seventeen million people, contribute to Wikipedia than people who reside across the entire continent of Africa, home to more than 1.2 billion people. Another way of looking at this imbalance in representation? Articles about the continent Africa, the cradle of humanity, home to more than fifty countries, thousands of languages, and thriving modern cities, represent fewer than 4 percent of all of the geotagged articles on English Wikipedia.[8]

It is not difficult to infer that the authors of these relatively few articles about African topics are statistically unlikely to be from Africa themselves, conjuring up a parallel world in which every article about Europe is written primarily by Latin Americans and every article about North America written primarily by South Asians. Of course, Wikipedia's articles should be written by people from all over, with space inclusive of many different perspectives. If only some people represent all people, we lose out on a more holistic and representative collection of knowledge.

Across the globe, this problem persists. Wikipedia's editor populations are stable or growing where real populations are not while editing communities in regions and countries that are experiencing rapid population growth remain relatively small. Hindi Wikipedia, representing the world's third-most spoken language, is only the fifty-third-largest Wikipedia, far smaller than languages with far fewer native speakers, such as Catalan and Finnish, or none (Esperanto).

Of course, no conversation about the need for increased contributor diversity in Wikimedia would be complete without acknowledging the lack of equitable gender participation in the Wikimedia communities. Often described as the "gender gap," the best available statistics about gender participation in the Wikimedia communities indicate that less than 20 percent of Wikipedia contributors identify as women. (The idea of closing the "gender gap" itself has always struck me as somewhat problematic as it implies a gulf between two equivalent sides and reinforces the idea of binary gender. An aspiration to equitable "gender diversity" might be more fitting.)

As of publication, there are roughly three hundred language versions of Wikipedia, ranging in size from very large and very active (English, currently the largest, at six million articles) to relatively small (Tulu, currently the smallest active Wikipedia, with about one thousand articles). Although opinions differ within the Wikimedia movement about whether we should strive for a Wikipedia in every language, it is certainly the case that more can be done to address knowledge parity across the Wikipedia language versions that exist today, whether through supporting organic community and article growth, optional machine translation, or even natural language generation.

If we believe that a better informed world is a world of greater understanding, better equipped to address our collective challenges, then the Wikimedia movement must reorganize ourselves to acknowledge who is not yet a part of our vision. If languages, regions, and people are missing and if contributors to the Wikimedia projects are still predominantly male, still predominantly from North America and Europe, and still predominantly white, then we must agree that our pursuit of free and open knowledge is definitionally incomplete. If Wikipedia editors don't represent the world's diversity, they cannot fully contribute to a representation of the world's knowledge.

The imperative of building a more representative and welcoming community extends beyond our own projects. In a future in which Wikimedia's knowledge extends well beyond the Wikimedia projects, a more inclusive and diverse Wikipedia editing community has positive repercussions that extend well beyond their participation on Wikimedia sites. Diversity of perspective not only enriches Wikimedia content, culture, and governance, it enriches the broader open knowledge ecosystem in which Wikimedia exists. It allows us and others to build more representative knowledge, more valuable and appropriate user experiences, and less biased machine learning models.

The Wikimedia 2030 direction recognizes the work of Wikimedia as a social movement and calls on us to center knowledge and communities that have been left out by structures of power and privilege. To truly do so, we must welcome people from every background and invest resources in breaking down the social, political, and technical barriers preventing people from accessing and contributing to free knowledge. This will support not only strong and diverse communities but also robust, resilient, and representative knowledge.

Conclusion

A world in which every single human can freely share in the sum of all knowledge is an impossible, asymptotic vision. This is because knowledge itself is always changing with every passing day, discovery, and reconsideration. Wikimedia can only ever get closer, but it will never be finished. The Wikimedia movement's direction for 2030 acknowledges that there is a step we can aim for along the way: supporting the people and institutions that produce free knowledge, building the technology that hosts and distributes it, and standing up for the policies and practices that make this work possible. This is how Wikimedia evolves while staying true to the values from whence it came.

We will be able to make this journey from the "encyclopedia anyone can edit" to the "essential infrastructure of free knowledge" because change is at the core of what Wikimedia is and does. Our capacity to change is Wikimedia's greatest strength. Every day, Wikipedia changes moment by moment in response to the global flow of knowledge. It changes to reflect current events, it changes as we learn new things about our world and ourselves, it changes as new voices enter the conversation and challenge dominant paradigms. It changes when there are typos and grammatical errors. It changes when new technologies demand new experiences. It changes because humans are often wrong, and we can only ever seek to improve.

Over the past twenty years, the Wikimedia community has managed to build an unintentionally ubiquitous resource, an integral piece of the fabric of modern society. But the continued growth and resilience of free knowledge is not an inevitability. History is a story of knowledge as scarcity, a tool of power and privilege. By comparison, the very idea of free knowledge is radical, subverting practices of gatekeeping that date back centuries. A belief in free and open knowledge is a belief that everyone has the potential to contribute to the world and that everyone has the ability to use knowledge well and wisely. Paraphrasing Wikimedian Marco Correa, former president of Wikimedia Chile, "The knowledge is neutral. The mission is not."

I'm reminded of a Wikimedia story, probably apocryphal, about a moment when the first edition of a major editorial encyclopedia first entered into the public domain. As the story goes, Wikipedia editors were thrilled—this newly available knowledge could now be fully integrated into Wikipedia, improving the accuracy and breadth of Wikipedia's own articles. Yet, when editors went to review what they could salvage, they found almost nothing. From Aristotle to zebras, our understanding of the world had kept evolving, and static knowledge had not kept up.

For Wikipedia to be as essential in the next twenty years as we have been for the first twenty, we will need to keep up with our world. We will need to make the changes that make Wikipedia easier to contribute to and more delightful to read. We will need to retool our platforms to support and serve knowledge on our sites and across the digital landscape. We will need to change to include more voices, more demographics, more diversity, more languages. We will need to change to recognize and respond more robustly to the risks and threats to free knowledge and its creators. We will need to embrace our role as the essential support system of free knowledge.

Wikimedia reminds us that the greatest thing we will ever build is the thing which we build with others. It reminds us that the world we seek is a work in progress and that each of us has a role to play in how we improve what lies before us. In 2001, we had no idea of what we could build together. I look forward to what we the world will build next.

Notes

1. Ed Erhart, "'My Favorite Website': Stephen Colbert's Complicated Relationship with Wikipedia," Wikimedia Foundation, September 8, 2015, https://blog.wikimedia.org/2015/09/08/colberts-complicated-relationship-with-wikipedia/.

2. Meta-Wiki, s.v. "Strategy/Wikimedia Movement/2018-20," accessed October 11, 2019, https://meta.wikimedia.org/wiki/Strategy/Wikimedia_movement/2018-20.

3. MediaWiki, s.v. "Wikimedia Product/Perspectives," accessed October 10, 2019, https://www.mediawiki.org/wiki/Wikimedia_Product/Perspectives.

4. Manos Antoninis and Silvia Montoya, "The World Is Off Track to Deliver on Its Education Commitments by 2030," *Data for Sustainable Development* (blog), July 9, 2019, https://sdg.uis.unesco.org/2019/07/09/the-world-is-off-track-to-deliver-on-its -education-commitments-by-2030/.

5. Danielle Antosz, "Mary Meeker's 2016 Internet Trends Report," *Search Engine Journal*, June 6, 2016, https://www.searchenginejournal.com/5-search-related-takeaways -mary-meekers-2016-internet-trends-report/165434/#close.

6. The Wikiverse Project: An Interactive 3D Visualization of Wikipedia, accessed October 10, 2019, https://www.wikiverse.io/.

7. Jonathan T. Morgan, "Designing Ethically with AI: How Wikimedia Can Harness Machine Learning in a Responsible and Human-Centered Way," Wikimedia Foundation, July 18, 2019, https://wikimediafoundation.org/news/2019/07/18/designing -ethically-with-ai-how-wikimedia-can-harness-machine-learning-in-a-responsible -and-human-centered-way/.

8. Mark Graham, "The Geographically Uneven Coverage of Wikipedia," Oxford Internet Institute, October 21, 2014, https://geonet.oii.ox.ac.uk/blog/the-geographically -uneven-coverage-of-wikipedia-2/.

Contributors

Phoebe Ayers is the librarian for electrical engineering and computer science at the Massachusetts Institute of Technology Libraries. She has been a Wikipedian since 2003, is a former member of the Wikimedia Foundation Board of Trustees, and is the coauthor of *How Wikipedia Works: And How You Can Be a Part of It* (No Starch Press, 2008).

Omer Benjakob is a journalist and researcher based in Israel. He was born in New York and raised in Tel Aviv. His work focuses on Wikipedia and the politics of knowledge in the digital age. He covers the online encyclopedia for *Haaretz*—Israel's sole paper of record—in English and Hebrew. His work has also appeared in *Wired UK*. His academic research focuses on Wikipedia's ties to science, and he works with scientists from the Weizmann Institute of Science and the Centre de recherches interdisciplinaires to map the growth of knowledge online. He's pursuing an MA from Tel Aviv University's Cohn Institute for the History and Philosophy of Science and Ideas.

Yochai Benkler is the Berkman Professor of Entrepreneurial Legal Studies at Harvard Law School and codirector of the Berkman Klein Center for Internet & Society at Harvard University. He has been a leading scholar on the impact of the internet on the networked economy and society since the 1990s, with a particular focus on commons, cooperation, and decentralization. His books include *Network Propaganda: Manipulation, Disinformation, and Radicalization in American Politics* (Oxford University Press, 2018) and *The Wealth of Networks: How Social Production Transforms Markets and Freedom* (Yale University Press, 2006). His work can be freely accessed at benkler.org.

William Beutler is the founder of Beutler Ink, a digital marketing agency specializing in Wikipedia engagement. As a volunteer Wikipedia editor for more than a decade, Beutler has played a leading role in fostering dialogue between the Wikipedia community and the public relations industry and is the author of a blog, *The Wikipedian*, that focuses on Wikimedia topics. He is also the creator of The Infinite Atlas Project, a multimedia work mapping the locations of David Foster Wallace's "Infinite Jest," and a cohost of podcasts about Stanley Kubrick as well as other unconventional film-makers. He is based in Washington, DC.

Siko Bouterse is an online community organizer, digital activist, and feminist who cofounded Whose Knowledge?. She grew up in the United States with family spread across three continents in both the Global North and Global South, and her interest in the internet began as a way to connect people across languages, cultures, and spaces. She joined the Wikimedia movement in 2011, becoming former director of commu-nity resources at the Wikimedia Foundation and a Wikipedian. Today Bouterse uses her white privilege to challenge injustice and inequality of many forms online, and is exploring antiauthoritarian education practices in partnership with her daughter.

Amy Carleton (BS, Simmons College; MA, PhD, Northeastern University) teaches writing and communication in the Comparative Media Studies/Writing department at the Massachusetts Institute of Technology. Her research interests include study-ing collaborative culture, design thinking, and online communities. Outside of aca-demia, her writing has appeared in the *New York Times, Washington Post, Atlantic*, NPR, *Los Angeles Review of Books*, and others. Currently she is working on a book project about the musician Prince and online fan culture.

Stéphane Coillet-Matillon is based in Switzerland and has owned a registered account on Wikipedia since 2004. Moving through the ranks on-wiki as well as off-wiki, he joined the Swiss chapter shortly after it was founded and was ultimately elected to its board of trustees in 2014. Luck, fate, and tragedy led him to become its ad interim executive director a year later. His mission there having been completed, he spun off Kiwix, the offline Wikipedia reader for people without internet access, and launched it as an independent entity in 2017. He still serves as its chief executive officer.

Robert E. Cummings serves as executive director of academic innovation and associ-ate professor of writing and rhetoric at the University of Mississippi. His research focuses on open educational resources generally and more specifically on teaching with Wikipedia in higher education as an open educational practice. He edits the open access journal *Wiki Studies*, which publishes peer-reviewed articles examining the intersection of Wikipedia and higher education. He serves on the board of direc-tors for Wiki Education, and his current research focuses on how the introduction of open educational resources in the classroom impacts teaching and learning practices.

LiAnna L. Davis is the chief programs officer and deputy director for Wiki Education. With more than nine years' experience in running programs connecting Wikipedia and academia, Davis is one of the world's leading experts in teaching with Wiki-pedia. She has played a pivotal role in creating Wikipedia education programs in eight countries worldwide and has supported the work of volunteers in more than fifty additional countries. She has a master's degree in communication, culture, and technology from Georgetown University and a bachelor's degree in communication studies from the University of Puget Sound.

Siân Evans is the information literacy and instructional design librarian at Maryland Institute College of Art and cofounder and co-lead Organizer of Art+Feminism Wikipedia Edit-a-thon. Her writing can be found in journals such as *Art Documentation* and *The Serials Librarian*, and her work with Art+Feminism has been covered by the *New York Times*, *Wall Street Journal*, and more. She believes that librarianship is information activism.

Heather Ford is an associate professor and head of discipline for digital and social media in the School of Communications at the University of Technology, Sydney. She focuses on the implications of the increasing deployment of algorithms and automation to organize and construct knowledge about events, people, places, and things. *Fact Factories* (MIT Press, 2020) follows the ways in which history is written as it happens on Wikipedia and about how facts travel through the infrastructure of the internet.

Stephen Harrison is an attorney and writer whose work has appeared in the *Atlantic*, *New York Times*, and *Washington Post*. He also writes "Source Notes," a regular column for *Slate* about the internet's knowledge ecosystem. In recent years, he has published feature articles about leading figures in the Wikimedia movement. He received his undergraduate and law degrees from Washington University in St. Louis and his master's degree from the University of Texas at Austin.

Heather Hart is based in Brooklyn and has received grants from Anonymous was a Woman, Joan Mitchell Foundation, Harpo Foundation, and Jerome Foundation as well as a fellowship from the New York Film Academy. Her work has been included in a variety of publications and exhibited worldwide, including at Storm King Sculpture Park, Socrates Sculpture Park, Seattle Art Museum's Olympic Sculpture Park, Studio Museum in Harlem, ICA Philadelphia, Art in General, The Drawing Center, PS1 MoMA, Museum of Arts and Craft in Itami, Portland Art Center, and the Brooklyn Museum. Hart is invested in creating site-specific liminal spaces for personal reclamation and in questioning dominant narratives and proposing alternatives to them. She received her BFA from Cornish College of the Arts and her MFA from Rutgers University. For more information, see heather-hart.com.

Benjamin Mako Hill is a social scientist, technologist, and activist. In all three roles he works to understand why some attempts at peer production—like Wikipedia and Linux—build large volunteer communities while the vast majority never attract even a second contributor. He is an assistant professor in the Department of Communication at the University of Washington and a founding member of the Community Data Science Collective. He is also a faculty associate at the Berkman Klein Center for Internet & Society at Harvard University. He has been participant in Wikipedia and Wikimedia communities for more than fifteen years.

Dariusz Jemielniak is a full professor of management at Kozminski University where he heads the MINDS (Management in Networked and Digital Societies) department;

a faculty associate at the Berkman Klein Center for Internet & Society; and a member of the board of trustees of Wikimedia Foundation. He published the first ethnography of Wikipedia, called *Common Knowledge?* (Stanford University Press, 2014). More recently, he wrote about *Collaborative Society* (with A. Przegalinska; MIT Press, 2020) and *Thick Big Data: Doing Digital Social Sciences* (Oxford University Press, 2020). He currently studies antiscience movements online.

Brian Keegan is a computational social scientist and assistant professor in the Department of Information Science at the University of Colorado Boulder. His research explores how sociotechnical systems like Wikipedia manage bursty disruptions arising from breaking news. The mediation of bursts through information technologies enables him to understand the antecedents, processes, and consequences of these disruptions. He is particularly interested in the increasing interoperability of online social infrastructures and their vulnerabilities to bursts. He received his PhD in media, technology, and society at Northwestern University and SB degrees in engineering and science and technology studies at MIT.

Jackie Koerner is the social scientist behind action research initiatives pertaining to equity and inclusion in community spaces. Fascinated by the world around her, she loves making sense out of complex social situations. To share that love, she employs humor and relatability to inspire others to get involved in social change. Her tenacious nature and sense of justice usually get her into trouble but always for good reasons. She lives in the midwestern United States with her husband, her two daughters, and many rescued pets. Learn more and get in touch with her at jackie koerner.com.

Alexandria Lockett is an assistant professor of English at Spelman College. She publishes about the technological politics of race, surveillance, and access. Her work appears in the journals *Composition Studies*, *Enculturation*, and *Praxis* and in the edited collections *Humans at Work in the Digital Age: Forms of Digital Textual Labor* (Routledge, 2019), *Black Perspectives on Writing Program Administration: From the Margins to the Center* (SWR Press, 2019), *Out in the Center* (Utah State University Press, 2019), and Bad Ideas about Writing (West Virginia University Digital Publishing Institute, 2017). An extended biography is available via her portfolio at www.alexandrialockett.com.

Jacqueline Mabey has been shaped by studies at Wilfrid Laurier University, McGill University, and the University of British Columbia and by diverse professional experience in commercial galleries, museums, and artist studios. Mabey works in a research-based curatorial model, exploring a set of recurrent themes: desire, power, visibility, vulnerability, and creative community. Mabey is cofounder and co-lead organizer of Art+Feminism Wikipedia Edit-a-thon and assistant curator at the Paul Robeson Galleries, Rutgers University–Newark. They work independently under the honorific failed projects (failedprojects.net).

Katherine Maher is the executive director of the Wikimedia Foundation, the nonprofit organization that operates Wikipedia and the Wikimedia projects. She is a longtime advocate for free and open societies and has lived and worked around the world, leading the introduction of technology and innovation in human rights, good governance, and international development. Maher has worked with UNICEF, the National Democratic Institute, the World Bank, and Access Now on programs supporting technologies for democratic participation, civic engagement, and open government. She is a member of the World Economic Forum's Global Council on Human Rights and a fellow at the Truman National Security Project.

Michael Mandiberg is an interdisciplinary artist who created *Print Wikipedia*, edited *The Social Media Reader* (NYU Press, 2012), founded the New York Arts Practicum, and cofounded the Art+Feminism. Their projects have been exhibited at the Los Angeles County Museum of Art, the Whitney Museum of American Art, the New Museum, and Musée d'Art Moderne de la Ville de Paris, among others. They have been written about widely, from *Artforum* to *Süddeutsche Zeitung*. Mandiberg is professor of media culture at CUNY College of Staten Island and is on the doctoral faculty at the CUNY Graduate Center.

Cecelia A. Musselman is associate teaching professor in the Writing Program at Northeastern University. She has been teaching with Wikipedia since 2006 and is an active member of the Boston-based Working Wikipedia Collaborative group of instructors and researchers. Musselman did her doctoral work in Uralic Studies with a special focus on the history of the Finnish language. She's also a potter, gardener, and sauna enthusiast.

Eliza Myrie received her MFA from Northwestern University and BA from Williams College. Myrie was in residence at Bemis Center, MacDowell Colony, and Arts + Public Life at the University of Chicago. Myrie lectures at School of the Art Institute and is a cofounder of the Black Artists Retreat [B.A.R.]. Her work has been supported by 3Arts and Propeller Fund and has been exhibited at Arts Club Chicago, Gallery 400, Vox Populi, Museum of Contemporary Art Chicago, and New Museum of Contemporary Art. Myrie considers laboring as a physical and conceptual endeavor that complicates assignations of value across gender, socioeconomic, and racial categories. For more information, see elizamyrie.com.

Jake Orlowitz is a seeker of well people and sane societies, an internet citizen, a digital project manager, and an ally and activist for radical culture change. Orlowitz founded and ran the Wikipedia Library research access and library outreach program and built the Wikipedia Adventure interactive learning tutorial. Orlowitz lives in Santa Cruz, California, with his wife and stepdaughter.

Ian A. Ramjohn is the senior Wikipedia expert at Wiki Education. He discovered Wikipedia in 2004 and was able to correct errors in the Wikipedia article about his native Trinidad and Tobago. The experience of sitting in the developing world and changing the way your country was presented in an international reference world was life-changing. He has a PhD in ecology from Michigan State University and a bachelor's from the University of the West Indies and has spent a decade teaching in higher education before joining Wiki Education in 2014.

Joseph Reagle is an associate professor of communication studies at Northeastern University. In 1998 and 2010 he was a resident fellow at the Berkman Klein Center for Internet & Society at Harvard University, and he taught and received his PhD at New York University's Department of Media, Culture, and Communication. As a research engineer at MIT, he served as an author and working group chair within the Internet Engineering Task Force (IETF) and World Wide Web Consortium (W3C) on topics including digital security, privacy, and internet policy. He has written about Wikipedia, online culture, and geek feminism. His latest book, *Hacking Life: Systematized Living and its Discontents*, was published by MIT Press in 2019.

Anasuya Sengupta is an Indian feminist activist, scholar, and cofounder of Whose Knowledge? who lives and works across multiple continents and online as a Wikipedian. She joined the Wikimedia Foundation in 2012, became chief grantmaking officer, and then began in earnest to edit and amplify marginalized knowledges on Wikipedia as a volunteer. She's led and supported social justice initiatives in India and the United States, particularly against caste-based and sexuality-based discriminations, religious fundamentalisms, and gender-based violence. She acknowledges the multiple positions of power and disempowerment she holds, especially as an "upper caste" savarna brown woman from the Global South.

Aaron Shaw is an associate professor of communication studies at Northwestern University and a faculty associate of the Berkman Klein Center for Internet & Society at Harvard University. Together with Benjamin Mako Hill, he cofounded the Community Data Science Collective.

Melissa Tamani is an art historian who graduated from the National University of San Marcos (Lima). She's developed a career in the fields of cultural management and museum education at various cultural institutions in Peru. She has been part of Art+Feminism since 2015, formerly as a regional ambassador in Latin America and currently as a lead co-organizer. She is also a promoter of Wikimedia culture in Peru, organizing and taking part in campaigns focused on gender, human rights, and ecology. The axes of her work are the empowerment of marginalized communities and the promotion of culture as a catalyst for social mobilization.

Rebecca Thorndike-Breeze teaches writing, rhetoric, and professional communication at the Massachusetts Institute of Technology's Comparative Media Studies/ Writing department. She grounds everything she does in a philosophy of extreme collaboration cultivated throughout her experiences with the Working Wikipedia Collaborative. She earned her PhD in literature from Northeastern University. Her interests range widely and include active learning pedagogy, improv comedy, rhetoric of science, animal studies, and theory of the novel. She has published essays on literary realism and modernism as well as Working Wikipedia Collaborative projects—in collaboration with her collaborators, of course.

Jina Valentine is an associate professor of printmedia at the School of the Art Institute of Chicago. She has exhibited at venues including the Drawing Center, the Studio Museum in Harlem, the CUE Foundation, Elizabeth Foundation, MCA Chicago, Southern Exposure, and Marlborough Gallery. Her work has received recognition and support from the North Carolina Arts Council, Joan Mitchell Foundation, Art Matters, and the Institute for Arts and Humanities at the University of North Carolina at Chapel Hill. Her interdisciplinary practice is informed by the intuitive strategies of American folk artists and traditional craft techniques, and interweaves histories latent within found texts, objects, narratives, and spaces. Valentine received her BFA from Carnegie Mellon University and her MFA from Stanford University. For more information, see jinavalentine.com.

Matthew A. Vetter is an assistant professor of English and affiliate faculty in the Composition and Applied Linguistics PhD program at Indiana University of Pennsylvania. His research asks questions related to technology, writing, pedagogy, and digital culture, with a specific interest in investigations of the ideological and epistemological functions of digital communities. Vetter's work has appeared in journals such as *College English, Composition Studies, Computers and Composition, Pedagogy*, and *Postdigital Science and Education*. He edits and teaches in Wikipedia as user:Matthewvetter and maintains a digital portfolio at mattvetter.net.

Adele Godoy Vrana is an Afro-Brazilian feminist, social justice activist, and cofounder of Whose Knowledge? who joined the Wikimedia movement in 2012. As the former director of strategic partnerships at the Wikimedia Foundation, she led initiatives to help increase access to Wikipedia in the Global South. A Wikimedian against all odds, she decided to stick around to make the point that black women belong everywhere, with or without an edit count. She first learned of Wikipedia in her mid-twenties when she couldn't afford to buy books and remains determined to make the knowledges of people like her visible, heard, and affirmed in this movement.

Denny Vrandečić is the founder of Wikidata, the Croatian Wikipedia, and cofounder of Wikibase and Semantic MediaWiki, used by the United Nations, the World Health Organization, the National Aeronautics and Space Administration (NASA), the Metropolitan Museum of Art, and other institutions. He works at Google AI and has worked previously on the Google Knowledge Graph, at Wikimedia Deutschland, and at the University of Southern California. Vrandečić gained a PhD while at the Karlsruhe Institute of Technology. He was a community-elected member of the board of trustees of the Wikimedia Foundation. His research interests are in massively collaborative knowledge creation. He lives with his wife and daughter in the San Francisco Bay Area.

Index

Note: Information in figures and tables is indicated by *f* and *t*.